Mastering Illiquidity

Risk Management for Portfolios of Limited Partnership Funds

Peter Cornelius
Christian Diller
Didier Guennoc
Thomas Meyer

A John Wiley & Sons, Ltd., Publication

Registered office
John Wiley & Sons, Ltd, The Atrium, Southern Gate, Chichester, West Sussex, PO19 8SQ, United Kingdom

For details of our global editorial offices, for customer services and for information about how to apply for permission to reuse the copyright material in this book please see our website at www.wiley.com.

Library of Congress Cataloging-in-Publication Data

Cornelius, Peter, 1960-
Mastering illiquidity : risk management for portfolios of limited partnership funds / Peter Cornelius, Christian Diller, Didier Guennoc and Thomas Meyer.
pages cm
Includes bibliographical references and index.
ISBN 978-1-119-95242-8 (cloth)
1. Private equity funds. 2. Portfolio management. 3. Risk management. I. Diller, Christian, 1976- II. Guennoc, Didier, 1967- III. Meyer, Thomas, 1959- IV. Title.
HG4751.C754 2013
332.63′27–dc23

2013004405

A catalogue record for this book is available from the British Library.

ISBN 978-1-119-95242-8 (hardback) ISBN 978-1-119-95280-0 (ebk)
ISBN 978-1-119-95281-7 (ebk) ISBN 978-1-119-95282-4 (ebk)

Cover image: Shutterstock.com

Set in 10/12pt Times by Aptara, Inc., New Delhi, India
Printed in Great Britain by CPI Group (UK) Ltd, Croydon, CR0 4YY

To our families:
Peter Cornelius: Susanne; and Heike and Paul
Christian Diller: Susanne, Moritz and Mara
Didier Guennoc: Brigitte, Lorenz-Gabriel and Ninon-Marie
Thomas Meyer: Mika Kaneyuki

Contents

Foreword

Over the last three decades, private equity has established itself as one of the most important asset classes for institutional investors. Despite going through boom and bust periods, investments in private equity have grown steadily over time. Two important economic forces have helped drive this growth.

First, illiquid assets, such as private equity, comprise an important part of the overall market portfolio and thus provide investors with important diversification benefits. The vast majority of assets around the world are private, and despite the recent growth of private equity these assets are still underrepresented in the portfolios of institutional investors.

Second, as institutional investors have grown larger and more diversified, it is becoming harder for institutions to exercise active ownership and governance in all the companies they own. This is a serious problem, since active ownership and governance are crucial in order to realize the full value potential of a firm. By investing part of their assets in private equity funds, large institutions can delegate their active ownership to skilled intermediaries, which in turn can acquire large ownership stakes in companies and act as active owners, while still allowing the institutional investors to maintain a high degree of diversification in their overall portfolios.

Recent research has confirmed that this model seems to work: firms seem to be run more efficiently under private equity ownership, and private equity has been a major contributor to institutional investor returns. Because of this, the long-term trend in private equity growth is not likely to reverse anytime soon.

Given its growth and importance, it is both worrying and surprising that private equity is so misunderstood. Despite the positive research evidence on the impact of private equity ownership on firms, the public perception of private equity is often quite negative. Private equity funds are depicted as vultures and asset strippers, who use financial engineering to squeeze out short-term profits from firms at the expense of employment and long-term growth. These perceptions have led legislators to impose misdirected regulation, such as the European AIFM directive, which at best simply imposes some additional red tape on funds, and at worst threatens the supply of capital to European small and medium-sized enterprises. A large part of the blame for this misunderstanding should fall on the private equity industry itself, which for too long believed it was fine to lack in transparency towards the public as long as it was transparent towards their investors.

It is even more worrisome, however, that investors themselves often misunderstand the private equity asset class. Many investors enter the private equity arena relying on their experience from investing in liquid stocks and bonds, without fully realizing that investing in illiquid assets requires a completely different skill set and investment approach.

Investors are often unable to appropriately assess and evaluate their returns from private equity. The type of short-term, quarter-by-quarter benchmarking that can be done for liquid investments fails to work for evaluating private equity. The regular net asset values reported by private equity funds are very different from market valuations, and relying on these for performance evaluation will be very misleading.

The true costs of private equity investing are also much less transparent, both because of the complex fee structures of private equity funds and the substantial organizational resources an institution has to devote to assess, execute, and monitor private equity investments. In addition, the opportunity cost of future liquidity commitments is often ignored. Numerous investors have experienced disappointing private equity returns, either because they felt forced to hold an excess of low-yielding liquid assets in order to meet future private equity fund commitments, or because they were forced to sell their private equity interests at fire-sale prices in the secondary market when they were not able to fulfill their commitments. These various costs will vary substantially across different types of investors, depending on their size, liability structure, and investment horizon. While the costs may be negligible for some investors, they may be insurmountable for others.

Evaluating private equity funds is also very different from evaluating liquid investment opportunities and asset managers. Liquid investment strategies are often about market timing, with investors swiftly responding to changes in relative risk premia across different assets and markets. Investment strategies that were successful in the past are unlikely to persist for long into the future, as capital can quickly move across liquid asset classes. Private equity investment, by contrast, is primarily about identifying consistent performers, who have the proprietary skills to add operational and strategic value to their investments over a long period of time.

The liquid investment mindset also leads investors to misunderstand the risks of private equity investments. For liquid assets, we have seen large leaps forward in terms of risk measurement and risk management in the last decades. Using modern portfolio theory, risk factors can now be estimated and incorporated in asset allocation models to capture exotic risk premia and improve diversification. Risk management tools such as VAR-models are estimated using high-frequency data in order to control and limit downside portfolio risks. These tools have also been picked up by regulators around the world and incorporated in capital regulations such as the Basle and Solvency rules.

Applying these standard models to private equity, however, often gives a highly misleading view of the real risks involved. Relying on fluctuations in infrequently updated net asset values are highly inappropriate for measuring risks, guiding strategic asset allocation, and forming the basis of risk management. In contrast, the liquidity risks are often either ignored or inappropriately modeled, leading to spectacular risk management failures and large costs to investors. In addition, if regulators fail to adjust their models, this can encourage institutions to take excessive illiquidity risk and result in the under-capitalization of such investors. Conversely, inappropriate regulation may penalize investors for taking perceived risks that in reality are not present or important.

Hence, the private equity industry faces a huge challenge in educating the public, investors, and regulators about this asset class. This is where this book fills an extremely important void. The authors, Cornelius, Diller, Guennoc, and Meyer, are some of the world's foremost experts on private equity investing. They uniquely combine extensive practical investment experience with deep knowledge of state-of-the-art research and methodologies. The authors provide an extensive coverage of all major aspects of the private equity market from an institutional investor's point of view, including fund structures, return and risk measurement, and risk modeling and management, in a way that is both advanced and highly practical. In addition, the book contains numerous discussions of more specialized topics, such as secondary markets and recent industry trends, such as securitization, which are enlightening and informative even for those very familiar with the private equity industry. The book should be required reading for those investing in private equity, novices and experienced investors alike. I congratulate the authors on an impressive and important effort!

Per Strömberg
Centennial Professor of Finance and Private Equity
Stockholm School of Economics
Stockholm April 1, 2013

Acknowledgements

Alternative investing in illiquid assets has become increasingly popular in the past few decades. For some long-term investors, especially family offices and endowments, the label "alternative" may no longer be appropriate as their exposure to private equity and real assets has risen to 20 – 30 percent, in some cases even more. While pension funds and insurance firms usually allocate a comparatively smaller share of their capital to alternative asset classes – reflecting, among other things, different liability profiles and regulatory requirements – their exposure has also increased considerably over time.

Alternative investing is expected to gain further momentum as investors chase yields in an environment where policy rates look set to remain low. Higher expected returns typically come with higher risk. But not only that. The nature of risks in alternative investing in illiquid assets is fundamentally different from risks that investors are exposed to when allocating capital to marketable assets. This is a key lesson investors have learned in the recent global financial crisis, which culminated in the collapse of Lehman Brothers in the fall of 2008. In light of this experience, a growing number of them have adopted new asset allocation models that focus on asset class-specific risk premiums.

Harvesting asset class-specific risk premiums requires asset class-specific risk management techniques. However, as far as investments in private equity funds and similar structures are concerned, the development of such techniques has not kept pace with the rapid increase in investors' exposure to these assets. Almost half a decade after the Great Recession, investors still find surprisingly little guidance in the existing literature in measuring risk in their illiquid portfolios and managing this risk efficiently. Meanwhile, regulators have identified the widening gap between the rise in alternative investing and the use of appropriate tools to measure and manage the risks associated with such investments as a key issue. New regulatory initiatives, such as Solvency II, encourage investors to develop their own proprietary models, in the absence of which they will have to adopt a standard model that imposes high capital requirements for private equity and similar assets.

In aiming at narrowing the gap between the growing importance of alternative investing and the availability of appropriate risk management tools, this book ventures, almost by definition, into unknown territory. Luckily, in our journey into terra incognita we were able to tap into the deep pool of knowledge of a wide range of investment professionals, risk managers and academics. All of them deserve our deep gratitude for making their invaluable insights and precious time available to us.

First and foremost, we would like to thank our fellow members of the working group on developing risk measurement guidelines, a group of practitioners that was set up by the European Venture Capital and Private Equity Association (EVCA) in the spring of 2010. Specifically, our sincere thanks go to Davide Deagostino (BT Pension Scheme); Ivan Herger (Capital Dynamics); Niklas Johansson (Cogent Partners); Lars Körner (Deutsche Bank Private Equity); Pierre-Yves Mathonet (formerly European Investment Fund and now ADIA); and the group's secretary Cornelius Müller (EVCA). Specifically, this working group was tasked to set up a framework for measuring and managing risk in private equity, within which investors may develop their own proprietary risk models in compliance with existing and emerging regulation. The initiative was supported by Dörte Höppner, EVCA's secretary general, to whom the authors, and indeed the entire working group, are deeply indebted.

Furthermore, we would like to thank the members of EVCA's Professional Standards Committee, and especially its chairman Vincent Neate (KPMG), for providing extremely helpful comments and suggestions throughout the process. The guidelines were finally approved by EVCA's Board, chaired by Vincenzo Morelli (TPG), in the fall of 2012. The authors would like to express their gratitude for the Board's support of the guidelines, which have evolved into the present study.

There are few areas where the symbiosis between academic research and practical applications is more intensive than in financial economics and risk management. In drafting EVCA's risk measurement guidelines, the working group greatly benefited from a first-class academic advisory board consisting of Ulf Axelson (London School of Economics and Political Science), Morten Sørenson (Columbia Business School) and Per Strömberg (Stockholm School of Economics and University of Chicago Booth School of Business). Their advice has been extremely important in ensuring the academic rigor the subject at hand requires. Professors Axelson, Sorenson and Strömberg have also served as an important sounding board in preparing the manuscript of this book, for which we are extremely grateful.

Other world-class academics have also commented extensively on earlier drafts or individual chapters and provided extremely useful guidance in developing a coherent risk management framework for illiquid assets. These include Oliver Gottschalg (HEC Paris); Robert Harris (University of Virginia); Tim Jenkinson (Oxford Said Business School); Christoph Kaserer (Technical University Munich); Josh Lerner (Harvard Business School); Ludovic Phalippou (Oxford Said Business School); and Peter Roosenboom (Rotterdam School of Management). All of them deserve our special thanks.

While this book aims to reflect the latest academic thinking on a subject that is constantly evolving, the main addressees of the present study are limited partners in private equity funds and similar structures. Many investment and risk management practitioners have shared their deep knowledge and experience with us and provided detailed comments on individual draft chapters or the entire manuscript. At AlpInvest Partners, we would like to thank the firm's partners for their continuous encouragement and their support in getting this project to the finish line. Furthermore, we have benefited greatly from specific comments and suggestions by Edo Aalbers and Robert de Veer of AlpInvest Partners' Portfolio and Risk team. At Montana Capital Partners, our sincere thanks go to Lara Lendenmann and Marco Wulff. We are also deeply indebted to John Breen (Sanabil); Pascal Cettier (Aeris Capital); Philippe Desfossés (ERAFP); Pieter van Foreest (APG); Ivan Popovic (Aeris Capital); John Renkema (APG); Alfred Rölli (Pictet); Christophe Rouvinez (Müller-Möhl Group); Pierre Stadler (Pictet) and Ashok Samuel (GIC). All of them have been extremely generous with their precious time in reading the manuscript and helping us determine best practices in measuring and managing risk in illiquid assets other investors will hopefully benefit from.

We also owe special thanks to our publishing team at Wiley, especially Werner Coetzee, Samantha Hartley and Jennie Kitchin. Sarah Lewis has done an outstanding job as our copy editor. Prakash Naorem of Aptara has very aptly led the production process, for which we are most grateful.

The greatest amount of gratitude is due to our families, however. Indeed, this book would not have been possible without their constant support and understanding and the time they have given us over the past few years. We would therefore like to dedicate this book to them.

Peter Cornelius
Christian Diller
Didier Guennoc
Thomas Meyer

1 Introduction

Investing in private equity, hedge funds and real assets – such as infrastructure, real estate, forestry and farmland, energy and commodities – has gained considerable momentum in recent years. These assets are often called "alternatives" as their investment history is still relatively short and, unlike traditional asset classes, they are rarely traded in public markets.[1] Investors have been attracted by the superior returns that alternative assets may offer. Moreover, as returns are found to be correlated less with traditional asset classes, alternative assets have been regarded as attractive investments helping asset allocators diversify their portfolios. At the same time, it has been argued that the potential returns of traditional asset classes have diminished. Specifically, public stock markets have become increasingly efficient, limiting investors' potential to achieve excess returns by investing in undervalued stocks. In the bond market, yields have declined substantially since the 1980s thanks to successful central bank policies aimed at reducing inflation expectations and restoring confidence in monetary policy.

1.1 ALTERNATIVE INVESTING AND THE NEED TO UPGRADE RISK MANAGEMENT SYSTEMS

At the end of 2011, private equity funds, hedge funds and funds investing in real assets were estimated to be managing around USD 4 trillion. This amount may still seem small compared with the size of the global equity and debt securities markets, whose volume totalled almost USD 150 trillion in 2010. However, the market for alternatives has grown much faster than traditional investments. Just three decades ago alternative assets totalled only a few billion US dollars, implying a compound annual growth rate of more than 25%. For some investors, especially endowments, foundations and family offices, alternative investing is no longer considered a niche strategy, but instead is part of their core portfolio. In fact, some asset allocators have invested as much as half their capital in alternatives, a few individual institutions even more. Pension plans, the largest investors in private equity, real assets and hedge funds, generally have a comparatively less pronounced exposure in terms of the total amount of assets under management (AuM). However, some of the largest pension funds worldwide, such as the California Public Employees' Retirement System (CalPERS), the Canadian Pension Plan Investment Board or the Washington State Investment Board, have invested 20% and more of their assets in alternatives.

The United States has remained the largest market for alternative investing, absorbing more than 50% of the capital deployed in private equity, real assets and hedge funds. At the same time, US investors have been the world's largest capital source for alternative investments. However, Europe and, more recently, advanced Asia and emerging economies have been playing catch-up, both as a destination and source of capital. As regards the latter, sovereign wealth funds

[1] Note that there is no universally accepted definition of alternative assets. Although often too small for institutional investors, alternatives may also include arts, rare books and maps, vintage cars and wine/vineyards.

(SWFs) have played a particularly important role, helping recycle their countries' current account surpluses and raising foreign exchange reserves by investing in asset classes whose liquidity characteristics make them inaccessible for central banks. Thus, alternative investing has become a global business, with cross-border transactions helping regional markets become increasingly integrated.

However, it appears that the development of investors' risk management capabilities has not always kept pace with their growing exposure to alternative assets. During the global financial crisis in 2008–2009, a significant number of investors, and especially those with a substantial exposure to alternative assets, were faced with an acute lack of liquidity. The sudden shortage of liquidity took investors by surprise. The majority of them had based their liquidity planning on cash flow models whose parameters were essentially static. However, as financial markets shut in the wake of the collapse of Lehman Brothers in the autumn of 2008, the model parameters shifted rapidly due to sharply reduced distributions from private equity funds and similar partnerships investing in real assets, the suspension of redemptions by hedge funds, and increased margin calls and collateral. Many institutional investors thus found that their short-term liabilities either proved to be much more inflexible than they had thought or rose unexpectedly in the face of the crisis.

The financial turmoil that spread rapidly around the globe made a key characteristic of long-term investing in private equity funds and similar structures suddenly highly transparent. Organized as limited partnerships, such funds are designed to shield fledgling portfolio companies in their early stages and those in need of being restructured from disruptive market influences, and to assure these companies' continued financing. This requires patient capital, with long-term investors in limited partnerships essentially locking away their capital for 10 years or even longer. While investors, or limited partners in private equity funds, were aware of the fact that they had to make long-term capital commitments in order to be able to harvest an illiquidity risk premium, during the crisis it turned out that many of them had underestimated liquidity risk in two important ways. First, capital calls, or so-called contributions, of committed capital to private equity funds and similar structures are unknown in terms of their timing and size. Although capital calls slowed substantially during the Great Recession, distributions fell even faster as exit markets essentially closed. Thus, limited partners were exposed to funding risk, which represents a key challenge in terms of liquidity management. Second, investors who had relied on the secondary market as a means to liquidate (parts of) their portfolios found out that transaction volumes fell sharply precisely when liquidity was needed most.

University endowments in the USA were hit particularly hard, and given their payout requirements several of them were forced into distressed sales of assets. However, the problems were by no means confined to university endowments. In fact, as we discuss throughout this book, even some of the largest pension funds were confronted with significant liquidity problems as funding risk and market liquidity risk in the secondary market surged to unprecedented highs. As investors attempted to avoid defaulting on their commitments amid an increasingly illiquid secondary market, they decided to sell liquid parts of their portfolios, such as public stocks, to generate liquidity (Ang *et al.*, 2011). In some cases, the pressure to divest was amplified by a substantially larger-than-expected decline in the mark-to-market value of investors' portfolios, triggering "sell" signals by their asset allocation models. In the event, many investors incurred significant losses (Ang and Kjaer, 2011; whose analysis is summarized in Chapter 6).

To be sure, the crisis did not generally undermine investors' belief in the benefits of alternative investing. While some investors did reduce their allocation to alternatives in an effort

Table 1.1 Allocation of pension funds to alternative asset classes, as a percentage of total assets under management

	2006	2008	2010
Real estate	5.2	6.7	5.6
Private equity	2.7	4.5	4.6
Commodities	0.4	0.6	1.0
Hedge funds	1.5	2.2	2.2
Other	1.0	1.7	2.1
Total	10.9	15.7	15.6

Source: IMF (2011).

to align assets more closely with liabilities and to comply with accounting and regulatory pressures, others maintained their allocations or even raised them, for example, to address underfunded liabilities (WEF, 2011). As far as pension funds are concerned, a recent survey by the International Monetary Fund (IMF, 2011) found that their overall exposure to alternative assets was virtually unchanged between 2008 and 2010 (see Table 1.1), as new investments essentially kept pace with distributions by limited partnership funds or offset other divestments. Importantly, the share of alternative assets in pension funds' total AuM thus remained significantly higher than prior to the crisis, when many investors increased their allocations to alternatives substantially. As a result, pension funds' average exposure to alternative assets in 2010 exceeded their relative allocation in 2006 by more than 40%, with private equity contributing particularly strongly to this increase.

Arguably, the most recent turmoil in Europe's sovereign debt market might have contributed to institutional investors' continuous commitment to alternatives. As the IMF (2012) points out, the debt crisis has reinforced the notion that no asset can be viewed as truly safe. Instead, recent rating downgrades of sovereigns previously considered to be virtually riskless have reaffirmed that even highly rated assets are subject to significant risks. The IMF (2012) estimates that the decline in the number of sovereigns whose debt is considered safe could remove some USD 9 trillion from the supply of safe assets by 2016, or roughly 16% of the projected total. This decline is accentuated by a reduction in the private supply of safe assets as poor securitization in the USA has tainted these securities and more stringent regulation has impaired the ease with which private sector issuers may produce assets that are deemed "safe".

At the same time, heightened uncertainty, regulatory reforms and crisis-related responses by central banks have driven up demand for safe assets. Given the shrinking set of assets perceived to be safe, growing global supply/demand imbalances are feared to increase the price of safety and compel investors to move down the safety scale as they scramble to obtain scarce assets. The IMF (2012) warns that safe asset scarcity could lead to global financial instability resulting from short-term volatility jumps, herding behaviour and runs on sovereign debt. In this environment, where global supply/demand imbalances may seriously distort the benchmark pricing of sovereign debt, investors may be compelled further to invest in alternatives to generate higher returns. Note, in this context, that in the first nine months of 2012 10-year US Treasury bonds averaged around 1.8%, implying significantly negative yields in real terms. Yields on 2-year US Treasuries averaged 0.28% during this period, while strong demand for German and Swiss 2-year bonds drove even nominal yields into negative territory. A third round of quantitative easing in the United States, unconventional monetary policy measures in the euro area, the United Kingdom and Japan, and further monetary easing in several emerging markets indicate that policy makers are committed to keeping interest rates low in the foreseeable future.

While investors have remained committed to alternatives, their experience in the recent global financial crisis has led many of them to reconsider their investment strategies with regard to private equity, hedge funds and real assets. Generally, this review has focused on two aspects of the allocation process. First, from a top-down perspective investors have revisited their asset allocation models in light of their liability profiles and risk appetite (WEF, 2011). Second, from an asset-specific point of view a growing number of investors have thought about alternative ways to achieve their target exposure to specific asset classes. As a growing number of investors have begun to adjust their asset allocation strategies, they have fostered visible changes in the alternative investment industry.

As far as portfolio construction is concerned, in the pre-crisis era most investors relied on models that were designed to construct efficient portfolios on the basis of historical asset returns, their variance and their correlation with returns in other asset classes. However, in the Great Recession such mean/variance approaches proved to be too static, as systemic risk rapidly pushed correlations upwards. As a result, gains from diversification often proved to be illusive, and investor portfolios turned out to be far less robust than the models had suggested.

Against this background, several investors have begun to implement less granular asset allocation frameworks that focus more on asset-specific risks as differentiating factors generating diversification benefits – as opposed to (less-than-perfect) return correlations that play a key role in the standard mean/variance approach. This applies to both traditional and alternative asset classes. As far as the latter are concerned, the risk factor allocation approach recognizes that private equity, hedge funds and real assets are subject to fundamentally different risks. Private equity, for instance, is subject to liquidity risk, in addition to equity risk. By comparison, investing in hedge funds is generally less illiquid than commitments to private equity funds. At the same time, however, hedge funds tend to be highly leveraged and hence subject to credit risk. As far as real estate is concerned, investors expect to be compensated for the term risk they take – a risk component which is absent in private equity investments. It is this heterogeneity of investment risk and the associated risk premiums that offers diversification gains and hence helps improve risk-adjusted portfolio returns.

1.2 SCOPE OF THE BOOK

Harvesting different risk premiums requires specific risk management approaches. In this book, we focus primarily on the illiquidity risk premium that structurally illiquid asset classes may offer. Two clarifications are in order. First of all, a broad range of asset markets may become illiquid in periods of severe financial stress. In the recent global financial crisis, the markets for corporate debt, collateralized debt obligations and securitization virtually shut down. There is a rapidly expanding literature on cyclical illiquidity, discussing its causes and effects and especially the role of banks (e.g., Shin, 2010; Tirole, 2011 and the literature discussed therein). In contrast to asset classes that may become illiquid thanks to financial turmoil and heightened risk aversion, investors in structurally illiquid asset classes, such as private equity and real assets, are aware *ex ante* of the risk they take. In fact, as we argue in this book, it is precisely this risk, and more specifically the associated risk premium, that attracts investors to these asset classes. Not all investors are able to harvest this risk premium, however. As a matter of principle, only long-term investors can, whose liability profile allows them to lock capital in for a prolonged period of time, usually 10 years or more. Harvesting the illiquidity risk premium requires specific risk management techniques, however, which are the subject of this book.

Second, we shall not consider hedge funds. While they are generally considered to be part of the alternative investment universe, they show a different risk profile compared with private equity and real assets. Although redemptions may be suspended in certain circumstances, the organization of hedge funds is fundamentally different from private equity funds and limited partnerships investing in real assets, making the former less illiquid. At the same time, hedge funds are subject to risks that are idiosyncratic to this asset class, requiring different risk management tools whose discussion is beyond the scope of this book.

This leaves us with long-term investing in private equity and real assets as two highly illiquid alternative asset classes. But this is still too broad a focus for what this book attempts to achieve. Instead, it is important to recognize that there are different ways to invest in private equity and real assets. As investors have revisited their exposure to alternative assets, and more specifically to private equity and real assets, some of them have decided to pursue alternative routes to fund investing. To begin with, some large investors have engaged in direct investments, essentially competing with partnerships in acquiring assets. Others have put increased emphasis on co-investments alongside funds they have committed capital to. While there is little systematic evidence on the significance of co-investments and direct investments in investors' portfolios, anecdotal evidence suggests that at least in individual cases (notably some Canadian pension funds) these forms play an important role. Yet others (i.e., some sovereign wealth funds) have acquired stakes in the management company of private equity firms. Finally, a rising number of investors have sought to set up managed accounts with asset managers instead of committing capital to limited partnerships.

As investors have looked into alternative ways of investing in private equity and real assets, many fund managers have adjusted their own business models. Several large private equity firms – such as the Blackstone Group, Carlyle Group or Kohlberg Kravis Roberts – have transformed themselves into alternative asset managers, offering their clients a broad range of products, including through managed accounts. A growing number of firms have gone public, enabling shareholders to get exposure to alternative investing without investing in their funds. Meanwhile, there is a range of derivative instruments on listed private equity, including exchange-traded funds (ETFs).

As important as these structural changes in the alternative investment arena are, the most common form of investing in private equity and real assets remains the limited partnership. In a limited partnership, investors serve as limited partners (LPs) committing capital to a fund, which is raised and managed by a general partner (GP). Such limited partnership funds typically have a lifespan of 10 years, with the possible extension of 2 years. For this period, LPs essentially lock in their capital, notwithstanding the emergence of a secondary market in recent years. At any given point in time, LPs have to be in a position to respond to capital calls by the GP, subjecting fund investments to significant funding risk.

Unfortunately, studies on managing illiquidity risk associated with investments in limited partnerships have remained rare. This may seem surprising in light of the growing importance of private equity and real assets in investors' portfolios and the experience of several LPs in the recent global financial crisis. It is therefore the objective of this book to narrow this gap by developing risk management guidelines drawing upon best practices.

1.3 ORGANIZATION OF THE BOOK

This book is organized in three parts. In **Part I**, we discuss illiquid investments in private equity and real assets from a market perspective. In **Part II**, we focus on risk measurement for portfolios of limited partnership funds targeting these asset classes. Finally, in **Part III**, we discuss some techniques for managing this risk and related issues.

1.3.1 Illiquid investments as an asset class

Our discussion starts by defining long-term assets that are subject to structural illiquidity, offering investors a risk premium. These assets constitute the universe of investment opportunities we address in this book, which have to be clearly distinguished from assets that may become temporarily illiquid in periods of financial turmoil. In **Chapter 2**, we provide an estimate of the size of the market for illiquid investments in private equity and real assets. These asset classes can be accessed through alternative routes, which, however, require strategy-specific risk management approaches. In contrast, limited partnerships provide a structural investment framework, which is largely agnostic with regard to the underlying asset class – presumably an important reason why limited partnerships have remained the dominant route for investors seeking exposure to private equity and real assets.

While, as we explain, the market for illiquid investments has grown rapidly over the last few decades, this market expansion has not been linear. Instead, there have been pronounced cycles around the long-term trend, which in part is explained by macroeconomic cycles and in part by asset-specific investment dynamics. Furthermore, we look at the global investor base of private equity, which is representative of the broader universe of illiquid asset classes. While pension funds and insurance firms dominate the investor base in terms of the absolute amount of money invested in private equity funds, endowments, foundations and family offices generally have a larger exposure to the asset class relative to the size of the portfolio they manage. As we will discuss in more detail, relative allocations are generally a function of investors' liability profiles, which vary across different classes of investors. Moreover, asset managers are subject to different regulations and accounting rules. However, even within specific investor classes allocations vary widely, reflecting different degrees of risk appetite.

Looking ahead, we discuss long-term trends in the asset management industry. Of particular importance for long-term investing is the secular shift from defined benefits (DB) pension plans to defined contributions (DC) plans. Given the transferability of claims under DC plans, investments generally require a high degree of liquidity. However, as we discuss in this chapter, this does not necessarily mean that DC plans are unable to invest in illiquid assets. Furthermore, we explore the potential role of emerging economies as suppliers of patient capital. While SWFs have attracted considerable attention as investors in private equity and real assets, we also look at pension funds and insurance firms. Their AuM grow at substantial rates as governments implement important pension reforms and incomes rise. Investments are still often restricted to domestic markets and to specific asset classes. To the extent that such restrictions are lifted and replaced by a prudent investing approach, pension funds and insurance firms in emerging economies could make an increasingly meaningful contribution to the global supply of long-term capital. A precondition for this to happen, however, is the introduction of a comprehensive risk management approach that encompasses illiquid asset classes.

Portfolio diversification is at the core of "prudent investing", a concept with far-reaching legal consequences. As we point out in **Chapter 3**, the prudent investor rule, as stipulated in the

"Prudent Investor Act" in the United States, has to be clearly distinguished from the "prudent man" rule. Importantly, the former explicitly recognizes that diversification is a key component of prudence, which includes the delegation of investment management to external managers. A portfolio may thus include assets which, on a stand-alone basis, might be considered too risky from the viewpoint of the prudent man rule. Note in this context that US pension funds were allowed to invest in private equity and venture capital funds only in 1979 when the US Department of Labor clarified its prudent man rule in a way that explicitly permitted fund managers to invest in high-risk assets.

As regulators have redefined what constitutes prudent investing, the emphasis has shifted towards the investment process as opposed to specific investments and allocations. As long as the investment process is considered to be prudent, investment managers enjoy considerable flexibility to (re-)design strategies in rapidly changing market environments. Arguably, this flexibility should reduce the risk of herding among investors who have to follow the same rules. But what exactly is a prudent investment process? In Chapter 3, we suggest a number of criteria that are simple and transparent and can be applied across different jurisdictions.

In **Chapter 4**, we discuss the basic structure of limited partnerships as the dominant vehicle through which investments in many alternative asset classes are made. Understanding this structure is critical for investors to measure their risk exposure correctly and manage it appropriately. As we argue, the high degree of illiquidity is not just a by-product of the limited partnership as a legal construct, but instead represents a central feature that enables the GP of a fund to harvest a premium for his LPs. This basic observation remains intact, despite the emergence of a secondary market in recent years. Although the absolute volume of transactions in the secondary market has risen appreciably, it is still very small relative to the total amount of assets managed by private equity funds and partnerships investing in real assets.

Investors have several alternatives to achieve exposure to private equity and real assets, including: through listed vehicles; investments in the management company of private equity firms or alternative asset managers; managed accounts; direct and co-investments. However, none of these alternative routes have seriously challenged the fund structure as the preferred choice for investors who seek exposure to private equity and real assets. In fact, today's limited partnership as a legal investment framework has precedents that can be traced back to ancient Babylon almost 5000 years ago.

While the limited partnership has a very long history, the key question for investors locking in capital for 10 years or more through such vehicles is whether they are adequately compensated for the illiquidity they accept. To be sure, the illiquidity risk involved in long-term investing in funds is far from trivial, as such commitments make it very difficult, if not impossible, for investors to continuously rebalance their portfolios, a key assumption in standard asset allocation models. In **Chapter 5**, therefore, we discuss recent attempts in the literature to measure risk and returns in private equity to get a better understanding of the illiquidity premium investors may expect.

Generally, the literature finds that GPs have achieved excess returns through a combination of strategic measures, operational measures and financial measures. This does not tell us, however, whether their LPs have actually enjoyed excess returns, given the management fees and the carry paid to the GP. While earlier studies actually raised doubts whether private equity has outperformed public equity net-of-fees, more recent work does suggest that there is a positive illiquidity premium to be earned.

However, it is important to note that the outperformance recent studies find is not adjusted for risk. As we discuss in more detail, the public market equivalent (PME) – a standard measure to compare returns of investments in private equity funds with similar (cash flow-based) investments in a public market index – implicitly assumes beta to be equal to one, implying the absence of market risk. To the extent that the true beta is under- or overestimated, the true PME is over- or underestimated. Fortunately, we receive some comfort from recent academic research that finds changes in beta have a strongly diminishing effect on the PME: thus, even if the true beta were 1.5 (the upper end of empirical estimates for buyout funds) instead of 1, which is implicitly assumed in PME-based comparisons, there would still be considerable outperformance of private equity. Similarly, it is found that PMEs are remarkably insensitive to the multiple of the public market returns. In fact, even if public market returns had been twice the S&P 500, the median PMEs would still be larger than 1 for the 1990s and 2000s vintages, suggesting that systematic risk does not explain the estimated outperformance of buyout funds.

It remains an open question, however, whether this outperformance is enough for the illiquidity risk investors take when committing capital to private equity and similar funds. Academic research that addresses liquidity risk explicitly in extended approaches of the Capital Asset Pricing Model (CAPM) has just begun to emerge. While this research puts the illiquidity premium in the range of 2–4%, more work is required to say with sufficient confidence whether these estimates provide a reasonable range for the risk illiquid investments in funds entail.

Notwithstanding the remaining uncertainty about the size of the illiquidity premium, a growing number of investors have begun to implement an allocation approach that seeks to generate diversification gains on the basis of a limited number of distinct risks. One risk is illiquidity, a factor that can be accessed through private equity and real assets. This renders private equity and real assets different compared with, say, high-yield bonds, which are primarily subject to term risk and credit risk. As we stress, however, each risk needs to be measured and managed carefully to harvest the premiums associated with the risks in each asset class.

In the final chapter of Part I, we focus on the role of the secondary market, which has sometimes been seen as a panacea for illiquidity in primary fund investments. We caution against such a view. As important as the emergence of a secondary market has been for investors seeking to mitigate the J-curve effect of their primary fund investments programme and improve the risk/return characteristics of their private equity holdings, it is not a game changer in terms of the basic characteristics of illiquid investments. In fact, as we argue in **Chapter 6**, it would be highly dangerous for investors to regard the secondary market as a substitute for proper management of liquidity risk. For starters, as we emphasized before, the secondary market has remained small relative to the overall exposure of investors to private equity and real assets. More importantly, liquidity in the secondary market tends to dry up precisely when sellers need it most. In the recent global financial crisis, transaction volumes fell sharply as buyers demanded huge discounts relative to the net asset value (NAV) of the portfolios the sellers wanted to liquidate. This experience casts doubt on the role of the secondary market in discovering the true price of illiquid investments. Putting in place an adequate risk management system that is designed for the specific risks in illiquid asset classes is therefore a key condition for investors venturing into private equity and real assets.

1.3.2 Risk measurement and modelling

In the second part of the book, we outline the main features of proper risk management based on current best practices. In **Chapter 7**, we set the scene by introducing risk as the potential deviation from an expected outcome. Risk, as we emphasize, can usefully be distinguished from uncertainty. Whereas risk generally refers to the probability of an event occurring, uncertainty is immeasurable, given that particular events are so infrequent or unique that no probability distribution can be determined. Typically perceived as a negative outcome – not least from a regulatory perspective – risk is usually calculated as the product of the probability of an event and the expected loss if the event occurs. However, investment strategies are generally subject to both downside and upside risks, requiring investors to navigate carefully through the potential losses without ignoring the opportunities that are associated with a particular allocation decision.

While risk is generally predicated on the notion of quantifiability, in practice risk managers often face substantial challenges in measuring risk in a statistically meaningful way. Frequently, we have to accept a considerable degree of subjectivity in quantifying risks. This is not least true in alternative investing where historical data remain rare and market-based valuations are not available. Not surprisingly, therefore, risk models for such assets have remained rare and subject to considerable controversy. Given the nature of investing in private equity and real assets, we argue that a new risk management approach is needed that embraces the lack of high-frequency market data by using all available information, including qualitative assessments.

At the core of any risk management approach lies the definition of the types of risk that need to be managed. From a broader portfolio standpoint, risk is generally seen as market risk and typically estimated in the CAPM framework, to help determine the desired allocation of capital to different asset classes. However, once an allocation to these asset classes is determined, investors have to manage their asset-specific risks. First and foremost, as we explain in **Chapter 8**, investors in limited partnership funds face the risk that the fund manager fails to return the invested capital in full (plus an expected return). Conceptually, this may be considered as a default, and with many practitioners viewing default risk as more relevant than market risk, there have been attempts to apply credit risk models to illiquid assets. However, such attempts are fundamentally flawed as they focus only on the downside, whereas in a portfolio of funds unrealized gains may serve as a buffer, a viewpoint that has long been accepted by the Basel Committee in the context of banks' equity portfolios.

As we emphasize throughout this book, the key differentiating factor between investments through limited partnership funds and investments in marketable assets is the high degree of illiquidity of the former. As far as commitments to funds are concerned, two dimensions of liquidity risk can be distinguished. First, investments are subject to market liquidity risk, in the sense that there might not be enough demand for purchasing assets in the secondary market. Second, investors face the risk of lacking sufficient liquidity to fund their commitments. Capital calls are made at short notice, requiring investors to have sufficient liquidity at any point in time to avoid defaulting on their commitments. However, hoarding cash comes at significant opportunity costs. Related to the illiquidity problem is the absence of market prices as the basis for risk measurement. Instead, we need to base such a measurement on suitable models. Thus, as we discuss further in Chapter 8, investors are well advised to run funding tests by monitoring key liquidity ratios or undertaking more sophisticated scenario analysis for future cash flows. LPs also need to employ such a funding test to confirm that they are able to honour all capital calls or, alternatively, are able to undertake orderly transactions under no duress, which obviously is a critical assumption for modelling the economic substance of investments in limited partnership funds.

In **Chapter 9**, we return to the issue of potential capital losses in fund portfolios. Specifically, we are interested in the maximum loss an investor could suffer within a given confidence interval – a question which can usefully be addressed in the framework of a value-at-risk (VaR) analysis.[2] Applying VaR analysis to illiquid assets, for which market prices do not exist, raises a number of important conceptual and statistical issues. In addressing these issues, we discuss two alternative approaches. The first approach is a VaR analysis based on (typically quarterly) changes in NAVs as reported by the funds in a portfolio. While this approach appears to be conventional and relatively easy to implement, its simplicity is deceptive and it has important limitations. Chief among these is the fact that changes in reported NAVs do not reflect the lifecycle characteristics of limited partnerships, such as the J-curve phenomenon and the future pattern of undrawn commitments. The second, alternative approach presented focuses on the volatility of cash flows. This approach uses historical cash flow data over the entire lifecycle of funds. These data can be used in a Monte Carlo simulation to generate cash flow scenarios for a portfolio of funds, taking into account correlations between portfolio segments, such as specific vintage years or strategies.

Working with cash flows is more akin to the needs of non-financial firms. While financial institutions employ VaR to determine their capital adequacy and measure tradable risks, real investments in fixed assets by non-financial firms cannot easily be liquidated. Instead, industrial companies tend to focus on the cash-flow-at-risk (CFaR) as a more relevant measure of their investment risk exposure. Specifically, the CFaR measures the maximum deviation of actual cash flows from a given level within a given confidence interval. Contrary to VaR, which is calculated for very short time periods, CFaR relates to longer periods, typically quarters or even years (i.e., intervals that are also relevant for investors in limited partnership funds). Importantly, the CFaR mirrors both cash inflows and cash outflows as key determinants of the funding test limited partners are required to meet at any given point in time.

This leads us to the importance of diversification within fund portfolios across different dimensions. As we discuss in more detail, significant gains are already achieved at relatively low levels of diversification, especially as far as investing over different vintage years is concerned. A key conclusion from this analysis is that continuous monitoring and management of diversification should be an integral part of a LP's risk management. There are two important caveats, however. First, as the degree of diversification increases – in the extreme case, an investor holds the market portfolio – the potential to achieve extraordinary returns declines. Second, in periods of financial turmoil cash flow correlations tend to rise, reducing the potential diversification gains with respect to managing liquidity risk – as opposed to the risk of actual capital losses we also consider in Chapter 9.

The estimation of the true VaR in portfolios of limited partnership funds is inextricably intertwined with the question of how undrawn commitments should be treated in this framework. The answer the standard finance model gives is simple – undrawn commitments can be ignored. According to what represents the main framework of finance theory, different investments and assets can be valued in isolation. Each investment has its own net present value (NPV), which is calculated by discounting future cash flows using an appropriate discount rate. Since undrawn commitments do not represent actual cash flows, they have NPV = 0 and hence should not matter.

[2] This approach is widely used in financial risk management and regulation, with maximum losses due to adverse movements in asset prices typically determined at the 99% or 99.5% level of confidence (implying an event occurring every 100 or 200 years, respectively).

However, undrawn commitments, which are contractually binding, obviously did matter during the recent financial crisis. In addressing this apparent conundrum, our discussion in **Chapter 10** starts by asking whether overcommitments to funds actually represent leverage. In fact, we find important commonalities between overcommitments and leverage, with both strategies being motivated by the objective to magnify returns. To the extent that overcommitments are used in order to achieve higher returns, they imply higher risk – just as in the case of leverage. Conversely, holding capital in low-yielding Treasury bills to always be in a position to respond to capital calls lowers or even eliminates risk – at the expense of higher returns. Investors may therefore choose a commitment strategy that is consistent with a risk/return profile according to their utility function. However, this suggests that undrawn commitments do play an important role, in contrast to the standard finance model where capital held in highly liquid assets has no economic value as negative cash flows are assumed to be financed through borrowing.

The important role undrawn commitments have played in the losses some investors have suffered during the recent financial crisis will no doubt continue to attract a substantial amount of attention from practitioners and academics alike. A key question that will need to be addressed concerns the treatment of such commitments in the standard finance model. Specifically, how can discount rates be determined in the presence of undrawn commitments? In addressing this question, the accounting view, which treats undrawn commitments as off-balance sheet items, needs to be reconciled with the economic perspective that recognizes the resources dedicated to private equity and the risk from possible overcommitment strategies. Finding a solution to this challenge looks set to rank prominently on the research agenda for years to come. As we argue in the final part of Chapter 10, a first possible step could lie in treating undrawn capital as a loan. Intuitively, one may think of a credit line from a bank used by the LP to fund his commitments. Alternatively, as here, it may be assumed that the GP draws down the capital entirely at the beginning of the fund's life and lends the money to the LP in order for them to respond to their capital calls.

Given the high degree of liquidity risk associated with investments in private equity and real assets, cash flow modelling is a key challenge that needs to be addressed in internal models. Generally, two approaches can be distinguished. Non-probabilistic models use a limited number of parameters and are preferable in cases where the modeller is confronted with important data constraints. A well-known example is the model developed by the Yale endowment's investment team, whose basic structure is presented in **Chapter 11**. While this model and its numerous variants that have been developed in recent years are relatively simple and easy to implement, they are subject to strict limitations. Importantly, non-probabilistic models do not provide for outcome ranges and hence are unable to capture the volatility of cash flows. As a result, they are appropriate only in exceptional circumstances, for instance in the case of large diversified and fully funded portfolios of fund investments.

By contrast, probabilistic models are generally more complex and pose important data challenges. Probabilistic models use extensive cash flow libraries to project the cash flows of a given investment portfolio, taking into account the maturity of the individual funds making up the portfolio. Probabilistic models can usefully be subjected to scenario analysis to determine the sensitivity of cash flows to deviations from the past. Scenarios are particularly useful to stress-test cash flow projections derived from probabilistic models in order to evaluate and quantify the impact of exogenous shocks. The experience that many investors had in the recent financial crisis leaves little doubt about the importance of cash flow modelling under alternative assumptions.

Risk models for funds can be constructed top-down or bottom-up. While probabilistic models using cash flow libraries tend to start with a top-down approach, a bottom-up analysis can refine projections and add considerable granularity. In this analysis, a key ingredient is the distribution waterfall as specified in the limited partnership agreement. The basic structure of the waterfall is presented in **Chapter 12**, on the basis of which we provide different examples of cash inflows and outflows under alternative assumptions about hurdle rates and carried interest. While these parameters determine the profit for the LPs, they are also highly relevant from a risk management perspective. Realistically, however, a bottom-up analysis may be too complex and resource-intensive for most investors, given substantial variations between funds in terms of the key parameters determining profit sharing between the GP and his or her LPs.

As important as quantitative risk measurement is, in illiquid asset classes risk managers often face important data constraints. This does not mean, however, that effective risk management cannot be done. Rather, the risk manager has to work with the set of information that is available to him or her, and this includes qualitative assessments. Understandably, many risk managers feel uncomfortable using qualitative data, as they fear that such information may be inconsistent and hence result in distorted conclusions. However, this discomfort can be mitigated, at least to some degree, by employing classification schemes for limited partnership funds.

As far as mutual funds are concerned, there are several external agencies that provide ratings aiming to provide a forward-looking prognosis based on a standardized valuation. As we argue in **Chapter 13**, independent ratings of limited partnerships are more difficult, as there are few objective criteria that can be used in a standardized fashion. Furthermore, there may be too few potential users, given the still relatively limited number of investors in private equity and real assets, making these asset classes less scalable in terms of external ratings. However, a growing number of LPs are using proprietary fund grading systems that, in an effort to exploit all available information, take into account qualitative assessments. Importantly, funds are benchmarked against their peers in such grading systems. Defining the appropriate peer group is therefore essential for the risk manager to extract information from the grading of funds and as a basis for quantifying risks, as we discuss in **Chapter 14**.

1.3.3 Risk management and its governance

In **Part III** we turn to the question of how the concepts discussed in this book can be applied in practice. The management of securitizations of private equity funds should be seen as a case study where such instruments were successfully used in the market place under the scrutiny of rating agencies. While in the risk-on/risk-off environment in the post-crisis era securitization in general has played a less prominent role, the principle of securitizing portfolios of illiquid funds is highly illustrative for effective risk management. As we discuss in **Chapter 15**, such structured vehicles represent a relatively simple case of asset liability management and are therefore instructive for LPs facing comparable issues, such as pension plans and insurance companies. Securitizations of portfolios of limited partnership funds demonstrate how one risk dimension can be transformed into another and how trade-offs between risk dimensions can be managed – equity versus debt, market risk versus credit risk, illiquidity versus liquidity, liquidity risk versus capital risk.

Focusing on the investment process as a defining criterion of prudent investing could easily lead to confusion over the role of the LP's risk manager versus the role of its compliance officer. In **Chapter 16**, therefore, we clarify the two functions as distinctly different parts of an investment firm's risk management system. Assuring conformity with regulatory requirements and dealing effectively with operational risk is fundamental for the long-term success of an investment firm. However, compliance has little, if anything, to do with the management of financial risks in the sense of trading off risks versus rewards in asset markets, which falls squarely into the remit of the risk manager. Put differently, compliance has to ensure that specific processes are followed in the way they were intended to work, but it is the role of risk management to help design such processes in the first place.

Ensuring that the risk manager can fulfil his or her role effectively requires appropriate governance structures. This raises a number of important issues. Where in the LP's organization should the risk management function be anchored? To whom should the risk manager report? Who is accountable in case of failures? And how should the risk manager be remunerated within the broader structure of the firm? These are only some of the thorny issues we discuss.

In addressing these and other issues, LPs should have a clear risk management policy in place that sets the framework for coordinating and executing the firm's activities in a risk-sensitive manner. Conceivably, as we examine in the final chapter of this book, this framework may consist of a set of clearly defined rules or may be based on rather general principles. However, while a pure rules-based system may be too rigid, a principles-based framework may be too weak or ambiguous. In practice, therefore, a combination of the two may be superior, a direction that is favoured by new regulatory initiatives, such as the European Alternative Investment Fund Manager (AIFM) directive. Importantly, as we point out in **Chapter 17**, risk management policy is a living instrument rather than a static set of checks and balances. Periodic reviews are necessary to ensure that an investment firm's risk management policy is consistent with the industry's best practices. In installing a risk management framework, it is important to note that its effectiveness is not least a function of its organizational setting. To be effective, the risk management function has to enjoy a high degree of independence versus the firm's operating units, must be equipped with adequate resources and must have access to all information. The firm's reporting system is equally important. This and the general complexity of risk models imply an appropriate IT system that allows the running of large-scale stress tests and scenario analyses.

For LPs, putting in place an effective risk management policy is a prerequisite for adopting internal model-based approaches to risk management. In fact, regulated investors – such as banks, insurance firms and pension funds – have a strong incentive to employ internal risk models, which allow them to reduce significantly their regulatory capital charges compared with the standard approach. For the internal model to be approved by the regulatory authorities, it has to pass a "use test", however. This entails, *inter alia*, explaining the rationale of the model, the underlying assumptions, the valuation methods and the data used. However, the use test also includes procedural questions, pertaining, for example, to the model's function in the broader governance system, its role as an integrated tool in decision-making processes and its adaptation to the investor's evolving risk profile.

Part I

Illiquid Investments as an Asset Class

2

Illiquid Assets, Market Size and the Investor Base

In setting the scene for this book, this chapter starts by defining the universe of illiquid assets. Specifically, we stress the structural nature of illiquidity as the major defining characteristic of the asset classes we cover in this book, as opposed to asset classes that may become subject to cyclical market liquidity breakdowns in periods of financial stress. This definition limits our focus to private equity and real assets consisting of real estate, infrastructure, oil and gas, and forestry.

The most common form of investing in private equity and real assets remains the limited partnership. As we discuss in greater detail in Chapter 4, limited partnership funds provide a particularly appropriate framework to harvest the illiquidity risk premium these asset classes offer. Specifically, fund structures allow the use of a common risk measurement and management approach that can be applied across different asset classes. Between 2000 and 2011, around USD 4 trillion were committed to private equity partnerships and funds targeting real assets. While this amount may seem small relative to investments in traditional asset classes, such as public stocks and bonds, we show in this chapter that illiquid investments represent a sizable share in the portfolios of some investor classes, especially those who are less constrained by their liabilities.

In the final part of this chapter, we look at recent trends in the community of long-term investors. A particularly important trend is the secular shift from defined benefit pension plans to defined contribution plans, with the latter requiring a significantly higher degree of liquidity in their investments. In this context, we also discuss the emergence of long-term investors in developing economies and their potential to at least partially offset the possible decline in the supply of patient capital from advanced economies.

2.1 DEFINING ILLIQUID ASSETS

Asset classes are subject to different degrees of liquidity, requiring different risk management approaches. Figure 2.1 shows a range of selected asset classes according to their degree of liquidity versus their time horizon (WEF, 2011, p. 14). Private equity and real assets represent one end of the spectrum, whose opposite pole comprises high-grade short-term and long-term government bonds and public equity (Figure 2.1). In the middle lie hedge funds, commodities and corporate bonds. Importantly, market size is not necessarily the key determinant of liquidity. For example, at the end of 2011 the outstanding amount of corporate bonds in the United States was USD 7,791 billion, not dramatically less than the stock of debt of USD 9,928 billion owed by the US Treasury.[1] Yet, as Chacko (2005) notes, the median corporate bond trades approximately only every two months, which makes this asset class

[1] Data are from the Securities Industry and Financial Markets Association (SIFMA) (2012).

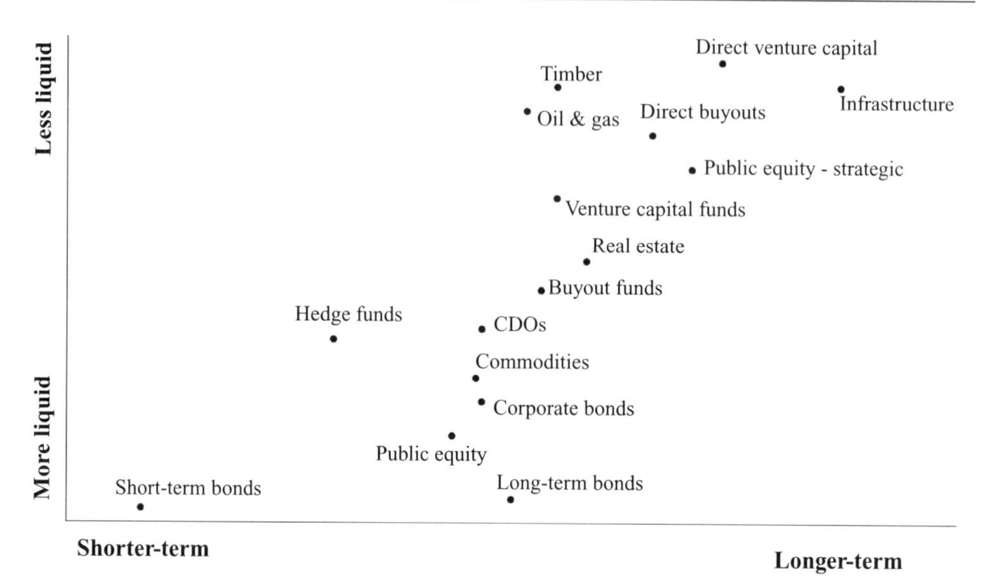

Figure 2.1 Investment horizon and asset class liquidity.
Source: WEF (2011); authors' estimates.

significantly less liquid than investments in US public equity, where the median stock trades every few minutes.

Private equity investments are sometimes narrowly defined as leveraged buyouts (LBOs) of companies. While companies may be privately held or publicly listed, LBOs generally involve firms that are already mature, generating revenues. This distinguishes LBOs from investments in start-up companies where earnings have yet to be generated. Such investments involve venture capital (VC), which especially in the United States is often seen as a separate asset class.

In this book, we follow a broader definition of private equity. Instead, we generally define private equity investments as investments in unlisted companies, irrespective of their maturity and earnings history. While start-ups and younger companies are privately held, acquisitions of mature firms frequently involve public-to-private transactions, where the acquired company is delisted by the new private equity owners.[2] Thus, from the perspective of this study, private equity is seen as a form of financing to which companies may turn during their entire lifecycle (Cornelius, 2011). In their start-up phase, firms often turn to venture capitalists as banks are usually unwilling to lend to companies that have yet to generate earnings. As companies expand, private equity investors may provide the necessary capital to support the growth process. In the more mature phases, leveraged buyouts aim to create value by redesigning corporate strategies, improving operations and optimizing the capital structure under tax considerations. Finally, firms that are experiencing economic difficulties may seek turnaround capital to re-establish prosperity.

Buyouts and VC transactions represent the most common form of private equity investments. They differ in a number of important ways. First, in a leveraged buyout the private equity

[2] Sometimes, private equity investors take minority stakes in publicly listed firms. These private investments in public equity (PIPEs) fall outside the scope of this book.

investor and the management team typically purchase all or the vast majority of the shares in the company. By contrast, venture capitalists usually acquire only minority stakes. Second, companies involved in a buyout are generally mature with predictable cash flows, which allows the investor to finance the transaction with a significant amount of debt, amplifying the expected return on his equity investment (as well as the risk, we hasten to add; see Axelson *et al.*, 2009). In VC deals, investments are usually made with equity capital only. Third, buyout capital is invested across a broad range of industries, whereas the vast majority of VC transactions are concentrated on technology-driven sectors, such as information technology, life sciences and clean technology.

Real assets are generally defined as physical or tangible assets, as opposed to financial assets whose value is derived from a contractual claim on an underlying asset, which may be real or intangible. Real assets include three broad categories: infrastructure, real estate, and natural resources, including farmland. These assets are often lumped together in investors' portfolios as an asset class providing protection against inflation, although there is a significant degree of heterogeneity in terms of their risk/return characteristics. As far as *infrastructure* is concerned, Fraser-Sampson (2011) distinguishes between economic (communications, transport, utilities) and social infrastructure (education, health, security). Infrastructure investments can be made to fund the planning and construction phases of a project. Such investments are sometimes called primary investments, distinguishing them from secondary investments, which are related to the operational period. Depending on the specific project, secondary investments often have a very long investment horizon, sometimes several decades. Therefore, they are sometimes likened to a bond where the investor acquires the right to receive a stream of income over time.

Real estate investments include a variety of assets, such as office buildings, industrial warehouses, shopping and apartment complexes. High-quality real estate holdings have in common with infrastructure investments that they generate significant and stable cash flows. In the case of real estate, cash flows are generated by long-term lease contracts with creditworthy tenants. As Swensen (2009) notes, real estate assets combine characteristics of fixed income and equity. As in the case of infrastructure investments, the investor acquires the right to receive regular payments as specified in the lease contract. At the same time, he has an equity-like exposure in the sense that there is residual value associated with leases for current or anticipated future vacant space.[3]

Finally, investments in *natural resources* focus especially on commodities, such as oil and gas, forestry and farmland. As far as the former are concerned, investments fall into two distinct categories. While holdings of proven oil and gas reserves generate cash flows that are highly correlated with energy prices, investments in exploration activities essentially represent real options. Usually, only the former are considered as real asset investments, given their protection against inflation. By contrast, investing in highly risky drilling operations is typically subsumed under an investor's private equity allocation. Forestry investments, finally, are unique in the sense that the cash flow stream is not based on the depletion of the underlying asset – provided, of course, that the timber owners manage holdings in a sustainable fashion. At the same time, timber shares the characteristic of inflation sensitivity, although the protection it offers is comparatively less, given the limited role it plays in the overall economy.

Private equity and real assets are *structurally illiquid* investments. Their degree of liquidity is low due to the long *ex-ante* lock-in period of investors' capital. This sets structurally illiquid

[3] Note that real estate investment trusts (REITS) are financial assets rather than real assets. Similarly, commodity futures represent financial assets, not real assets.

investments apart from other asset classes whose degree of liquidity is generally relatively high, but *ex post* – that is, after the investment decision is made – may deteriorate sharply in periods of financial stress. The recent financial crisis in 2008–2009 provides plentiful examples of *cyclical illiquidity*. During this period, various markets (including money markets, corporate debt, securitization, collateralized debt obligations (CDOs)) completely shut down, while a significant number of hedge funds limited or stopped redemptions. To be sure, in these markets liquidity was not simply a question of a seller reducing prices to a level where he would find a buyer who was willing to step in. Instead, there were no bids at any price as whole classes of investors simply decided to exit entire markets (Tirole, 2011). Various explanations have been offered for market liquidity breakdowns, among which adverse selection has probably received the greatest amount of attention.[4] While *cyclical*, or *dynamic*, liquidity risk has attracted a great deal of attention from academics and regulators alike (see, for example, Ang *et al.*, 2011), this discussion is beyond the scope of this book.

There are many ways to invest in private equity and real assets, which are discussed in detail in Fraser-Sampson (2011). This includes investments in listed private equity, quoted real estate investment trusts (REITs), or simply exchange-traded funds tracking infrastructure or oil and gas companies. However, by offering ways that make investments in these asset classes more liquid, investors who choose these routes are arguably disabled to access potential liquidity risk premia. From the viewpoint of this book, such investments are of little interest. Nor do we consider direct investments in these asset classes. Recently, direct investments, especially in private equity, have gained in popularity, not least in an effort to reduce costs associated with investments through limited partnerships. However, direct investments – and to a lesser degree co-investments alongside funds – have been limited to large investors and hence have remained the exception. The risk profile of such investments varies substantially across individual sub-asset classes, requiring highly heterogeneous risk management techniques.

Therefore, the discussion in the remainder of this book is confined to investments through fund structures, the most common form of investing in private equity and real assets. This includes funds-of-funds and secondary funds organized as limited partnerships. In such partnerships, the general partner manages the fund and the limited partners provide most of the capital. Generally, private equity partnerships are closed-end funds with a typical lifespan of 10 to 12 years. During this period, capital commitments are drawn down by the GP to pay for investments made by the fund. Investors cannot withdraw their capital before the fund liquidates itself, and failing to meet the GP's capital calls essentially means that the LP is in default. In fact, as we explain in Chapter 4, the very characteristics of limited partnerships, which make investments highly illiquid, are essential for enabling investors to harvest a risk premium.

2.2 MARKET SIZE

Between 2000 and 2011, LPs committed around USD 4 trillion to nearly 10,500 partnerships targeting private equity and investments in real assets (Figure 2.2). Taking into account investments that have already been liquidated, funds managing private equity and real assets are

[4] This possible explanation goes back to the "lemons problem" we discuss in greater detail in Chapter 4 in the context of limited partnerships.

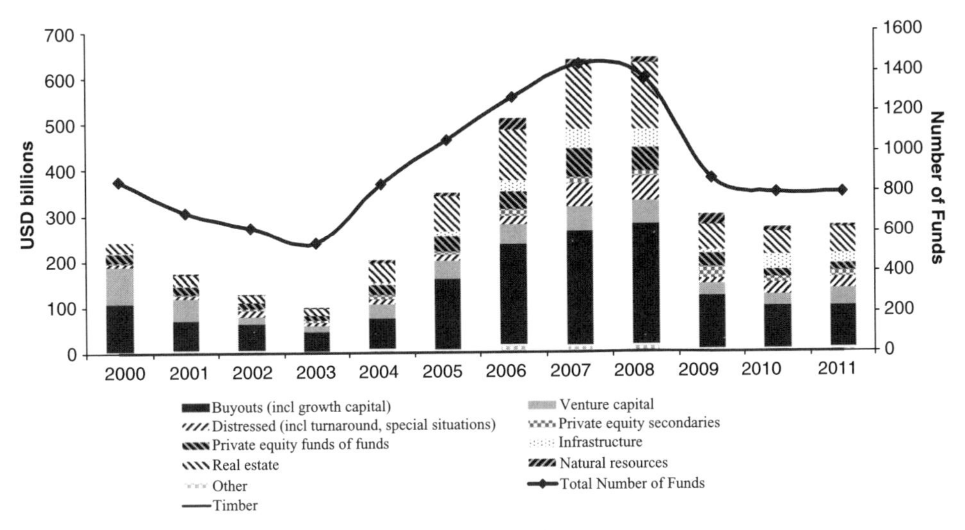

Figure 2.2 Global fund commitments to illiquid assets, by asset class.
Source: Preqin.

estimated to have managed around USD 2.25 trillion at the end of 2011.[5] Of this amount, around 60% was managed by private equity funds (buyout, growth capital, VC, distressed, turnaround and special situations, mezzanine). Furthermore, private equity funds-of-funds and secondary funds managed another 11%, while AuM of partnerships investing in real estate, infrastructure and natural resources funds are estimated to have totalled USD 660 billion at the end of 2011, or nearly 30% of all AuM of limited partnership funds.

The United States has remained by far the largest market for investments in private equity and real assets, accounting for almost 60% of all inflows to limited partnership funds between 2000 and 2011 (Figure 2.3). Europe represents the second largest market, with a global share of 23%. Although the market for illiquid investments in the rest of the world has remained comparatively smaller, economies outside the United States and Europe have been playing catch-up in recent years as magnets for private equity and real assets. Whereas such markets had attracted just around 10% of global investments at the beginning of this century, by the end of the first decade their share had more than doubled.

Almost half of the global capital inflows to private equity and real assets funds during the period from 2000 to 2011 occurred in just 3 years. Between 2006 and 2008, commitments to illiquid assets surged as more partnerships were formed and individual fund sizes ballooned. However, although the past cycle was particularly pronounced, it was not unique. While in all cycles macroeconomic shocks have played an important role, research by Gompers and Lerner (2000) and Diller and Kaserer (2009) suggests that the particular characteristics of illiquid investments through partnerships have contributed to the pronounced cyclicality of fundraising.

Figure 2.4 looks more specifically at commitments to US buyout funds, the largest market for private equity investments. To emphasize their cyclicality, inflows to these partnerships

[5] Hedge funds are estimated to have managed around USD 1.7 trillion at end-2011. Thus, alternative AuM as described in Chapter 1 amounted to around USD 4 trillion.

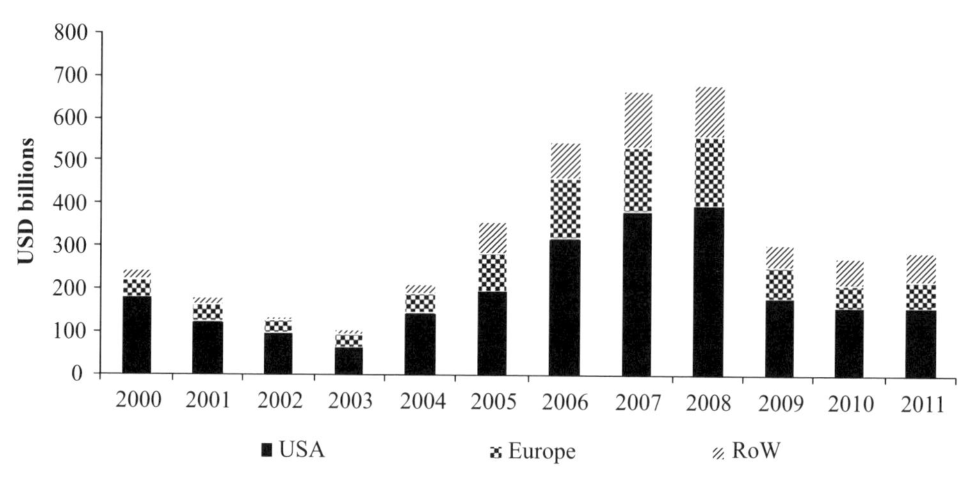

Figure 2.3 Global fund commitments to illiquid assets, by region.
Source: Preqin.

are shown not only in absolute terms but also as a share of the capitalization of the US stock market, which itself has been subject to considerable fluctuations due to cyclical changes in valuations. While this share has averaged one-third of a percentage point in 1980–2011, during the first buyout wave in the late 1980s it had already risen to 0.6%. This substantial increase was dwarfed in the most recent wave when commitments to buyout funds reached 1% of public market capitalization.

The cyclicality in commitments to limited partnerships has been attributed to imbalances between the supply of, and the demand for, private equity capital. Following a market correction, which usually coincides with an economic downturn, capital inflows to private equity

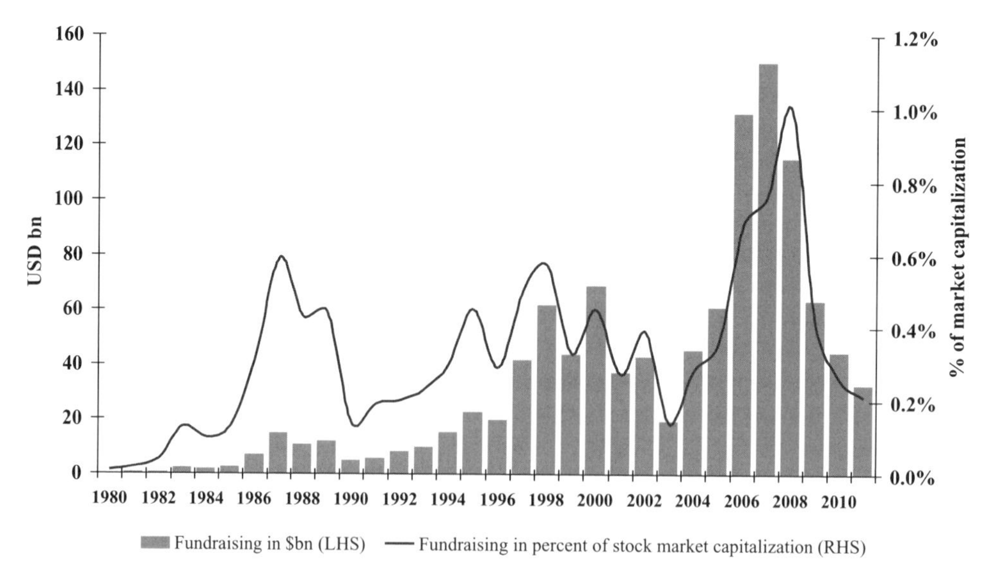

Figure 2.4 Commitments to US buyout funds.
Source: Thomson; Preqin; Federation of World Exchanges.

funds tend to be small, limiting the amount of capital fund managers can deploy. As a result, less money is chasing a finite number of attractive deals. In this phase, purchase prices tend to be low. As economic growth begins to recover, earnings start to improve. While interest rates are still low, yield spreads usually narrow as investors' risk appetite gradually returns. This permits portfolio companies to refinance their debt at cheaper cost and make dividend payments to investors. However, as private equity returns recover, inflows to funds rise. As this process gains momentum, fund managers find it increasingly difficult to source attractive transactions, causing average returns to fall (Gompers and Lerner, 2000). Investors' return expectations are increasingly disappointed, prompting them to adjust their commitments to new funds in an effort to de-risk their portfolios. This adjustment sets the stage for a new cycle.

Illiquidity plays a decisive role in what has become known as the "money-chasing-deals" phenomenon. As Ang and Sorenson (2011) explain – and we shall return to this issue in Chapter 5 in greater detail – optimal asset allocation approaches usually assume continuous portfolio rebalancing. In a frictionless world, an investor continuously sells assets that have risen in value and buys assets that have fallen in value in order to maintain constant portfolio weights. However, the discrete nature of commitments to private equity funds and the illiquidity of such investments render continuous rebalancing impossible. Instead, adjustments are made infrequently, resulting in pronounced investment cycles. As we shall see later, the cyclicality has important implications for cash flows and hence for the management of liquidity risk.

Although illiquid investments have attracted increased attention as an asset class for long-term investors, their relative significance has remained small. In 2011, the global stock of illiquid investments through limited partnerships was estimated to have totalled USD 2.25 trillion. This is equivalent to around 5% of the market capitalization of global stock markets. If we add the global outstanding stock of public and corporate bonds to the global market capitalization of publicly listed stocks to get a sense of the importance of illiquid investments relative to traditional (and generally marketable) assets, the ratio drops to less than 2% (Figure 2.5). Even in the United States, the largest market for illiquid investments by far, investors' exposure to private equity and real assets accounts for just 3.3% of the stock of debt securities and public equity market capitalization.

2.3 THE INVESTOR BASE

Figure 2.6 depicts the market for illiquid assets, where capital supplied by institutional investors is channelled (mostly) through limited partnerships to companies and investment projects in the real estate, infrastructure and natural resource sectors.

Investing in fund structures in private equity and real assets requires patient capital that limits the universe of investors to those with an appropriate liability structure.

2.3.1 Current investors in illiquid assets and their exposure

Given their liability structure, the most important investors in illiquid assets, measured by their total amount of investments in such assets, are pension funds, life insurers, family offices, endowments, foundations and sovereign wealth funds. Although banks are less predestined as long-term investors, they have also provided significant amounts of capital – sometimes in an effort to cross-sell other services related to M&A transactions (Lerner *et al.*, 2007). However, new regulations such as the Dodd–Frank Act in the United States will make it more difficult for banks to invest from their own balance sheets.

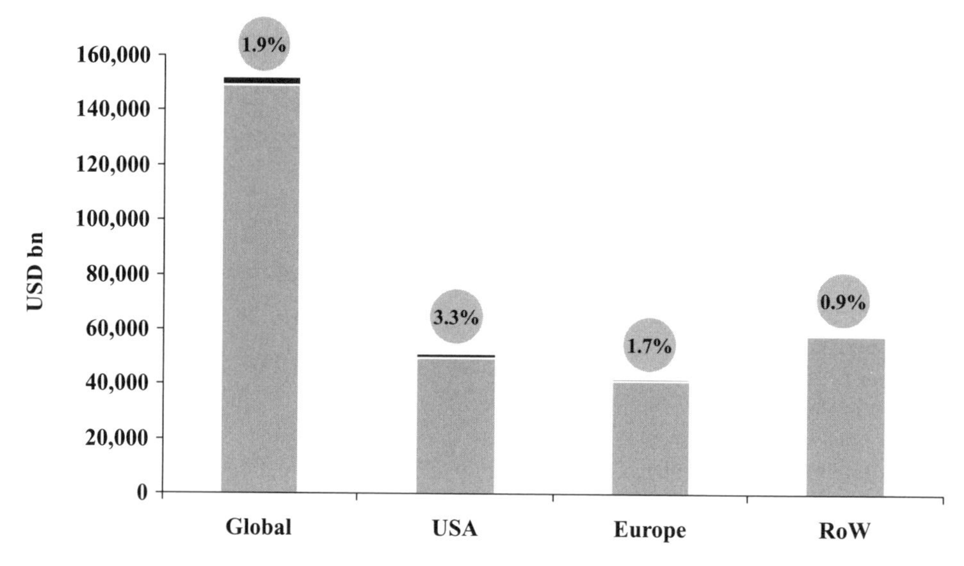

Note: Size of equity markets measured by market capitalization; size of debt markets measured by outstanding debt issued by sovereign and corporate borrowers. Percentages refer to stock of illiquid investments relative to size of equity and debt markets at end-2010

Figure 2.5 Stock of illiquid investments and size of equity and debt securities market.
Source: Preqin; IMF.

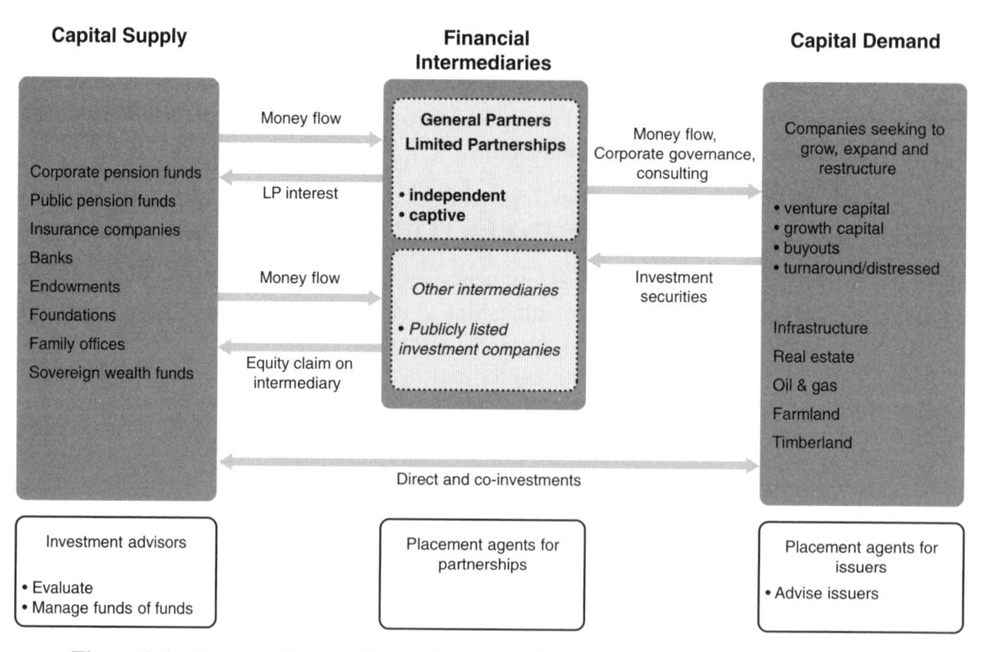

Figure 2.6 Financial intermediation through limited partnerships in illiquid investments.

Table 2.1 Number of limited partners in private equity funds, as of October 2012

	North America	Europe	Asia	RoW	Total
Public pension funds	319	160	16	18	513
Private pension funds	297	205	15	58	575
Insurance companies	150	106	56	22	334
Banks	33	105	66	47	251
SWFs	5	2	11	16	34
Family offices	227	155	33	21	436
Endowments/foundations	1,072	102	7	15	1,196
Others	400	414	244	186	1,244
Total	2,503	1,249	448	383	4,583

Source: Preqin. Note that "others" includes funds-of-funds, secondary funds, investment companies, investment trusts, government agencies and corporate investors.

Table 2.1 shows the number of known investors in private equity funds by investor category. According to information reported by Preqin, a data vendor, there were almost 4,600 private equity investors worldwide. While the true number of investors is likely to be even larger, there is reason to assume that those investors that are not included in Table 2.1 are probably smaller institutions. Around 25% of identified investors in private equity funds are endowments and foundations, the overwhelming majority of which are based in the United States. This investor group is particularly well positioned to invest in private equity and other long-term assets, as they face relatively few investment constraints. Unlike many other investor types, endowments and foundations are generally not affected by regulatory policies, and although they usually face significant yearly payout requirements for beneficiaries, these are proportional to the assets. One of the most well-known long-term investors is the Yale University Investments Office, which, under David Swensen's leadership, raised its allocation to private equity to 21.3% in 2010 from just a bit more than 2% in 1999 (Lerner and Leamon, 2011). Real assets accounted for another 15.6% in 2010, implying that more than one-third of Yale's capital was allocated to illiquid assets.

Yale's substantial exposure to long-term assets and absolute return strategies has been copied by many other endowments as the "Yale approach to investing". While not all of them have such a significant allocation to non-traditional instruments as Yale does, endowments are generally more willing to accept the idiosyncratic risks of illiquid assets than most other investors.

Family offices are even less constrained in their asset allocation. On the liability side, they face minimal yearly payouts, allowing them to focus on wealth preservation and accept short-term mark-to-market losses. There is little consistent information on their exposure to long-term assets in general and especially to private equity, but Preqin reports some individual cases where family offices have allocated a third and even more to private equity funds.

Unlike endowments, foundations and family offices, DB pension funds face fixed payments with an average duration of 12 to 15 years, with regulatory and accounting constraints limiting the share of illiquid assets in their portfolios. On an (AuM) unweighted basis, US public pension funds currently target an exposure to private equity of about 7.5%, US corporate pension plans somewhat less. In Europe, public pension funds and private pension funds are reported to have a target allocation of 4.5% and 4%, respectively. However, these averages mask a substantial degree of variation, with some large North American pension investors, such as CalPERS, CalSTRS, Ontario Teachers' Pension Plan and Washington State Investment Board, having built up double-digit exposures to private equity.

Life insurance companies, which are confronted with similar liability structures, typically have a somewhat lower exposure to private equity than pension funds. Their investment decisions are largely constrained by accounting pressures, combined with regulatory requirements they have to comply with. In contrast to pension funds, publicly listed life insurance companies tend to have a higher focus on stable quarterly results, which might be another explanation for their relatively lower allocations.

Sovereign wealth funds, finally, have generally been set up to invest a country's foreign exchange reserves in asset classes whose risk characteristics make them inaccessible to central banks. Serving as a store of wealth for future generations, SWFs usually do not have clearly defined liabilities. Facing minimal yearly payments, they are much less constrained by accounting and regulatory pressures than pension funds and insurance companies and are therefore particularly well positioned as long-term investors.

Some SWFs, such as the Abu Dhabi Investment Authority (ADIA), the China Investment Corporation (CIC) or the Kuwait Investment Authority (KIA), manage huge portfolios. Little is known about the structure of their asset holdings, but recent research by Bernstein *et al.* (2009) suggests that many SWFs have been involved in a significant number of direct VC and buyout transactions. ADIA, for example, the world's largest SWF, publishes a target exposure to private equity of 2–8%, which includes not only direct investments but also commitments to funds. Likewise, the Government of Singapore Investment Corporation (GIC) targeted an allocation of 10% to private equity.

Overall, endowments and foundations are the most important private equity investors in terms of the number of institutions as well as in terms of the average percentage of their AuM they allocate to private equity. However, their investment portfolios are dwarfed by pension funds, insurance companies and many SWFs. For instance, Yale University Investments Office, the second largest university endowment, currently manages a portfolio of around USD 20 billion, not even a tenth of the assets managed by CalPERS, the largest American pension fund. Thus, we find an inverse relationship between the size of investment portfolios and investors' exposure to private equity (Figure 2.7). This relationship holds not only for private equity investments but also for illiquid investments more generally (Figure 2.8).

Unfortunately, there is no reliable and consistent information about the amount of capital committed to private equity funds by investor class on a global basis. However, data collected by the European Venture Capital and Private Equity Association (EVCA) for the European fundraising market suggests that (European as well as foreign) pension funds have accounted for almost 25% of the capital raised by European private equity funds between 2005 and 2010. Insurance firms added another 8%, while endowments and foundations and family offices were responsible for 2% and 3%, respectively (Figure 2.9). Thus, the denominator effect – the amount of AuM in investors' portfolios – has clearly dominated the numerator effect – the percentage of a given portfolio allocated to private equity.

2.3.2 Recent trends

While pension funds have been the most important investors in private equity and real assets, their role as suppliers of long-term capital might be curtailed by the secular shift from DB pension schemes to DC plans. In the United States, the share of corporate DB plans has fallen to around 35% in 2010 from 65% in the mid-1980s. As far as public and private plans in the

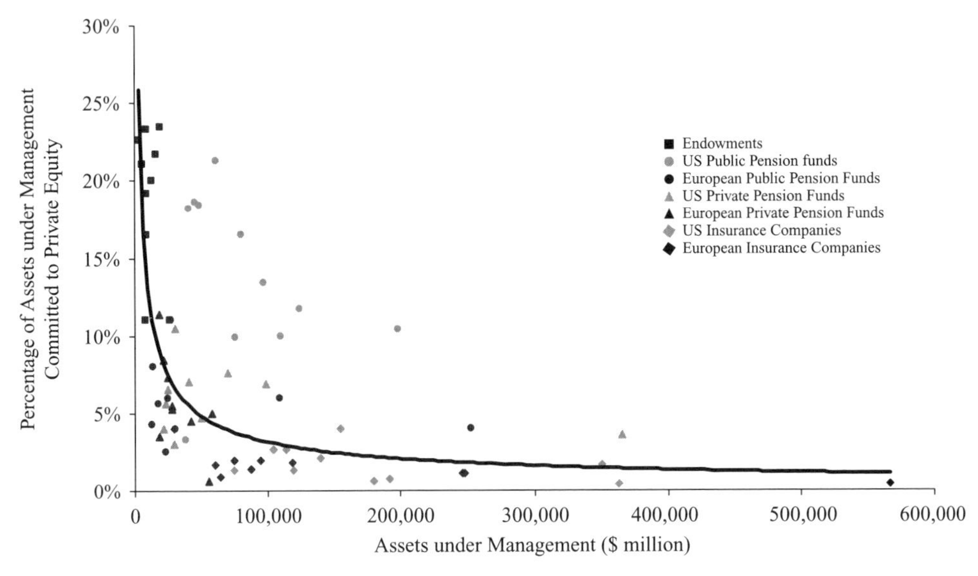

Figure 2.7 Commitments to private equity by large institutional investors.
Source: Preqin.

USA are concerned, the share of DC plans has already climbed to almost 40% (OECD, 2011). In several other OECD countries – such as Australia, Denmark, Italy and New Zealand – DC plans dominate. And in the many emerging economies, the entire pension system is based on defined contributions.

The secular shift from DB to DC plans implies a significant redistribution of risks from employers to employees. In contrast to a DB plan, it is the contributions, rather than the

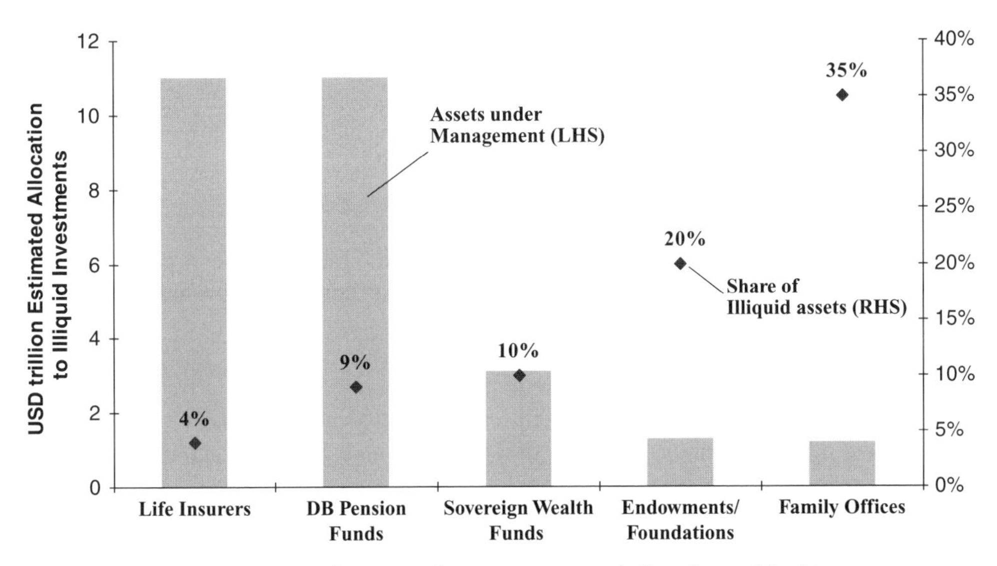

Figure 2.8 Long-term investors' assets under management and allocation to illiquid assets.
Source: WEF (2011).

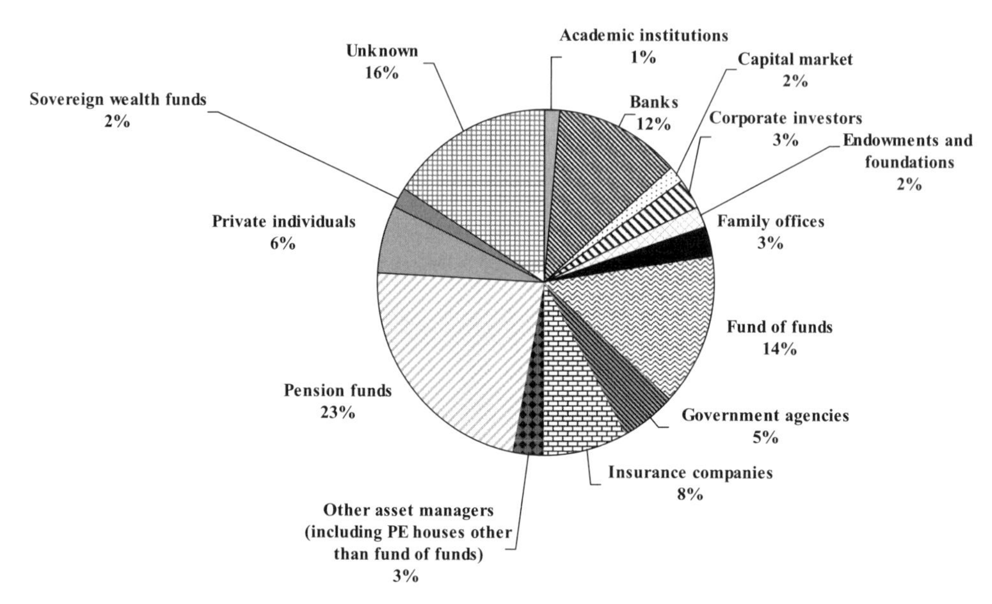

Figure 2.9 Sources of commitments to European private equity funds, 2005 to 2010.
Source: EVCA.

benefits, that are fixed in a DC plan. On the other hand, DC plans are always funded, whereas the employee faces the risk of employer insolvency under a DB plan. From an investment perspective, the key difference lies in the fact that under a DB plan employers are under no obligation to pay benefits that might be expected but have yet to actually accrue. Thus, DB benefits are not portable from one employer to another, a critical precondition for such plans to make long-term investments.

By contrast, an employee covered under a DC plan has substantially greater flexibility. Usually, she is able to leave the plan assets under the administration of a previous employer, transfer the assets to a new employer's plan or transfer the assets to an individual retirement account. This requires DC plans to be able to provide a valuation of each member's assets at short notice, either for information purposes or to enable members to move their pension account to a different scheme. Thus, investments in DC plans are generally restricted to assets with a clear market price so that they can offer equitable treatment to those subscribing to or withdrawing from the fund and those remaining in the fund. Liquidity, therefore, becomes a critical consideration – it must be possible to price the assets fairly and allow the employee to take her investments with her.

Private equity and real assets generally do not meet these criteria, implying that DC plans are unable to harvest the illiquidity risk premium such asset classes may offer. However, as we shall discuss in Chapter 5, such premiums can be significant, which has motivated some to think about possible solutions. One proposal has been made by the Myners Report (2001, p. 106):

> "There could also be more innovative approaches which would permit defined contribution schemes to invest in private equity. It is not the role of this review to design products, but for example, one could envisage an approach under which defined contribution investors would

direct regular sums of money into a feeder fund. While this fund was accumulating, the assets would be invested in a passive equity fund. Once sufficient funds were accumulated and establishment of the private equity vehicle was complete, the index portfolio would be liquidated as and when required to finance new investments by the private equity fund. The defined contribution investor would either receive funds back on realisation from the private equity portfolio or the scheme promoter would establish a facility where proceeds would again be invested in a passive portfolio pending establishment of a new private equity vehicle. This brief description does not tackle all the possible issues raised by such a vehicle, but it serves to indicate that there is scope for greater innovation in this area."

In fact, a variant of the Myners approach is in operation in Chile, whose pension system is 100% DC-based. At the end of 2011, Chile's six privately managed public pension funds (AFPs) controlled nearly USD 150 billion in AuM. In recent years, several international GPs – including Blackstone, HarbourVest, KKR, Lexington Partners, Partners Group and Southern Cross – have raised capital from five of these AFPs. Specifically, these GPs have registered a local feeder fund, which is a publicly traded listed vehicle, on the Chilean stock exchange, allowing the pension plans to meet their monthly liquidity requirements (for details, see EMPEA, 2011).

Whether similar solutions can be found in other jurisdictions will be a critical factor for the future supply of long-term capital. According to a recent study by the World Economic Forum (WEF, 2011), AuM of family offices, endowments, foundations and SWFs look set to rise. But this expected increase will only partly offset the negative effect of the shift from DB to DC plans and the continued de-risking of investment portfolios of pension plans and life insurers in response to regulatory and accounting changes in the post-Lehman era (Figure 2.10). Thus, the WEF study concludes that the net effect will be negative.

Institution	Expected change in AUM	Impact of emerging constraints
Family office	↑ - Sales of family business - Increasing wealth of HNW families	↔ - Reducing appetite for investments with uncertain long-term outcomes
Endowments/ foundations	↑ - Increasing donations from HNW families	↔ - Increasing pressure from trustees and beneficiaries resulting in a movement away from illiquid assets
Sovereign wealth funds	↑ - Excess reserves and account surpluses continue to be transferred to SWFs - Numerous countries have expressed interest in creating a SWF	↔ - Pre-crisis movement into riskier and illiquid investments has slowed down
DB pension funds	↓ - Shift from DB plans via plan closing, sales and increase in DC - Ageing populations in countries with established pension systems increases payouts	↓ - Trend towards mark-to-market accounting - Stricter funding and solvency requirements - Decreased sponsor appetite for pension volatility - Maturing liabilities
Life insurers	↔ - Increased wealth, in particular in emerging markets, will increase assets - Ageing population will increase payouts	↓ - Emerging regulation (e.g. Solvency II) discouraging longer-term risky investments

Figure 2.10 Drivers of future long-term investing capacity.
Source: WEF (2011).

	United States	West. Europe	Japan	China	Other devel-oped	Other Asia	Latin America	MENA	RoW	Total
Households	3.9	2.9	0.6	16.2	6.6	10.0	15.6	22.8	16.2	4.4
Institutional investors										
• Pensions	4.1	5.2	6.8	27.3	5.6	19.4	24.0	14.0	24.3	5.1
• Insurance	5.1	4.4	2.6	30.0	2.3	18.9	21.7	15.5	18.0	4.4
• Endowments & foundations	4.9	7.3	6.8	--	13.2	--	16.6	--	--	5.5
Corporations										
• Banks	5.0	7.4	7.1	21.2	20.0	14.3	13.7	20.7	32.8	8.5
• Nonfinancial corporations	9.2	3.4	2.9	17.7	10.4	15.5	18.2	18.7	16.1	9.6
Governments										
• Central banks	37.0	18.7	11.6	33.0	6.5	15.0	12.6	22.6	21.9	18.6
• Sovereign wealth funds	0.0	9.0	--	7.7	3.6	8.1	20.4	12.0	1.0	7.7
• Other government	--	--	--	14.7	--	9.2	11.2	10.2	13.4	12.5
Total	4.8	4.4	3.3	19.2	7.6	15.7	16.1	21.0	19.7	6.3

Figure 2.11 Increase in financial assets, 2000 to 2010 (compound annual growth, %).
Source: McKinsey Global Institute (2011).

Importantly, the WEF study assumes that DC plans are unable to provide long-term capital. The Chilean example shows, however, that this does not have to be the case. While the role of pension funds as long-term investors in advanced economies is further diminished by rising payouts due to ageing, AuM of pension funds in emerging economies looks set to continue to rise rapidly as pension reforms are broadened and deepened. A recent study by the McKinsey Global Institute (2011) estimates that pension assets managed by DC plans and individual retirement accounts rose by 27% p.a. and 19% p.a., respectively, in China and other Asian emerging markets – albeit from a still relatively low basis.[6] In Latin America, the growth rate averaged 24% p.a. (Figure 2.11). To the extent that the liquidity and portability issues can be addressed effectively, these funds could represent an increasingly important pool of capital for investments in private equity and real assets.

Another potentially mitigating factor lies in the further liberalization of quantitative investment restrictions that DB plans and insurance firms in emerging markets are still subject to. Such restrictions may apply to particular asset classes, such as private equity and other alternatives, or foreign investments, or both. Quantitative investment restrictions may be motivated by prudential considerations as well as national objectives. As regards the latter, pension investments often serve to help develop domestic debt markets and are sometimes used as a source of funding for social investments, including housing loans and the construction of hospitals, schools and other infrastructure (Borensztein *et al.*, 2006). Investment restrictions come at a cost, however, as they limit potential diversification benefits and tend to lower risk-adjusted investment returns.

[6] To be sure, the potential for playing catch-up remains huge. In China, for instance, pension assets (excluding assets managed by the national reserve fund) totalled just 7% of GDP, compared with 100% in the United States.

In emerging economies, the costs of sub-optimal diversification are particularly significant as the growth of pension and life insurance assets outpaces the growth of domestic securities markets (Chan-Lau J.A., 2004). While asset managers have to deal with portfolio risk concentrated in a few government securities and corporate names, the low volumes of corporate bond and equity issuance in many emerging economies' pension funds heighten the risk of asset price bubbles, as increased AuM chase a limited number of securities. Apart from limiting potential diversification gains, quantitative investment restrictions affect asset managers' ability to match their assets with the liabilities of their institutions. This is particularly critical for pension funds. As we discuss in greater detail in the following chapter, the OECD Guidelines on Pension Fund Asset Management (OECD, 2006) therefore counsel against specific ceilings that undermine diversification strategies aimed at reducing risk:

> "Portfolio limits that inhibit adequate diversification or impede the use of asset–liability matching or other widely accepted risk management techniques and methodologies should be avoided. The matching of the characteristics of assets and liabilities (like maturity, duration, currencies, etc.) is highly beneficial and should not be impeded."

A still small, but rising number of governments in emerging economies have begun to follow the OECD's recommendations and started to liberalize quantitative restrictions on foreign investments and/or riskier asset classes. This process has generally commenced with a focus on asset classes as opposed to foreign investments. Investors in some countries may now invest – at least domestically – in long-term asset classes that hitherto were outside their permissible universe. In other cases, ceilings on particular asset classes have been increased, allowing more meaningful strategies. Within the (more generous) limits, investment decisions are guided by the principle of a "prudent investor" standard, as we will discuss in the next chapter. According to the OECD guidelines, this standard requires the governing body of the pension plan or fund to undertake investments with care, the skill of an expert, prudence and due diligence. As long as fund managers fulfil their fiduciary duties and operate under appropriate internal controls and procedures to effectively implement and monitor the investment management process, they may now be able to access risk premia and exploit diversification benefits by investing patient capital.

To be sure, lifting investment restrictions is a necessary but not sufficient condition for pursuing long-term strategies. If the United States were the appropriate benchmark, one would expect a significant increase in long-term investing – within the limits set by the regulatory bodies. In fact, as soon as the US Department of Labor clarified the "prudent man" rule in 1979 and explicitly allowed pension fund managers to invest in high-risk assets, including buyout and VC funds, pension funds reallocated a growing share of their AuM to illiquid asset classes. This set the stage for the rapid development of the US and global private equity industry, whose AuM ballooned from a few billion in 1980 to an estimated USD 1.4 trillion in 2011.

A counterexample is Brazil, where pension funds may now generally invest up to 20% of their assets in domestic private equity funds and up to 10% in foreign private equity funds, although they are still prohibited from investing in foreign currency-denominated funds. Internal restrictions may impose additional ceilings. However, current actual allocations are generally much lower than legal and internal investment restrictions. One example is PREVI, Brazil's largest pension fund, which manages more than USD 90 billion for Banco do Brazil. As of 31 March 2011, PREVI's exposure to private equity totalled only USD 555 million, or 0.7% of AuM, all of which was invested by domestic private equity funds. One possible explanation for this very small allocation to private equity might lie in the absence of appropriate risk management tools for illiquid asset classes, which has prevented the pension fund managers from accessing the risk premia potentially associated with such investments.

2.4 CONCLUSIONS

In this chapter, we have defined the universe of asset classes which constitutes the focus of this book. While most asset classes can become illiquid in periods of severe market stress, only a subset is structurally illiquid and hence appropriate only for long-term investors who are able and willing to accept *ex ante* long lock-in periods for their capital. These asset classes include private equity, real estate, infrastructure and natural resources, especially oil and gas and forestry. Their high degree of illiquidity results from the specific characteristics of limited partnership funds, the most common form of investing in private equity and real assets. Commitments to such funds totalled more than USD 4 trillion in 2000–2011. While this amount appears small relative to the size of traditional asset markets, for some investors illiquid investments are no longer a niche strategy. This applies especially to endowments, foundations and family offices, which have built up a substantial exposure to private equity and real assets, in some cases dwarfing their investments in public equity.

Nevertheless, DB pension plans and life insurance companies remain the most important providers of long-term capital, although sovereign wealth funds have gained substantially in significance as their AuM has continued to rise and their allocations to illiquid assets have expanded thanks to a liability structure that is generally conducive to long-term investing. While pension plans and insurance firms typically allocate a comparatively smaller share to illiquid assets than endowments, foundations and family offices, the total size of their portfolios is generally much larger. Given the dominance of DB pension plans and life insurance firms as suppliers of patient capital, this chapter has finally looked at recent trends in the institutional investor community. Specifically, we have focused on the secular shift from DB funds to DC funds, with the latter facing important constraints on investing in illiquid assets due to the portability of pensions under such schemes. As we have argued, the impact of this shift might be mitigated to some degree by the growing pool of capital accumulated in emerging markets. However, the extent to which such pools will be invested in long-term assets will be influenced substantially by investors' risk appetite and their ability to appropriately measure and manage risk in their portfolios.

3 Prudent Investing and Alternative Assets

"A prudent man sees danger and takes refuge; but the simple pass on, and suffer for it."
Proverbs 27:12. World English Bible

Long-term investors in illiquid assets seek to harvest special risk premia – notably an illiquidity risk premium – and achieve portfolio diversification gains. In pursuing these goals, however, many investment managers are not entirely free in their investment decisions. For example, pension funds and insurance companies as fiduciaries are generally subject to regulation that aims to limit the risk for their beneficiaries (and in systemically important cases, the broader economy). Thus, investment decisions take place within a legal framework that attempts to achieve a balance between two objectives – the maximization of returns and the protection of capital (Möllmann, 2007). In principle, there are two broad regulatory approaches to investing: first, the qualitative description of managerial behaviour according to the "prudent investor rule" and second, the explicit setting of quantitative restrictions (Franzen, 2010).

The general perception of what constitutes prudent investing has developed over time. Initially, "prudent investments" were largely defined by legal lists. In many jurisdictions, this rather static approach was eventually replaced by the *prudent man rule.* While the prudent man rule focuses on individual investments, over time this rule has increasingly been seen as still too narrow. With modern portfolio theory (MPT) showing that diversification may reduce risk at a given level of returns (and vice versa), the prudent man rule has been transformed into the *prudent investor rule*, which emphasizes investment risk at the portfolio level rather than at the level of single assets. Within a given portfolio, the treatment of alternative assets may vary considerably, for regulatory reasons and because of internal policies. According to one approach, quantitative investment rules are set that represent statutory restrictions on the extent to which trustees can seek exposure to unregulated markets and derivatives. While it is generally acknowledged that this is a "crude" system, it is often felt that restricting the share of invested capital per asset class works better than more sophisticated approaches from a risk management standpoint (Spiteri, 2011). This approach still exists in many countries, especially in emerging economies, and reflects a clear focus on protecting the capital for the beneficiaries. However, quantitative investment rules may lead to complacency and encourage concentrated investments in underperforming assets.[1] As a result, investment restrictions on individual assets are increasingly criticized for producing sub-optimal investment results and even being imprudent from a portfolio perspective. It is expected that changes in regulation result in a larger share of capital being allocated to alternative asset classes.

In this chapter we address the question of "what is 'prudent'?" in the context of alternative assets. This discussion is not limited to the regulatory perspective but raises wider issues, for example, regarding the role of the risk manager. Is this role limited to enforcing existing regulations or internal investment rules setting limits on the investor's exposure to individual asset classes? Or should the risk manager be the guardian of prudence in a broader sense, ensuring the protection of capital from a portfolio standpoint?

[1] Franzen (2010) points out that German "Pensionskassen" do not exploit their legal risk-taking limit.

3.1 HISTORICAL BACKGROUND

During the Middle Ages, real estate was the primary form of wealth but feudalism imposed stringent restrictions on a landowner's ability to transfer land to their family upon death. As Hayden (2008) explains, the concept of a trust was created to bypass such feudal restrictions by allowing the transfer of the title to a third-party trustee. This trustee could then transfer the title to specified beneficiaries according to the grantor's instructions. Initially, the trustees did not actively manage property over longer periods but only served as transfer agents.

3.1.1 The importance of asset protection

Over time, the importance of asset protection became increasingly recognized and consequently the trustees also became more involved in management, buying and selling trust assets to achieve better returns for the beneficiaries. Trustees also began managing assets other than land. For example, in 1719 the British Parliament authorized trustees to invest in the shares of the South Sea Company. However, in reaction to the "South Sea Bubble", the standards of prudence in trust investment were tightened.

The Court of Chancery developed a legal list of what were considered as proper investments. With the sole obligation of a trustee being the preservation of capital, the emphasis was on "safe" investments. However, the universe of "safe investments" was rather limited, at least in the view of the judges and legislators, consisting of long-term fixed-return obligations such as government bonds and first mortgages (Langbein and Posner, 1976). Assets that were not on the list were viewed as "improper", and English and many American jurisdictions prohibited all trust investments in the securities of private enterprises until late in the nineteenth century.

3.1.2 The prudent man rule

The instruments that were open for investment generated poor returns thanks to high rates of inflation. At the same time, financial innovation led to new capital markets, raising increasing doubts about the concept of "safe investments". Eventually, this concept was abandoned and replaced by the so-called "prudent man rule" as a new standard for governing investments by fiduciaries. As a legal doctrine it can be traced back to a case heard before the Supreme Judicial Court of Massachusetts in 1830.[2] In this case, the judge suggested that trustees:

> "observe how men of prudence, discretion and intelligence manage their own affairs, not in regard to speculation, but in regard to the permanent disposition of their funds, considering the probable income, as well as the probable safety of the capital to be invested."

The prudent man rule was originally formulated as a general statement of care, skill and caution. It aimed to give trustees sufficient flexibility to address particular circumstances. However, over time this flexibility was gradually limited by case law and influential treatises. This resulted again in certain investments and techniques being deemed "speculative" and therefore "imprudent". Implicitly, this also rendered the application of modern portfolio management practices impossible.

[2] Harvard College v. Armory, 9 Pick. (26 Mass.) 446, 461 (1830).

The most important objective of the prudent man rule was the preservation of capital. The primary responsibility of the fiduciary was therefore not to lose any capital due to potentially speculative and risky investments. In performing their duties, fiduciaries were required to undertake appropriate due diligence for each individual investment, which had to be judged on the basis of its own risk/return characteristics – as opposed to its role in a diversified portfolio. The prudent man rule thus developed into a set of court-defined rules specifying what is generally imprudent, with several courts finding certain types of investment (such as second mortgages or new business ventures) intrinsically speculative and thus outside the universe of prudent investments. The various constraints and narrow judicial interpretations severely limited the types of investment that could be made and essentially again just left government securities and high-grade corporate bonds.

3.1.3 The impact of modern portfolio theory

Since the last revision of the prudent man rule in 1959 there has been a series of innovations in investment products that eventually became mainstream investments for a broad range of investors. Importantly, this includes the emergence of the venture capital and buyout industry and the proliferation of the limited partnership as the main vehicle to invest in private equity. Such investments were initially considered to be imprudent and inappropriate for pension funds. However, in 1979 the US Department of Labor clarified its prudent man rule under the Employee Retirement Income Security Act (ERISA) in a way that explicitly allowed pension funds to invest in assets that were perceived to be highly risky, including venture capital (Gompers and Lerner, 2001). This set the stage for a substantial increase in commitments to VC funds. Whereas new VC partnerships attracted only slightly more than USD 400 million in 1978, 8 years later more than USD 4 billion was invested, with pension funds accounting for more than half of all contributions.

The clarification of the prudent man rule in 1979 took place against the background of the increasing acceptance of MPT, whose whole purpose was to control risk by combining diversified assets rather than following an approach based on the appropriateness of holding a single asset. While an asset may fail the requirements of the prudent man rule in the sense that it may be too risky on a stand-alone basis, it may help mitigate portfolio risk thanks to its diversifying properties. Perhaps not surprisingly, therefore, the inherent conflict between MPT and the prudent man rule soon led to legal disputes.

The main problem was caused by the fact that fiduciaries could be held liable for a loss in one investment, irrespective of whether it was a prudent investment in the context of the portfolio taken as a whole and the performance of the other investments. For example, in First Alabama Bank of Montgomery v. Martin,[3] the Supreme Court of Alabama applied the prudent man rule analysis and evaluated each security transaction in isolation. Both the relevant market conditions and the fact that the assumption of risk for some stocks would likely result in higher returns on the entire portfolio were disregarded and the 17 disappointing stocks were found to be speculative. Hayden (2008) suggests that if MPT had been applied and notably the effects of individual transactions on an entire portfolio had been evaluated, the First Alabama court would likely have reached an opposing result.

[3] 425 So. 2d 415, 427 (Al. 1982), cet. denie4 461 U.S. 938 (1983).

3.2 PRUDENT INVESTOR RULE

As the clarification of the prudent man rule by the US Department of Labor already foreshadowed in 1979, the modern interpretation of "prudence" follows the lines of financial economics where investors seek to maximize the risk-adjusted total return on investment, with capital appreciation being placed on an equal footing with dividends and income. In evaluating expected returns, trustees are required to recognize the importance of protecting a portfolio against inflation. Consistent with this, the relevant level for measuring (risk-adjusted) performance is the entire portfolio rather than the returns of individual investments.

3.2.1 Main differences

As a consequence of these developments, the prudent man rule is no longer the standard in evaluating investing. Instead, it has been replaced by what has been labelled the "prudent investor rule", which includes the concepts of due diligence and diversification. This is, for example, expressed in the US "Prudent Investor Act",[4] which differs from the prudent man rule in four major ways (FDIC, 2005):

- Consistent with MPT, the entire investment portfolio is considered. This allows trustees to include riskier investments in their portfolio without fear of being held liable, after the fact, for the losses on any one investment. An investment needs to be consistent with the overall portfolio objectives determined by the beneficiaries' needs at the time of the acquisition, but hindsight is not a factor when judging prudence.
- Consequently, diversification of investments is a key factor for prudence. Trustees are still allowed to invest in a single asset class, but they must be prepared to justify that decision. Furthermore, the investment process should at least reflect the consideration of alternative asset classes.
- No particular asset class is mandatory, and there is no minimum number of asset classes that must be considered. While there is no category or type of investment deemed inherently imprudent, speculation and outright risk taking is not prohibited by the prudent investor rule. That said, the trustee is permitted – and even encouraged – to develop greater flexibility in overall portfolio management.
- Because of the increased complexity implied by these responsibilities, a trustee is not only permitted but literally obliged to delegate investment management and other associated functions to third parties.

Möllmann (2007) contrasts the prudent investor rule with what has often been described as a "draconian regime" of fund regulation, where outcome measures and quantitative rules apply. In a report commissioned by the European Commission – famously known as the "Pragma-Report"[5] – quantitative investment rules for pension funds were criticised for being

[4] The PIA was adopted in 1990 by the American Law Institute's Third Restatement of the Law of Trusts and reflects a MPT and "total return" approach to the exercise of fiduciary investment discretion. The PIA was followed by the Uniform Prudent Investor Act (UPIA) in 1994. See 7B Unif. Law. Ann. 56 (1998 Supp.).

[5] As it was authored by Pragma Consulting.

"in the way of optimisation of the asset allocation and securities selection processes and, therefore, may lead to sub-optimal return and risk taking" (Franzen, 2010). Meanwhile, such quantitative restrictions have mostly been abolished, and there is an increasing trend towards some form of prudent man rule in investment regulations and away from quantitative restrictions.

3.2.2 Importance of investment process

The "prudent investor rule" is a legal doctrine that focuses on the investment process, as opposed to labelling an investment or course of action as prudent or not. It is important to note that hindsight is no longer a component of the investment standard: if the process followed was prudent, i.e. based on what was known and not known at the time of the decision, then the decisions made are prudent, regardless of subsequent results.

With this reinterpretation the standard of prudence has shifted towards diversification, including alternative assets, with fiduciaries expected to engage actively in (corporate) governance. Trustees are now required to conduct an ongoing investment process that is, in substance and procedure, more complex and sophisticated than was previously required by law (Maloney, 1999). The broader universe of possible investment options and the application of MPT bring additional complexity: trustees not only have to evaluate the expected return and risk of holding an individual investment but also to assess its impact on the entire portfolio. This requires monitoring expected returns, standard deviations and correlations of all individual investments in the portfolio. Clearly, these responsibilities imply a different skill set compared with the traditional prudent man rule, and given the increased investment obligations for fiduciaries, delegation has become an integral part of the investment process. In fact, no individual professional or advisory firm can claim to be fully informed about the universe of possible investments and how they interact.

Consequently, under UK law, for example, trustees are not required to have professional investment knowledge; instead, they are legally obliged to obtain proper advice in relevant areas. As Hayden (2008) explains, trustees are "virtually compelled by considerations of efficiency" to delegate to qualified and supervised agents and may now be deemed imprudent for failing to do so in some situations. This has paved the way for the huge influence of investment consultants (Franzen, 2010). However, trustees still must act in a prudent manner in selecting and supervising them.

Given the emphasis that the prudent investor rule puts on the fiduciary's behaviour, it may not be surprising that what actually constitutes appropriate behaviour has remained subject to discussion. Many observers see the vagueness of the term as an important advantage, as it gives the investment manager the flexibility he needs in an ever-changing market environment. Others, however, have taken a more critical view, raising the questions of how and by whom reasonable behaviour should be defined (Möllmann, 2007). This question is particularly relevant, given that regulations – especially pertaining to the pension fund industry – often seem to set contradictory objectives. On the one hand, for example, a minimum return has to be guaranteed while, on the other hand, the trustee's investment capabilities are restricted. As Spiteri (2011) puts it:

> "... it's like they are being asked to travel at 100 miles per hour and are then handed a bicycle as their mode of transport."

3.3 THE OECD GUIDELINES ON PENSION FUND ASSET MANAGEMENT

While the interpretation of prudence in investment decisions continues to differ widely, even in sophisticated and mature markets, considerable effort has recently been made to develop a set of guidelines that can be applied universally by the pension fund industry. Published by the OECD (2006), these guidelines refer to a prudent person standard, under which a pension fund's governing body is "expected to undertake obligations related to the investment management function with the requisite level of skill to effectively carry out that function, and absent that level of skill or knowledge, to obtain the external assistance of an expert". Importantly, the prudent person standard does not necessarily make portfolio limits redundant. As the guidelines make clear, such portfolio limits are generally intended to help implement the prudential principles of security, profitability and liquidity at the regulatory level rather than the pension fund level. However, to reiterate the guidelines emphasize that:

> "portfolio limits that inhibit adequate diversification or impede the use of asset–liability matching or other widely accepted risk management techniques and methodologies should be avoided. The matching of the characteristics of assets and liabilities (like maturity, duration, currencies, etc.) is highly beneficial and should not be impeded."

In Annex II of the OECD guidelines, it is recommended that policy makers and regulators "take account of and give proper consideration to modern and effective risk management methods, including the development of assets/liabilities management techniques". Effectively, although the guidelines explicitly consider regulatory limits on individual asset classes, they urge that any such limits be set from the perspective of a portfolio approach rather than individual investments. Consistent with this approach, the guidelines highlight the need for implementing "*a sound risk management process* to appropriately measuring and controlling *portfolio risk* and the overall risk profile of the pension fund" (authors' emphasis).

3.4 PRUDENCE AND UNCERTAINTY

The prudent investor rule is usually associated with market-based portfolio management and supervision. Acting with prudence is deeply embedded in the principle of fiduciary duty, which forms a fundamental aspect of the Anglo-Saxon regulatory approach. Whereas investment risk has long been considered as the risk to the beneficiaries' capital, in the current context risk is generally perceived as falling short of a predetermined benchmark. Arguably, this shift in the definition of investment risk may have contributed to the observed herd behaviour in the investment community, with many large institutional investors just "hugging the benchmark". Note, however, that the gravitational forces in investment approaches still differ across jurisdictions. In the United States, "expertise" and "prudence" are legally required in pension fund management. According to Franzen (2010), the governance structure of US pension funds clearly incentivizes risk taking on behalf of the pension fund fiduciaries:

> "It seems doubtful if the heavily bond-geared portfolios of some continental European pension funds would pass the prudence test in the United States."[6]

[6] Hayden (2008) confirms that under the US Uniform Prudent Investor Act (UPIA), investing an entire portfolio in bonds would likely be a breach of duty.

3.4.1 May prudence lead to herding?

The problem is, as Teresa Ghilarducci (labour economist and widely recognized expert on retirement security) observes, that these concepts "are whatever passes for standard practice by members of the pension fund industry" and that US law and supervisory authorities require "the industry to abide by the standards the industry itself defines" (Blackburn, 2002). However, from the viewpoint of individual investors, it "... is better to fail conventionally than to succeed unconventionally", as Keynes famously observed, and requiring individual investors to follow industry standards in terms of asset allocation could, as *The Economist* has phrased it, boil down to "... requiring investors to buy tulips in 17th-century Holland because everyone else was doing so" (Buttonwood, 2008).

Against this background, we suggest four tests to determine whether an investment approach can be considered prudent:

- Assuming that a portfolio approach is taken, the portfolio should comprise assets that are fully understood. This requires that the investment in a particular asset is undertaken on the basis of thorough due diligence, a process that itself requires the necessary skills and experience. Unless an investment has been subjected to an appropriate due diligence process, it should be considered imprudent.
- There needs to be a researched and formalized investment strategy that is consistent with legal provisions and the objectives set by the beneficiaries (i.e., profile of liabilities, liquidity needs, risk tolerance, etc.).[7]
- Individual investments need to be consistent with the investment strategy. Whether an investment makes sense and whether it is prudent can only be assessed in the context of this strategy.
- The portfolio composition and its individual assets are monitored and deviations are reacted upon. In particular, over the long timeframes that are typical for alternative assets, investment strategies will typically need to be adjusted due to unforeseen market developments.

As far as alternative investing is concerned, investors face the important challenge that standard portfolio models have been developed for efficient markets where permanent rebalancing is possible. Many of the assumptions made in these models are violated in the context of alternative investing. Furthermore, data are usually of questionable quality or do not exist at all. All these factors result in a high degree of uncertainty that often appears to make many trustees feel uncomfortable when allocating a significant share to alternative investments.

3.4.2 May prudence lead to a bias against uncertainty?

Increasingly, the main responsibility of trustees lies in the overall asset allocation (Maloney, 1999). In most advanced markets, there are no *a priori* restrictions. However, while any investment can be chosen, there is no "safe" investment that protects a trustee from liability. In theory, the prudent investor rule incentivizes trustees to allocate more to alternative assets that have the potential to yield higher returns. But investors tend to prefer current and presumably more reliable information compared with valuations made on expectations in the future. While investors try to tackle this uncertainty through rigorous due diligence, in an

[7] According to Maloney (1999), under the UPIA a trustee must determine the appropriate risk profile for a trust and then develop and implement an investment strategy for the portfolio.

environment characterized by uncertainty there are clear limits to identifying and quantifying risks. For trustees there may be another dilemma: is it acceptable to forgo financial returns because the asset in question cannot be integrated in the traditional MPT-based models and therefore only a very small fraction of capital, if any, is allocated to that asset? In principle, at least, this could imply a lower living standard for the beneficiaries than they could potentially enjoy.

3.4.3 Process as a benchmark for prudence?

Therefore, regulations like ERISA in the United States[8] provide a safe harbour from liability if the trustee has given "appropriate consideration" to the facts and circumstances of the investment and its relationship to the needs of the pension plan (Maloney, 1999). In other words, such regulation is process- rather than rule-oriented, implying that actions are more important than outcomes which may be achieved through reckless behaviour. Trustees need to provide information on decision processes rather than just ensuring that the composition of the asset portfolio complies with quantitative restrictions. However, while the emphasis on processes aims at limiting downside risk, it is less clear to what extent the quality of processes actually drives investment performance. A challenge lies in assessing the quality of different practices themselves. What exactly do we mean by prudence, and how can different levels be distinguished?

Importantly, new approaches are developing in this area, for example, based on ISO/IEC 15504 (Software Process Improvement and Capability Determination, also known as SPICE). ISO/IEC 15504-4:2004 provides guidance on how to utilize a conformant assessment of processes to determine their capabilities and also guide their improvement.[9] For each process, ISO/IEC 15504 defines a capability level on a defined scale.[10] While originally this set of standards addressed the IT industry and related business management functions, it has become a universally recognized standard that is no longer limited to software development processes and in recent years it has also been applied by the investment industry.[11]

3.4.4 Size matters

What has been said so far applies to institutional investors whose investment decisions are not constrained by the size of the asset class. However, there are some large institutional investors where this assumption does not hold. The extreme example is Norway's government pension fund, the world's largest pension reserve fund, whose AuM has increased to more

[8] ERISA was enacted in 1974. The policy makers' central objective was to ensure adequate investment returns necessary for defined benefit plan participants.

[9] See http://www.iso.org/iso/iso_catalogue/catalogue_tc/catalogue_detail.htm?csnumber=37462 [accessed 4 August 2011].

[10] Scale with levels from 0 to 5: 0 – incomplete process, 1 – performed process, 2 – managed process, 3 – established process, 4 – predictable process, 5 – optimizing process. The capability of processes is measured against nine process attributes (process performance, performance management, work product management, process definition, process deployment, process measurement, process control, process innovation, process optimization) that get assessed on a four-point rating scale (not achieved (0–15%), partially achieved (>15–50%), largely achieved (>50–85%), fully achieved (>85–100%)).

[11] The Luxembourg Centre de Recherche Public's Henri Tudor has been leading an initiative called "Banking SPICE", with the objective of developing structured governance tools and providing a commonly accepted framework for process assessment and improvement in the finance and banking industry. See http://www.tudor.lu/ and http://www.bankingspice.com/web/Introduction.html [accessed 4 August 2011]. Together with one of the authors, Henri Tudor has been applying this framework to the European Investment Fund's valuation process to ensure that each of its private equity funds is valued appropriately, objectively and in a timely manner, reflecting current market conditions (as described in Mathonet and Meyer, 2007, ch. 7).

than USD 600 billion. Managed by Norges Bank Investment Management, the fund started out by investing in government bonds only. However, as the fund continued to grow in size, it was allowed to buy shares in 2007. With stocks representing 60% of the fund's portfolio, it holds around 1% of global equities. In an effort to diversify the portfolio further, the fund was allowed in 2008 to invest in emerging markets, and more recently property was added to the permissible universe of assets. However, no investments have been permitted in private equity. Based on an evaluation of the potential benefits of venturing into private equity by Phalippou (2011), the government decided not to invest in this asset class at this point in time. In a recent interview with the *Financial Times* (20 August 2012), Yngve Slyngstad, chief executive of the fund, explained that its abstinence was essentially explained by the fund's sheer size and the relatively small amounts of capital managed by private equity funds: "We are too large to make a significant allocation to alternative assets." Relatively few players fall into this category. For most, it is the balance between prudence and uncertainty that represents the main challenge.

3.5 CONCLUSION

Modern standards of prudent investing aim to incentivize risk taking while discouraging recklessness. The danger lies in applying rules without understanding them and their limitations. In a similar context the quantitative analyst and author Emanuel Derman refers to the late Fisher Black, a leading academic in financial economics as well as a well-known practitioner: "He suggested traders at banks should be paid for the plausibility story they told behind the strategy they used, rather than for the results they obtained, thus rewarding intelligence and thinking rather than possible luck" (Dunbar, 2001). This puts emphasis on the process rather than the outcome – this is of particular relevance in the case of alternative investments where forecasting regularly fails and affects, as we will discuss in the following, the role of the risk manager. A clearly defined and sound risk framework is essential for a prudent operation and represents an important pillar of prudent management practice. The approaches and choices made can even affect the stability of the financial system as a whole. Franzen (2010) quotes a regulator: "You want efficiency in the system and that is what 'prudence' really is."

4 Investing in Illiquid Assets through Limited Partnership Funds

Understanding the key characteristics of limited partnerships is critical for effectively measuring and managing the risks of investing in private equity and real assets. In this chapter, therefore, we explain the basic characteristics of this structure, which has remained the most common form for long-term investing in these asset classes. As we shall see and also discuss in more detail in Chapter 5, the very features of this structure are essential to reap the illiquidity risk premium that private equity and real assets offer to investors. Limited partnerships have not remained uncontroversial, however, which explains why alternative investment forms have emerged, including listed vehicles, direct and co-investments, and deal-by-deal investments. However, notwithstanding its constraints, the limited partnership structure has stood the test of time and provides a superior framework for long-term investing, which is typically associated with a high degree of uncertainty.

4.1 LIMITED PARTNERSHIP FUNDS

Limited partnership funds are unregistered investment vehicles that pool capital for investing in private equity and real assets. These funds are set up by fund management companies – also referred to as "firms" – to attract institutional investors. Funds fulfil a number of functions. They allow the investment process to be delegated to fund managers, who have significant experience in screening, evaluating and selecting investment opportunities with high expected growth potential. This potential is generally reaped through a combination of strategic, tactical and financial measures, requiring particular skills in controlling, coaching and monitoring portfolio companies' management. Finally, fund managers source, exit opportunities and realize capital gains on disposing investments. In managing a fund, managers are usually supported by advisory committees and a network of industry experts, sharing knowledge and other non-financial resources.

4.1.1 Basic setup

A partnership is a contract between two or more individuals who agree to carry on an enterprise, contribute to it by combining property, knowledge or management, and share its profit. The most basic form of partnership is a general partnership. In a general partnership, all partners manage the business and are personally liable for its debts, as every partner is both an agent and a principal of the firm, thus binding the firm and the other partners. As these liabilities can be significant, another "asymmetric" form for investment vehicles has evolved: the limited partnership (see Figure 4.1). In a limited partnership, the "limited partners" relinquish their ability to manage the business. At the same time, however, their liability for the partnership's

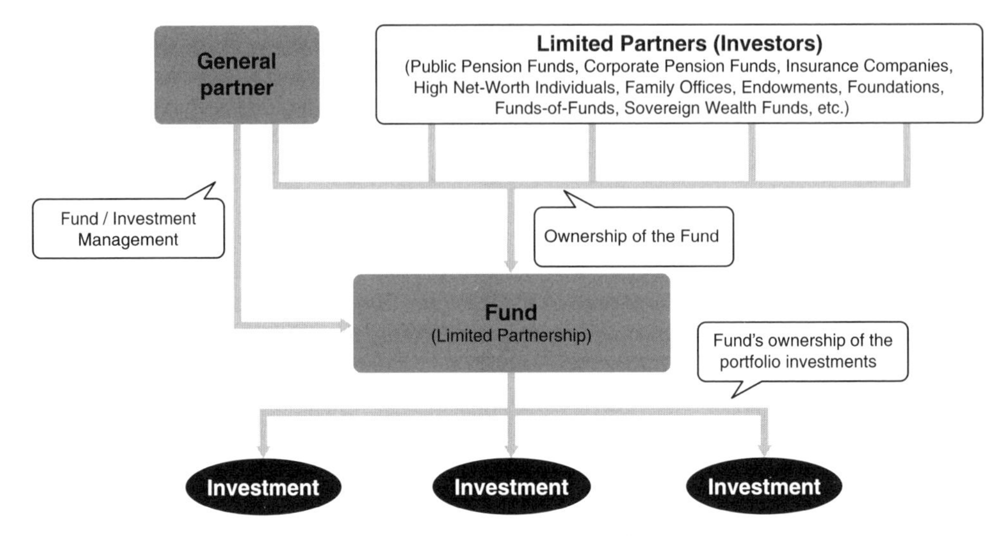

Figure 4.1 Basic limited partnership fund structure.

debts is limited. Additional factors that have played an important role in the emergence of the limited partnership as a dominant investment vehicle for long-term investors lie in tax considerations and regulatory requirements, with a high degree of transparency allowing investors to be treated as investing directly in the underlying assets.

The limited partnership was expressly designed to be tax effective under US law. Commonly, domestic private equity funds in the United States are limited partnerships under the law of the State of Delaware. A Delaware Limited Partnership is a separate legal entity that continues as such until it is dissolved and winds up its affairs pursuant to the partnership agreement. While limited partnerships organized in Delaware are not generally required to register with any regulatory authority, the management company of the fund, which is normally organized as a separate entity, may be subject to registration as an investment advisor.

Importantly, limited partnerships under the law of the State of Delaware are tax transparent, i.e. "look-through" entities. This allows the limited partners to be taxed on capital gains in their own jurisdiction, which is a major advantage for those who are wholly or partly tax exempt in their home jurisdiction. Because cash flows freely both in and out of the fund as investments are bought and realized, investors do not suffer any tax leakage they may not be able to reclaim. Moreover, limited partnerships satisfy various legal requirements for regulated investors (for example under the Employment Retirement Income Security Act (ERISA) in the United States).

Similar structures exist in other countries. In the United Kingdom, the largest market for private equity investments in Europe, funds organized as limited partnerships must be registered under the Limited Partnerships Act of 1907. Under UK law, the liability of the limited partners is limited to the amount of capital in the partnership as long as they do not take part in its management. UK limited partnerships are similarly tax transparent, a key advantage for investors in such funds.

Consistent with common practice, in this book we use the term "general partner" to refer to the firm as an entity that is legally responsible for managing the fund's investments and with unlimited personal liability for its debts and obligations. "Fund managers" are the individuals involved in its day-to-day management. The group of fund managers forms the fund's "management team" which includes the carried interest holders, i.e. those employees or directors of the general partner that are entitled to share in the "super profit" made by the fund. The term "limited partners" refers to the fund's passive investors.

4.1.2 The limited partnership structure

Whereas terms and conditions, investor rights and obligations are defined in specific non-standard partnership agreements, the limited partnership structure – or comparable structures used in different jurisdictions – has evolved over the last decades into a "quasi-standard".

- Investors – who are mainly institutions with appropriate liability structures (see Chapter 2) – serve as LPs, committing a certain amount of capital to the fund. As LPs, they have little, if any, influence on the day-to-day management of the fund. However, LPs are given some oversight of the fund, i.e. by inviting them to serve on advisory boards or on special committees while still being protected from general liability.
- Depending on the strategy followed, funds have a contractually limited life ranging from typically 7–10 years up to 15 years. No early redemption rights are granted to the LPs. Moreover, secondary sales of the fund's shares are generally subject to the approval of the GP.[1]
- The fund manager's objective is to realize all investments before or at the liquidation of the partnership. Limited Partnership Agreements (LPAs) often have provision for an extension of 1 or 2 years (sometimes even longer).
- The main part of the capital is drawn down as "contributions" during the "investment period", typically 3 to 5 years, when new investment opportunities are identified. Sometimes, there is provision for an extension of 1 year. During the "divestment period", only the existing and successful investments will be further supported with some follow-on funding in order to maximize the value creation until the final exit. The manager's efforts during this time are concentrated on realizing or selling the investments and "distributing" the proceeds to the LPs.
- Management fees are a function of the size of the fund and the resources required to implement the proposed strategy. They generally range from 2.5% of committed capital for funds of less than €250 million, between 1.0% and 1.5% for large buyout funds, to 50 bps and 150 bps for funds-of-funds. The fees are often scaled down once the investment period has been completed and adjusted according to the proportion of the portfolio that has been divested.
- Furthermore, some GPs charge transaction and monitoring fees to the companies they have acquired. These fees are not easily visible to the LPs as they are taken directly out of the portfolio companies.
- Management fees are supposed to cover the expenses of running a private partnership. The fund manager himself typically earns a relatively low base salary. His main financial incentive results from the "carried interest" (often simply referred to as "carry") he may earn. Carried interest usually amounts to 20% of the profits realized by the fund, although a small number of GPs (mostly top US VC firms) charge higher carry of up to 30%. Funds-of-funds, by contrast, are paid less carry.

[1] Note that the Carlyle Group has recently decided to pre-approve the sale of stakes by the LPs in their most recent buyout fund to five secondary fund managers in an effort to address possible liquidity concerns by their investors.

- Carried interest is usually subject to a "hurdle rate". Only if this hurdle rate is met or exceeded do GPs receive carry. While in the United States carry is usually determined on a deal-by-deal basis, subject to a claw-back clause in the LPA, in Europe carry is not normally paid out until all LPs' capital has been returned and the hurdle rate is met. Thereafter, normally 100% of additional returns go to the GP. This catch-up period ends when the agreed carried interest split is reached. After that point, distributions are shared according to the agreed split.
- Fees and carried interest have a meaningful impact on the net returns for LPs. While carried interest is related to the performance of a fund, management and transaction fees are not. Metrick and Yasuda (2009) estimate that on average about 60% of a GP's compensation is due to non-performance-related management and transaction fees.
- GPs usually invest a significant share of their personal wealth in the fund to ensure a close alignment of interest with the LPs.
- Commitments are drawn down as needed, i.e. "just-in-time" to make investments or to pay costs, expenses or management fees. Funds typically do not retain a pool of uninvested capital, and the timeframe for LPs to respond to the GP's capital call is generally very short, often only 10 days or even less.
- When realizations are made or interest payments and dividends are received, they are distributed to investors as soon as practicable. Thus, the fund is "self-liquidating" as the underlying investments are realized. However, LPs typically have no right to demand that realizations be made, and these returns come mostly in the second half of the fund's life up to its final liquidation (Figure 4.2). Distributions can also be made "in kind" in the form of securities of a portfolio company, which normally requires that these securities are publicly tradable.

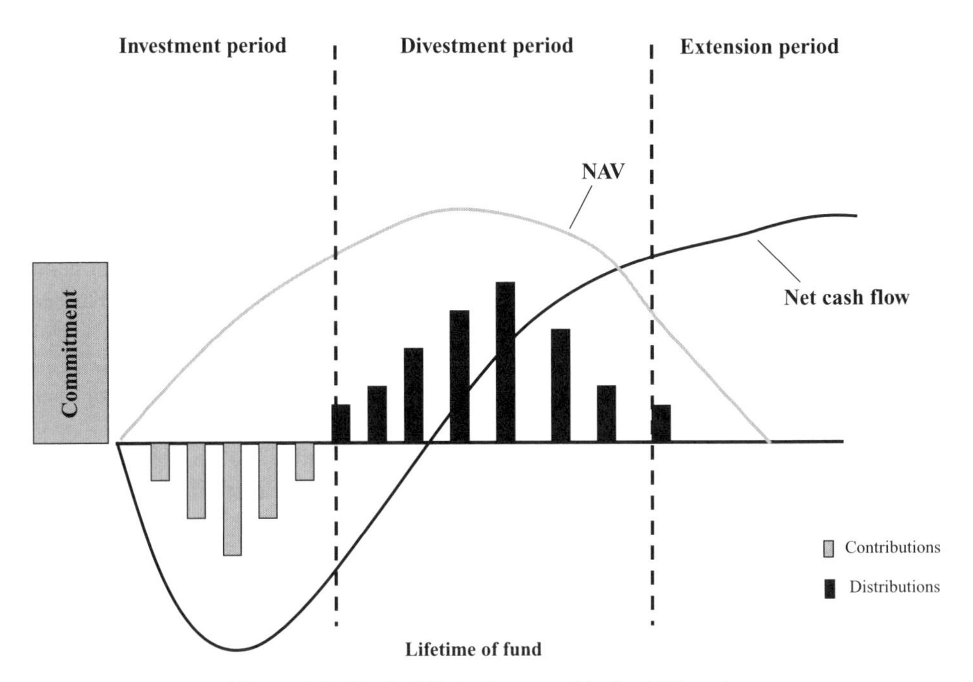

Figure 4.2 Typical limited partnership fund lifecycle.

- These broad principles generally also apply to funds-of-funds. The manager of a fund-of-funds acts as a GP. The GP earns a management fee and participates in the investment profits, subject to a hurdle rate. At the same time, the fund-of-funds serves as a LP in the partnerships it commits capital to. While funds-of-funds add a cost layer, they may be especially attractive for institutional investors who lack the skills and experience in selecting the best funds, have only limited access to them, lack the resources to monitor different market segments on a global basis and/or lack the necessary (but often overlooked) portfolio and risk management systems.

The LPA defines the legal framework and the terms and conditions for the limited partnership fund. It mainly addresses the allocation of capital gains or losses among partners; the allocation of interim distributions; management fees to the general partner; possible investment restrictions; and major governance issues. The management company enters into agreements with all employees and with the general partners. One management company can act as a "group", managing several such partnerships in parallel.

4.1.3 Is "defaulting" an option for limited partners?

Theoretically, as Litvak (2004) argues, LPs have the option to abandon their investment simply by defaulting, in which case the exercise price of the option is the default penalty that should be weighted against the undrawn commitments that can be saved. Litvak concludes that the threat of capital withdrawal is a useful contractual tool to reduce agency costs between investors and low-quality firms. However, Fleischer (2004) points out that default involves a "reputational" penalty investors suffer when they exercise this "walk-away" option. This penalty may be substantial as a defaulting investor might not be allowed to invest in other capital funds. In practice, the repercussions of becoming a defaulting investor go beyond the penalties described in the limited partnership agreement. Fleischer (2004) argues that the reputational costs of a default may vary among the different investor types within a fund. Pension funds, university endowments and other repeat players care deeply about their reputation, while some individuals and corporate investors might be indifferent. The private asset market has been described as relying heavily on informal relationships and the reputation of its participants. Repeatedly defaulting damages a LP's reputation as a reliable investor and almost certainly undermines future attempts to participate in partnership funds, especially those that are oversubscribed. The negative consequences for defaulting investors in this networked industry can thus substantially outweigh the potential savings that may arise from simply walking away from an underperforming fund. Instead, as we discuss in Chapter 6, a LP is likely to prefer to sell its stake in a fund in the secondary market.

4.2 LIMITED PARTNERSHIPS AS STRUCTURES TO ADDRESS UNCERTAINTY AND ENSURE CONTROL

Despite its virtues, the limited partnership structure has often been criticized. Importantly, it has been argued that in a typical partnership managers need to show quick results to prove they deserve commitments to a new fund they plan to raise. However, this works against the *raison d'être* of investments in areas where patient capital is particularly needed. One frequently cited example is VC, where deals are sometimes found to be exited prematurely relative to what would have been the optimal holding period of the investment. In principle, the solution may be sought in "evergreen funds"; that is, funds which do not mature but instead have an – at least theoretically – infinite lifetime. But why does the alternative asset industry still use what Love (2009) calls "archaic LP structures that are spectacularly ill-suited" to long-term investing? One answer may be sought in the liability structure of DB pension plans and insurance firms, the largest investors in limited partnerships. Their horizon typically involves 10–15 years, which more or less coincides with the lifetime of a limited partnership fund. More generally, however, it is the particular way the limited partnership addresses uncertainty and grants control rights to investors.

4.2.1 Addressing uncertainty

The question "why are funds not evergreen?" could be compared to the question "why do publicly quoted companies pay dividends?" According to the dividend irrelevance theory, dividend payments should have little, if any, impact on the stock price as investors can always liquidate a portion of their portfolio of equities if they prefer cash.[2] For instance, Apple, the world's most valuable company in terms of market capitalization (third quarter 2012), did not pay dividends for 17 years until 16 August 2012, when a new dividend programme entered into force. However, dividends may serve an important signalling function with respect to the financial well-being of a company.

Similarly, there is a strong argument to be made for self-liquidating funds in private equity and real assets. Take VC, for example, where valuations are notoriously difficult and are often viewed by investors with considerable doubt. To be sure, it is not that the fund managers are not seen as trustworthy; rather, it is the recognition that in any appraised asset class valuations are highly judgmental. The only way to give investors confidence is by exiting portfolio companies, thus liquidating investments and showing investors that valuations are "real".

In coping with the extreme uncertainty of innovation or with a rapidly changing economic environment, the fund's limited lifetime forces its managers to regularly return to the capital markets and ask existing or new investors to back the next fund. Rather than having a "magic formula" to guarantee success, fund managers periodically need to convince investors that they provide superior investment opportunities. This results in high evolutionary pressure and requires fund managers to listen closely to their investors and adapt rapidly.

4.2.2 Control from the limited partner perspective

While fund managers may prefer evergreen funds as such structures give them the opportunity to raise fresh capital on a permanent basis, investors often shy away from being locked up under such conditions. In contrast to evergreen funds, limited partnerships follow a fundraising cycle in the sense that GPs return to the market at – more or less – regular intervals to raise capital for a new fund. Typically, this interval is around 4 years, although it became significantly shorter during the last investment boom in the mid-2000s.

The future of the GP depends essentially on the success of his fundraising efforts. To the extent that funds become smaller, management fees decline, requiring the general partner to reduce its cost base. In the extreme case, where no new funds are raised at all, full liquidation eventually becomes inevitable as management fees on old funds under management dry up.

[2] In fact, little or no dividend payout is more favourable for investors, as taxation on a dividend is higher than on a capital gain.

Heikkilä (2004) views this periodic liquidation of private equity funds as essential from the viewpoint of their limited partners, because the exit and reinvestment cycle allows them to withdraw capital from less competent fund managers or managers whose industry expertise has become obsolete. It also allows setting back the clock for new investors, who do not need to value and pay for an existing portfolio. The fund management team's track record and reputation are critical for the successful closure of follow-on funds. Typically, limited partnership agreements do not allow follow-on funds with the same strategy by the same manager before the end of the investment period or before a high percentage of the active fund is invested.

LPs can exercise "evolutionary pressure" through the selection and monitoring process, which is an essential component of the "alternative asset ecosystem". Obviously, this pressure would not exist if investors in funds also had management control. The separation of the GP and LP functions in a limited partnership is therefore a critical governance characteristic of such structures.

4.3 THE LIMITED PARTNERSHIP FUND'S ILLIQUIDITY

The liquidity of an asset – or lack of it – is generally viewed as its ability to be sold and converted into cash with a minimum loss in value. This loss in value corresponds to transaction costs. There is no specific amount attached to these transaction costs that would draw a line between liquid and illiquid assets. Therefore, assets are in relative terms more or less liquid than others. As we discussed in the previous chapter, illiquidity can occur even in capital markets that may be considered "deep". One example is the corporate debt market. But even in the public stock market, where trades typically occur on a high-frequency basis, there may be situations where positions for a specific security are too large compared to its daily trading volumes. Apart from this "blockage factor", some assets have very specific characteristics, making it difficult for the seller to find an acquirer.

Limited partnership funds belong to the most illiquid assets. As explained above, their illiquidity is known *ex ante*, as opposed to asset classes whose liquidity may dry up *ex post* in periods of financial turmoil. Investors in limited partnerships deliberately accept illiquidity in order to harvest an illiquidity risk premium (Pastor and Stambaugh, 2003; Acharya and Pedersen, 2005). With the required return being inversely related to the liquidity of an asset, the risk premium for limited partnerships tends to be relatively high (see Chapter 5). Importantly, the high degree of illiquidity of limited partnerships is not just an unintended consequence of its general contractual structure. Instead, illiquidity is the purpose of such investment vehicles, preventing the emergence of a secondary market as an accounting standard setter.[3]

4.3.1 Illiquidity as the source of the expected upside

Thanks to the institutional capital provided outside listed markets, unquoted portfolio companies are able to sustain difficulties or successes without having to release information that could be detrimental to the success of the investment due to the adverse behaviour of competitors, suppliers or clients. Information is provided to the LPs in strict confidence relating to specific

[3] According to the IASB, an active secondary market is characterized by quoted prices that are readily and regularly available from an exchange, dealer, broker, industry group, pricing service or regulatory agency, with those prices representing actual and regularly occurring market transactions on an arm's length basis.

aspects of the development of underlying investments. In fact, in private equity a key purpose of the fund structure is to shield fledgling portfolio companies in their early stages and those that are being restructured in turnaround situations from disruptive market influences. Similar considerations apply to explorations and green field projects that are particularly susceptible to sudden changes in investor sentiment and with a high risk of being cut off from sources of funding. To allow the value of such investments to increase, financial resources need to be provided on a sustained and predictable basis within a reasonably long timeframe. From this perspective, it is conceptually problematic to look at the market value of a fund's underlying investments, especially at an early investment stage. This implies that market values come to existence and thus risk are controlled at the level of the fund rather than the level of the underlying investments.

4.3.2 The market for lemons

From a strictly legal viewpoint, limited partnership shares are illiquid, although – as we discuss in Chapter 6 – secondary transactions do take place in practice. However, the secondary market may to some degree be subject to what is known as the "lemons problem". Coined by Akerlof (1970) more than four decades ago, the "lemons problem" exists because of asymmetric information between the buyer and the seller. In the used car market – the example Akerlof gives – the buyer usually does not know beforehand whether it is a good car or a bad one (a "lemon"). Therefore, his best guess is that the car is of average quality, and he will be willing to pay for it only the price of a car of known average quality. This means that the seller of a good used car will be unable to get a high enough price to make selling that car worthwhile. As a result, he will not place his car on the used car market.

The same dynamic can be observed in other markets, which are subject to asymmetric information. In asset markets, where there are doubts about asset quality, the exit of the highest-quality seller leads to a reduction in the market price. His exit triggers another exit wave by sellers with somewhat lower-quality assets, resulting in a further decline in the market price. Eventually, and sometimes quickly, the market may turn from an efficient, high-volume one to a transaction-less market (Tirole, 2011).

Investors who are not a LP in a limited partnership fund are faced with the lemons problem, because they have less information on the quality of the fund. This lack of information makes them less willing to pay what may actually be a fair price for a fund share and under certain market conditions they might not be willing to buy a share at all. Importantly, this does not mean that the fund is actually a "lemon". But information asymmetries can result in significant spreads between the asking price and the bid price, potentially resulting in few or even no transactions.

The extent to which the "lemons problem" plays a role in secondary transactions in the private equity market remains unclear. Some specialized players maintain proprietary databases with detailed intelligence on funds and pro-actively seek to source deals. Information asymmetries, to the extent they exist, should be relatively small. In fact, in individual cases potential buyers may even possess superior information about a fund or a portfolio of funds a LP wants to sell.

A related issue concerns the potentially adverse signal a secondary transaction may send to the investor community in terms of the perceived quality of the fund and its manager. However, this issue can be addressed by selling only a part of a stake in the fund, ensuring that the seller maintains his role as a LP. Signalling his confidence in the fund manager and maintaining his relationship with the GP, the LP retains the option to commit to new partnerships formed in the future.

4.3.3 Contractual illiquidity

Notwithstanding the restrictions regarding the transferability of shares stipulated in the limited partnership agreement, GPs usually give their consent to secondary transactions. However, Lerner and Schoar (2002) argue that private equity fund managers, by choosing the degree of illiquidity of the security, can influence the type of investors the firm will attract. This allows them to screen for "deep-pocket" investors who have a comparatively low probability of facing a liquidity shock. Such investors can ease the GP's fundraising efforts in future fund-raising rounds. Importantly, GPs also face a lemons problem, in the sense that information about a LP's quality is asymmetric between existing LPs in their funds and the rest of the investor community (Lerner and Schoar, 2002).

4.3.4 Inability to value properly

Settlement prices in the secondary market are determined by a host of different factors, including asymmetric information, negotiation skills of the seller and the buyer, the pressure to close a deal, to name just a few. Furthermore, there may be different preferences. For example, whereas the seller may place a higher premium on short-term liquidity, the buyer may attach greater importance to the long-term performance, irrespective of holding period. Since the true economic price for an underlying asset cannot be observed, market participants have to rely on particular appraisal techniques. Indeed, many alternative assets may be described as an appraised asset class, where the market value is determined by a small number of experts rather than a large number of sellers and buyers.

4.3.5 Endowment effect

The "endowment effect", also known as the "divestiture aversion effect" or "status quo bias", may also contribute to the illiquidity of funds. In behavioural economics, the endowment effect refers to the experimental observation that people generally attach a considerably higher value to a good that they own than the price they are prepared to pay to acquire that good (Thaler, 1980). Thus, subjective considerations often stand in the way of trading an asset. A frequently cited example of the endowment effect is a family's reluctance to sell an old painting, which has been in their possession for a considerable amount of time, (more or less) regardless of the price that is being offered.

While the endowment effect has been shown in various behavioural experiments, it is less clear to what extent this effect exists in financial markets where traders are motivated by the objective to maximize profits (Arlen *et al.*, 2002). Instead, behavioural biases may be attributed to "loss aversion", i.e. investors' tendency to attach greater importance to losses than to gains. In private equity and real assets, however, it is important to take into account that interactions between LPs in a fund and the fund manager are particularly close, which differentiates these asset classes from publicly traded assets. With access to funds sometimes being restricted and mutual trust being built up over several years, investors in a fund may be reluctant to terminate a relationship – unless there are overwhelmingly clear reasons to do so. Thus, the endowment effect may well play a role in illiquid asset classes, given their particular market characteristics (Blake, 2008).

4.4 CRITICISMS OF THE LIMITED PARTNERSHIP STRUCTURE

Investors in private equity and real assets are generally aware of the illiquid nature of limited partnerships. They deliberately accept illiquidity to harvest a premium, with the limited partnership providing an adequate framework. Illiquidity in private equity and real assets thus does not represent a market failure but is an essential characteristic to generate excess returns. Nevertheless, it is sometimes argued – especially in market downturns – that the limited partnership model is broken and destined to disappear (e.g., Scott, 2012).

Furthermore, some fund managers have argued that periodic fundraising requires a substantial amount of time and resources, which could be better spent on sourcing and making investments. In fact, this was an important motivation behind the public listing of investment vehicles at the peak of the last cycle, with the capital raised by the private equity firms being invested in their funds. Moreover, in many situations – notably early-stage VC transactions – the usual lifetime of limited partnership funds may not be sufficient to develop the underlying portfolio companies owned by the fund and reap their full potential. Therefore, some GPs have called for a longer fund life or have advocated, as discussed before, evergreen structures.

LPs have also expressed concern about the limited partnership as the dominant investment vehicle in private equity and real assets, albeit from the opposite angle. Locking up capital for a period of 10 years or more plays a key role in this regard, given investors' reduced ability to rebalance their portfolios. This consideration is particularly important in periods of heightened economic uncertainty.

Another factor emphasized by some LPs, such as David Swensen of the Yale University Endowment, is the less-than-perfect alignment of interest between LPs and GPs. As mentioned earlier, Metrick and Yasuda (2009) and Phalippou (2009) find that non-performance-related management fees account for around 60% of the total compensation of fund managers. Among other things, this compensation structure, which has come under increased pressure from LPs after the recent downturn, has been identified as a possible disincentive for GPs to divest underperforming portfolio companies.

Finally, the limited lifespan of limited partnerships does not allow an investor to build up reserves. As Achleitner and Albrecht (2011) point out, listed stocks can be held over very long time periods, allowing them to build up considerable reserves. These reserves, called unrealized capital gains and losses (UCGL), are linked to inflation and the overall growth of the economy. They are of considerable importance for life insurance companies, which can smooth returns and help achieve the predictable and stable investment results expected by both shareholders and life insurance holders by realizing UCGLs.

4.5 COMPETING APPROACHES TO INVESTING IN PRIVATE EQUITY AND REAL ASSETS

Consequently, investors are continuously looking for ways to avoid or mitigate the limited partnership's existing or perceived shortcomings.[4] In addition to the evergreen funds discussed

[4] For the purpose of this discussion we focus on institutional financing and ignore the continuous innovation and experimentation with vehicles such as business angel networks, pledge funds, crowd funding, etc. mainly found at the boundary between formal and informal capital markets in early-stage entrepreneurial investing.

before, a range of competing approaches have been marketed to investors over the years. However, these approaches have generally produced mixed results.

4.5.1 Listed vehicles

Listed vehicles appear to be a way to combine the advantages of alternative assets with relatively high liquidity. Resembling investment-trust structures, listed vehicles address the hurdles of regulatory requirements, tax efficiency and transparency. Furthermore, they provide immediate access to a diversified portfolio and management expertise. Moreover, institutional investors that are new to alternative assets often use such products to gain insights into the market before deciding to set up their own investment programme.

However, liquidity may be strictly limited for listed vehicles as well, given that share price discounts can make it difficult, if not impossible, to divest without incurring significant losses. While the lack of liquidity should generally be reflected in the market price, extreme discounts are not unusual, with thin markets resulting in high bid–ask spreads. Potential buyers who are interested in acquiring relatively large positions will typically find it difficult to find sellers. This may take a prolonged period of time, possibly pushing up prices significantly. Likewise, potential sellers may incur considerable losses as the market is able to absorb the increased supply only at considerable discounts.

Furthermore, while listed vehicles increase investors' flexibility in tactical asset allocations and permit them to accelerate their exposure to alternative investments, interests are less well aligned compared with traditional partnerships where investors exercise tight control over the use of funding. Essentially, listed vehicles display the same characteristics as public stocks, where control is much less direct than in limited partnerships.

Finally, a distinction has to be drawn between investments in listed vehicles and investments in publicly listed alternative asset managers themselves. As far as the latter are concerned, investors hold shares in the management company, which may serve as a GP in limited partnerships. In fact, several of the largest private equity firms, which have transformed themselves into alternative asset managers, have gone public (e.g., Blackstone Group, Carlyle Group, KKR). However, to the extent that investors acquire shares in the management company, they are exposed to all asset classes the management company is involved in, such as private equity, infrastructure, real estate, credit and hedge funds. This may or may not be in the interest of the investor. The same applies to investments in benchmarks of publicly listed private equity, such as the LPX 50 index, which includes both listed vehicles and listed management companies.

4.5.2 Direct investments

Private equity and real assets are relatively expensive asset classes, with the compensation structures in traditional limited partnerships having a profound impact on returns for LPs. Thus, some investors have looked for alternative ways to get exposed to alternative assets while avoiding paying high management fees and carried interest. However, cost savings may not be the only reason for pursuing direct investments. Other factors, such as better market timing, may also play an important and sometimes even the primary role (Fang *et al.*, 2012). A prominent example of a limited partner going direct is OMERS PE, the private equity investing arm of the Ontario Municipal Employees Retirement System, a CD 55 billion pension system. In 2004, OMERS PE initiated a major shift from private equity fund investments to direct investments, with the latter targeted to ultimately represent 85% of their total exposure to private equity (Witkowsky, 2012). This strategy has found followers especially in other Canadian pension funds, which increasingly act as investment companies, spearheading an approach that pushes for more control and cost reductions.

Fang *et al.* (2012) find that direct investments have actually significantly outperformed standard fund investment benchmarks. Nevertheless, important questions remain as to the applicability of this approach within a wider investor community. In fact, it has been tried before: such "captive" structures represented an important category of investors until the end of the 1990s in Europe. However, the share of these players in the market decreased significantly because of a number of challenges namely: (i) to create a governance structure that gives investment authority and decision-making power to the investment professionals; (ii) to attract other investors in the structure, given the potential conflicts of interest with the parent company; (iii) to build and retain a team of talented individuals; and (iv) to manage the difficult interaction of these entities with the rest of the parent company. However, addressing these challenges in an appropriate way may also entail significant costs, and it is not clear whether running an in-house direct investment programme that can reasonably expect to achieve the same gross returns will actually be cheaper than investing through funds as intermediaries.

4.5.3 Deal-by-deal

Some firms offer their investors the option to come in on a deal-by-deal basis, an approach that shares certain characteristics with the direct investment approach. At first glance, this seems highly attractive from a LP's standpoint as it gives them the possibility to: (i) opt out, for example, in situations where they are liquidity-constrained; (ii) reduce management fees; and (iii) build up a portfolio that is more in line with their targeted asset composition. However, following a deal-by-deal investment approach requires fast decision-making processes and investment professionals with direct investment experience, something which is beyond most institutional investors' capabilities. From the fund manager's perspective, the deal-by-deal model is also subject to considerable challenges. Importantly, fund managers need to ensure that their investors who participate in such non-binding arrangements are not just strategic "deal-flow watchers" but are sufficiently committed. Overall, deal-by-deal arrangements have failed to gain traction in most markets and there are few signs that this will change in the foreseeable future (Romaine, 2012). Thus, the Middle East, where deal-by-deal arrangements have traditionally played a more prominent role, looks set to remain an exception.

4.5.4 Co-investments

Co-investing has emerged as an increasingly accepted way of getting around the shortcomings of the limited partnership structure. Co-investing entails the syndication of financing between a fund and one or more of its LPs. In principle, this brings complementary capabilities of GPs and LPs together. A fund may be too small to acquire an asset whose risk-adjusted returns are viewed to be particularly attractive. At the same time, its LPs may lack the required industry-specific knowledge and the networking capabilities to source such deals.

In contrast to direct investing, co-investing involves transactions that are sourced, pre-screened, structured, and priced by the fund manager. While LPs generally do not pay fees and carry for co-investments, the role such investments play in investors' allocation approaches can vary significantly. Some LPs follow a passive and nearly automatic approach and rely more or less entirely on the fund managers. Others, however, behave nearly like a direct investor, with co-investments being best described as a form of syndication. In any case, invitations to co-investments are often confined to the largest LPs in a fund, and running a meaningful co-investment programme typically requires a significant primary fund franchise. At the same time, selecting among the universe of invited deals requires experience and skills that are akin to those needed for direct investments, which explains why co-investors in private equity transactions and similar deals in real assets are often large and sophisticated institutions.

4.6 A TIME-PROVEN STRUCTURE

The limited partnership has resulted from the extreme information asymmetries and incentive problems that arise in the market for many alternative assets. Although this partnership structure is often seen as an innovation that has been developed for VC investing and subsequently for other forms of private equity and real assets more generally, its origins date back to ancient times. Partnerships have existed throughout most of recorded history. Indeed, for unusually large or especially risky enterprises it is natural to pool resources to be better able to exploit investment opportunities. Combining resources helps partners achieve an outcome that is greater than the sum of the individual investments. Importantly, this insight cuts across cultures and legal systems, prompting Borden (2009) to suggest that humans have a natural tendency to form partnerships to conduct business. His analysis reveals that ancient and modern partnerships, in all their forms, have numerous common characteristics.

- One example is the relationship between the Sumerian "damgar" merchants and their agents, the "shamallu", which existed in ancient Babylon as early as 2750 BC. The arrangement between these parties provided for independent action by the shamallu, as well as profit sharing and liability allocation between the shamallu and the damgar, and in several ways has parallels to the medieval commenda and modern partnerships. Documents show that as early as 1947 BC trade partnerships, so-called "tapputum" existed that required partners for some defined business project to make equal capital investments and to use the contributed capital for purchasing merchandise and for reselling at a profit. The structure allowed for debt financing of the operations and provided for joint liability or joint and individual liability of the partners. This Babylonian tapputum possessed characteristics of the medieval commenda.
- According to Hansmann *et al.* (2005), ancient Rome failed to develop general-purpose commercial entities, but found a type of multi-owner firm known as the "societas publicanorum". This fourth-century BC type of partnership consisted of groups of investors, known as "publicani", who bid on state contracts for projects or collection of taxes. Upon accepting the bid, the state paid a portion of the contract and the rest when the contract was completed. Investments could not be withdrawn, nor could the firm's assets be liquidated before the contract with the state was fulfilled. Hansmann *et al.* (2005) argue that multi-owner structures for amassing capital in ancient Rome were absent because they were not needed, as significant wealth was already concentrated in certain families. Only a few undertakings – such as the construction of public works or the manufacture of armaments – were too capital intensive even for a wealthy Roman family, with the multi-owner societas publicanorum filling the gap.
- Although partnerships can be traced to ancient history, many scholars attribute the origins of modern partnership law to either Byzantine or Arabic origins. Partnerships were based on a statute in the Code of Justinian and on the Rhodian Sea Law, a seventh-century body

of regulations governing commercial trade and navigation in the Byzantine Empire. This "Lex Rhodia" focused on the liability for lost or damaged cargo and divided the cost of the losses among the ship's owner, the owners of the cargo and the passengers, thus serving as a form of insurance against storms and piracy. It was effective until the twelfth century and greatly influenced the maritime law of the Italian cities from the eleventh century onwards.

- It appears that Arabian contract law has provided at least one of the bases for the partnership structures widely used today. The "mudāraba" is a form of commercial contract whereby an investor – or a group of investors – entrust capital to a "mudārib", i.e. an agent, who trades in it and then returns the principal along with a predetermined share of the profits to the investors (Brunnhuber, 2007). The mudāraba form of financing a venture has developed in the context of the pre-Islamic Arabian caravan trade. As such, it appears that its roots are indigenous to the Arabian Peninsula as a critical part in the long-distance caravan trade for the Hejaz region.
- Consequently, the mudāraba's conceptual approach appears to be particularly relevant in the context of long-distance international trade. According to Brunnhuber (2007), Islamic contract law has had a long tradition of defining and sharing investment risks among the relevant parties to a business venture. One conceptual underpinning of Islamic finance is commonly perceived to be the prohibition of interest taking, not unlike other belief systems like Christianity or Hinduism that at some point in their history have disallowed the charging of interest. The common perception is that interest in a standard loan is quasi risk-free, because the lender is guaranteed a return, independent of whether the underlying business transaction is successful or not. In contrast to this, Islam stresses the need to share rather than to transfer risk.
- With the Arab conquest, the mudāraba spread to Northern Africa and the Near East, and ultimately to Southern Europe. Partnerships were introduced into Europe as Italian merchants increasingly traded in the Eastern Mediterranean, thus becoming familiar with business practices in this region and adopting the "commenda". Indeed, researchers have demonstrated a very strong correlation between the structures of the mudāraba and the commenda. The commenda contract had a sedentary investor, known as the "commendator", who advances capital to a travelling associate, known as a "tractator".
- The commenda both combined financing with insurance, as the recipient of the financing was freed of any obligation to the provider of the financing if ship or cargo was lost. The contract ended when profits were distributed after the merchant returned. The commendator received a portion of the profits, but had no liability for losses, was not guilty of usury and, in turn, could diversify risk by entering into commenda contracts with many different merchants. A commenda was not a common form of long-term business venture as most long-term businesses were still expected to be secured against the assets of their individual proprietors. Instead, the commenda was "self-liquidating", i.e. it ended upon the completion of a venture or the death of the tractator.
- Colbert's Ordinance on Commerce of 1673 and the Napoleonic Code of 1807 reinforced the commenda's limited partnership concept in European law. Britain enacted its first limited partnership statute in 1907. In the USA, limited partnerships became widely available in the early 1800s.

While a number of legal restrictions made them unpopular for businesses, in the early twentieth century limited partnerships were increasingly used to raise capital for prospecting new oil fields. The establishment of the first VC limited partnerships in the USA dates back to the late 1950s and 1960s. In 1959 Draper, Gaither and Anderson adopted this structure and raised what, in all likelihood, was the first limited partnership in the VC industry.[5] This model for VC investments is arguably the most successful worldwide and is followed in many international markets. Indeed, many see the limited partnership as an ideal vehicle for investing in private equity and real assets.

4.7 CONCLUSION

Limited partnerships formed by GPs and LPs are a particular form of financial intermediation that entails the asymmetric sharing of risks and rewards and represents a time-proven response to dealing with uncertainty. The efficiency, scalability and strong controls associated with modern large corporations are traded off against the flexibility of and the communication within small teams that allow a much quicker adaptation to changing market conditions and newly arising opportunities. While the limited partnership has frequently been pronounced dead, such pronouncements have thus far proved premature. To be sure, the limited partnership may have important shortcomings, which lie not least in their self-liquidation and their limited lifespan. However, no superior structure has evolved yet. To paraphrase Sir Winston Churchill, the limited partnership may be the worst form of investing in private equity and real assets except all those other forms that have been tried from time to time. Limited partnerships have been around for thousands of years in one form or another. Surprisingly, however, they are still poorly understood in terms of their risk properties from the standpoint of a diversified investment portfolio. Instead, investments in limited partnerships are often treated in the same way as investments in traditional asset classes. As we discuss in the remainder of this book, such treatment may have unintended consequences. Instead, a risk management approach is needed that reflects the specific characteristics of the limited partnership.

[5] The long-term success of this firm, later renamed Draper Fisher Jurvetson, contrasts with the demise of the VC firm ARD (American Research and Development). General George Doriot, the pre-WWII Harvard Business School professor, organized ARD as a publicly traded, closed-end investment company subject to the Investment Company Act of 1940. This closed-end structure was, according to Hsu and Kenney (2004), plagued by three main problems:

1. Its structure as an investment fund pressured ARD's management to generate a steady stream of cash.
2. It also inhibited the provision of competitive compensation for ARD's investment professionals. This reduced their incentives and eventually led to their resignation.
3. Closed-end investment funds often trade at a discount to their value in terms of cash and marketable securities, thus making them targets for corporate raiders.

ARD was a pioneering organization whose business model ultimately failed while the limited partnership had a better fit with the business environment.

5

Returns, Risk Premiums and Risk Factor Allocation

Investors who invest in illiquid asset classes expect to achieve higher returns, compensating them for the lack of liquidity they have to accept. From a portfolio standpoint, the illiquid nature of investments in limited partnership funds makes it difficult, if not impossible, to continuously rebalance an investor's portfolio – a key assumption in standard asset allocation models (Ang and Sorensen, 2011; Ang *et al.*, 2011). Shares in limited partnership funds cannot easily be liquidated, despite the development of a secondary market in recent years, as we discuss in Chapter 6. In addition to market liquidity risk, investors face funding risk, or commitment risk, as they have to be able to respond to capital calls at any given point in time. Since capital calls and distributions are stochastic, investors may suddenly become overcommitted or undercommitted, moving investors away from their optimal portfolio and reducing diversification benefits (Phalippou and Westerfield, 2012). Measuring and managing funding and market liquidity risk is essential for investors in illiquid asset classes, an issue we return to in the second part of this book.

Quantifying the risk premium in illiquid asset classes is subject to considerable conceptual and statistical challenges. While the literature on investment returns of illiquid assets has expanded significantly in recent years as more data have become available, most studies have focused on comparing such returns with returns of liquid assets. However, as we discuss in this chapter, studies focusing on risk-adjusted returns, and especially on returns adjusted for liquidity risk, have remained rare and their results should still be viewed with considerable caution as this literature continues to evolve. Despite the significant difficulties in measuring risk in private equity and real assets as illiquid asset classes, a growing number of institutional investors are adopting an asset allocation approach that aims explicitly at harvesting asset-specific risk premiums. More specifically, as we outline in the second part of this chapter, the risk factor allocation strategy seeks to exploit diversification gains from uncorrelated investment risks – as opposed to uncorrelated returns as emphasized in traditional mean–variance approaches.

5.1 RETURNS AND RISK IN PRIVATE EQUITY

Many asset allocators construct their portfolios according to a two-step process. In the first step, investors generally determine the desired share of each asset class in the overall portfolio. In the second step, investors then design particular investment strategies within each asset class (Sharpe, 2007). In this chapter, we are primarily concerned with the first step. As we have seen in Chapter 2, illiquid asset classes are essentially limited to long-term investors with appropriate liability profiles. Their long-term liabilities allow them to invest in illiquid asset classes that promise higher returns in compensation for a higher degree of illiquidity. But do illiquid asset classes actually generate comparatively higher (risk-adjusted) returns? In addressing this question, the natural starting point is to compare private equity returns with public equity returns; two asset classes that are identical in terms of their position in the capital structure of companies, but subject to fundamentally different degrees of liquidity.

5.1.1 Comparing private equity with public equity returns

As far as leveraged buyouts are concerned, GPs usually employ a combination of three measures to create value and achieve superior returns for their LPs:

- *Strategic measures* include buy-and-build initiatives, divestments of non-core businesses and development of new products and markets, aimed at enhancing EBITDA growth and usually leading to multiple expansions.
- *Operational measures* are focused on improving product quality and sales effectiveness, reducing overhead costs and optimizing the company's value chain.
- *Financial measures* aim at maximizing capital efficiency and optimizing the company's capital structure.

In implementing strategic, operational and financial measures, GPs pay particular attention to effective governance structures, ensuring that the company's management's interests are fully aligned with the owners' interests. Management teams of portfolio companies are therefore incentivized by giving them a large equity upside through stocks and options. At the same time, the management team is usually also exposed to the downside by requiring executives to make a meaningful investment in the company.

There is ample evidence from the 1980s that buyouts have led to considerable gains in operational performance and increases in firm values or both (for a review of the literature, see Kaplan and Strömberg, 2009). Unfortunately, there is still much less evidence from the 1990s and the most recent buyout boom. An exception is Guo *et al.* (2011), who study 192 buyout transactions completed between 1990 and 2006. Surprisingly, they find that gains in operational performance were substantially smaller than documented for deals of the 1980s, which appears to contradict the growing emphasis on operational measures relative to financial leverage. Overall, however, Guo *et al.* find that returns to either pre- or post-buyout capital invested are positive and significant, a result which is consistent with earlier studies of buyout transactions in the 1980s. Importantly, the value creation appears to be long-lasting: Cao and Lerner (2009) who study reverse leveraged buyouts (initial public offerings (IPOs) of firms that had previously been bought out by private equity investors) find that such transactions outperformed non-private equity IPOs even after five years.

As far as European buyouts are concerned, Kaserer (2011) analyses 332 mid-market buyout transactions from 1990 to 2011. Employing a novel approach to decompose the returns into different value drivers – earnings growth, multiple expansion and financial leverage – he finds that around two-thirds of gross returns in European buyout transactions are attributable to strategic and operational measures aimed at increasing earnings. By contrast, multiple expansion was found to be negligible. While the leverage effect was estimated to contribute another third, it was statistically insignificant, leading Kaserer (2011) to conclude "... that if there is any benefit to leverage, it may be reaped by the seller instead of the buyer in a buy-out transaction".

Somewhat different results are reported by Achleitner *et al.* (2011), who studied performance drivers of European and North American buyout transactions completed between 1986 and 2010. Specifically, the authors provide evidence that returns have been more broadly based, with multiple expansion playing a meaningful role in addition to operational improvements and leverage. Finally, Acharya *et al.* (2013) examine 395 buyout transactions in Western Europe between 1991 and 2007. Correcting for leverage, they find abnormal performance to be significantly positive on average, driven by greater growth in sales and greater improvement in EBITDA to sales ratio (margin) relative to those of quoted peers.

Notwithstanding the role of individual value drivers, there is general agreement that buyout transactions have generated profits for private equity funds. But this does not necessarily mean that investments in private equity partnerships represent attractive investments for LPs. To begin with, sellers may capture a significant amount of the value a private equity firm creates as the latter generally pays a significant premium in buyout transactions. Furthermore, as we discussed in the previous chapter, GPs receive significant compensation from their LPs in the form of management fees and carried interest. What matters for LPs are the partnership's distributions net of fees and carried interest, as opposed to the gross returns the GP achieves.

There are a growing number of studies which aim to measure the net-of-fees returns of private equity funds and compare them with the returns a LP would have received if he had invested the same amount of capital in a public market index (for an overview, see Diller and Wulff, 2011). Using a dataset from Thomson Venture Economics (TVE) consisting of 169 (largely liquidated) US buyout funds that were raised before 1995, Kaplan and Schoar (2005) compared how much a LP earned net of fees with what the investor would have earned in an equivalent investment in the S&P 500. In order to make the performance comparable, the authors employ a measure known as the public market equivalent. This measure is calculated by investing (or discounting) all cash outflows of a fund at the total return to a public market index (in this study the S&P 500) and comparing the resulting value with the value of the cash inflows (all net of fees) to the fund invested (discounted) using the total return to the public market index. Thus, the PME circumvents a well-known problem with IRRs, which lies in the reinvestment hypothesis of the underlying cash flows.[1] The PME has a value of 1 if an investment in a limited partnership achieves exactly the same returns as an investment in the public stock market. The PME is larger (smaller) than 1 if an investment in a limited partnership outperforms (underperforms) an investment in the public stock market.[2]

For the buyout funds in their sample, Kaplan and Schoar (2005) report a PME of 0.97, indicating that, net of fees, such partnerships have slightly underperformed the public market. The underperformance was somewhat higher (PME = 0.93) when average returns were measured on a size-weighted basis. Thus, Kaplan and Schoar (2005) did not find the outperformance often given as justification for investing in private equity as an illiquid asset class.[3] Using a slightly updated version of the Kaplan and Schoar dataset, Phalippou and Gottschalg (2009) obtained qualitatively similar results. In fact, assuming that the market value of non-liquidated mature funds equals zero (complete write-offs), their findings suggest an even greater degree

[1] In reporting their returns in terms of IRRs, private equity funds implicitly assume that cash proceeds have been reinvested at the IRR over the entire investment period. For example, if a fund reports a 40% IRR and has returned cash early in its life, it is assumed that the cash proceeds were invested again at that rate. In practice, however, such investment opportunities are rare.

[2] Rouvinez (2007) proposes a PME approach that is based on the IRR methodology. In this approach, he uses the original contributions to a fund and scales the distributions in such a way that the final NAVs of the two cash flow streams – from the private and public markets – are identical. Based on these two new cash flow streams, the IRRs can be calculated and compared. Rouvinez's results suggest an outperformance of 300 bps for funds raised between 1980 and 2003. Day and Diller (2010) estimate an outperformance of private equity compared with the S&P 500 of more than 600 bps.

[3] However, under plausible assumptions about management fees and carried interest, Kaplan and Schoar (2005) explain that gross PMEs would be at least 13% higher than the estimated net PMEs. As a result, gross PMEs would be well above 1, both on an equal and size-weighted basis.

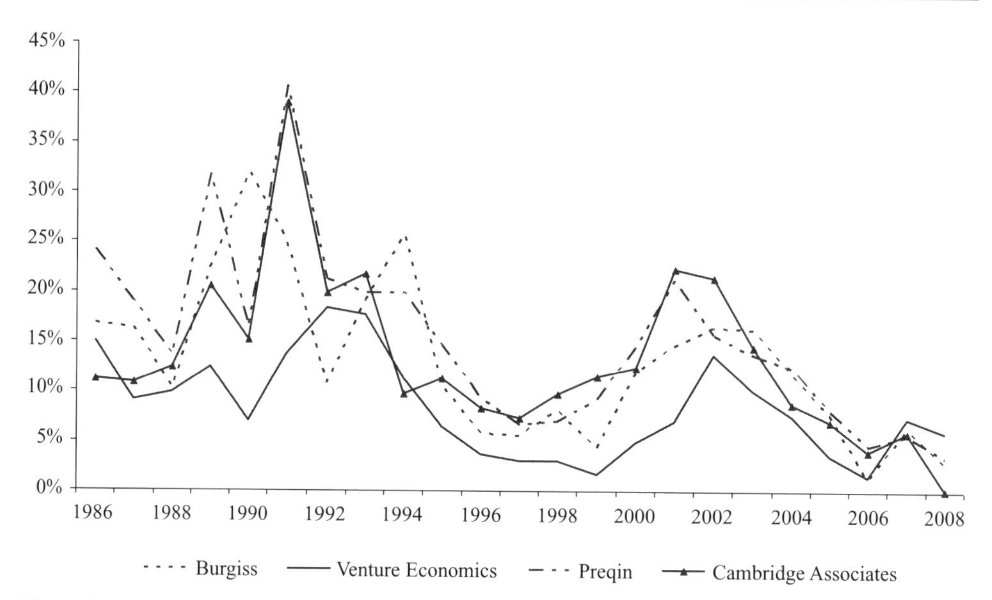

Figure 5.1 Comparing four different benchmarks for US buyout fund returns (IRR, net of fees). *Source:* Harris *et al.* (2012).

of underperformance of buyout funds on a net-of-fees basis. The sobering conclusion one might draw from these studies is that even on a risk-unadjusted basis, investments in private equity are rather unattractive. This conclusion gains even more weight if one factors in that private equity investors accept a high degree of illiquidity. Thus, it seems that from a return perspective commitments to buyout funds make sense only if investors are able to commit capital to upper-quartile funds for which significant outperformance is found.

Turning to VC investments, which are typically unleveraged, the picture appears comparatively brighter, at least for the period before the tech bubble. Based on a TVE sample of 577 VC funds, Kaplan and Schoar (2005) calculate a size-weighted PME of 1.21, indicating that LPs in such funds received significantly higher returns than a similar investment in public stocks would have generated. For all private equity funds in their sample, Kaplan and Schoar (2005) thus report a size-weighted average PME of 1.05, implying a slight outperformance of private equity as an asset class compared with a public market investment.[4]

More recent research suggests that private equity has probably outperformed by a wider margin than earlier studies (Kaplan and Schoar, 2005; Phalippou and Gottschalg, 2009) found. As mentioned above, these studies used a dataset from TVE, which, however, shows on average considerably lower private equity returns than other data providers – such as Burgiss, Cambridge Associates, Preqin and State Street (Harris *et al.*, 2010, 2012; Cornelius, 2011). As Figure 5.1 shows for US buyout funds, IRRs reported by different data providers follow a similar pattern over time, but differ by several hundred basis points in individual vintage years. These variations are due to the very nature of the data – namely that information about fund returns is private. While some data providers rely on voluntary and Freedom of

[4] Diller and Kaserer (2009) show a PME of 1.05 for European private equity funds (buyouts and VC) covering vintages from 1980 to 2003.

Information Act (FOIA) disclosures by GPs and LPs (Preqin, Thomson), others obtain data from LPs who use them for back-office services and fund investment monitoring (Burgiss, Cambridge Associates). While no database contains all funds ever raised, arguably the former are particularly prone to selection bias and problems with data updating.

The suspicion that TVE may have understated the true returns of private equity funds finds support in recent research by Stucke (2011), who analyses in detail the return data reported by the vendor. More specifically, he finds that the NAV for a significant number of funds in the TVE dataset were not updated, presumably because Thomson stopped receiving data from GPs/LPs and simply repeated the last known NAV in subsequent quarters. This was the case in a significant number of funds, with fund-level IRRs falling with the passage of time in the absence of recorded cash flows. Correcting for this inertia, Stucke (2011) finds significantly higher fund returns than were reported in earlier research.

Harris *et al.* (2012) use a dataset provided by Burgiss, a back-office service provider. This dataset is not only particularly comprehensive in terms of the number of funds constituting the benchmark, but is also arguably less prone to selection bias and problems with data updating. Their results suggest that earlier studies are likely to have understated the performance of private equity funds, particularly for buyouts. In fact, the degree to which the performance of buyout funds is likely to have been understated is far from trivial: Harris *et al.* (2012) estimate an average outperformance versus the S&P 500 of between 20% and 27% over the life of the average US buyout fund, or more than 3% per year. On an unweighted basis, the authors find an average PME of 1.22 for the vintage year period from 1984 to 2008; on a capital-weighted basis, the estimated average PME is 1.27. In fact, of the 25 vintage years in the sample, only five had average PMEs of less than 1 (see Figure 5.2) As far as VC funds are concerned, the authors find that this asset class has outperformed public markets substantially in the 1990s, but underperformed in the 2000s.

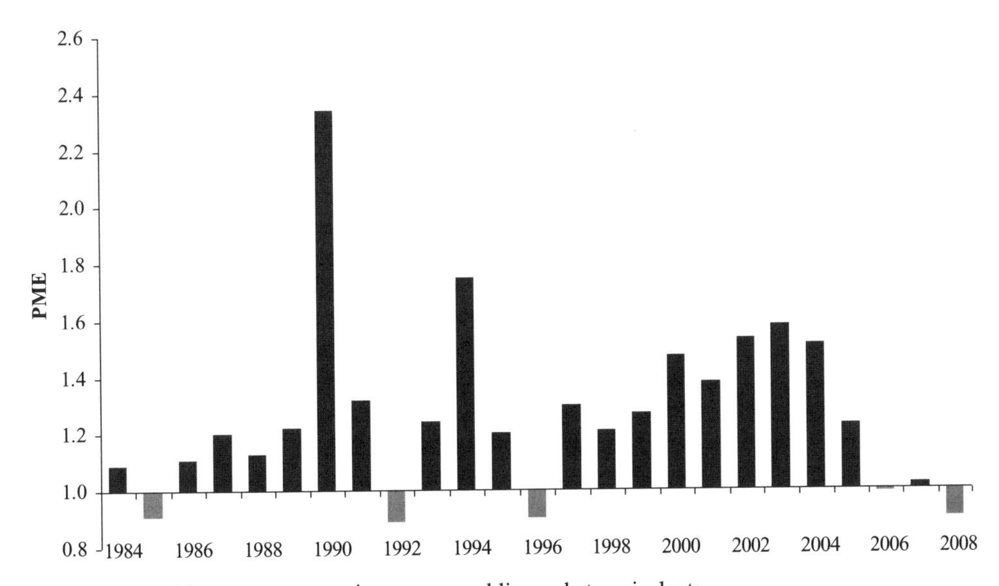

Figure 5.2 US buyout returns – vintage year public market equivalents.
Source: Harris *et al.* (2012).

The results obtained by Harris *et al.* (2012) are materially similar to those reported by Robinson and Sensoy (2011), whose analysis is based on data provided by a large LP. Their database includes not only US buyout funds but also international partnerships. Although PMEs from Burgiss and Robinson and Sensoy differ for individual vintage years, both studies agree that buyout PMEs exceed on average 1.0, indicating that private equity funds have generated superior returns compared with public equity investments.

Similar conclusions are also drawn by Higson and Stucke (2012), who use cash flow data provided by Cambridge Associates. Their sample includes US buyout funds raised between 1980 and 2008. As far as liquidated funds from 1980 to 2000 are concerned, the authors report excess returns of about 450 bps per year; excess returns increase to over 800 bps if the sample is extended to partially liquidated funds up to 2005. Importantly, however, the cross-sectional variation is found to be considerable, with just over 60% of all funds doing better than the S&P 500 and excess returns being driven by top-decile rather than top-quartile funds. Furthermore, the authors find a significant downward trend in absolute returns over all 29 vintage years in their sample.

While the Harris *et al.* (2012) and Higson and Stucke (2012) papers find significant outperformance, the question arises as to whether the S&P 500 represents an appropriate benchmark for private equity returns. Based on data by Capital IQ, a leading data vendor, Phalippou (2012) stresses that 95% of the enterprise values reported for leveraged buyout transactions are below USD 1,175 million, which is close to the largest stock in the Fama–French small cap index. According to Harris *et al.* (2012), however, the relative performance of US buyout funds is surprisingly insensitive to the benchmark. In fact, the authors obtain essentially identical results when they calculate PMEs on the basis of the Russell 2000, which measures the performance of US small-cap stocks.[5]

An even thornier issue pertains to risk. While the recent literature suggests that US buyout funds have outperformed public equity investments, in and of itself this tells us little as to whether LPs are adequately compensated for the greater risk they take when committing capital to private equity partnerships.

5.1.2 Market risk and the CAPM

Investment risk is generally perceived as the variance of returns over time. The greater the variance, the riskier the asset class. Other things being equal, asset classes whose returns are more stable will receive a larger portion of an investor's portfolio (and vice versa). Put differently, investors are willing to allocate capital to asset classes with a higher variance of returns only if they get compensated through higher expected returns. The relationship between the returns and their variance is expressed by the Sharpe ratio, which, in its original form (Sharpe, 1966),[6] is calculated by dividing (i) the historical excess return, $E[R]$, over

[5] Significantly different results are reported by Phalippou (2012), who uses cash flows provided by Preqin for 392 US funds raised between 1993 and 2010. He finds PMEs of close to 1 if returns are benchmarked against a small-cap mutual fund managed by Dimensional Fund Advisor, which offers passive low-cost exposure to small-cap stocks. The largest market capitalization considered by the fund was USD 1,130 million, as of December 2011, corresponding to an enterprise value that is higher than that of the 95th largest leveraged buyout reported by Capital IQ.

[6] Recognizing that the risk-free rate changes with time, Sharpe himself later revised the ratio as follows: $S = (E[R - R_f])/\sigma$, with $E[R - R_f]$ representing the expected value of the excess of the asset return over the benchmark return and σ being the standard deviation of the excess of the asset return, $\sqrt{\mathrm{var}[R - R_f]}$.

the riskless rate of interest, R_f (typically the 3-month treasury bill rate) by (ii) the standard deviation of its excess return, σ:

$$S = \frac{E[R] - R_f}{\sigma}$$

It is one of the greatest achievements in finance theory, however, to show that at least part of the risk is diversifiable, or idiosyncratic. What matters in the portfolio context is the extent to which asset returns are correlated, an insight that has its roots in the groundbreaking contributions by Markowitz (1952), Treynor (1962), Sharpe (1964), Lintner (1965) and Mossin (1966). Based on this insight, MPT attempts to maximize expected portfolio returns for a given amount of portfolio risk (or, equivalently, to minimize portfolio risk for a given level of expected returns), by carefully allocating capital to diverse asset classes. In efficient and complete markets with no restrictions, the optimal allocation is determined in such a way that the expected rate of return of an asset reflects the systematic, or non-diversifiable, risk of the asset in a broader investment portfolio. This risk is usually called market risk or beta risk. This is the essence of the CAPM, which stipulates that the price paid for an asset is determined by the degree to which the market portfolio's risk/return characteristics improve when the asset is added to it.

Public market equivalents, as calculated by Kaplan and Schoar (2005) and Harris *et al.* (2012), implicitly assume that market risk in private equity is 1. This might or might not be correct. Buyout deals are leveraged, with an average debt-to-equity ratio in US and European transactions of roughly 60:40 over the past 10 years. Leverage amplifies returns as well as losses, which, other things being equal, would suggest a beta of greater than 1. In other words, a beta of 1 would require other factors (e.g., structural and operational improvements in portfolio companies) just offsetting the impact of leverage on returns.

Some studies have attempted to estimate market risk and excess returns in buyouts and VC explicitly. However, the nature of private equity investing, the reporting of returns and the limited availability of performance data make this a difficult task.[7] First of all, standard asset-pricing models have been developed for marketable assets that are traded in transparent, liquid and essentially frictionless markets. These assumptions hardly apply to private equity investing (or similar investments in real assets). Second, private equity returns are observed infrequently, with the standard databases potentially subject to sample bias due to the over-representation of well-performing funds. Thus, the estimated alphas and betas may need to be adjusted to provide meaningful measures of returns and risk for private equity investments.

While some studies have used fund-level data to measure alpha and beta, others have employed deal-level data. As far as the former are concerned, Ljungqvist and Richardson (2003) examine cash flow data from a large LP investing in funds raised between 1981 and 1993, with the sample consisting of 19 VC funds and 54 buyout funds. They find an average fund IRR (net of fees) of 19.81%, compared with the average S&P 500 return of 14.1% during this period, implying a considerable outperformance of the former. In order to estimate beta risk, Ljungqvist and Richardson then assign each portfolio company to one of 48 broad industry groups and use the corresponding average beta for publicly traded companies in the

[7] Specifically, the CAPM assumes that all investors have access to the same information and agree about the risk and expected return of all assets. Further, it is assumed that there are no taxes or transaction costs and the market portfolio consists of all assets in all markets, where each asset is weighted by its market capitalization. There are no preferences between markets and assets for individual investors, who choose assets solely as a function of their risk/return profile. Finally, all assets are infinitely divisible as to the amount which may be held or transacted.

same industry. For buyouts the authors obtain a beta of 1.08, for VC investments they estimate a beta of 1.12. Given the estimated returns and the market risk in private equity, Ljungvqist and Richardson (2003) interpret the 5–6% excess returns as an illiquidity premium. Note, however, that these results are not adjusted for higher (lower) leverage used for buyouts (VC) compared with the S&P 500.

Driessen *et al.* (2011) present a new empirical method to estimate alphas and betas from fund-level cash flows. Using data from 272 mature buyout funds raised between 1980 and 2003, the authors find betas of 1.3 to 1.7 depending on the specification of the underlying model. While buyout funds in their sample have a slightly negative alpha of 0.4–1%, the estimates are statistically insignificant. As far as VC funds are concerned, the Driessen *et al.* sample contains 686 partnerships. The authors find betas of 2.4 to 2.7, with negative alphas of 0.7–1%.

Other academic studies use company-level data. Such data may be advantageous in the sense that they contain more disaggregated information, which may lead to more precise estimates of risk and allows for an analysis of risk and return as a function of individual company characteristics. However, researchers using company-level data face their own set of challenges. To begin with, company-level cash flow data exclude management fees and carried interest paid by the LPs. As a result, estimated risks and returns reflect the gross-of-fees risks and returns of the investments, not those earned by the LPs. Second, company-level data require continuous-time specifications, whereas the standard CAPM is designed on a discrete-time basis, implying that it does not compound over time. However, while this is a standard problem in empirical finance, Ang and Sorensen (2011) point out that the continuous-time specification can no longer be interpreted as the abnormal arithmetic return, as in the standard discrete-time version of the CAPM. Instead, as they suggest, the abnormal return (i.e., the "alpha") can be obtained by adding 0.5 times the square of the estimated volatility: $\alpha = \delta + 0.5\sigma^2$.

As far as VC investments are concerned, there are two major studies that use company-level data: Cochrane (2005) and Korteweg and Sorensen (2011). Using VC company data, both studies find high volatility, which leads to high arithmetic alphas. In fact, Cochrane reports an estimated alpha of 32% annually, which appears very high, given return estimates using fund-level data. At the same time, he finds a slope of 0.6–1.9 for the systematic risk, which appears low. By contrast, Korteweg and Sorensen obtain substantially higher betas, in the range of 2.6 to 2.8. Consistent with this, the authors find alphas that are positive but modest. While the alphas in the late 1990s are found to have been very high, they were negative in the 2000s, a result which is broadly in line with return estimates using fund-level data (e.g., Harris *et al.*, 2012).

Studies on buyouts using deal-level data have remained even rarer. An exception is Franzoni *et al.* (2012), who use data from CEPRES, an independent advisory firm originally set up as a joint venture between Deutsche Bank and the University of Frankfurt. Their sample includes around 7200 buyout investments between 1975 and 2006. Depending on the specification of the model, the authors find betas of 0.9 to 1.4 and alphas of 0.4% to 9.3%.

Our brief review of recent academic research suggests that there remains considerable uncertainty as to the (excess) returns and market risk in private equity. Systematic risk estimates vary considerably, and to the extent that the true beta is over- or underestimated, the true PME is under- or overestimated. So how sensitive are the PME estimates we reported above to variations in the beta values? One way to look at this is suggested by Harris *et al.* (2012), who estimate PMEs under the assumption that an alternative investment earned, respectively,

1.5 times and 2 times the return on the S&P 500. This assumption is made to estimate the possible impact of levering up investments in public stocks to levels that are found in financial sponsor buy-side transactions. Interestingly, the PMEs turn out to be remarkably insensitive to the multiple of the S&P 500 return, which leads the authors to conclude "... that systematic risk does not explain our PME results for buyout funds".

Similar results are obtained by Robinson and Sensoy (2011), who use a proprietary database from a large LP. Specifically, by varying beta they lever the S&P benchmark return used in the PME calculation for buyouts to trace out the "levered PME" beta relation for each fund. While at low levels an increase in beta has a significant impact on the PME, the authors find strongly diminishing effects as beta is raised further. For example, raising the beta from 1 to 1.5 (the high end of buyout beta estimates in the literature) lowers the average levered PME from 1.18 to 1.12 – still a significant outperformance relative to public equity.

5.1.3 Stale pricing and the optimal allocation to private equity

To the extent that academic studies employ cash flow data from largely or fully liquidated funds to estimate risk and returns in private equity, they do not have to worry about stale pricing, a well-known phenomenon in illiquid asset classes. Stale pricing refers to the fact that reported fund returns are generally based on a combination of actual cash flows and NAV calculations of the residual value of the fund for partnerships that are not yet fully liquidated. Despite important industry-led efforts and more stringent accounting rules,[8] NAV calculations remain to a certain degree subjective. Furthermore, valuations are infrequent and usually available only with a delay. However, as market value changes that are not directly observable usually feed only gradually through the reported data, GPs' estimates of remaining values generally represent "smoothed" series.

The disadvantage of using fully liquidated funds is, of course, that the data which can be used is by definition relatively old, given the typical lifespan of a limited partnership. Given that markets may be subject to structural shifts, practitioners typically prefer using more recent data. One example is VC investing, where fund returns in the 2000s appear to have fallen substantially short of their spectacular performance in the late 1990s. However, to the extent that investment portfolios are determined on the basis of fund-level data that include a significant number of relatively young partnerships, it is important for asset allocators to adjust reported returns for stale pricing. Unless corrected for, stale pricing leads to artificially low correlations with the rest of the investment portfolio. Given the uncertainty surrounding true asset pricing and beta measures for private equity and other illiquid assets, LPs may therefore hold portfolios whose risk/return profile is sub-optimal. To the extent that the true beta is underestimated, investors will be overexposed to private equity (and vice versa).

To see how, Conroy and Harris (2007) employ fund-level data obtained from TVE to calculate efficient portfolios consisting of private equity (buyout funds), public equity (S&P 500 for large firms and NASDAQ for smaller firms) and bonds.[9] In a standard CAPM framework, they estimate that the optimal allocation to private equity would be 20%, if the representative investor targets annual returns of 10%. With this allocation, the investor's overall portfolio

[8] For instance, the International Private Equity Valuation (IPEV) Guidelines, which have recently been revised to take into account the evolution of fair value accounting requirements and practices around the globe, especially as promulgated by the Financial Accounting Standards Board (FASB) in the United States and the International Accounting Standards Board (IASB).

[9] Return and risk estimates for buyout funds are based on quarterly TVE data from 1989 to 2005.

would have an estimated standard deviation of 5.8%. With an expected portfolio return of 12% the optimal allocation to private equity would need to be raised to 50%, implying an increase in the standard deviation to 6.6%.

In a second step, Conroy and Harris (2007) "de-smooth" reported private equity returns in order to deal with the well-known stale price problem in illiquid asset classes. Instead of using raw data reported by GPs, the authors propose "de-smoothing" returns by using a standard Dimson (1979) approach, which takes the current observed reported return as a weighted average of current and past true returns.[10] However, while this method focuses on the risk (variance), it accepts the reported returns as the true reflection of the performance of individual funds and the asset class overall. Recalculating the variance–covariance of private equity, Conroy and Harris (2007) find the true risk of private equity to be significantly higher. In fact, the estimated beta jumps from 0.53 using raw data to 1.17 using adjusted data. With private equity being considerably riskier than unadjusted estimates imply, the portfolio weight attached to private equity is considerably smaller at any given expected portfolio return. For instance, with an expected portfolio return of 10%, private equity would be allocated 14%, six percentage points less than implied by the unadjusted raw data.[11]

Conroy and Harris's (2007) findings support early research by Gompers and Lerner (1997), who examine the investments of one single private equity firm (Warburg Pincus) between the first quarter of 1972 and the third quarter of 1997. Using raw data, they find an arithmetic average annual return (gross of fees) of 30.5%, with a beta of 1.08. However, when they mark-to-market the portfolio and regress the "refreshed" returns on market returns, the beta in the CAPM regression increases to 1.44.[12] Although the intercept in the regression is still positive, the authors caution that "the stated returns of private equity funds may not accurately reflect the true evolution of value, and the correlations reported by Thomson Economics and other industry observers may be deceptively low. To ignore the true correlation is fraught with potential dangers."

5.1.4 Informed judgments and ad hoc adjustments to the mean–variance framework

Instead of using econometric techniques to correct for stale pricing and other anomalies in illiquid assets, some investors, such as the Yale Investment Office (Swensen, 2009), use informed judgments in making adjustments to the observed historical return and volatility characteristics and correlations with other asset classes. For example, whereas the historical correlation coefficient of private equity and US public equity returns is estimated at 41% using raw data, in their asset allocation the Yale Investment Office assumes a coefficient of 70%. As Swensen (2009) puts it: "Assuming that private equity investments generate 12 percent returns with a risk level of 30 percent represents an appropriately conservative modification of the historical record of 12.8 percent with a 23.1 percent risk level." Similarly, the correlation coefficient between returns on real assets and public US stocks is adjusted upwards to 20%

[10] Getmansky *et al.* (2004) suggest an alternative approach of "de-smoothing" the volatility of private equity returns. Applying this methodology to a dataset of European private equity funds increases the volatility of returns to 35% per year as described in Diller (2007). Alternative methods are discussed in Kaserer *et al.* (2003).

[11] Diller and Jäckel (2010) calculate returns and volatility using a dataset of 1717 US buyout and VC funds raised between 1983 and 2005. The study assumes that private equity distributions are fully reinvested, employing an approach proposed by de Zwart *et al.* (2007). Diller and Jäckel (2010) find a standard deviation of 23% compared with 16% for public stocks, whereas private equity outperformed by 2.5% per year, achieving average returns, net of fees, of 14.13%. The correlation between private equity and the public market index was estimated at 63%.

[12] In quarters where there is neither an investment nor a write-down, Gompers and Lerner (1997) adjusted the portfolio value by the change in the matched industry public market index.

from 1% using raw data. At the same time, the Yale Investment Office uses lower expected returns compared to the reported historical performance of the asset class.

However, in modifying the risk and return assumptions about non-marketable assets and adjusting the correlation matrix between them and other assets, investors should be aware that even relatively small changes can lead to rather dramatic changes in portfolio weights. Especially in illiquid assets, it may be difficult to implement such weights, given their long-term nature and the potentially limited availability of investment opportunities in individual market segments. In addressing this problem in practical applications, it has been suggested by Black and Litterman (1992) to implement an approach that is sometimes described as the "CAPM in reverse". Specifically, their model takes into account that investment managers tend to think in terms of weights in a portfolio rather than balancing expected returns against the contribution to portfolio risk. The starting point in the Black–Litterman approach is the market equilibrium returns, which provide a neutral reference point in the sense that they clear the market if all investors have identical views. However, the model allows investors to deviate from the neutral market equilibrium by explicitly formulating their own return expectations and specifying the degree of confidence they have in the stated views. The optimal portfolio is then simply a set of deviations from neutral market capitalization weights in the directions of portfolios about which views are expressed.

Furthermore, in adjusting their mean–variance framework, investors should take into account dynamic risk – a key lesson learned from the recent global financial crisis. While the CAPM is static in the sense that correlations are assumed to remain unchanged, in reality risk in the system as a whole may rise, shifting otherwise "normal" correlations of returns among asset classes rapidly upwards. Such shifts may lead to a serious underestimation of risk in portfolio construction. As Spence (2009) explains, an important part of portfolio risk is not stationary. This risk is systemic, and when risk in the system as a whole rises, "normal" correlations of returns among asset classes shift rapidly upwards. If this happens, diversification and hedging models and risk mitigation strategies are bound to malfunction. At the same time, as we discussed above, dynamic risk caused havoc with investors' cash flow models, and when the parameters of these models suddenly shifted due to reduced distributions, the suspension of redemptions, increased margin calls from hedge funds and collateral, some investors were faced with an acute lack of liquidity. Given this experience, a growing number of investors factor in a dynamic risk component and add a complementary part of liquid investments to their illiquid allocations.

5.1.5 Extensions of the CAPM and liquidity risk

While the CAPM has remained the workhorse of asset pricing and is still widely used as a framework for thinking about investments, its various limitations have motivated researchers to develop new approaches. One important limitation in empirical applications arises from the fact that the CAPM uses only one variable (beta) to describe the relationship between returns of a portfolio and returns of the market as a whole. A major extension of the CAPM is the Fama–French (1993) model, which uses three variables. Specifically, the model adds two factors to the CAPM to reflect a portfolio's exposure to small caps and value stocks, two assets that are found to have done better than the market as a whole. In empirical applications, the Fama–French three-factor model has a significantly higher explanatory power than the CAPM, with small caps and value stocks having higher expected returns than large caps and growth stocks.

Another important extension of the CAPM has been suggested by Pastor and Stambaugh (2003), who add a fourth factor to take into account liquidity risk in a portfolio. Specifically, the Pastor–Stambaugh model predicts that market-wide liquidity is an important factor for pricing stocks. Acharya and Pedersen (2005) develop a theoretical model for the liquidity premium in asset pricing, concluding that negative liquidity shocks are associated with both lower contemporaneous and higher predicted future returns.

The Fama–French and Pastor–Stambaugh extensions have been developed for marketable assets, just like the original CAPM. However, recently some researchers have applied these models to private equity as an illiquid asset class. Franzoni *et al.* (2012) find a significant beta on the liquidity risk factor, implying a risk premium of about 3% annually.[13] In interpreting their results, the authors note that due to their high leverage buyouts are sensitive to the capital constraints faced by the providers of debt to private equity, who are primarily banks, hedge funds and collateralized debt obligations (CDOs). In times of high risk aversion and low market liquidity, private equity fund managers tend to find it more difficult to refinance their investments, potentially undermining the performance of their funds.

The liquidity risk premium estimated by Franzoni *et al.* (2012) for VC and buyout funds is broadly in line with what practitioners generally view as an adequate compensation for the illiquidity of their investments in private equity partnerships. Factoring in this liquidity premium, the findings by Harris *et al.* (2012) and Higson and Stucke (2012), combined with Robinson and Sensoy's (2011) sensitivity analysis, suggest that private equity represents an attractive asset class for investors. However, this conclusion is not undisputed. As an alternative approach to estimating the liquidity risk premium, Sorensen *et al.* (2012) calibrate a model of the LP's portfolio choice problem, including the illiquid private equity investment. For a representative LP, they find a substantial illiquidity premium. The cost of illiquidity is similar in magnitude to the combined costs of management fees and carried interest. Moreover, they argue that the public market equivalent measure typically used to evaluate the performance of private equity does not appropriately capture the costs of the risk and illiquidity of these investments. However, more work is needed on risk and liquidity to put this conclusion on a more robust basis.

5.1.6 Liability-driven investing and risk factor allocation

As we have discussed in Chapter 2, accessing the illiquidity risk premium requires an appropriate liability structure as well as an appropriate risk management. Importantly, however, the CAPM – and its various extensions – essentially ignore the liability side of the investor. Strictly speaking, therefore, it is appropriate as an allocation tool only for investors who have virtually no liabilities that lead to predetermined payouts. In practice, family offices and foundations come closest to this type. All others, however, have to take into account their liabilities when allocating capital to different asset classes. An increasing number of pension plans and life insurers are therefore adopting some form of liability-driven investing (LDI) in a consistent framework of asset liability management (ALM),[14] moving away from assets-only frameworks.

[13] Metrick (2007) provides some estimates for venture capital. In a simple textbook example of the Pastor–Stambaugh model, he estimates the average return to the liquidity factor at 3% per year for the sample period from 1966 to 2004. However, splitting the sample period into different sub-periods, Metrick (2007) obtains a return of nearly 6% since 1980.

[14] There is a rapidly expanding literature on ALM. Readers with a particular interest in the technical details of ALM are referred to Hoevenaars (2008), whose work has influenced the strategic asset allocation approach of ABP Investments, one of the world's largest pension asset managers in the pension industry. For a discussion of private equity in an insurance company's asset allocation within an ALM framework, see Achleitner and Albrecht (2011).

Basically speaking, LDI approaches focus on managing the size and composition of the asset pool and the related liability with respect to their sensitivities to changes in interest rates, inflation and other factors determining the capital market environment (Cambridge Associates, 2011). Thus, LDI frameworks take into account risks that affect both sides of investors' balance sheets. The importance of this approach became particularly obvious in the recent financial crisis, which turned out to be the perfect storm for DB pension plans. The combination of sharp declines in equity prices and market-based liability discount rates led to a serious deterioration in the funding status of many pension plans. This situation is often exacerbated in periods of economic stress when sponsors experience declining cash flows and more expensive access to capital markets to fulfil their legal or contractual obligations of making plan contributions.

In allocating capital in an LDI framework, investors have to define their risk-free or risk-neutral position. To be sure, this position is different from assets-only investment approaches where the risk-free asset is generally considered high-quality government bonds (e.g., US Treasuries). Instead, in an LDI framework the risk-neutral asset pool is defined in such a way that it perfectly hedges the investor's liability. This pool serves as a benchmark for evaluating the trade-off between expected returns and risk, given the risk appetite of the investor. The risk appetite itself depends on the individual circumstances of the investor. As far as pension funds are concerned, for example, key variables include: the size of the plan liability relative to the size of the sponsor's balance sheet; the potential size of future contributions relative to the sponsor's projected free cash flow; and the correlation between the sponsor's operations and the return of risky assets and changes in interest rates (Cambridge Associates, 2011).

Consistent with this approach, some institutional investors have decided to create two portfolios – a hedging portfolio and a growth portfolio. The hedging portfolio aims to minimize the volatility between the size of the asset pool and the related liability, which is known as "surplus risk". For DB pension plans, this risk is generally a function of changes in interest rates and inflation, both of which affect the liability value for the sponsor. In hedging surplus risk, investors typically buy fixed-income instruments with interest rates that in the ideal case have exactly the same derivation as the discount rate. In cases where benefits are indexed to inflation, hedging portfolios usually rely on inflation-linked bonds and inflation swaps. The exact structure of the hedging portfolio is determined by whether the investor's approach focuses on simply matching durations or cash flows, or a hybrid approach between the two.

The growth portfolio aims to generate excess returns in order to reduce contributions. In pursuing this objective, a growing number of investors have shifted to a risk-focused asset allocation approach that may be better suited to capture potential diversification benefits. Importantly, investors who have already adopted this approach typically employ simplified asset allocation frameworks that emphasize risk factors as key drivers of return. Institutions that are moving into this direction include some of the world's largest asset allocators, such as CalPERS, the Canadian Pension Plan Investment Board,[15] the Danish pension fund ATP, the Norwegian Sovereign Pension Fund and the sovereign wealth funds of New Zealand and Alaska. In fact, some investors have allocations to as few as four or five broad categories,

[15] For details, see the Harvard Business School case study on the Canadian Pension Plan Investment Board (Hardymon *et al.*, 2009).

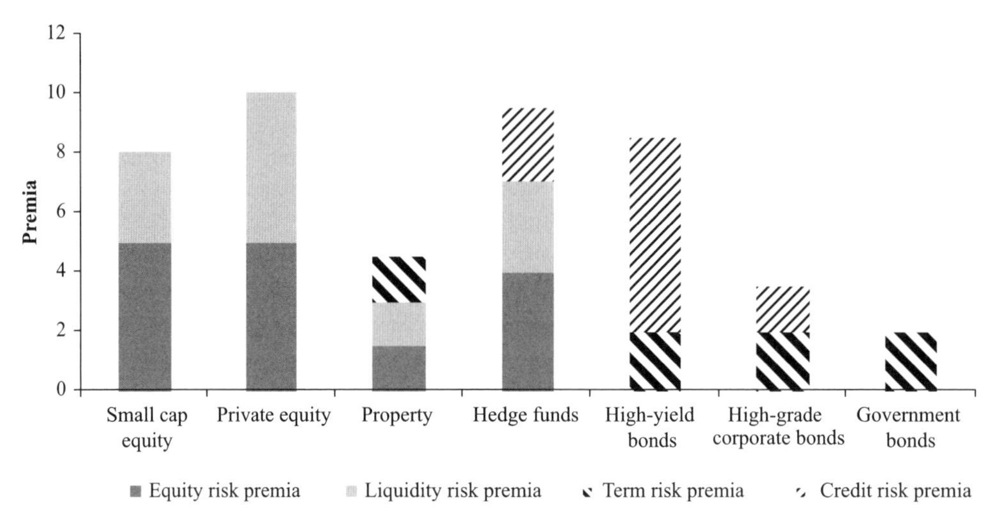

Figure 5.3 Portfolio diversification through risk factor allocation.
Source: WEF (2011).

as opposed to highly granular asset class buckets that were common in the pre-crisis era. In a risk factor allocation, illiquidity risk is explicitly taken into account, alongside other risk factors such as equity risk, term risk and credit risk. Each risk factor offers a particular reward for investors (see Figure 5.3). Accessing these premia requires investments in specific asset classes, whose allocations are determined in an ALM framework. As far as private equity is concerned, returns are generated from both an equity risk premium and an illiquidity risk premium.

As the WEF (2011) emphasizes, the increasing switch to a risk factor allocation approach within an LDI framework has been motivated not least by the disillusionment about traditional investment strategies. In the pre-crisis era, investors' attention had focused on choosing increasingly granular asset class buckets, which however limited their insight into the underlying drivers of risk and return in their portfolios. Instead of delivering the stable returns the well-diversified strategies had promised, many investors found themselves short of liquid assets they could call upon during the crisis. Unlike traditional CAPM-based strategies, the risk factor allocation approach treats asset classes as ways of accessing the key underlying risk and return factors. The attractiveness of this approach lies in its intuitive simplicity.

It is too early to tell whether the risk factor allocation approach will actually help investors generate superior returns on a risk-adjusted basis. The international investor community is therefore following closely CalPERS' experience. Introduced in mid-2011, its "new alternative asset classification" follows a risk-based asset allocation strategy with two hedging portfolios to protect against extreme market risks and rising inflation. The rest of the portfolio is a combination of growth-oriented assets that include public and private equity and real assets. The new and old asset allocation targets are shown in Table 5.1. For each asset class a strategic plan is developed, an issue we return to in Part III of this book.

Table 5.1 CalPERS alternative asset classification

			Allocation (%)	
Risk class	Asset class	Objective	June 2009	July 2011
Income	Global fixed income	Deliver stable income	20	16
Growth	Public and private equity	Positively exposed to economic growth	63	63
Real	Real estate, infrastructure, forestry	Help preserve the real value of the pension fund	10	13
Inflation-linked	Commodities and inflation-linked bonds	Provide hedging against inflation	5	4
Liquidity	Cash and nominal government bonds	Supply liquidity when needed	2	4

Source: CalPERS; IMF (2011).

5.2 CONCLUSIONS

Long-term investors in illiquid asset classes accept higher risk as they are unable to rebalance their investment portfolios on a continuous basis, a key assumption in standard asset allocation models. Thus, investors generally demand a higher premium in compensation for this risk. In this chapter, therefore, we have reviewed the literature on risk-adjusted returns in private equity, an asset class that is essentially identical to public equity in terms of its role in a company's capital structure, except for its substantially high degree of illiquidity. Our results can be summarized as follows:

- On a risk-unadjusted basis, private equity investing through limited partnerships is found to outperform public equity by a significant margin.
- While return comparisons between private equity and public equity are generally based on public market equivalents that implicitly assume beta to be 1, the majority of studies that focus on market risk explicitly find betas of greater than 1.
- However, sensitivity analyses suggest that under reasonable assumptions for beta, PMEs for private equity are still greater than 1, implying outperformance on a risk-adjusted basis.
- Studies that focus specifically on liquidity risk find premiums in the range of 2–4%.

Despite important efforts to estimate returns to private equity and the risk associated with investments in this asset class, our review of the literature suggests that it is too early to say with sufficient confidence whether the apparent outperformance of private equity is sufficient to compensate investors for the risks they take and whether the investments outperform on a risk-adjusted basis. This uncertainty has important implications for investors' asset allocation strategies. Whereas in the pre-crisis era most investors followed a traditional CAPM-based approach that sought to diversify risk in an increasingly granular way, more recently a rising number of asset allocators have begun to adopt a risk factor allocation approach that embraces risk explicitly. Critically, as we discuss in the second part of this book, such an approach is particularly predicated on the development of well-functioning internal risk management systems.

6
The Secondary Market

Secondary transactions refer to the buying and selling of pre-existing limited partnership interests in private equity and other alternative investment funds. These interests include both commitments that have already been drawn down by the GP and unfunded commitments. Importantly, the transfer of investor commitments between LPs in the secondary market must not be confused with secondary buyouts or similar transactions where a deal is exited by selling the underlying portfolio company to another fund.

The emergence of a secondary market for stakes in limited partnerships has been hailed as the advent of liquidity in an otherwise illiquid asset class. With liquidity risk being reduced, it is generally expected that the broadening and deepening of the secondary market will help fuel the growth of the primary market for investments in private equity and real assets. While long-term allocators who are already exposed to these asset classes may be encouraged to increase their current allocations, a higher degree of liquidity, so the argument goes, could expand the universe of potential investors who would otherwise be constrained by the liability profile of their balance sheets. Furthermore, the growth in secondary transactions has often – and mistakenly – been viewed as a superior means of price discovery compared with subjective NAV estimates of invested capital.

Indeed, the secondary market for fund investments has gained substantial momentum over the last decade and represents one of the most important developments in the recent history of alternative investing. Undoubtedly, the secondary market would not have reached its current level of significance if it had not brought about important advantages for both sellers and buyers of interests in limited partnerships. However, as we caution in this chapter, the secondary market has not materially altered the fundamental characteristics of fund investments and hence the challenges investors face in measuring and managing the particular risks that come with commitments to limited partnerships remain essentially unchanged.

Our discussion starts with a brief description of the micro structure of the secondary market, introducing the different actors on both sides of the market and discussing the intermediation of transactions between sellers and buyers. Next, we debate the different factors that motivate private equity investors to sell and buy assets in the secondary market. These factors have a considerable impact on the supply of, and the demand for, funds in the secondary market. Pricing of stakes in a fund or a portfolio of funds is of particular interest, as the price reflects the valuation of the acquisitions the funds have already made as well as the unfunded commitments to this fund or the portfolio of funds. Then, we look at the behaviour of secondary prices over the cycle and the volume of assets that changed hands over the past decade. Finally, we discuss the interactions between the primary and secondary markets and their impact on portfolio construction under risk considerations.

6.1 THE STRUCTURE OF THE SECONDARY MARKET

6.1.1 Sellers and their motivations to sell

Sellers in the secondary market are LPs in private equity funds or similar structures set up to invest in real assets. There are different reasons why LPs decide to sell their stakes in such funds. Broadly speaking, we may differentiate between sales that are motivated primarily by liquidity constraints and those that are related to the strategic repositioning of an investor's portfolio. Understanding these different reasons is important to assess the informational content of transaction prices in the secondary market.

Liquidity-motivated sales

As far as liquidity-motivated sales are concerned, the desire to transfer stakes in a limited partnership is usually cyclical. Box 6.1 discusses the case of the Harvard Management Company, which attracted considerable public attention as it decided to sell a portfolio of illiquid fund stakes worth USD 1 billion during the recent financial crisis. To be sure, the endowment of Harvard University was not alone. In fact, many other LPs with a substantial exposure to private equity and other illiquid asset classes found themselves in a situation where distributions dried up at a time when margin calls on other investments, such as hedge funds, rose and redemptions were reduced or even excluded. In this situation, a number of LPs with large unfunded commitments ran a significant risk of defaulting on possible capital calls and decided to liquidate their position partially or even entirely.

Box 6.1 Liquidity constraints and the sale of limited partnership interests: experience from the global financial crisis 2008–2009

The collapse of Lehman Brothers in the autumn of 2008, the largest bankruptcy in history, resulted in the deepest global recession in at least three generations. As market participants became extremely risk averse, financial markets for risky assets shut, while yields on safe assets fell to record lows. Investors' cash flow models were generally not designed to cope with this tail risk, and many long-term asset allocators found themselves short of liquidity as distributions of private equity funds dried up, which coincided with increased margin calls and the suspension of redemptions by hedge funds and similar vehicles.

Confronted with significant unfunded commitments and an acute shortage of liquidity, many investors sought to sell stakes in private equity funds in the secondary market. However, given the huge amount of macroeconomic uncertainty, the profound lack of liquidity and the massive degree of risk aversion, there were few buyers. As NAVs were only gradually adjusted in line with the rapidly deteriorating operating performance of underlying portfolio companies and the continued decline in public markets, there was a wide gap between sellers' and buyers' price expectations. In the first half of 2009, this gap proved unbridgeable for many portfolios, causing a steep decline in the volume of secondary transactions. For the year as a whole, the total amount of stakes changing hands in the secondary market was more than 50% lower than in the previous year.

While institutions seeking to liquidate (parts of) their private equity holdings included a wide range of investors, US university endowments are reported to have been particularly keen to reduce their exposure, which in individual cases accounted for more than 20%

of their total assets under management. A case that has attracted particular attention and been followed intensively in the media is the Harvard Management Corporation (HMC), which manages the endowment of Harvard University. In mid-2008, the endowment stood at USD 36.9 billion, making it the biggest endowment of any university. At that point in time, private equity represented 13% of HMC's total portfolio, a relatively moderate share compared with other large endowments. However, HMC's total exposure to illiquid asset classes was far larger, with investments in real assets (real estate, infrastructure, forestry, oil and gas) accounting for more than 30%.

Prior to the financial crisis, HMC contributed as much as USD 1.2 billion per year to Harvard's budget, accounting for more than one-third of the university's total annual operating income, nearly equivalent to the contributions from tuition and sponsored research combined. Thus, the university came to rely on HMC in their planning for hiring, expansions and new facilities. This reliance was predicated on the assumption of steady cash flows from "harvested" private investments. However, while this assumption was based on historical observations, it proved fundamentally wrong in 2008–2009 when exit markets shut amid deepening financial stress.

What made things even worse was that HMC had a substantial amount of unfunded commitments, which under normal market conditions would have been financed with distributions. However, during the crisis distributions dried up, and with cash reserves actually negative – implying that the endowment overall had been leveraged – HMC was forced to liquidate assets to avoid defaulting on their previous commitments to private equity funds as well as other investments they could not easily get out of. In the event, HMC decided to liquidate some equity and fixed-income investments at what turned out to be the worst possible time. Desperately needing additional liquidity, HMC decided to put USD 1.5 billion of fund investments with unfunded commitments for sale – at a time when secondary private equity funds were on average bidding 50–60% of NAV of private equity assets. With the liquidity crisis sending shock waves through the university, HMC also issued debt in the capital markets of more than USD 1 billion in another effort to raise liquidity.

To be sure, HMC was not unique. As Ang and Kjaer (2011) report, CalPERS (the largest US pension fund) lost USD 70 billion during the market turmoil in 2008–2009. Referring to an article in the *Wall Street Journal*,[1] Ang and Kjaer attribute these losses to the sale of public equity holdings to raise cash in order to meet CalPERS' obligations from private equity and real estate investments. While CalPERS' equity weight was 60% at 30 June 2007, it shrank to 52% by 30 June 2008 and to 44% by 30 June 2009 – missing to a significant degree the substantial subsequent rebound in public equity markets. The experience led CalPERS to adopt a new asset allocation framework using risk factors (IMF, 2011). This new framework became effective in July 2011.

Such fire sales are not new. As a matter of fact, liquidity risk has played an important role for the secondary market to come into existence in the first place. As Talmor and Vasvari (2011) argue, secondary transactions started to emerge after the stock market crash in the fall of 1987 and the global recession at the beginning of the 1990s when economic conditions resulted in

[1] Karmin and Lublin, "Calpers sells stock amid rout to raise cash for obligations", *Wall Street Journal*, 25 October 2008.

an intensive need for liquidity among investors. For the same reason, investors also wished to reduce their funding obligations on committed capital, as their inability to meet the capital calls of the GPs would have implied a default with serious consequences. As the demand for illiquid assets is typically weak in periods of economic turmoil, sellers usually have to accept significant discounts to the NAV in distressed transactions, an issue we return to in Section 6.3.

Strategic sales

As the secondary market has matured, it has been increasingly used by private equity investors to manage their portfolio holdings actively. Sell-side LPs may decide to divest their entire stake in a particular fund or even offer their entire portfolio of fund investments. Others, however, may decide to sell only a certain share of their stake in a partnership, signalling their continued confidence in the fund manager. Which option sell-side LPs pursue essentially depends on their individual objectives.

Sometimes, LPs are dissatisfied with the performance of a fund or a portfolio of funds and lose confidence in a management team. Selling their stakes in such funds can generate capital that may be redeployed into new opportunities (Meyer and Mathonet, 2005). Conversely, a LP may want to lock in returns if he believes that the fund manager is not likely to materially increase the performance of the underlying portfolio companies further during the remainder of the lifetime of the fund (Almeida Capital, 2002).

Another strategic reason to sell may lie in an unintended overexposure to private equity. This so-called denominator effect usually arises in periods of financial stress when prices of marketable instruments adjust much faster than valuations of illiquid investments, resulting in a higher-than-targeted share of the latter. In fact, many investors prefer to apply ranges to target allocations for their illiquid asset classes, which is a pragmatic approach to avoid over-reacting to relatively short-term developments in public markets. Bringing the actual portfolio weights in line with an investor's asset allocation targets may prompt a sell-off of parts of his illiquid investments. Alternatively, an investor may allow the portfolio to readjust more gradually by postponing new commitments to asset classes to which he is overexposed. However, investors who choose this route risk having underdiversified portfolios in terms of vintage years, a particularly important dimension of diversification.

Related to this are adjustments and "tactical" shifts in an investor's approach. For instance, while many pension funds have built up highly (even overly) diversified investment portfolios over many years, some have decided to rationalize these portfolios by focusing on their core relationships and utilizing their resources more efficiently.

Furthermore, there may be regulatory reasons for LPs to seek early exits through the secondary market. Regulatory changes, such as those pertaining to banks (Basel III, European Capital Adequacy Directive IV, Volcker Rule), insurance companies (Solvency II) and pension funds (IORP Directive), may impose quantitative restrictions on certain asset classes or affect their attractiveness through changes in specific capital requirements to protect an investor's portfolio against possible but unexpected losses due to financial shocks. As the opportunity costs of holding illiquid investments rise as a result, the investor may decide to sell in the secondary market. Importantly, secondary transaction volume has consistently been led by financial institutions between 2008 and 2011 (Figure 6.1).

Secondary sales may also be considered in the context of a broader reorientation of an investor's portfolio of fund investments. For instance, in cases where overall allocation targets

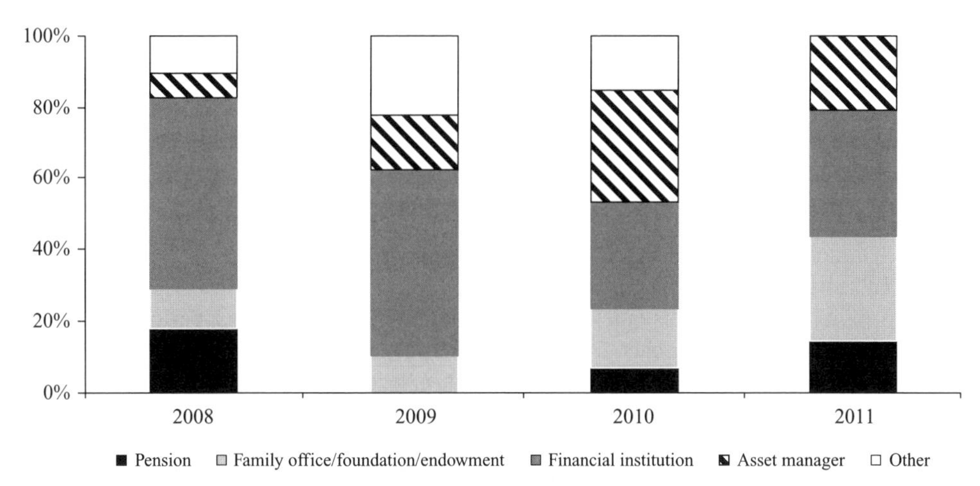

Figure 6.1 Sell-side secondary market transactions by institution.
Source: UBS.

are already met, a restructuring in favour of particular market segments, such as emerging markets, could be achieved much faster through a sale of funds targeting private equity and real assets in advanced economies.

Finally, sales are sometimes motivated by a change in group strategy, which often occurs following a period of poor investment results in challenging market conditions and in the context of changes in corporate control, senior management shifts or other corporate-level events (Meyer and Mathonet, 2005). In such situations, LPs sometimes decide to sell their fund investment portfolios wholesale, exiting entire asset classes or at least sub-asset classes, such as VC after the tech bubble burst in the early 2000s.

6.1.2 Buyers and their motivations to buy

On the buy side, the secondary market has historically been dominated by dedicated secondary funds and other funds-of-funds. In recent years, however, a growing number of non-traditional buyers have entered the market, including pension funds, insurance companies, endowments, foundations, family offices, SWFs as well as hedge funds. Their reasons to buy illiquid assets through secondary transactions are as diverse as those for sellers to dispose of their holdings. To begin with, in certain market conditions there are distressed assets offered at significant discounts – for those who have at their disposal a sufficient degree of liquidity to meet the unfunded commitments of the fund investments.

An important advantage in this context is the fact that secondary investments are subject to less uncertainty when compared with commitments to primary funds, which represent "blind pools" of capital. At the time of making a commitment, a primary investor does not know how his capital will eventually be deployed by the fund – apart from the broad investment guidelines specified in the limited partnership agreement. By the time a secondary transaction takes place, a significant share of the fund's capital has already been invested in portfolio companies. Prospective buyers can analyse them in detail and already have indicators that help to distinguish between companies which developed according to plan and those which did not.

Note, however, that this advantage can be significantly reduced, and even eliminated, in early secondary transactions. Sometimes called "purchased primaries", such transactions take place at a very early stage of the fund. In extreme cases, the buyer agrees to buy the seller's commitment at a point in time when the fund has not yet made any acquisitions at all. Purchased primary transactions are often distressed sales, which allow the buyer to acquire a stake in a fund or portfolio of funds from an LP who faces a non-trivial risk to default on future capital calls from the fund managers. These transactions were mainly seen during the financial crisis of 2009, but their volume has decreased significantly over recent years.

Other LPs might be interested primarily in secondary transactions as a means to get exposure to private equity and real assets quickly without committing capital over a period of 10 to 12 years, which is typical for primary fund investors. Given that it normally takes several years for a fund to reach the cash flow break-even point, a secondary acquisition of a 4-year-old fund reduces this period significantly and potentially even eliminates it. Furthermore, the entire holding period is typically reduced to 6 to 8 years before the fund liquidates itself. The different dynamic in the secondary market can be employed as a means to counteract the J-curve effect of primary fund investments. This effect describes a well-known phenomenon in private equity and similar asset classes, whereby capital outflows at the beginning of the lifetime of a fund results in negative IRRs, before turning positive when the fund begins to divest assets, resulting in capital inflows for the LP (see Figure 6.2 and Box 6.2). This mitigating effect is of particular relevance for investors with a relatively young portfolio, where positive net cash flows can be expected only in the medium term. Take, for example, secondary transactions that were realized and intermediated by UBS (Figure 6.3). Almost one-third of the funds in which stakes were acquired in the secondary market in 2011 was from the vintage year 2007. If we add funds from the vintage years 2006 and 2008, almost three-quarters of the funds in which stakes were acquired in 2011 were between 3 and 5 years old.

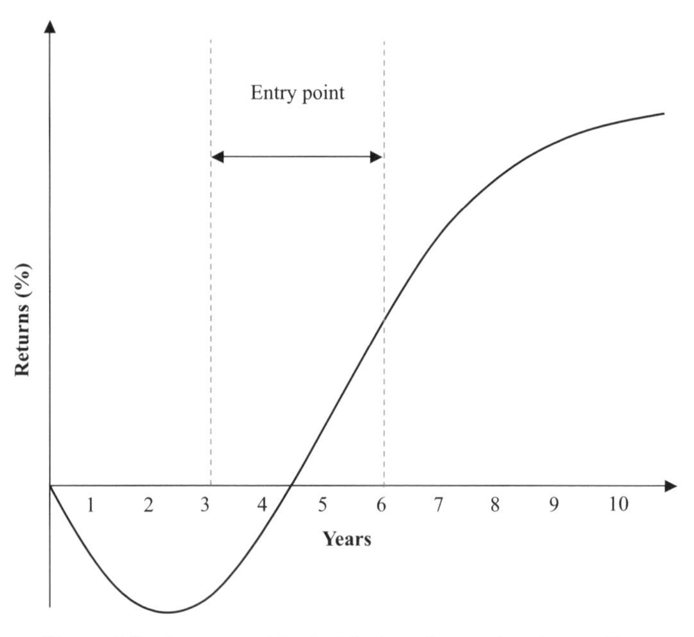

Figure 6.2 J-curve and typical timing of secondary transaction.

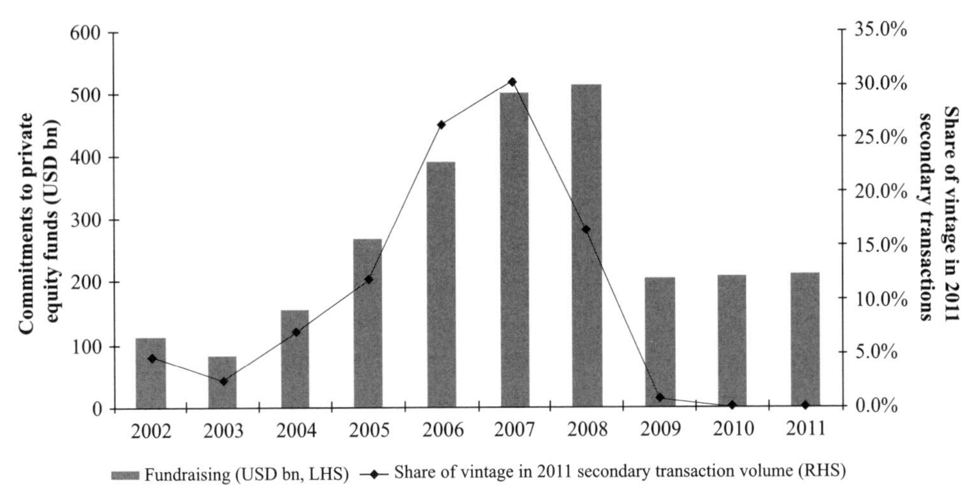

Figure 6.3 Global private equity fundraising and relative vintage distribution of 2011 secondary transaction volume.
Source: UBS; AlpInvest Partners.

Box 6.2 The J-curve

The J-curve is explained by the limited partnership funds' structure with the set-up costs and management fees, as well as by the valuation policies followed by the fund managers (Mathonet and Meyer, 2007). The term "J-curve" is referred to in various ways, notably related to the development of a fund's cash flows, its NAV or its performance.

The "cash flow J-curve" is explained by the fact that from the LP's perspective, net cash flows are increasingly negative during the early years (i.e., during the fund's investment period). Afterwards there is a reversion in the pattern, with cash flows becoming positive during the fund's divestment period until its maturity.

The "NAV J-curve" describes the evolution of the NAV vs. the NPI, which tends to decrease during the early years before improving in later years of the fund's life. Like in the case of the "performance J-curve" – where cash flows as well as valuations have an impact – this to some degree can be explained by uncertainty inherent in the underlying investments and projects and the resulting biases even when applying fair valuation techniques.

The J-curve is often said to be more pronounced for VC funds, because here it takes several years for value to be created – a phenomenon the Ewing Marion Kauffman Foundation has recently taken a critical look at. Mulcahy *et al.* (2012) caution LPs to be sceptical regarding the J-curve argument often brought forward by GPs to explain the fund's underperformance as just being a temporary phenomenon. Their analysis concludes "that the J-curve effect is an elusive outcome, especially in funds started after the mid-1990s".

However, it is undeniable that limited partnership funds follow a distinct lifecycle that can create systematic biases and distortions which need to be factored in when modelling risks for such assets, as we discuss in Part II of this book.

Moreover, investments in the secondary market allow LPs to reach their target allocation of private equity and real assets significantly faster than commitments to primary funds only. In addition, given the substantial cyclicality in the fundraising market, secondary investments offer LPs an opportunity to maintain a more steady investment pace.

Further, it is sometimes argued that secondary investments may help LPs gain access to oversubscribed funds in the primary market. Particularly successful funds with an outstanding track record frequently do not accept investors unless they have already committed capital to previous funds. In fact, sometimes secondary transactions are closely linked to the raising of a new fund by the GP. In a *stapled transaction*, a secondary buyer acquires an interest in an existing fund from a current LP and, at the same time, makes a commitment to the new fund being raised by the GP. However, whether or not a secondary investment qualifies an LP as an existing investor is up to the GP. Even if the GP agrees on the secondary transaction concerning existing partnerships, there is no guarantee that he admits the LP to his successor funds.

Finally, secondary investments also improve investors' ability to build diversified portfolios. While in the primary market the potential to diversify across geographies, industries, fund sizes, investment strategies and vintage years is limited to current and future vintage years, investments in the secondary market enlarge this potential to past vintage year – albeit at valuations that reflect the set of information at the time of the transaction.

6.1.3 Intermediation in the secondary market

Although the secondary market has seen a significant increase in volume of transactions over the last 10–15 years (see next section), it has remained highly opaque. At the most fundamental level, potential sellers need to find a potential buyer and those who are eager to purchase stakes in private equity and real asset funds in the secondary market need to identify potential sellers. Importantly, while transactions in secondary markets are usually initiated by sellers, in the secondary market for stakes in private equity funds it is not uncommon for buy-side LPs to pro-actively source deals. However, market transparency has generally remained low, despite recent efforts by various data vendors to build specific internet platforms for secondary transactions. Information about market conditions is often spurious, and little is known about prices at which transactions finally settle.

Furthermore, the secondary sales process in and of itself can be highly complex and time-consuming. While transactions involving individual funds or small portfolios are usually negotiated bilaterally, intermediated auctions have become increasingly common for larger and more complex transactions. This process is facilitated by financial intermediaries who are today involved in the majority of deals in the secondary market. Used mainly by sellers, intermediaries help identify buyers and structure fund interest offerings. Financial intermediaries are either specialized secondary advisors (e.g., Campbell Lutyens, Cogent Partners, UBS) or placement agents, generally charging a transaction fee between 1% and 2% of the value of the transaction (Talmor and Vasvari, 2011).

Financial intermediaries ensure that the sales process is competitive. Typically, a number of LPs are contacted to sound out their potential interest. In cases where a large portfolio is sold, intermediaries may divide it into different subsets to improve the chances of finding interested buyers. LPs make bids in a managed auction for the particular stakes they want to purchase, which are based on confidential information the intermediary provides about the holdings of the fund(s) and their valuation. Many secondary auctions involve two rounds. After a first round of bidding, a subgroup of potential buyers is invited by the seller and the intermediary to the second round. In the second round, interested buyers have the opportunity to revise their bids in light of new information they might have acquired in the process. While the set of information the intermediary provides is the same for all interested buyers, large LPs with diversified portfolios often have an important competitive advantage in the sense that they have superior proprietary information about the fund manager, his previous track record and the quality of the current investments.

Taking into account the diverse motivations of buyers and sellers, intermediation in the secondary market has become increasingly complex. Although traditional secondary transactions account for the majority of deals, *structured secondaries* have gained in importance in recent years. Structured secondaries may entail the creation of a new structure to hold the assets, the delegation of managing the assets to a new team, different payment structures or the seller's participation in the upside of the portfolio. For example, as Talmor and Vasvari (2011) explain, the seller may keep some or all of the fund interest on its balance sheet, with the buyer agreeing "to fund all future capital calls of the seller's portfolio in exchange for a preferred return against future distributions of the seller's portfolio."

6.2 MARKET SIZE

The secondary market has grown significantly over the last 10 to 15 years, as the primary market has expanded substantially during the period and sellers and buyers have pursued a more active management approach of their alternative investment portfolios.

6.2.1 Transaction volume

It is estimated that the global volume of secondary transactions increased 10-fold between the turn of the century and 2011 (Figure 6.4). According to Cogent Partners (2012), a financial

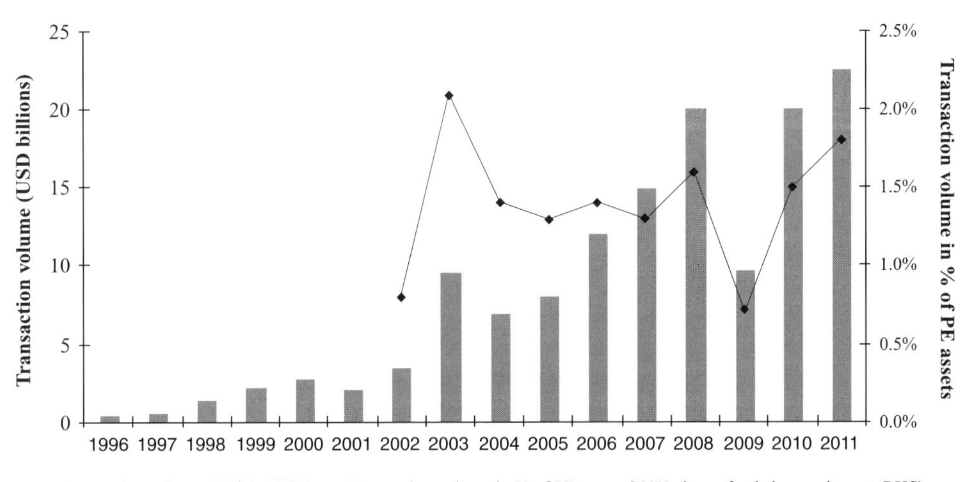

Figure 6.4 Secondary transaction volume.
Source: Cogent Partners; UBS; AlpInvest Partners.

intermediary, stakes in private equity funds valued at around USD 23 billion changed hands in 2011, the second straight year in which the market volume eclipsed USD 20 billion. It is important to emphasize that the total supply was significantly larger, however. Partners Group (2011), for instance, notes that they had sourced a secondary deal flow of over USD 60 billion in 2010, implying that around two-thirds of the assets LPs wanted to dispose of in 2010 failed to find a buyer.

The failure to find a buyer for a transaction implies that the price does not fall far enough to clear the market, an issue we return to in Section 6.3. A key issue is information asymmetries, which give rise to the "lemons problem" we introduced in Section 3.3.2. Typically, the seller knows much more about the quality of his portfolio than the potential buyer, who in the absence of better information may assume that the fund or portfolio of funds he is offered to buy is of average quality. This means that the seller of a high-quality portfolio may be unable to get a sufficiently high price to make selling the portfolio worthwhile. Thus, the "lemons problem" may prevent a transaction from happening, explaining why the offered amount in individual years has by far exceeded the amount of commitments that actually changed hands. Note that the "lemons problem" has been an important impediment despite the fact that potential buyers are normally confined to large and sophisticated investors who often know the portfolios they are offered well, for example, because of primary commitments to the same partnerships.

Historically, around 3–5% of outstanding LP exposure comes to market, which represents the pool from which potential buyers can fish. In the end, 1.3–1.6% of the outstanding exposure – calculated as the sum of NAV and unfunded commitments – is actually traded each year (Figure 6.5). Thus, the rapid growth in the secondary market mirrors the substantial expansion in the primary fundraising market in past years. Note that a significant part of the total underlying pool of assets in 2011 is due to partnerships formed during the peak years between

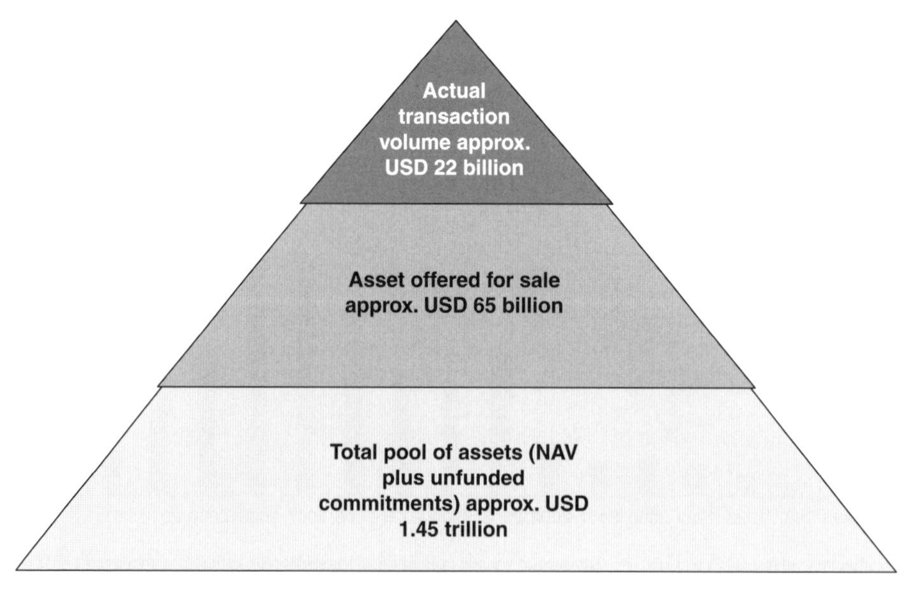

Figure 6.5 Asset pool and transaction volume, 2010.
Source: AlpInvest Partners; Partners Group; UBS.

2005 and 2008. In these four years, commitments to private equity funds (excluding real asset funds) totalled nearly USD 1.7 trillion. As we showed in Figure 6.3, these vintage years accounted for around three-quarters of the total transaction volume in the secondary market in 2011.

The rapid growth in secondary transactions has not followed a steady trajectory, however. Instead, there have been important fluctuations around the longer-term trend. For instance, in 2003 the volume of transactions nearly tripled in absolute terms and increased 2.5-fold relative to the underlying base pool of assets. This jump is explained by a combination of factors. First of all, the overall volume during that year reflects one of the largest deals in the history of the secondary market – the acquisition of Deutsche Bank's private equity investments in the United States and Europe by MidOcean Partners, a firm formed in the same year through a management spinout transaction. Several investors provided the capital to acquire Deutsche Bank's private equity assets, including some of the largest players in the secondary market (e.g., AlpInvest Partners, Coller Capital, Harbourvest Partners and Paul Capital Partners, as well as some large pension funds). This single transaction alone amounted to more than USD 1.8 billion, or nearly one-third of the total transaction volume during that year.

Although unique in terms of its size, the Deutsche Bank/MidOcean transaction was probably motivated by similar reasons that also encouraged others to sell at least part of their private equity portfolios or even exit the asset class altogether. Despite the economic recovery from the recession at the beginning of the decade, many LPs had growing doubts about the performance of their private equity portfolios, which typically included a significant or even dominant share of VC funds. While such funds had performed spectacularly well in the run-up to the tech bubble, after the bursting of the bubble a growing number of LPs lost confidence that the pre-bubble performance could be repeated. At the same time, commitments to primary private equity funds dried up and started to recover in earnest only in 2004. Importantly, for the first time the sellers in the secondary market included a pension fund, the State of Connecticut Retirement Plans and Trust. The sellers were willing to accept significant discounts relative to the NAV, an issue we shall return to in the following section.

Conversely, the volume of secondary transactions more than halved in 2009 compared with the previous year before returning to its previous level in the following year. At the beginning of 2009, global market conditions had deteriorated to unprecedented levels in response to the largest bankruptcy in history, the collapse of Lehman Brothers in the fall of 2008. Prices for risky assets deteriorated sharply and correlations jumped, triggering a massive flight to safety, with yields on US Treasuries pushed to record lows. The interbank market essentially froze, prompting central banks around the world to inject massive amounts of liquidity through unconventional measures. Investors' cash flow models were generally not designed to cope with this tail risk, and many long-term asset allocators found themselves short of liquidity as margin calls were raised, distributions dried up and many hedge funds limited redemptions.

In this environment, the supply of stakes in private equity funds skyrocketed, but given the huge amount of macroeconomic uncertainty, the profound lack of liquidity in the market and the massive degree of risk aversion among investors, there were few potential buyers. As NAVs were only gradually adjusted in line with the rapidly deteriorating operating performance of underlying portfolio companies and the continued decline in public markets, there was a wide gap between sellers' and buyers' price expectations. In the first half of 2009, this gap proved unbridgeable for many portfolios, except for a few transactions where sellers were

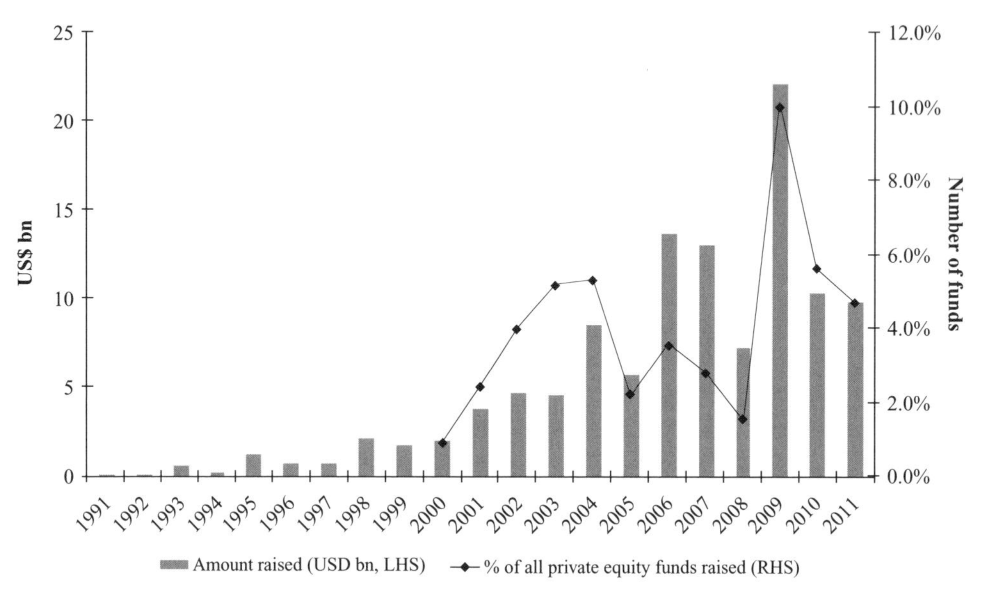

Figure 6.6 Secondary funds raised.
Source: Almeida; Preqin.

particularly distressed. Only when global markets stabilized around the middle of the year and NAVs caught up with economic reality did transaction volumes in the secondary market regain momentum.

6.2.2 Fundraising

While commitments to private equity funds in the past determine the pool of assets that might be supplied today, on the buy side the secondary market has also seen substantial growth in recent years. In the post-crisis years 2009–2011, institutional investors made commitments of around USD 42 billion to specialist secondary funds, the largest amount in any 3-year period since the secondary market started to emerge (Figure 6.6). Although the history of the secondary market is still quite short, it appears that commitments to secondary funds have been less cyclical than commitments to primary funds. Instead, fundraising has followed an upward trend, with significant year-on-year variations. For instance, whereas commitments in the primary fundraising market fell sharply in 2001–2003, commitments to secondary funds continued to increase. As a result, the share of secondary funds in the overall fundraising market surged from less than 1% in 2000 to more than 5% in 2003. Although the upward trend of capital flowing into secondary funds remained intact during the boom years 2005–2007, commitments to such partnerships were dwarfed by funds committed in the primary market. Thus, the share of secondary funds in the overall fundraising market fell back to less than 2%. More recently, however, the secondary market reached new highs as the commitments to primary funds remained subdued in the post-crisis era.

Preqin estimates that specialist secondary funds had at their disposal resources of more than USD 30 billion at the end of the first quarter of 2012. This dry powder reflects commitments investors had already made, but which had not yet been drawn down by the fund managers.

Note that this amount does not include potential resources from non-traditional buyers, nor does it include new commitments to secondary funds. As regards the latter, Preqin reports that there were 26 secondary funds in the market at the end of the first quarter of 2012, targeting a total amount of almost USD 23 billion. Of these funds, almost 50% already had at least a first close. Thus, from a buyer's standpoint the market seems to be poised for further growth, subject to cyclical variations around a longer-term trajectory.

6.3 PRICE FORMATION AND RETURNS

6.3.1 Pricing secondary transactions

Prices serve a critical function in markets by balancing supply and demand. In market conditions where supply exceeds demand, prices tend to adjust downwards to attract additional buyers and discourage sellers just enough to achieve a market equilibrium. Conversely, if demand exceeds supply prices are pushed upwards, attracting additional sellers and discouraging buyers until supply and demand are equated. While this general principle also applies to the secondary market for stakes in private equity and real asset funds, it is important to identify the peculiarities of that market to understand the informational content of secondary pricing. Specifically, investors, risk managers and regulators alike are interested in the following question: To what extent do secondary prices reveal fair market values that can be used to price portfolio holdings in illiquid assets for which there are no market prices?

Traditionally, fair market values are determined on the basis of the NAV of a fund or portfolio of funds. As Meyer and Mathonet (2005) point out, NAVs can be considered fair only if they are equal to the present value of the fund's overall expected cash flows. However, these cash flows include not only those that are related to the investments a fund has already made, but also future cash flows that are associated with the undrawn commitments the buyer needs to fund. While prices in the secondary markets are generally expressed in terms of discounts or premiums relative to the fair market value, sellers and buyers may have different views about the benchmark against which such discounts or premiums apply. As far as the former are concerned, the reference is usually the NAV of the capital that has already been invested by the fund manager. Conversely, potential buyers tend to view the fair value of a fund as applying to the total commitment – including those that have yet to be funded.

From the perspective of a potential buyer, one method to assess the fair value of a secondary transaction is based on a top-down analysis, using historic cash flows of a large number of funds from internal or public databases (Meyer and Mathonet, 2005; Diller and Herger, 2009). These historic cash flows are employed to model future cash flows, taking into account specific assumptions about the funds' characteristics. Such assumptions may be derived from internal grading systems (see Chapter 14 for details), with the economic value of the portfolio being determined under alternative scenarios. The secondary price from a buyer's perspective is then estimated by discounting the expected future cash flows, based on the buyer's expectations about the asset's performance:

$$P_0 = \sum_{i=0}^{n} \frac{\mathrm{CF}_i}{\left(1 + \mathrm{IRR}_{\mathrm{buyer}}\right)^i}$$

with P_0 denoting the secondary price offered by the buyer, CF_i the fund's expected cash flow at time i, n the fund's maturity and $\mathrm{IRR}_{\mathrm{buyer}}$ the buyer's expected IRR.

With the price a potential buyer is willing to pay reflecting expected cash flows from both funded and unfunded commitments, the buyer's offer will generally be different from the NAV reported by the GP, which is usually the reference point for the seller. The discount can be expressed as follows:

$$\text{Discount}_t = \frac{\text{NAV}_t - P_{0,t}}{\text{NAV}_t}$$

Few players will rely exclusively on a top-down analysis. Instead, most buyers of secondary assets will determine the price they are willing to pay for a given portfolio on the basis of a bottom-up analysis. In this analysis, the NAV reported by the GPs is of limited relevance, as the underlying assets are sold only in the future. Instead, the analysis takes into account the expected exit value and exit timing for current portfolio investments, projected future capital calls and the return on future investments made using such drawdowns, and the legal structure of the fund. These variables are used to conduct a discounted cash flow (DCF) analysis, helping determine the buyer's desired return on the transaction (target return of discount rate).

Following a bottom-up approach to determining the price for a given portfolio can be extremely resource-intensive. For instance, to determine the expected value of a privately held company at the time of sale, the buyer needs to analyse a set of key variables for each company in the portfolio, such as EBITDA, the company's degree of indebtedness (net of excess cash on the balance sheet) and the fund's ownership in the company. Further, the buyer must make critical assumptions about the remaining holding periods of the companies, the EBITDA growth rate, the rate of debt paydown and the future EBITDA multiple. While previous investments by the GP may provide some guidance, for example, with regard to typical holding periods, the outcome of this analysis can be highly sensitive to the underlying assumptions. Thus, buyers typically find it advisable to subject their estimates to different scenarios about the macroeconomic environment and its implications for EBITDA growth rates, interest rates and exit multiples.

If valuations of buyout portfolios are already difficult and subject to substantial uncertainty, valuing venture portfolios is even more challenging by an order of magnitude. As we discuss in different parts of this book, venture investments typically have a wide range of potential outcomes, with a significant number of write-downs and write-offs offset by a few successful and highly successful transactions. For LPs it is generally not possible to assess the probability of individual companies falling into either category. Thus, secondary buyers considering VC assets are generally much more reliant on information they receive from the fund manager and are usually guided by his reputation and track record.

As far as unfunded commitments are concerned, buyers usually first determine the split between commitments used for future investments as opposed to those used for fund fees and expenses. In determining the value future capital calls may generate, a buyer will closely examine the GP's quality and historical returns. Depending on these factors, the unfunded part may be considered to be an asset or a liability. As far as the expected speed of the future capital calls are concerned, the buyer will typically be guided by historical data.

Finally, based on his analysis the buyer needs to determine his target rate of return, or the discount rate. This target rate varies across market segments, with mezzanine funds usually having a lower target rate than buyout funds, which in turn have a lower target rate than VC funds, reflecting their specific risk characteristics. Furthermore, target rates mirror market conditions, which vary over time. Target rates dropped on average below 15% at the peak of the last cycle, according to Cogent Partners' semi-annual trend analysis, but they climbed to 30% in late 2008 and early 2009 amid extreme uncertainty about the macroeconomic outlook and the global financial markets. While these numbers might have fallen for larger players participating in auctions, the target rate is generally viewed to be still high for other market segments. For example, at the smaller end of the market with less intermediation and transparency, target returns are believed to be less cyclical and typically at a higher level.

In this context, tactical considerations may also play a role. As Talmor and Vasvari (2011) note, for example, buyers have not been in a rush to bid aggressively for mega-funds raised in 2007 and 2008, given the huge amount of capital committed to these partnerships. Assuming that a certain percentage of the stakes will eventually come to market, they can simply wait in the hope of purchasing the assets at a more attractive price. Further, some LPs may have been investors in a fund through a primary transaction. While this increases their visibility and may provide an important competitive advantage, they may face constraints by exceeding self-imposed concentration limits.

Let us turn now to the seller's side. From a seller's perspective, a key issue is the deviation of the price a buyer offers from the fund's NAV provided by the GP. In the case where a buyer is offering to purchase a stake in a fund at a discount to the partnership's most recently reported NAV, a transaction at that discount would create a loss on the seller's books. While realizing a loss is painful for any investor, Talmor and Vasvari (2011, p. 201) point out that this issue may be particularly important for alternative asset allocators as their compensation is typically tied more closely to performance. Finding a market-clearing price may be aggravated further by different target rates of return used by sellers and buyers. The former tend to employ lower discount rates than potential buyers, which reflects, *inter alia*, a risk premium indicative of their informational disadvantage. This discrepancy may be particularly large if the seller is a pension fund which, for actuarial reasons, uses a low target rate of return.

Reflecting the different supply and demand dynamics and the formation of price expectations among sellers and buyers, prices have varied significantly over the cycle (Figure 6.7). In 2003,

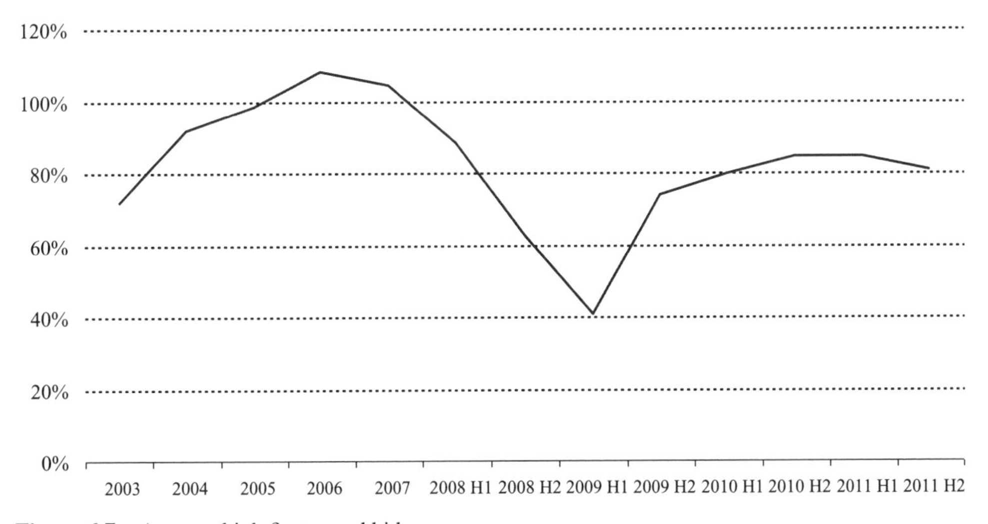

Figure 6.7 Average high first-round bid.
Source: Cogent Partners.

the average high first round bid for assets intermediated by Cogent Partners hovered around 70% relative to the NAV. Despite this large discount, the transaction volume jumped almost threefold as shown in Figure 6.4. Obviously, sellers were willing to accept even large losses as they were seeking liquidity and restructuring their portfolios for strategic reasons. In the first half of 2009, the gap between the average high first round bid and the NAV widened to a record high of around 60%. At the same time, bid spreads (defined as the average high bid for a given asset divided by the average low bid for such asset) increased to record levels, reflecting the huge degree of uncertainty in valuing assets and the large variety in the perceived quality of the supply pool, with unfunded commitments representing a substantial share. However, in this buyers' market, the huge discounts offered by potential purchasers were accepted only by a few distressed sellers who were forced to liquidate assets. Others, however, who were less desperate decided not to sell. Thus, a large amount of assets potentially up for sale failed to find a buyer, with the volume of transactions falling by more than 50% compared with the previous year.

As Partners Group (2011, p. 5) points out, a key issue in the price formation process lies in the inertia of NAV reporting. Discounts offered by buyers were particularly large at the peak of the crisis, as many of the deals brought to market were still priced off September and December 2008 NAVs. However, given the further large drop in public valuations and the rapid deterioration in macroeconomic and financial market conditions, these NAVs were quickly outdated. However, as NAVs were increasingly adjusted downwards by GPs in line with prevailing market conditions, bid–ask spreads in the secondary market narrowed again and set the stage for a recovery in the volume of transactions. More recently, discounts have stabilized around 80% for first-round bids, with settlement prices presumably exceeding such bids by a non-trivial margin. At the same time, bid spreads have narrowed again, as the quality of supply has become more consistent and macroeconomic uncertainty has receded.

We may juxtapose the bids in the secondary market with the premiums and discounts at which listed private equity vehicles trade (Figure 6.8). Compiled by Preqin, these discounts/premiums are generally based on the latest available NAV and are composed of just 100 listed vehicles. The overall picture is fundamentally the same as the one depicted in Figure 6.7. Following a period of small premia for buyout and VC funds during the peak years, large discounts emerged in 2008 which troughed in the first quarter of 2009 at the height of macroeconomic and financial uncertainty. Thereafter, discounts narrowed, trading at around 20% – more or less in line with what is observed in the secondary market.

6.3.2 Returns from secondary investments

Returns from secondary investments are driven by the supply/demand conditions in the secondary market at the time when the secondary transaction takes place. Portfolio companies held by the fund(s) under consideration are valued in light of the information that is available when the stake(s) in the fund is (are) offered to the potential buyer, resulting in a possible discount or premium to the NAV. While unfunded commitments are generally treated in finance theory as NPV = 0, potential buyers, as we have argued above, might attach a different value to them. This value takes into account information about the fund manager that was not available at the time when the primary investment was undertaken. Thus, it is important to recognize that secondary investments are unable to rewrite history by providing access to market opportunities at historic valuations. Instead, secondaries represent a stand-alone market segment that should be seen as a complement to a primary fund programme.

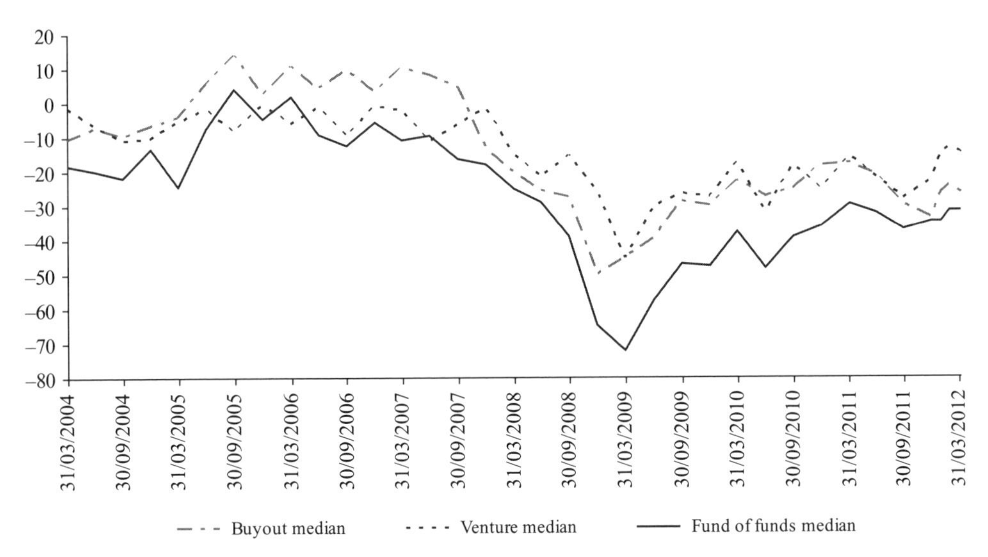

Figure 6.8 Listed private equity: discount/premium by type.
Source: Preqin.

Given the valuation dynamics in the secondary market, how do returns compare with primary fund investments? In addressing this issue, we focus on returns of secondary funds expressed as IRR as well as TVPI. These returns are benchmarked against a portfolio consisting of all private equity funds raised in a given year for which cash flow data is available. The data are taken from Preqin, a leading data vendor, and refer to partnerships in the area of buyouts, venture capital, growth capital, mezzanine, turnaround, special situations and distressed. Essentially, our benchmark aims to mirror the broadest possible universe of investment opportunities a LP could have chosen from. Our sample period ranges from 1998 to 2008. The results are shown in Table 6.1.

On a capital-weighted basis, secondary funds have outperformed our benchmark in most vintage years when returns are measured by the funds' IRRs. While their TVPIs are generally lower due to their shorter life, the strong IRR performance has contributed significantly to the rising amount of commitments to secondary funds in recent years. Essentially, LPs who are faced with the decision of where to allocate capital compare expected returns from secondary funds with those in their primary fund programme. What is interesting from the point of view of our discussion in this chapter, however, is that the returns generated by secondary funds in a given vintage year are related to purchases of stakes in primary funds raised in previous years. Take, for example, secondary funds raised in 2004. Weighted by the capital they raised, secondary funds returned an IRR of 21.2%. A substantial share of their acquisitions consisted of stakes in primary funds raised between 1998 and 2001. Their performance, however, was comparatively significantly weaker, ranging from 6.7% in 1998 to 18.6% in 2001. This gap is explained by the particular market characteristics of the secondary market and confirms that returns reflect the set of information that was available to the sellers and buyers at the time of the secondary transaction rather than the fundamental value of the underlying assets.

Table 6.1 Performance of secondary funds

	Private equity primary funds										Secondary funds									
			IRR (%)				TVPI						IRR (%)				TVPI			
Vintage year	Sample size	Cap. called (%)	Weighted average	Median	Q1	Q3	Weighted average	Median	Q1	Q3	Sample size	Cap. called (%)	Weighted average	Median	Q1	Q3	Weighted average	Median	Q1	Q3
1998	185	97.4	6.7	7.2	14.4	−1.3	1.43	1.34	1.69	0.87	7	98.5	8.7	7.0	–	–	1.32	1.27	–	–
1999	183	96.5	5.2	6.7	13.8	−4.3	1.40	1.34	1.81	0.69	5	95.9	12.2	12.3	–	–	1.32	1.25	–	–
2000	294	97.2	10.9	8.0	17.1	−2.3	1.59	1.35	1.86	0.85	6	96.0	12.8	13.6	–	–	1.55	1.61	–	–
2001	179	97.6	18.6	10.6	24.0	1.1	1.86	1.49	1.97	0.98	4	94.8	21.1	–	–	–	1.67	1.61	–	–
2002	151	99.7	19.5	11.2	22.8	2.2	1.70	1.42	1.85	0.94	7	94.0	18.1	17.8	–	–	1.54	1.56	–	–
2003	124	97.8	17.4	9.0	21.5	0.9	1.76	1.32	1.73	0.92	9	88.1	28.1	23.6	32.9	16.8	1.73	1.91	1.97	1.46
2004	154	95.4	13.6	8.2	14.6	−0.1	1.64	1.36	1.77	0.97	8	90.2	21.2	15.3	–	–	1.46	1.61	1.70	1.28
2005	254	93.9	10.3	7.7	13.7	2.6	1.44	1.30	1.60	1.03	13	93.8	11.4	7.1	11.3	6.2	1.32	1.27	1.40	1.22
2006	283	91.9	3.7	6.8	11.4	0.8	1.17	1.20	1.40	0.97	11	87.4	5.6	4.3	6.5	1.1	1.16	1.13	1.22	1.04
2007	307	78.4	6.4	8.0	16.2	0.9	1.21	1.19	1.39	0.97	10	71.7	14.0	13.0	16.2	10.0	1.31	1.31	1.34	1.23
2008	264	69.6	9.2	8.0	15.7	0.8	1.22	1.15	1.34	1.00	15	71.2	18.8	21.3	24.2	15.6	1.31	1.34	1.44	1.27

Note: Valuations as of 31 March 2012; capital called refers to weighted average. Primary funds include buyouts, VC, growth capital, mezzanine, turnaround, special situations and distressed.
Source: Preqin.

6.4 CONCLUSIONS

As we have discussed in this chapter, a secondary market has emerged over the past two decades that allows investors to sell their commitments to limited partnerships in order to generate liquidity or pursue strategic objectives. These commitments usually include those that have already been drawn down by the GP as well as those that are still unfunded. Often intermediated by specialized investment banks, these commitments are bought by investors who are primarily attracted by the potential discount at which a transaction may take place, the shorter period during which the invested capital is locked in and the portfolio diversification properties of secondaries.

The emergence of secondary transactions has usually been portrayed as a market response to the illiquidity of fund investments that constrains the universe of investors to those with appropriate liability profiles. As significant as the development of the secondary market may be for constructing efficient portfolios, this chapter has cautioned that it should not be perceived as a game changer in terms of risk management in illiquid investments. To begin with, although the secondary market has expanded rapidly in recent years, it has remained small relative to the primary market, with only a few percent of primary commitments being transacted in the secondary market. Second, the secondary market, just as other financial markets, may dry up precisely at the time when it is needed most. The year 2009 provides an important example. Although a maximum amount of supply came to market, the actual transaction volume collapsed as sellers were not prepared to accept discounts of 60% and in individual cases even more, unless they were under exceptional pressure to create liquidity.

For similar reasons, it appears doubtful that secondary market prices can be used as benchmarks for fair market value. Secondary prices are not observable. Transactions are confidential and the final settlement price is generally known only to the buyer and the seller (and the intermediary to the extent that a transaction has been facilitated by a specialist agent). The secondary market price reflects current market conditions for those who participate in the market, either as sellers or as buyers. But this tells us little about the underlying value of the portfolio which is held until maturity. While distressed sellers are forced to accept substantial discounts from buyers that are less constrained, the observed dynamic in the secondary market rather underlines the importance of appropriate risk management.

Part II
Risk Measurement and Modelling

7

Illiquid Assets and Risk

Investors who seek higher returns generally have to accept higher risk. To the extent that the efficient market hypothesis holds, it is impossible for investors to find risk-adjusted excess returns, with risk being defined in the standard CAPM context. In practice, of course, "... no market prices assets precisely at fair value all of the time". However, "most markets price most assets with reasonable efficiency most of the time, providing few opportunities for easy gains" (Swensen, 2009). Any mispricing of risk gives rise to relative-value trading strategies, which help ensure that excess returns are arbitraged away.

The high degree of efficiency in markets for marketable assets encourages investors to seek investment opportunities in less transparent and efficient markets. As Swensen (2009, p. 82) argues, these markets are typically illiquid, "... since rewarding investments tend to reside in dark corners, not in the glare of floodlights". However, as long-term investors venture into illiquid markets, such as private equity and real assets, the question immediately arises as to how risk should be defined and measured, an issue we already discussed in Chapter 5. To begin with, market prices are not observable. Instead, quarterly returns reported by limited partnership funds are based on subjective NAVs, which poses substantial challenges in terms of estimating risk-adjusted returns. And even if researchers find ways to get around this issue, for example, by working with cash flow data, time series for returns tend to be very short in most market segments other than US buyouts and US venture capital.

Investors thus face an important dilemma. In traditional markets, there are few opportunities to enjoy excess returns. By contrast, non-traditional markets which are usually relatively illiquid are more likely to be subject to inefficiencies, which may provide room for excess returns. However, in such markets, it is difficult to employ standard allocation models, which rely on a particular concept of measurable risk that does not easily apply to illiquid assets.

Against this background, this chapter starts by distinguishing between risk and uncertainty as different types of probability situations. In this context, we emphasize the importance of subjective elements in assessing risk in illiquid investments as opposed to working purely with objective probabilities. Turning to managing risk, finally, we discuss the relation between risk management and due diligence, emphasizing that these are clearly distinct, but complementary functions of the investment process.

Notwithstanding the issue of how risk in illiquid assets is defined and measured, our discussion accepts the general principle that risks and rewards are positively related. This principle is important as it implies risk management should be unbiased in the sense that it focuses on both downside *and* upside risks. In fact, as Damodaran (2007) observes, the Chinese symbol for "risk" is a combination of danger and opportunity. However, while the basic principle of a two-sided risk management approach applies to illiquid assets as well, particular skills are required to address the specific challenges investors face in committing capital to private equity funds and similar structures.

7.1 RISK, UNCERTAINTY AND THEIR RELATIONSHIP WITH RETURNS

In a single-asset portfolio, finance theory usually defines risk as the variance of returns of a specific investment. In a multi-asset portfolio, as the MPT shows, risk can at least partly be diversified away to the extent that asset returns are less than perfectly correlated. In empirical applications of the CAPM, risk is measured on the basis of historic movements of asset prices, which by definition requires the availability of appropriate time series. In private equity and real assets, this condition is hardly satisfied. First of all, the very nature of these asset classes implies that there are no observable market prices, which poses substantial challenges in terms of calculating market risk in the context of the CAPM. There are different approaches in the literature to deal with this problem but, as we reviewed briefly in Chapter 5, empirical estimates vary significantly. Thus, some investors continue to rely on informed judgment in formulating their mean–variance assumptions (Swensen, 2009, pp. 118–119). Furthermore, to the extent that academic research has attempted to estimate risk-adjusted returns, such efforts have focused predominantly on already more established private markets, such as US buyouts and US venture capital. By contrast, for many other market segments (such as distressed investing, mezzanine or growth capital in emerging economies) there are virtually no data that could be used in empirical investigations.

The challenges that arise in applying the CAPM to illiquid assets, such as private equity funds and similar partnership structures, raise a fundamental issue. How do we assess *risk* in illiquid asset classes where market prices cannot be observed and hence are subject to substantial *uncertainty*?

7.1.1 Risk and uncertainty

In addressing this issue, it is useful to go back to Knight (1921), who distinguishes three different types of probability situation: (i) *a priori* probability; (ii) statistical probability; and (iii) estimated probability.

- *A priori* probabilities can be derived deductively from inherent symmetries. Examples are games of chance where outcomes have a defined universe and there is an exhaustive set of events. Instances are completely homogeneous, with equal probability for each event to materialize.
- In the case of statistical probability, instances are not homogeneous and, consequently, probabilities assigned to each event are not equal. Without a defined universe, statistical probabilities are derived from empirical classifications of instances (i.e., the tabulation of current and past data). This, however, is based implicitly on the assumption that the distribution found in the past will hold in the future.
- In the case of estimates, there is no valid basis for classifying instances. Outcomes are unique or so infrequent that it is meaningless to tabulate them as a measure of their probability.

Knight (1921) associates "risk" with the first two categories, whereas "uncertainty" is linked to the third. As far as uncertainty is concerned, strict reasoning needs to be complemented with judgment and intuition, which makes any assessment subject to a wide margin of error. In fact, even the probability of error cannot be determined as instances are more or less unique, preventing statistical techniques from being applied to calculate probabilities. Thus, dealing with uncertainty implies a "probability judgment", in contrast to *a priori* and statistical probabilities. In this sense, investments in private equity and real assets are arguably subject to uncertainty rather than risk.

While the differentiation between risk and uncertainty is conceptually useful, in practice we often find a continuum from "measurable" risks to uncertainty (i.e., "immeasurable" risks). As far as illiquid assets are concerned, recent contributions to the literature may be interpreted as efforts to make risk measurable by extracting information from non-market (cash flow) data whose nature would classify such investments as uncertain in the Knightian sense. However, more research is needed to confirm that the recent academic findings provide reasonable estimates for practical applications in risk management. The crux is this, however: to the extent that a data-driven frequentist approach (Bénéplanc and Rochet, 2011, p. 29) is possible in measuring risk in illiquid assets, their potential to generate excess returns is set to diminish and eventually disappear. Until then, risk managers in illiquid assets will need to rely to a large extent on a subjective approach to deal with uncertainty in the absence of sufficient observations that can be used to derive objective probabilities.

7.1.2 How objective are probabilities anyway?

Since the seminal work by Knight (1921), the concept of risk is inextricably linked to how we understand probability (Rebonato, 2007). However, the Knightian view that probabilities can be employed objectively to estimate risk as long as such probabilities are based on a sufficiently large sample of observations has not remained undisputed. Holton (2004) refers to statisticians Leonard J. Savage and Bruno de Finetti as advocates of the subjective interpretation of probability. According to Savage, it "is unanimously agreed that statistics depends somehow on probability. But, as to what probability is and how it is connected with statistics, there has seldom been such complete disagreement and breakdown of communication since the Tower of Babel."[1]

According to their objective interpretation, probabilities can be determined through the application of logic or estimated through statistical analysis. "Investors 'just know' the objective probabilities attached to the different possible future states of the world" (Rebonato, 2007, p. 26). This may not be entirely satisfactory, however: "If we want to describe how human beings *actually* make their choices in the presence of uncertainty, we had better make sure that we truly understand how probabilities are *actually* used in decision making – rather than how stylized hyperrational agents endowed with perfect God-given statistical information *would* reach these decisions" (Rebonato, 2007, p. 26; italics in original). Thus, according to the subjective interpretation, probabilities reflect human beliefs in the sense of investors' own views on uncertainty.

Nevertheless, risk managers tend to prefer quantitative analytics as the most effective approach to both measuring risk and implementing risk management programmes. Only the (apparently) objective quantification allows measuring risks accurately and comparing different asset classes in terms of their risk profile. Thus, according to this view, the ability to objectively quantify risk is a prerequisite for the credible involvement of the risk manager in the investment process. Qualitative techniques are often dismissed as "generalizations", "hunches", "intuition" and "gut feel" and some "war quants", Hubbard (2009) even suggests

[1] Quoted from Savage, L.J. (1954) *The Foundations of Statistics*. John Wiley & Sons, New York.

that they are no better than having no risk management programme at all. Instead, the solution is usually sought in creating databases with detailed information on individual assets and extracting risk-relevant information from non-market data (Lorenz *et al.*, 2006). This search for objectivity, however, may be "... an illusory attempt to materialize our true probabilistic beliefs" (de Finetti).

To be sure, objective probabilities require stationary environments. However, as we discussed in Chapter 5, the risk/return properties of individual assets may shift dramatically during periods of financial turmoil. Risk models based on data that reflected "normal" market conditions became largely obsolete, if not dangerous. Thus, the selection of the sample period, which is a subjective decision of the risk manager, has a profound impact on the estimated risk of an asset. In some sense, therefore, investors are confronted with a version of Heisenberg's "uncertainty principle", aimed at measuring probabilities in a static market with a relatively high degree of precision or accepting imprecision when estimating probabilities in changing market conditions.

7.1.3 How useful are benchmark approximations?

In illiquid assets, even static market data are usually spurious, which raises the question as to whether certain assets can be used as an approximation. An obvious candidate for private equity funds seems to be indexes of publicly listed private equity, such as the LPX 50 index. According to Sanyal (2009), "... it (*the LPX 50 index*) is one of the best proxies since PE-VC funds are not regularly traded and have data limitations". European regulators, such as EIOPA, have sympathized with this view, proposing the LPX 50 index in determining risk weights under the Solvency II standard approach. However, this view ignores that private equity funds are set up deliberately in a way to allow fund managers to harvest an illiquidity premium and hence possess fundamentally different risk profiles compared with publicly listed private equity firms or specific vehicles for which daily market prices are quoted.

Similarly, several researchers have employed the NASDAQ as an approximation for (US) venture capital and small-cap indexes, such as the Russell 2000, for US buyouts. However, there are similar reservations against such approaches. While they are easy to implement, there are important doubts as to whether they provide meaningful insights in the risk/return profile of private equity, an asset class that is usually accessed through fundamentally different vehicles. The same question can be raised, for example, with regard to the applicability of REITs to investments in real estate partnerships.

As far as private equity investments in emerging markets are concerned, historical returns data are almost entirely missing. On what basis do limited partners determine their decision as to how much capital they want to commit to partnerships in such markets? Essentially, there are three approaches, none of which is satisfactory. First, investors simply take a market-neutral position in the sense that their exposure to private equity and real assets in emerging markets resembles the relative investment volume in these markets. For instance, an investor would invest 20% of his allocation to private equity in funds targeting emerging markets, if such markets absorbed 20% of private equity commitments worldwide. While this allocation may be considered as a market equilibrium portfolio in the Black–Litterman (1992) sense, it does not say anything about the relative attractiveness of emerging markets as a destination for private equity capital. Investors may deviate from the market view, and the Black–Litterman approach presents an appropriate framework for deriving portfolio weights based on investors' proprietary risk-adjusted return expectations and the degree of confidence they have in their stated views. However, this leaves open the question of how such views are formulated.

Alternatively, investors may use public equity indexes for emerging markets, such as the MSCI EM index or national market indexes. However, in so doing they run into the same issues as we have mentioned above. Finally, investors may base their risk-adjusted return expectations on data from more mature markets, notably the USA, adjusted for a risk premium. This approach fails to recognize, however, that private investments in emerging markets and more advanced markets may follow fundamentally different dynamics. In private equity, for example, the majority of transactions in emerging economies are growth capital deals, with GPs frequently taking a minority position. Leverage is hardly used. Furthermore, the universe of fund managers tends to be significantly more diverse, with international private equity firms competing with a rapidly growing number of local GPs. In many markets, exit markets are still embryonic and country risk is perceived to play a comparatively more important role. Sudden swings in international investors' risk appetite can lead to significant fluctuations in emerging markets' exchange rates. For all these reasons, it is doubtful if data from more advanced markets can provide any meaningful guidance.

Generally, the more the benchmark resembles the specific characteristics of investments in limited partnerships, the more meaningful the results will be. However, researchers looking for close benchmarks are likely to face comparable problems in terms of data availability and their reliability. Thus, there is an important trade-off investors are confronted with. To the extent that investors decide to invest in illiquid asset classes – the dark corners of the market, as Swensen (2009) has put it – they will need to accept that measuring and managing risk will have to rely to a considerable extent on subjective assessments.

7.1.4 Subjective probabilities and emerging assets

These considerations suggest complementing the standard treatment of risk in the CAPM, which is predicated on the frequentist approach in the Knightian sense, with a subjective approach that emphasizes the risk investors accept when venturing into new markets where CAPM-type risk measures do not exist. In this sense, risk has to do with the "newness" of the investment, with investment decisions being taken in the absence of information about historical returns, distributions and correlations. As Knight (1921) observes, business decisions deal "... with situations which are far too unique, generally speaking, for any sort of statistical tabulation to have any value for guidance".

An obvious example is venture capital, where venture capitalists back companies at a very early stage of their lifecycle. Typically, a significant percentage of companies backed by a fund will lose money, with the fund's returns driven by a small number of very successful deals, sometimes called "home runs". As Kaplan *et al.* (2009) find, failures and successes are predominantly determined by a venture capitalist's ability to pick the right business (the market for a particular product or service and the technology) rather than the management team, which can – and often is – replaced in case of underperformance. However, whereas management teams usually have a track record, which is an important variable in the venture capitalist's decision process, the market potential for a new product or new technology is essentially unknown and hence fraught with substantial investment risk.

Investors in limited partnership funds face similar challenges. As we discussed in Chapter 2, there were very few investors in private equity funds as recent as the early 1980s. Their total exposure was just about USD 2 billion, which is roughly equivalent to what a single fund may raise today, adjusted for inflation. Limited partners committing to this new asset class were venturing into unknown territory, without any guidance by historical returns and their variance. Thirty years later, private equity is an established asset class, and many large institutional investors are exposed to it to varying degrees. However, within the asset class new niches emerge, such as private equity in developing economies. It is the newness of investing in private equity funds or infrastructure funds targeting such markets that is inevitably associated with risk, which is deliberately sought by investors chasing excess returns.

The ability to harvest excess returns depends on the investor's success in identifying new market opportunities and learning how to succeed in new markets. This is true for fund managers as well as the limited partners in their funds. Importantly, the decision not to pursue new investment strategies in order to avoid risk is no guarantee of stable, if unexciting, returns. As markets mature and become more competitive and transparent, the potential for achieving excess returns diminishes. In this context, some observers (e.g., Fraser-Sampson, 2006, p. 92) have pointed, for example, to the outperformance of buyout funds in the European market relative to the United States for most of the 1990s and early 2000s. A key factor, in Fraser-Sampson's view, were market imperfections in the former. Whereas GPs' "... ability to source deals proactively and be able to transact it on an exclusive basis was still very much alive in Europe...", at that time it had already largely disappeared in the USA. However, investors backing fund managers targeting European companies had little, if any, objective information they could have used to formulate a view on the risk they would take.

Similar considerations motivate limited partners to continue to adjust their investment strategies in favour of emerging markets, notwithstanding the absence of historical return data and standard risk metrics, such as the variance and correlation of asset prices. Instead, they rely mostly on subjective considerations and qualitative indicators in assessing the risk of venturing into new markets. However, in so doing, they depart from standard risk management practices, which are generally understood to be a purely quantitative discipline consistent with regulatory frameworks, such as Basel II/III or Solvency II.

7.2 RISK MANAGEMENT, DUE DILIGENCE AND MONITORING

7.2.1 Hedging and financial vs. non-financial risks

Mirroring the particular concept of risk applied in the CAPM and in MPT, the focus of risk management is often narrowly defined. Managing financial risks is often equated with hedging risks, a view that is not easily applicable to investments in illiquid investments. Damodaran (2007) identifies several reasons why hedging is frequently viewed synonymously with managing risks. First of all, the majority of risk management products have been developed for risk hedging, including insurance instruments, derivatives or swaps. Risk hedging typically generates substantial revenues and, not surprisingly, is therefore considered as the "centrepiece of the risk management story". Second, Damodaran (2007) argues that human nature tends to remember losses (the downside of risk) more easily than profits (the upside of risk). As a result, extreme losses, for example, caused by market meltdowns, whet investors' appetite for risk-hedging products focusing on downside risks. Third, he points to the well-known principal/agent problem. While managers tend to prefer to hedge risks, the principal may actually prefer to take a risk. We will revisit this issue in greater detail in Chapter 16, where we discuss the role of the risk manager.

Apart from the reasons that Damodaran (2007) gives why risk management is often narrowed down to hedging, one may argue that regulation is likely to have played a role as well. Financial regulation often favours risk-hedging solutions through which regulated investors may enjoy lower capital requirements. Regulatory tightening, which typically occurs in the aftermath of financial crises, provides additional incentives for risk hedging. However, to the extent that risks are non-quantifiable, their treatment becomes vague and even murky. Frequently, this is the case with non-financial risks. For example, assessing risks related to environmental, social and governance issues (ESG) relies to a considerable extent on information whose nature is essentially qualitative. This poses important challenges not least from a regulatory standpoint, explaining why non-quantifiable (sometimes referred to synonymously as non-financial) risks are often treated as an afterthought. The narrow definition of risk management is also caused by the apparent preference of auditors and regulators for tangible and precisely quantifiable information.

7.2.2 Distinguishing risk management and due diligence

Another clarification is in order. Risk management must not be confused with due diligence, although the latter is often regarded as a major risk management tool in the alternative asset industry. In fact, discussions around this subject show significant confusion regarding risk *management* (that builds on risk *measurement*), due diligence and monitoring.

Generally speaking, due diligence covers all activities associated with evaluating an individual investment proposal. Meyer and Mathonet (2005) and Talmor and Vasvari (2011) provide a detailed overview of the fund due diligence process. This process entails investigating and evaluating the investment premise of specific partnerships, aiming "... to arrive at better investment decisions by following a rigorous stepwise investigation of specific investment opportunities" (Talmor and Vasvari, 2011, p. 81). Importantly, due diligence is both quantitative and qualitative, focusing, among other things, on the proposed investment strategy the fund in question intends to follow; the organization of the management company; the specific skills and attributes of the team, and its track record; and the legal terms and conditions.

Due diligence is undertaken by the LP's deal teams. To the extent that risk management is involved in the process, this will typically happen relatively late (i.e., close to the final investment decision), for example, to provide a second opinion on the proposal put forward. However, by focusing on a concrete investment proposal, it is outside the scope of the deal teams to examine the potential impact of the investment from a portfolio standpoint. This is precisely where risk management comes in (Table 7.1). More specifically, it is the responsibility of the risk manager to evaluate the expected risk-adjusted return profile of the portfolio and the extent to which this profile is likely to be affected by new investments. Unlike due diligence, which is concerned with a concrete investment proposal, risk management is an ongoing process, covering all aspects of financial risks, including capital risk and liquidity/funding risk (see Chapter 8). As far as co-investment and secondary investment decisions are concerned, risk management typically also focuses on the potential impact of the investment opportunity on the sectoral concentration and foreign exchange exposure of the portfolio.

Investment decisions reflect the set of information that was available at the time when the due diligence and risk management work was undertaken. However, even the most thorough due diligence process cannot fully eliminate investment uncertainty, especially taking into account the long life of limited partnerships spanning 10 years or more. Much can happen during this period, which is difficult – if not impossible – to anticipate. A significant number of

Table 7.1 Main conceptual differences

Risk management	Due diligence	Monitoring
Focus on portfolio of funds	Focus on individual fund	Individual funds and portfolio of funds
Main responsibility of risk manager	Main responsibility of investment manager	Responsibility of investment manager for individual funds, of risk manager for portfolio of funds
Frequently executed with coverage of entire portfolio of funds	One-off with detailed analysis of individual fund proposal	Frequently executed
Ongoing activity (pre- and post-investment)	Mainly pre-investment for investment decision making	Ongoing activity (post-investment)
Quantification of financial risks	Accepting or rejecting investment proposal	Gathering information
Unbiased (i.e., fair) assessment of the portfolio of funds' status	Conservative bias with stringent cut-off criteria	Quick reaction and input into the risk management system
Coverage of all relevant risks for portfolio of funds, notably funding and liquidity risk (see Chapter 8)	Focus on achieving high performance for individual investment proposal, i.e., capital risk	Focus on protecting investment in individual fund and mainly on operational risk

partnerships in private equity and real assets in each vintage year fail to meet investors' return expectations and a non-trivial share of them even fail to return the invested capital (Chapter 10). It is unlikely that such funds include only LPs whose due diligence was sloppy in the first place.

As important as due diligence is, important factors may be overlooked or misjudged, and the fund's original characteristics may change over time, for instance due to "style shift". This necessitates continuous monitoring, which could be seen as "in between" risk management and due diligence, with shared responsibilities between the LP's risk management and its investment managers.

Monitoring is part of a control system for the investment as well as the risk management process (see Figure 7.1). Monitoring of a fund should not be confused with the management of portfolio companies or projects, an activity which is exclusively the responsibility of the GP.

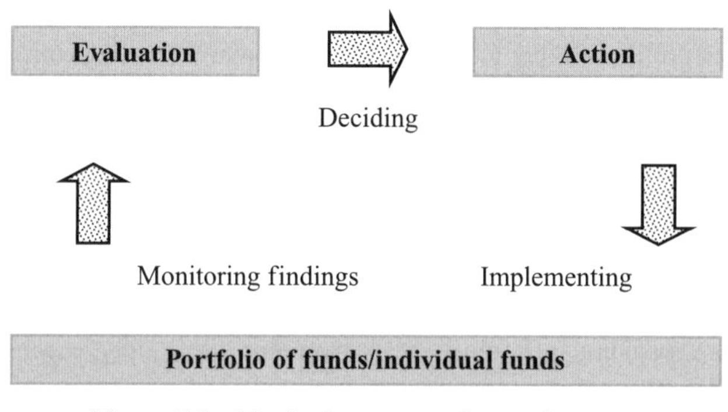

Figure 7.1 Monitoring as part of control system.

By contrast, LPs manage their portfolio of funds and monitor the fund managers (Meyer and Mathonet, 2005). This entails identifying performance-relevant issues by engaging with the GP and other LPs in a partnership, for instance through annual meetings or advisory boards. From the perspective of LPs, monitoring may be described as “ongoing due diligence” to gather information that can be used in the decision process as to whether to invest in one of the GP’s follow-on funds. This information also provides important input for risk measurement purposes. Risk managers primarily monitor the development of the entire portfolio of funds and coordinate possible corrective actions with the investment managers.

7.3 CONCLUSIONS

This chapter has started from one of the most basic observations in finance, namely that higher returns are inevitably associated with higher risk. Even if the efficient market hypothesis may not always hold, it will be difficult for investors in traditional markets to find risk-adjusted excess returns. This experience has motivated an increasing number of investors to venture into alternative asset markets, which are less transparent and efficient and hence provide a greater potential for generating excess returns.

However, this immediately raises the question as to how returns and risk in these markets are measured. As far as investments in illiquid limited partnership funds are concerned, market prices cannot be observed, and in the absence of market prices standard risk measures cannot easily be calculated. Thus, investors face a dilemma. While excess returns in traditional markets hardly exist, the calculation of risk-adjusted returns in non-traditional, illiquid markets is subject to substantial challenges. As a result, traditional risk management and portfolio construction techniques, which are based on the frequentist approach in the Knightian sense, are difficult to apply.

What to do? Academic research has focused on developing methods to extract information from non-observable valuation data that can be used in the traditional CAPM framework. However, such studies have remained rare, and their results suggest that there remains considerable uncertainty about the riskiness of illiquid investments. Furthermore, constrained by the availability of data, much of the available research has focused on market segments that already have a relatively long history, such as US buyouts and US venture. By contrast, there is very little, if any, research on the risk/return profile of investments in partnerships targeting emerging markets, distressed assets or mezzanine. Inevitably, therefore, investors who venture into the dark corners of financial markets have to accept that their investment decisions will need to rely to a significant degree on their subjective qualitative risk assessments. This raises important questions not only from the perspective of the investor, for example, with regard to the treatment of illiquid investments within broader asset allocation and risk modelling. It also raises important issues from a regulatory viewpoint, with financial regulation being embedded typically in quantitative risk models.

In this context, finally, we clarified that risk management should not be confused with due diligence, with the latter focusing on individual investment opportunities rather than examining the entire portfolio, which falls under the auspices of risk management. While the two functions are separate, they complement each other, including during the ongoing monitoring process.

8

Limited Partnership Fund Exposure to Financial Risks

Over the past few decades, investors have increased substantially their exposure to private equity and real assets, predominantly through commitments to limited partnership funds. At the same time, important efforts have been made to improve financial risk management. Arguably, these efforts were to a large extent motivated by repeated financial crises, such as the stock market crash in October 1987; the financial turmoil associated with the balance of payments crises in several emerging markets in the late 1990s and early 2000s; the bursting of the tech bubble in 2000; the sub-prime debacle in the USA that led to the collapse of Lehman Brothers and the Great Recession; and, most recently, the European sovereign debt and banking crisis. However, as Bongaerts and Charlier (2009) argue, the academic literature at the intersection of financial risk management and private equity has remained surprisingly close to an empty set. Similarly, contributions by practitioners have remained rare, with Weidig and Mathonet (2004) and Diller and Herger (2008) representing notable exceptions.

Similar observations can be made on the regulatory side. While the last couple of decades have seen important changes in bank regulation, which have been accompanied by a rapidly expanding literature on the subject, there is very little on the regulatory treatment of private equity and real assets. The Basel Committee on Banking Supervision (BIS, 2001) mentions that investing in private equity usually takes the form of commitments to such partnerships, but remains vague as to the implications for risk management. As far as the insurance industry is concerned, the European Insurance and Occupational Pensions Authority (EIOPA, 2012) does propose particular capital requirements for private equity under Solvency II, but fails to recognize the particular characteristics of limited partnership funds. However, ignoring the specific characteristics of such structures is bound to result in inappropriate capital requirements, which has motivated the EVCA to establish a working group to develop guidelines as to how limited partners in closed-end funds may measure their risk exposure.

Building upon this work,[1] the present chapter identifies the various types of financial risk LPs in limited partnership funds are exposed to. Our emphasis is on those risks that are specific to the particular characteristics of such funds. Thus, we do not discuss risks that are of a general nature, regardless of the particular way of investing. For example, operational risk (including legal and reputational risk) is common to all activities and not specific to investments in funds.[2] Instead, we concentrate on capital risk and liquidity/funding risk as the two major components of financial risk LPs face. As far as funding risk is concerned, we propose a funding test as a critical tool for LPs to manage their liquidity positions in light of undrawn commitments.

[1] For disclosure reasons, three authors of the present book (Cornelius, Diller and Meyer) were members of the EVCA working group.

[2] As far as Basel III is concerned, regulatory capital is calculated for three major components of risk that a bank faces: credit risk, operational risk and market risk. Other risks are not considered to be fully quantifiable at this stage. Solvency II considers market, credit, liquidity, insurance and operational risk, and for the AIFM Directive market, credit and liquidity risk are viewed as "financial risk".

Finally, given the increased amount of cross-border investment flows in private equity and real assets, we discuss the significance of foreign exchange risk.

8.1 EXPOSURE AND RISK COMPONENTS

In standard risk models, financial risk is measured by two variables: (i) the probability of a (negative) event and (ii) the loss an institution may suffer due to that event relative to the institution's total exposure. In credit risk models, for instance, the expected loss is the product of the probability of default and the loss given default (LGD). In quantifying financial risk, it is therefore imperative to determine the institution's exposure and the risks to which its exposed capital is subject.

8.1.1 Defining exposure and identifying financial risks

Turning to investing in private equity and real assets, let us first focus on the question of measuring an LP's exposure to such asset classes. This question is far less trivial than it might seem. Generally speaking, the risk exposure of limited partners is determined by their share in a fund or portfolio of funds (EVCA, 2011). However, given the particular characteristics of self-liquidating partnerships, an LP's exposure may change continuously, depending on how the exposure is actually measured. Importantly, this does not even require that the LP buys or sells shares in the fund. In practice, there is no common policy among LPs, who use one or several of the following measures to determine their exposure: the fund's NAV, its net paid-in capital, the NAV plus the undrawn commitments, the net paid-in capital plus the undrawn commitments or just the fund's commitment. All these measures have shortcomings and do not give a full picture of the risks. A fund's NAV or its net paid-in capital, for instance, does not capture the funding/liquidity risk caused by its undrawn commitments. If (undrawn) commitments are taken into account, the total exposure may exceed the investor's available resources due to overcommitments (Section 8.3).

This confusion comes out clearly from an online conversation among risk managers, as summarized in Box 8.1.

Box 8.1 A conversation among risk practitioners

For years, practitioners have been struggling with the question of how to integrate private equity and real assets into the traditional risk management framework. An exchange of blogs on a website for risk managers mirrors this confusion.[3] The thread had its starting point in the question of how one can possibly measure risk in the absence of observable market prices. While banks were generally believed to use stock prices of listed firms or stock indices as approximations for the value of non-listed firms in their portfolios, this approach was questioned by one blogger who argued that it ignored the idiosyncratic risk of the asset. The discussion can be summarized as follows.

- One participant thought that quantitative modelling would not be of much value. In fact, there was no point in trying to quantify all risks. Instead, it was more important to rely on the experience and intuition of the investor in assessing risk in illiquid funds.

[3] Blog on "private equity – risk measurement", posted by Tim Hellmann, 21 February 2005. See http://www.riskarchive.com/link/ar05-1.htm [accessed 14 October 2008].

- This view was supported by another blogger who believed that such assets do not lend themselves to the quantification of risk. In his view, there are insurmountable challenges arising from the absence of an organized market for these investments: daily pricing, standard performance metrics or disclosure requirements. Furthermore, he stressed that mark-to-market events were rare.
- Given the long investment horizon of commitments to limited partnership funds and the substantial challenges in calculating risk-adjusted returns, the best – and, according to one blogger, perhaps the only – thing risk management could do was to choose investments and fund managers wisely. "After that, about all you can do is monitor [sic] IRR by vintage year and track it against whatever benchmarks you set . . . and hope for the best."
- The literature known to the blogger who had posed the original question was in line with these responses, confirming that one theoretically would need to forecast future cash flows. However, the blogger recognized that every approach to it would be flawed or biased and it would be "almost impossible to have a quantitative measure for the risk." Unfortunately, this was of little help to him as "the banks need some kind of pseudo measurement" even if it makes little sense.[4] Would there be an approach to mitigate the identified shortcomings and generate a model for risk measurement that is as good as possible?
- One respondent proposed to throw "together some garbage spreadsheet and tell them it is based on extreme value theory." Another suggested using rules of thumb of the kind that if the private equity portfolio generates a return of less than 6 percentage points per year below the Wilshire 5000 or Russell 3000, the portfolio is subject to "high" risk. If it generates a return of 9+ percentage points greater than the index, so the argument put forward in the blog, it has "low" risk. Anything in between represents a "moderate" level of risk.

Overall, the blogs suggest that risk managers were more concerned with developing "pseudo risk metrics" to address particular regulatory requirements rather than designing sound risk management practices. In this spirit, the bloggers came to the conclusion that regulators believe that "private equity investments are at least 8.5 times more risky than investments in residential mortgages. Under this flawed rationale, you can simply track the price volatility of residential mortgages and multiply it by 8.5 to estimate the risk in your private equity portfolio."

The frustration with measuring risk in limited partnerships that is expressed in the blogs seems to be shared more widely. Interviewing a consultant, Kreutzer (2008) reports that managing risk in private equity was essentially a function of proper due diligence and relationship management: "You really want to know people that you're doing business with. You can quantify leverage on earning streams but it can be monkeyed with. It's not an easy thing to

[4] This view resembles an anecdote in Danielsson (2008): "A well-known American economist, drafted during World War II to work in the US Army meteorological service in England, got a phone call from a general in May 1944 asking for the weather forecast for Normandy in early June. The economist replied that it was impossible to forecast weather that far into the future. The general wholeheartedly agreed but nevertheless needed the number now for planning purposes." To have numbers seems to be more important than whether the numbers are meaningful and useful.

approach scientifically." In the consultant's view, the attempt to quantify risk in a systematic way was probably "a waste of time".

In Chapter 10, we address the issue of undrawn commitments in greater detail. While undrawn commitments are usually treated as an asset whose NPV is zero and hence are ignored, the experience of many investors during the recent global financial crisis suggests that undrawn commitments do matter in determining an investor's exposure to financial risks associated with investments in limited partnership funds in private equity and real assets.

Let us now turn to the second component of financial risk management, the identification and quantification of financial risks, given an LP's exposure to illiquid investments. As we discuss in the following, we can distinguish between two main types of risk in fund investments, i.e. (i) capital risk – the risk that their invested capital plus an expected return is not returned and (ii) liquidity risk – the risk that the investor's liquidity position does not allow him to respond to capital calls (funding risk) as well as the risk that he is unable to liquidate his shares in the secondary market (market liquidity risk), disabling permanent portfolio rebalancing.

8.1.2 Capital risk

In assessing the capital risk of fund investments, it is important to distinguish between the LP's commitment to a self-liquidating partnership and the GP's acquisition of assets. As far as private equity is concerned, the acquisition of a portfolio company obviously represents an equity investment in the company's capital structure. However, it is less clear how fund investments by LPs should be treated. Arguably, they share certain credit characteristics in the sense that investors provide capital that may or may not be returned to them after a period defined in the LPA. Thus, shares in a fund, which are highly illiquid, are subject to what may be considered as default risk (Meyer and Mathonet, 2005). Consistent with this view, rating-like approaches have been developed for evaluating the risks of limited partnership funds (see Chapter 13). Such approaches, which group funds into different risk categories, are widely used in the industry and have been endorsed by the Basel Committee (BIS, 2001).

However, in the context of limited partnership funds, there is no common definition of a default event. Theoretically, a default for a fund could be defined as the failure to pay back capital to the LPs. Alternatively, a GP could already be in default if he fails to meet a certain hurdle rate of return. The problem with such definitions is, though, that the default event can only be determined at the end of the fund's lifetime and therefore does not form an "annualizable event" in the true sense.[5]

Nevertheless, a number of practitioners and researchers have tried to apply existing credit portfolio models to private equity. Krohmer and Man (2007), for example, use a dataset provided by the Center of Private Equity Research (CEPRES). Their sample includes 252 private equity funds with 16,097 investments in 12,008 portfolio companies in 1971–2006. They employ a default model that is based on Wilson's CreditPortfolioView™. In their model, a default is defined as a total loss with an IRR of –100%, with the PD/LGD of funds being determined by simulating the development of portfolio companies. As far as venture capital is

[5] At the fund level it is difficult to obtain a sufficiently broad and unbiased sample to estimate a probability of default and loss given default (PD/LGD). Publicly available databases on private equity are typically subject to an important survivor bias and most datasets provide only aggregated figures that are of limited use. BIS (2001) discusses a PD/LGD approach but in a conversation with some of the authors in the early 2000s the Basel Committee explained that they did not see this as applicable to funds. They did agree that a PD/LGD approach could potentially be applied to debt-funded direct investments, as followed by Bongaerts and Charlier (2009).

concerned, Krohmer and Man (2007) find a default rate of 30%, significantly higher than for buyouts (11.5%).

These estimates appear high, especially when compared with studies by Weidig and Mathonet (2004) and Diller (2007). A key issue that limits the applicability of credit risk models to limited partnership funds lies in the fact that such models only reflect downside risk. Aggregating the PD/LGD figures for individual funds, without taking into account the upside potential of other funds, is bound to lead to excessive overall risk weights for portfolios of funds. Diversified portfolios of funds are significantly less risky than a single fund as the upside of well-performing funds compensates for the losses from "defaulting" funds – implying that economic capital should be allocated to fund portfolios rather than individual partnerships. Indeed, the Basel Committee has long accepted that unrecognized and unrealized gains (or latent revaluation gains) on equity investments can act as a buffer against losses (BIS, 2001). We shall return to this issue in greater detail in Chapter 9.

8.1.3 Liquidity risk

The financial crisis beginning in 2008 highlighted again the importance of managing liquidity risk. In response to this market turmoil, the Basel Committee on Banking Supervision issued principles for sound liquidity risk management (BIS, 2008):

> "Liquidity is the ability of a bank to fund increases in assets and meet obligations as they come due, without incurring unacceptable losses. [...] effective liquidity risk management helps ensure a bank's ability to meet cash flow obligations, which are uncertain as they are affected by external events and other agents' behaviour."

In fact, regulators now generally see liquidity risk management as of paramount importance and require that regulated investors have a sound process for identifying, measuring, monitoring and controlling liquidity risk:

> "This process should include a robust framework for comprehensively projecting cash flows arising from assets, liabilities and off-balance sheet items over an appropriate set of time horizons."

Liquidity risk can generally be defined as the potential loss due to time-varying liquidity costs. Investors in limited partnership funds take substantial exposure to liquidity risk: undrawn commitments can be seen as economic obligations, and LPs have to apply liquidity management processes along the lines described by the Basel Committee. In general, "liquidity" comprises market liquidity (Stange and Kaserer, 2009) and funding liquidity.

Market liquidity

Market liquidity risk arises from situations in which a party interested in trading an asset cannot do it because nobody in the market wants to trade that asset or only at a price that is far away from its – or its "last observed" – fair value (Dowd, 2001; Buhl, 2004; Amihud and Mendelson, 2006). Market liquidity risk can be reflected, for example, in steep discounts to valuations, in the need to hold liquid cash reserves or by the need to hold on to assets over longer periods than desired. Thus, investors in limited partnership funds will usually require an illiquidity premium that compensates them for the inability to constantly rebalance their portfolios – a critical assumption in standard asset pricing models.

Funding liquidity

Funding liquidity can be defined as the ability to settle obligations immediately as they come due. Funding liquidity risk relates to the possibility that, over a specific horizon, investors are unable to honour their obligations or can only meet them at an uneconomically high price (Drehmann and Nikolaou, 2008). Typically, LPs have to respond to a fund's capital call within a short timeframe of just 10 days or even less. This requires them to either keep sufficient cash reserves at any point in time or to liquidate other assets at short notice. As already discussed, a LP who is unable to meet his obligations by providing funding in response to a capital call would become a defaulting investor and, in the extreme, might lose his entire invested capital in the fund. The LP's ability to either hold on to his commitment to a fund and thus extract its full long-term value or to conduct an orderly secondary transaction at a fair price depends on keeping this funding risk under control.

Box 8.2 Development of distributions from private equity funds

Prior to the recent global financial crisis of 2008, liquidity management of larger fund portfolios arguably did not pose a critical challenge for investors as distributions were common and large. Many investors had increased their private equity commitments amid rapid economic growth, low interest rates and rising valuations. However, the picture changed dramatically when distributions dried up almost completely as valuations tumbled and exit markets shut. Although drawdowns also slowed significantly as the financial crisis deepened, cash outflows increasingly outpaced cash inflows, causing mounting problems for many investors' cash-management approaches. Especially hard hit were investors pursuing overcommitment strategies.

According to data provided by Thomson Reuters (as of September 2011), distributions fell from a record high of USD 120 billion in 2007 to USD 51 billion in 2008 before more than halving again to USD 24 billion in 2009. While capital calls decreased as well, their decline was comparatively less pronounced. For 2009, Thomson Reuters reports that capital calls from private equity funds totalled USD 58 billion in 2009, exceeding distributions by a factor of 2.4. Thus, many investors required additional funding from other sources to honour their capital calls in order to avoid fire sales in the secondary market.

Typically, LPs use the distributions from mature funds to respond to capital calls from less mature funds within their portfolio (see Box 8.2). This works well for portfolios of funds that are well diversified over time and under "normal" market conditions. However, as experience during the recent global financial crisis has shown, cash flow models may break down in periods of severe market dislocations, unexpectedly forcing investors to seek additional financing to cover the shortfall.

8.1.4 Market risk and illiquidity

Capital risk and liquidity risk in fund investments have received surprisingly little attention in the literature, which we have reviewed briefly in Chapter 5. Instead, to the extent that academic studies have attempted to measure risk in private equity, they have focused on market risk in the framework of standard asset-pricing models, such as the CAPM. Much of this debate has concentrated on the empirical problems of estimating alphas and betas (infrequent observations of valuations, potential sample biases in available databases) and their interpretation, given the restrictive assumptions of such models (transparent, liquid and low-friction markets).

From a more fundamental standpoint, the question arises as to how relevant market risk really is for investors in limited partnership funds. Implicitly, it is assumed that the short-term variation of valuations of illiquid fund investments – however measured – matter for LPs as much as the variation of prices of their portfolios of marketable instruments. This view may be disputed on the grounds that long-term investors in limited partnership funds deliberately decide to lock in capital for a period of 10 years and more. At the time when LPs make commitments to such funds, they have usually no intention of selling their stakes before maturity and should therefore be less concerned about quarterly changes in the NAV of their fund investments.

However, as we have seen in Chapter 6, LPs do sell their stakes in the secondary market. Sometimes, such sales are motivated by a strategic reorientation, but in the majority of cases divestment decisions have been driven by liquidity problems. Interim valuations therefore do matter, even if LPs intend to hold their fund investments until the end of the partnership's life. Market risk and liquidity risk are therefore closely intertwined, which has encouraged researchers to examine the impact of illiquidity on portfolio construction (e.g., Ang *et al.*, 2011), and more specifically on the optimal holdings of private equity. As regards the latter, Ang and Sorensen (2011) argue that "(o)ne way of interpreting the risks and returns of PE investments, especially for illiquidity risk, is for an investor to consider PE from an investor-specific asset allocation context". This is exactly what we propose in the following section – to conduct a funding test to ensure that the LP's specific funding needs are always met.

8.2 FUNDING TEST

As we discussed in Chapter 6, the secondary market is an imperfect price discovery mechanism for a limited partnership fund's fair market value. In the absence of observable market prices, risk managers have to turn to model-based approaches. Models, however, are generally based on the critical assumption that the LP is able to hold on to his assets or, alternatively, is able to sell his assets under normal market conditions. However, the question arises as to how a fair market value can be determined in a distressed sale. Unfortunately, industry valuation guidelines provide little guidance on this important question.[6] Against this background, it is critical for LPs to ensure that they do not have to sell in a situation of distress and always have sufficient resources available to respond to capital calls for the remaining undrawn commitments through a so-called "funding test". Although the total amount of undrawn commitments is known, the amount and timing of individual drawdowns are not.

There are various approaches to a funding test, ranging from the simple monitoring of key ratios to a more sophisticated scenario analysis for future cash flows. Ratio analysis focuses on setting key accounting variables in relation to each other and monitoring their behaviour over time in an effort to extract risk-relevant information. It is a quantitative technique for comparing a firm on a relative basis to other firms or to the market in general. Changes

[6] See, for example, EVCA (2005). The International Private Equity and Venture Capital Valuation Guidelines establish an industry standard for determining a fair value for these specific illiquid assets.

in ratios can help signal in which direction the portfolio is developing. Key ratios that are indicative of a LP's funding risk are the current ratio (CR), the adjusted current ratio (ACR), the overcommitment ratio (OCR) and the outstanding commitment level (OCL) (Mathonet and Meyer, 2007).

The CR is a standard tool to analyse a firm's capacity to finance its short-term liabilities by its short-term resources:

$$\text{CR} = \frac{\text{current assets}}{\text{current liabilities}}$$

The CR can be interpreted as a measure of a firm's ability to survive over the near term by being able to meet obligations with the available liquidity. A CR of 100% means that even without doing any business, the firm could theoretically survive for 1 year. A low CR is a signal that the available liquidity would be insufficient. However, over the long term a high CR could also be an indication of inefficient use of the firm's resources. In any case, it is obviously risky to overcommit for a CR below 100%.

However, for portfolios of limited partnership funds the CR is of limited explanatory power as it ignores the undrawn commitments.

- In the short term, a LP will have to pay a part of its current undrawn commitment, which can be considered as a short-term liability (percentage times undrawn commitments).
- Furthermore, the percentage of the distributions that will be received by the LP has to be taken into consideration (percentage times paid-in).

These items are reflected in the ACR:

$$\text{ACR} = \frac{\text{current assets} + (\% \times \text{paid-in})}{\text{current liabilities} + (\% \times \text{undrawn commitment})}$$

The projected amount of distributions as a percentage of the current paid-in depends on the maturity of the portfolio of funds. This figure, and the share of the undrawn commitments to be disbursed in the short term based on the current cumulative outstanding commitment, can be determined based on the analysis of historical data.

The OCR is defined as the ratio of undrawn commitments of limited partnership funds relative to available resources. Undrawn commitments are the aggregated commitments for individual funds, whereas the definition of resources available depends on the individual investor. For funds-of-funds, the resources available are simply the commitments from their investors. For insurance companies, banks and other institutional investors, "resources available" are liquid assets – or sometimes even clearly predefined and fixed future income streams – that have been allocated for fund investments in private equity and real assets.

$$\text{OCR} = \frac{\text{undrawn commitment}}{\text{resources available for commitments}}$$

The calculation of the OCR thus depends on the definition of "resources available". The most conservative case for an investor would be to avoid all risk and cover all undrawn commitments through available resources in the form of cash. However, in reality only very few LPs invest their undrawn capital risk-free. Therefore, the challenge for investors is to find the appropriate OCR. To some degree, overcommitments are unavoidable as the committed capital is only called over several years and for some funds not even the full commitment is drawn.

An OCR below 100% typically suggests an inefficient use of resources. Above 100%, the ability of an overcommitted investor to honour its commitments and to avoid default decreases proportionally to an increase in the OCR. Opinions vary in terms of the degree of overcommitments that would still be seen as prudent. Generally speaking, OCRs in the range of 105–115% would still be seen as relatively prudent. In practice, however, OCRs of between 125% and 150% are not untypical (Mathonet and Meyer, 2007), a level that warrants increasing attention. As long as there is no additional funding, the expected distributions of the existing portfolio put a natural limit on commitments to new funds given the availability of funding. Consequently, the long-term average return of the asset class puts a ceiling on pursuing overcommitment strategies.

Financial analysis typically differentiates between short-term, medium-term and long-term liquidity ratios. We suggest monitoring three different ratios:

- OCR1, mirroring immediately available cash; i.e. through cash holdings or liquidity facilities.
- OCR2 as the sum of OCR1 assets and potential proceeds from selling highly liquid assets, for example, high-grade sovereign bonds and equities.
- OCR3 as the sum of OCR2 assets and proceeds from selling assets that can be liquidated over a timeframe of several weeks, such as corporate bonds.

Therefore:

$$\text{OCR1} \geq \text{OCR2} \geq \text{OCR3}$$

Comparing the undrawn commitments to the total commitments provides information on the maturity of the portfolio. The OCL is defined as:

$$\text{OCL} = \frac{\text{undrawn commitments}}{\text{total commitments}}$$

Assuming that there is no change in the investment and commitment strategies, the current OCL can be indicative of the capital expected to be drawn down over the following financial year. It is important to maintain a reasonable OCL over time as it represents a future liability.

Obviously, the monitoring of these ratios can only be a first line of defence (see Box 8.3). A proper funding test should be based on the assessment of several cash flow scenarios (Figure 8.1). Without being able to honour all capital calls over the portfolio of funds' entire lifetime, the investor would either default on investments or sell parts of his portfolio, and in the extreme case the entire portfolio, on the secondary market. Depending on the market cycle, selling a stake in a fund or a portfolio of funds may be possible only at substantial discounts, putting the LP in a different risk position.

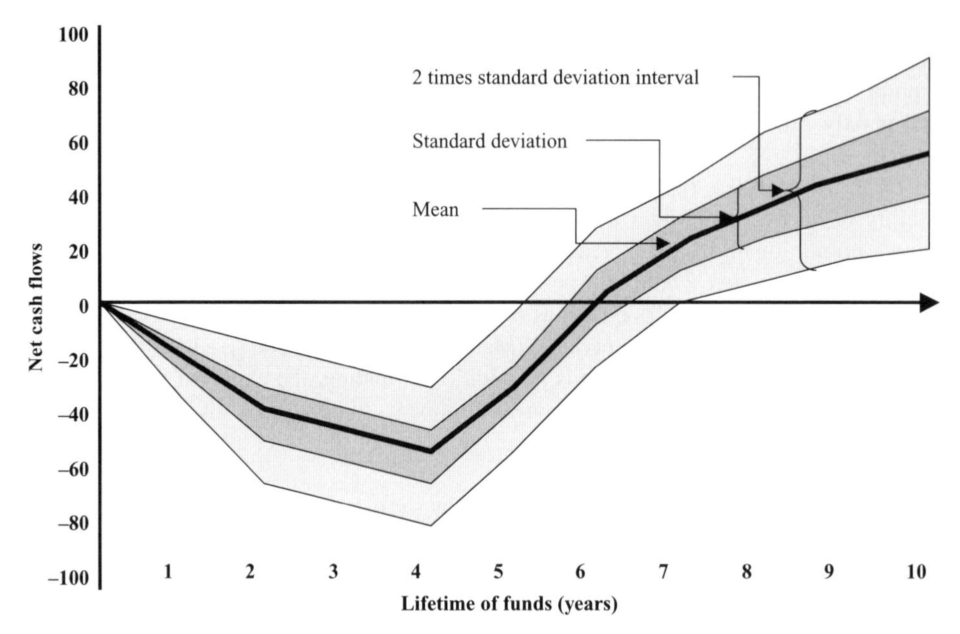

Figure 8.1 Cash flow projection for a portfolio of 10 private equity funds.

Box 8.3 Monitoring the overcommitment ratio

How can we use these ratios? We limit our discussion to the OCR and assume two different investors who are planning to invest in the same private equity programme.

- Investor A is an insurance company that invests 4.4% of its total assets in illiquid assets. The insurance company receives quarterly net inflows from its operative businesses of EUR 75 million, which will be directed to all asset classes. Overall, the insurance company has total assets of EUR 2 billion with an allocation of 75.6% to bonds, 15% to equity and 4.4% to illiquid assets. The remainder, 5%, is held in cash.
- Investor B is an endowment, which has a total available cash volume of EUR 55 million. In addition, a liquidity facility of EUR 10 million is arranged.

Both investors have made capital commitments to a portfolio of 10 funds, with a total commitment size of EUR 150 million over the last three vintage years. An amount of EUR 50 million has already been drawn by the GPs, leaving EUR 100 million as undrawn commitments.

Both investors would like to analyse if their current cash holdings are enough to live through different market scenarios. As a first indication, we can calculate the different OCRs for each investor.

- Investor A has an OCR1 of 100% as the cash holdings amount to EUR 100 million. In addition, a continuous net cash inflow decreases OCR2 to more than 57% (and even lower when taking all highly liquid bonds and equities into account). Hence, investor A has no liquidity issues and it can be expected that he will be able to hold its portfolio through various market phases without any problems.

- Investor B has an OCR1 of 154% and is hence running an overcommitment strategy. As there are currently no other sources of income other than the cash account and expected private equity distributions, it is a significant risk that the investor B (endowment) runs out of liquidity.

To assess the probability of investor B becoming a defaulting LP, we need to take a closer look at various cash flow scenarios taking future distributions into account (see Figure 8.1). Under normal market conditions, the cash requirements for such a portfolio of private equity funds are expected to be near the mean case – which is the black line in the middle of the grey area – a total cash requirement of EUR 55 million. This amount could be provided by both investor A and B.

However, under adverse market conditions, cash requirements can rise substantially. Although contributions and distributions should be in balance over the long term, under such a scenario exits and further financing required for portfolio companies may deviate substantially in the short and even medium term. In a distressed market environment, the acquisition of assets by private equity funds typically slows amid heightened investment uncertainty. However, the pace of investment activity is likely to slow less than the pace of distributions, which may come to a grinding halt as exit markets shut. In fact, the pace of drawdowns may be unchanged as GPs try to take advantage of lower entry prices amid deepening market dislocations as they may need to contribute more equity due to the lack of investors' demand for leveraged loans and high-yield bonds. As a result, (net) cash requirements may rise significantly.

Given the simulation of cash flows under alternative scenarios, cash reserves (including liquidity facilities) of EUR 65 million would be sufficient for covering possible outcomes in the range of the standard deviation (as visualized in Figure 8.1). However, there is a serious default risk for investor B. In a scenario similar to a 2 times standard deviation, investor B would face a shortfall of EUR 11 million, given net cash flow requirements of EUR 76 billion. To avoid a default, investor B would be forced to sell parts of his private equity portfolio in the secondary market or liquidate other assets – realistically those that have deep and liquid markets.

8.3 CROSS-BORDER TRANSACTIONS AND FOREIGN EXCHANGE RISK

The preceding discussion has taken a general view of financial risks investors in limited partnership funds are exposed to. An additional risk dimension arises, however, if investments involve cross-border transactions which are subject to foreign exchange risk. As long as national markets for private equity and real assets were largely separated, this type of investment risk did not matter much. However, as markets have become more integrated and LPs have committed capital to foreign currency-denominated funds, which in turn make cross-border acquisitions, investors have increasingly become exposed to currency fluctuations. Thus, we dedicate a special section to this particular type of risk, which interacts with both capital and liquidity risk.

8.3.1 Limited partner exposure to foreign exchange risk

Exchange rate changes are particularly relevant over longer time spans. Thus, LPs who want to diversify their alternative investment portfolios internationally have a keen interest in monitoring and managing their foreign exchange exposure.

Foreign exchange risk is often thought to lie in sudden jumps in bilateral rates in the wake of balance of payments crises. These crises typically occur if a country pursues a fixed exchange rate policy that can no longer be defended as reserves are being depleted amid unsustainable current account deficits and capital outflows. Reinhardt and Rogoff (2009) give a comprehensive overview of balance of payments crises, most of which, at least in the last couple of decades, have occurred in emerging economies (e.g., Mexico, 1994; Asia, 1997; Russia, 1998; Brazil, 1999; Argentina, 2001. A notable exception is the foreign exchange crisis in the United Kingdom in 1992, which forced the country to leave the European exchange rate mechanism). These currency crashes have significantly reduced, or entirely wiped out, foreign investors' returns.

However, foreign exchange risk is by no means limited to investments in emerging economies. While virtually all advanced countries today maintain flexible exchange rate regimes that make a sudden collapse much less likely, their foreign exchange rates do move significantly, reflecting inflation differentials, divergent monetary policies as well as speculative capital flows, for example, associated with carry trades. Take, for example, the USD/EUR rate, which links the world's two most important markets for private equity and real assets. In 2001, 2 years after the introduction of Europe's single currency, a US investor had to pay 0.82 US dollars for 1 euro. In 2008, the exchange rate had nearly doubled to almost 1.60. Between mid-2002 and mid-2003, the value of the US dollar fell by 26% relative to the euro, a movement which would have qualified as a currency crash according to Frankel and Rose's (1996) definition.

8.3.2 Dimensions of foreign exchange risk

Foreign exchange risk has several dimensions for investors in limited partnership funds. To begin with, an investor who commits capital to a foreign currency-denominated fund is exposed to currency movements between the point in time when he makes a commitment in a currency that is not his home currency and when the GP draws down the capital. Suppose that the currency in which the fund is denominated has appreciated against the investor's home currency. As a result, the contributions in the investor's home currency exceed the original commitment to the fund, which may cause liquidity problems. Conversely, the LP may find himself underexposed to private equity and real assets relative to his target exposure.

Second, exchange rate movements affect the performance of a foreign fund when the returns are converted into the investor's home currency. An investor based in the Eurozone is interested in returns in euros, just as much as a US-based investor is interested in returns in US dollars rather than in local currency returns. To the extent that the home currency has appreciated over the lifespan of the fund, the impact will be negative, other things being equal. However, the impact may also be positive if the home currency depreciates during the lifespan of the limited partnership.

At a third level, investors are exposed to foreign exchange risk to the extent that the fund itself makes acquisitions in foreign currencies. Suppose, for example, a Eurozone pension fund commits capital to a euro-based partnership, which uses part of its capital to acquire sterling-denominated assets in the United Kingdom and dollar-denominated assets in the United States. To make things even more complex, consider now the following situation where the European pension fund commits capital to a US-based private equity fund, which in turn acquires assets in Latin America in local currency.

The foreign exchange risk LPs take when committing to foreign currency-denominated funds may be mitigated by cross-border acquisitions undertaken by the partnerships they have invested in. For instance, several global USD-denominated funds backed by European limited partners have actually acquired European assets. However, foreign exchange risk at the fund investment level may also be amplified by foreign exchange risk at the portfolio company level, depending on the timing and direction of investments.

There is even a fourth level of foreign exchange risk, to the extent that portfolio companies are engaged in foreign transactions through trade and treasury operations. However, this risk is not different from the foreign exchange risk publicly listed companies may be exposed to. Furthermore, at the company level, foreign exchange risk is typically hedged and will therefore not be considered specifically in the rest of the book.

8.3.3 Impact on fund returns

How relevant is foreign exchange risk for LPs in terms of the fund returns in local currency? Using quarterly cash flows from a large number of partnerships of a Eurozone-based fund-of-funds investor, Cornelius (2011) estimates that the foreign exchange effect is indeed sizable. For example, IRR returns on investments made in USD-denominated funds in 2002 were reduced by more than 5 percentage points as of 30 September 2009 thanks to the depreciation of the US dollar against the euro during this period. Given that the long-term average of private equity returns (net of fees) has been around 15%, this implies that foreign exchange rate movements may have a significant impact on portfolio performance in the investor's home currency. Admittedly, some of the losses calculated by Cornelius (2011) have probably been recouped more recently as the US dollar regained ground in 2011–2012. However, the overall picture is clear – foreign exchange risk matters, and not only for cross-border commitments to funds in emerging economies.

As Cornelius (2011) shows further, foreign exchange rate risk also matters for GPs who invest abroad. The returns of the fund in the fund's currency may be boosted by favourable currency movements – or vice versa. For example, a US-based fund, which acquired a European company in 2001 and sold this company in 2006, would have made a significant foreign exchange gain thanks to the appreciation of the euro during this period. This raises a number of fundamental questions. How should a LP benchmark funds in their due diligence? Should returns due to currency movements be considered as sheer luck and hence irrelevant for the GP's track record? And how should currency gains (and losses) be treated from the point of view of carried interest?

While it is relatively straightforward to calculate *ex post* the impact of foreign exchange rate changes on the performance of funds, it is far more difficult to measure the exact degree of foreign exchange risk a given portfolio is exposed to. The LP knows, of course, the share of capital he has committed to foreign currency-denominated funds. And he also knows on a look-through basis the foreign exchange exposure that arises from cross-border investments made by the funds. What he doesn't know, however, is the foreign exchange risk his unfunded commitments are subject to. Although the limited partnership agreements typically provide some guidance as to how much a fund can invest outside their home markets, ceilings have become increasingly flexible to allow GPs to chase attractive deals across different markets.

8.3.4 Hedging against foreign exchange risk?

As far as limited partners are concerned, the particular characteristics of investments in illiquid funds render traditional hedging instruments largely irrelevant.[7] Using forward contracts, futures, currency swaps and options requires knowing the timing and the amount of cash flows that are subject to foreign exchange risk. This is generally not the case, however. Cash flow libraries can only provide an approximation of expected contributions and distributions, which is not sufficient to employ standard hedging instruments. This challenge applies especially to relatively young portfolios that consist of a limited number of funds. Furthermore, foreign exchange hedging is expensive, adding to the challenges LPs face when making commitments to international funds, which themselves operate across borders.

Thus, long-term investors are left with two options. The first option is just to "go naked". As Froot (1993) has argued, currency hedges have very different properties at long horizons compared with short horizons. In fact, at long horizons fully hedged international investments may actually have greater return variance than their unhedged counterparts. Suppose, for example, a US real estate fund makes an acquisition in the Eurozone. Suppose further that the euro depreciates in the short term due to unanticipated disturbances that lead to currency-induced losses in the value of the investment for the US-based investor. With the price level remaining unchanged in the short run, the euro also depreciates in real terms. However, if purchasing power parity holds in the long run, the price level in the Eurozone should increase relative to the United States, resulting in a real appreciation of the euro. To the extent that the value of the investment is linked to the national price level, the price effect should offset the currency effect in the long term. Thus, the investment is "naturally hedged" over long horizons.

The second option is a currency overlay. This option is usually pursued by large international investors who employ currency overlays for their entire portfolios, not just their portfolio of alternative investments. Currency overlay strategies are typically delegated to an external or in-house specialized manager who decides on the positions taken in currencies and manages currency risk. With currencies regarded as financial prices, the client usually determines a benchmark hedge ratio that reflects the investor's desired neutral currency exposure. How currency overlay strategies can be designed is discussed, for example, in Solnik and McLeavey (2009).

8.3.5 Foreign exchange exposure as a potential portfolio diversifier

Modelling cash flows for limited partnership funds, as we discuss in Chapter 11, enables LPs to undertake a risk component analysis that offers additional insights regarding foreign exchange risk. A simple way to show the impact of exchange rate changes on capital risk lies in the recalculation of cash flows at a historically fixed exchange rate. Importantly, investing internationally can increase the volatility of cash flows but may also decrease the capital risk of a portfolio of funds thanks to potential diversification effects. Whether an investment in a fund that is raised in a foreign currency reduces overall risk for the LP essentially depends on the behaviour of exchange rate movements relative to the fund's cash flows. In this context, it

[7] From a GP's perspective, hedging may be a more feasible option under certain circumstances, given that the timing of deals and their exits are determined by the fund manager. In fact, the timing may be influenced by the GP's view on possible exchange rate misalignments. For instance, if the GP is of the view that the currency in which the foreign investment is made is overvalued and is likely to mean-revert against the GP's home currency, he is likely to bring forward the divestment, other things being equal.

is important to note that exchange rate expectations are typically an important variable in the GP's investment and divestment decisions. While limited partnership agreements tend to be relatively vague in terms of a fund's foreign currency exposure and its management – beyond certain ceilings for investments in currencies other than the fund's currency – it is important for LPs to monitor closely their foreign exchange risk at the portfolio level with a view to their liquidity needs.

8.4 CONCLUSIONS

At the most basic level, the proper management of financial risks in illiquid assets requires (i) knowing an investor's exposure to such assets and (ii) identifying the risks this exposure is subject to. As trivial as this seems, there remains substantial confusion about both dimensions.

While we have emphasized the importance of undrawn commitments, an issue we return to in Chapter 10 in greater detail, much of the debate in the present chapter has focused on the definition of financial risks. As we have argued, LPs in limited partnership funds are subject to two key risks – capital risk and liquidity risk. Capital risk refers to the risk that a fund fails to return the investor's capital, but as we have discussed this risk should be seen from a portfolio perspective instead of taking a fund-specific view that is akin to a credit risk assessment.

Liquidity risk arises from the fact that shares in a fund cannot easily be liquidated in the secondary market (market liquidity risk) and that capital calls and distributions are uncertain with respect to their timing. This does not mean that market risk, the focus of academic research in the context of standard asset pricing models as well as from a regulatory standpoint, is unimportant. In fact, market risk, capital risk and liquidity risk are closely intertwined. Arguably, however, long-term investors are less concerned about short-term fluctuations in asset valuations in asset classes where they deliberately lock in capital for 10 years and more.

If there had been a need to stress the importance of liquidity risk, the recent global financial crisis would have been the perfect proof. Against this background, this chapter has emphasized the role of funding tests based on key financial ratios and scenario analysis. This discussion will be taken up again in Chapter 12, where we focus on cash flow projections.

Finally, we have focused on foreign exchange risk, a special risk that is associated with cross-border transactions in different currencies. Foreign exchange rate risk has several dimensions, and each dimension has important implications for the performance of fund investments, the underlying cash flows, and hence capital and liquidity risk. While a LP's ability to hedge foreign exchange rate risk is strictly limited, it is critical for him to monitor this exposure closely from a portfolio standpoint with regard to the impact of exchange rate movements on the portfolio's overall risk level.

9 Value-at-Risk

The VaR concept has become a standard approach in the toolkit of financial risk managers and regulators. Generally, the VaR is interpreted as the maximum mark-to-market loss a given portfolio can suffer for a given time horizon and a given confidence level. In essence, the VaR aims to calculate the portfolio impact of rare events. For instance, on a 1-year horizon and at a typical confidence level of 99.5%, the estimated loss should occur only once every 200 years, given historical market movements of asset prices (for a general overview of the VaR concept, see Jorion, 2006).

The VaR has been criticized for a number of reasons. For instance, it has been claimed that the VaR gives a false sense of confidence as it ignores tail risk and may even lead to excessive risk taking. Rather than making VaR control the chief concern, it has been claimed that it is far more important for risk managers to worry about portfolio losses that may be suffered if the VaR is exceeded. While we agree with most of the criticism, we believe that the VaR may still provide important insights for a risk manager as long as he is aware of the shortcomings of the approach. We concur with Jorion and Taleb (1997), who argue that "the greatest benefit of VAR [sic] lies in the imposition of a structured methodology for critically thinking about risk. Thus the process of getting to VAR [sic] may be as important as the number itself".

While we have little to add to this debate, we start from the observation that VaR has become an integral part of financial regulation ever since financial institutions were allowed to use VaR in regulated capital modelling in 1996.[1] Given increasing requirements regarding risk reporting and integrated risk management practices, it is probably only a question of time until VaR will be extended beyond traditional asset classes. However, this raises important questions as to how VaR can be estimated for portfolios of limited partnership funds, which are highly illiquid and for which market prices are not observable.

9.1 DEFINITION

For a given portfolio of funds, probability and time horizon, the VaR at time t_0 is defined as the loss on the portfolio over a given time horizon $[t_0, t_1]$ and for a given probability level $\alpha, 0 \leq \alpha \leq 1$. In order to calculate VaR, it is generally assumed that there are normal economic conditions and no changes in the composition of the portfolio of funds.

While regulators require confidence levels of typically 99–99.5%, this may not be meaningful for illiquid assets, given the limited number of data points risk managers typically work with. The danger of putting this threshold too high is that risk parameters cannot be validated empirically. Potential losses may be less extreme but more frequent than

[1] See for example Hendricks (1996), Duffie and Pan (1997) and Dowd *et al.* (2004). As the VaR approach was originally designed for investment banks heavily involved in trading, one may ask to what extent it is applicable to illiquid asset classes. However, concepts like credit-VaR demonstrate that related risk measures can be derived in a similar fashion as market risk.

those associated with once-in-200-year events. As Mittnik (2011) argues, a focus "on such extreme risks is like asking a medical doctor to determine the right dosage of treatment and providing her with a thermometer that only indicates temperatures of 42 degrees Celsius and higher".

Generally, the proper measurement of risk of limited partnership funds requires the "fair" valuation of such investments. Thus, risk modelling should fulfil the following criteria:

1. Risk models need to be *complete*, in the sense that all relevant risk parameters are taken into account.
2. Financial risk in limited partnerships is generally modelled with regard to specific return variables, normally the IRR or the multiple. The outcome of risk modelling must be *reconcilable* with the cash flow scenarios, which form the basis for the risk estimates.
3. Risk measures should be *unbiased* with respect to the specific characteristics of a fund's life, notably the well-known J-curve pattern. For the entire population of the funds in a portfolio at a given stage of their life, the weighted average NPV must be zero.
4. Other things being equal, the range of projected outcomes for returns should narrow as funds mature. Thus, risk in illiquid investing in limited partnerships is subject to a *monotonic* decline over the life of a fund.
5. Back-testing a risk model requires asset prices to be *observable*. While prices of marketable instruments can be observed though market transactions, risk models for illiquid assets need to rely on approximations or be based on observable liquidity events.
6. Measuring risk in illiquid fund investments needs to take into account that risk can be mitigated through diversification or amplified by overcommitment strategies. Risks are *inter-related* (which is ignored in the PD/LGD approach, for instance).

These criteria raise an important issue – how can we define the value that may be potentially at risk? And how do market fluctuations affect that value?

In principle, there are two methods for valuing assets. The first is the current market valuation as evidenced by prices observed in recent transactions, or an estimate of what that price might be. The second is the present value (PV) of the estimated future cash flows from that asset. In liquid markets, arbitrage ensures that the two methods are closely aligned. However, illiquidity and other market inefficiencies may cause the two methods to diverge, sometimes even substantially.

9.2 VALUE-AT-RISK BASED ON NAV TIME SERIES

In finance, risk is generally measured by the volatility of the price of an asset. Consistent with the standard mean–variance approach, risk in private equity and similar asset classes is usually calculated using (quarterly) changes in the NAV of a pool of funds (e.g., McCrystal and Chakravarty, 2011; for a more detailed discussion on estimating market risk in private equity, see Chapter 5). In estimating private equity returns and their volatility, researchers and investors typically employ time series provided by commercial data vendors (e.g., Preqin, Thomson VentureXpert) or special service providers (Cambridge Associates, Burgiss). Alternatively, market indices of publicly listed private equity are sometimes used.

9.2.1 Calculation

Calculations of returns from NAV time series are typically based on a chained modified Dietz formula. According to this formula, the investor has NAV_{t-1} at the beginning of the period, $t-1$, which ends at time t. The return R^t_{t-1} of this period is defined as

$$R^t_{t-1} = \frac{NAV_t - NAV_{t-1} - \sum_{i>t-1}^{i\le t} \text{Contributions}_i + \sum_{i>t-1}^{i\le t} \text{Distributions}_i}{NAV_{t-1} + \sum_{i>t-1}^{i\le t} \left(\text{Contributions}_i \times \left(1 - \frac{i-t_1}{t-t_1}\right)\right) - \sum_{i>t-1}^{i\le t} \left(\text{Distributions}_i \times \left(1 - \frac{i-t_1}{t-t_1}\right)\right)}$$

An investment in a new company increases the NAV. Conversely, exiting a company decreases the NAV of the fund, even if no changes in the valuation of the remaining portfolio companies take place. Over that period, the fund draws down and distributes capital, resulting in a change in the NAV reported at the end of the period. The market value of a portfolio is assumed to be

$$MV_t = MV_{t-1} \times \left(1 + R^t_{t_1}\right)$$

with the return of the first data point in the history set at 0. The thus-defined time series allows estimating the volatility of a portfolio by taking the standard deviation of the log return of the market values, given by

$$\log\left(\frac{MV_t}{MV_{t-1}}\right), \quad t = 1, \ldots, n-1$$

The yearly standard deviation can be derived from the standard deviation of the quarterly log-returns, essentially "annualizing forward" (Figure 9.1):

$$\sigma_{4t} = 2\sigma_t, \quad t = 1, \ldots, n-1$$

Figure 9.2 shows the annual change in NAV of private equity funds between 1980 and 2010 as reported by Thomson Reuters. While the NAV jumped by 59% in 1999, negative changes

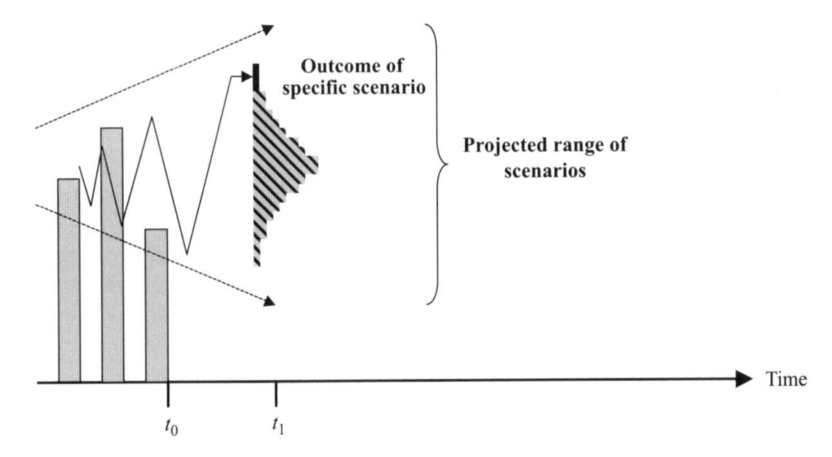

Figure 9.1 Annualizing quarterly returns forward.

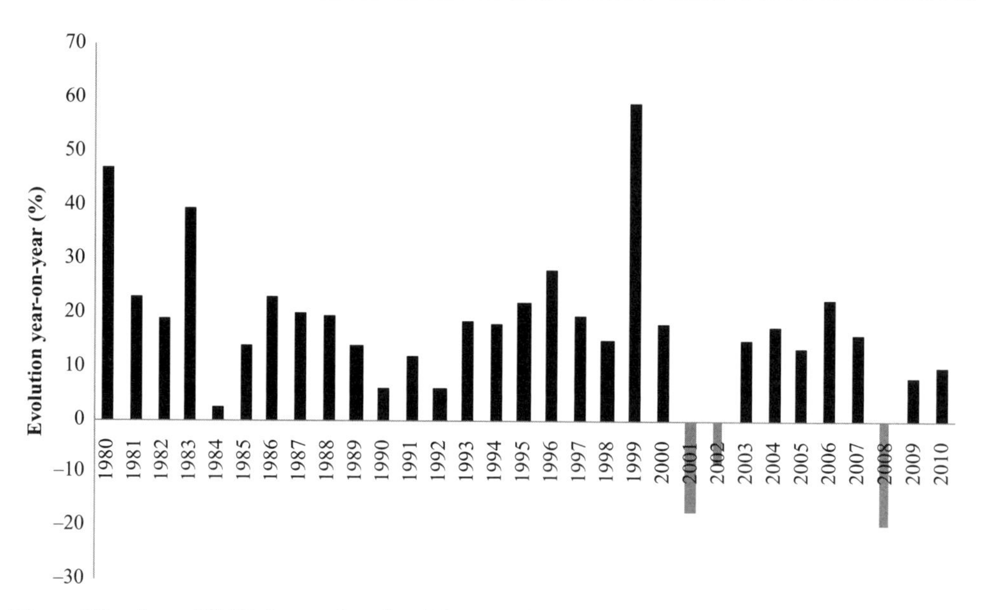

Figure 9.2 Annual NAV changes based on Thomson Reuters data from 1980 to 2010.
Source: Thomson Reuters.

are reported in the context of the bursting of the tech bubble in 2001–2002 and the recent financial crisis in 2008.[2]

Changes in the NAV of a portfolio of funds can be used to calculate a return index. An example is Preqin's Private Equity Index, which is updated quarterly for buyout funds and venture capital partnerships. A recent EVCA (2012) study uses a similar sample of funds tracked by Preqin, as well as data provided by Pevara – another data vendor. The total sample includes almost 2000 partnerships, for which quarterly and monthly changes in the NAV are calculated for the period 1980–2010 (Figure 9.3). The quarterly and monthly NAV changes are then employed to calculate the VaR at the 99.5% level of confidence.

Importantly, the EVCA study was prepared in response to Solvency II, a new regulatory initiative for European insurance companies. In determining the solvency capital requirement (SCR), the European Insurance and Occupational Pensions Authority (EIOPA) has proposed a VaR calibrated to a 99.5% confidence level over a 1-year horizon covering all risks faced by an insurer. Employing the LPX 50 index of publicly listed private equity, EIOPA has calculated a stress factor of 49% to be applied to "Other Equity" encompassing, *inter alia*, private equity, hedge funds, commodities and infrastructure.[3] However, as shown by EVCA (2012), the proposed stress factor appeared too high. Instead, using a NAV-based index of private equity funds a shock factor of less than 38% was calculated, with a correlation coefficient between private and public equity of 50–75% depending on the methodology.

[2] The estimated average return for the sample period is 16.3% with a volatility of 15.3%. Similar results are obtained by Kaplan and Schoar (2005), Studer and Wicki (2010) and Kaserer and Diller (2004b).

[3] Initially, an even higher stress factor of 59% was proposed.

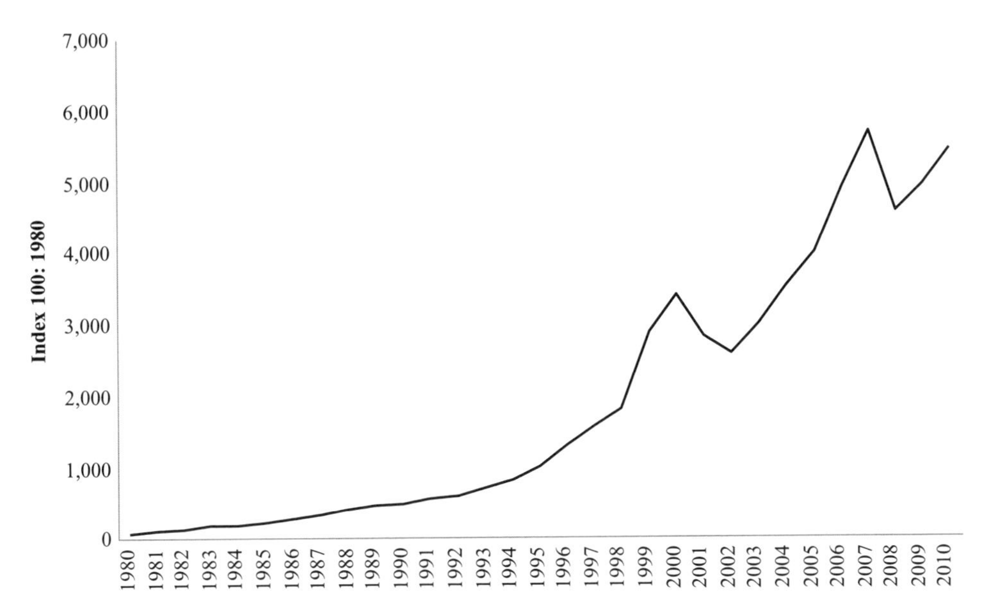

Figure 9.3 Index based on quarterly NAV changes.
Source: Thomson Reuters; authors' calculations.

Modelling market risk for private equity in a similar way as for public equity has a clear advantage in the sense that it uses the same "language" that risk managers of institutional investors, such as pension funds and insurance firms, as well as regulators are familiar with. Employing NAV-based time series appears straightforward and attractive, as quarterly returns are thought to be easily comparable to public indices, for example with regard to estimating correlations. However, the apparent simplicity of this approach may be deceptive for a number of reasons.

9.2.2 Problems and limitations

To begin with, the frequency of changes in the NAV of a fund or portfolio of partnerships is relatively low. Given that NAVs are usually available only on a quarterly basis, the number of data points is usually very limited. Even in the US private equity market, the market with the longest history, the sample period includes only around 30 years, or around 120 quarterly observations. For less developed alternative asset markets, notably in emerging economies, the sample period is typically substantially shorter. This raises important econometric issues.

Furthermore, NAVs are subjective appraisal-based valuations instead of observable market prices. Given the appraisal value effect, NAV time series tend to understate volatility, an effect that is known as stale pricing, which is closely related to the time lag effect (Emery, 2003; Woodward and Hall, 2003). Since risk is generally measured by the variance of returns, the naive use of NAVs may lead to the underestimation of risk of investing in private equity funds and similar partnership structures in other asset classes (and the overestimation of risk-adjusted returns). In addressing the stale price problem, NAV time series need to be de-smoothed, an issue we have already discussed in Chapter 5 (Geltner *et al.*, 2003). There are various statistical techniques to adjust NAV-based time series for stale pricing, for instance Dimson (1979) or Getmansky *et al.* (2004).[4] However, it is important to recognize that the adjusted time series can only be approximations of the true valuations that are not observable.

Apart from the econometric challenges risk managers face in working with NAV time series, there are several more fundamental reservations against such an approach (Mathonet and Meyer, 2007). Importantly, the NAV ignores a fund's lifecycle characteristics, such as the J-curve effect, the future use of undrawn commitments, the future management fees and the fund manager's value added (or value destroyed). The NAV time series approach aims to project the fund's future development based on a limited history. This may not be an insurmountable problem for relatively mature funds, where value is largely derived from existing portfolio companies and where undrawn commitments can essentially be ignored (EVCA, 2011). However, as far as immature funds are concerned where undrawn commitments are still substantial, using only NAVs violates the criteria for proper risk modelling in the sense that the model is neither "complete" nor "unbiased".

Moreover, changes in a fund's underlying portfolio do not translate directly into cash flows to and from LPs. While the increase in a portfolio company's valuation may increase the probability of an exit, the decision to sell remains at the discretion of the fund manager. Consequently, the NAV time series approach cannot easily be reconciled with a cash flow scenario of the funds' in- and outflows.

Additionally, the concept of market risk at the portfolio company level can be problematic from the perspective of a fund's LPs. Suppose, for instance, the NAV of a 2-year-old fund drops by 10%. There remain 8 years for the NAV to recover. The situation is fundamentally different for an 8-year-old fund where the relative impact on the remaining LP's share would be significantly stronger, given the shorter remaining life of the fund. Thus, NAV-based risk measures are inconsistent with our criterion that risk in illiquid investing in limited partnerships should be subject to a monotonic decline over the life of a fund. Importantly, therefore, employing a NAV volatility-based modelling approach may result in overestimating risk, potentially leading to a sub-optimal underallocation to private equity and real assets.

Although the modified Dietz formula described above captures cash in- and outflows in the portfolio, it does not differentiate between funds and their underlying positions. Since LPs committing to a primary fund are investing in a "blind pool", a NAV can only be reported after the fund has already started its investment activity – i.e., after risk management would theoretically have had the strongest impact. A key risk for LPs lies in the funding risk represented by the undrawn commitments, which are essentially ignored. In fact, as we have argued in Chapter 4, limited partnerships serve the purpose of shielding fledgling portfolio companies in their early stages as well as more mature companies in need of being restructured from adverse market developments.

An index can be a suitable proxy for the risk of the portfolio of funds held if the composition of the index is representative of the investor's own portfolio composition and diversification. This is a reasonable assumption for public equity where portfolio managers track an index. However, the composition of a specific limited partner's portfolio is typically significantly different from market indexes calculated on the basis of data provided by standard data vendors or service providers. This will especially be the case for smaller, less diversified LPs who are more exposed to risk.

[4] Conroy and Harris (2007) employ the Dimson approach. Diller and Jäckel (2010) follow Getmansky *et al.* (2004).

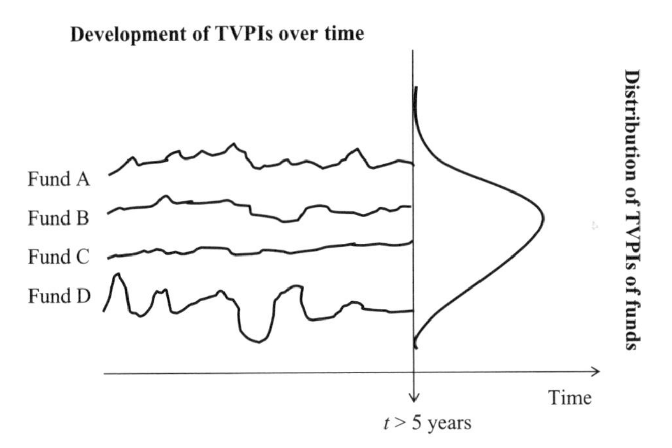

Figure 9.4 Calculation methodology based on the terminal wealth dispersion.

Finally, since NAVs are appraisal-based and observable market prices do not exist, risk models employing this valuation metric cannot be back-tested in the true sense. By contrast, liquidity events are observable and a model could therefore be tested against a fund's cash flows. In many ways, cash flow projections appear to be a more appropriate approach for building a VaR model as they capture other risk dimensions, notably liquidity and funding risk.

9.3 CASH FLOW VOLATILITY-BASED VALUE-AT-RISK

An alternative to the NAV volatility-based approach is to focus on the variability of outcomes over the full lifetime of the portfolio of funds and base the VaR calculation on cash flow information (Kaserer and Diller, 2004a; Diller, 2007; Diller and Herger, 2008). The important advantage of a cash flow-based approach lies in the fact that undrawn commitments are properly reflected in the VaR.

Instead of employing time series of returns, a cash flow-based approach is interested in the "terminal wealth dispersion", which relates directly to expected return and volatility levels.[5] Since market valuations are not regularly available for limited partnership funds, the time period relevant for risk assessment is the entire lifetime of the portfolio of funds. Ideally, only fully liquidated funds should be considered in the empirical risk analysis of cash flows. However, given the limited number of such funds, it is common to include also mature funds, which are still active but exceed a set threshold for the minimum age in the underlying data sample.[6] Calculating their cash inflows and outflows and reflecting the last reported NAV results in the calculation of the total value to paid-in (TVPI). Based on the outcomes for the TVPI for each fund, a probability density function can be determined (see Figure 9.4).

[5] However, Kaserer *et al.* (2003) emphasize several challenges. For instance, since the terminal wealth dispersion gives an average rate of return over a longer period of time, no dependency with market movements can be detected. Similarly, the approach does not allow for estimating correlations within the asset class.

[6] As far as private equity is concerned, Diller and Herger (2008) define mature funds as those with an age of at least 5 years.

For mature funds, the NAV has a lower weighting, because the investment period is already complete and the first distributions and exits have already occurred. Therefore, this approach not only takes into account the changes in NAV but also reflects the cash flow behaviour. The risk profile for a portfolio of funds is derived from the returns of comparable mature funds (Weidig and Mathonet, 2004). This avoids to a large degree issues related to too few data points, such as autocorrelation and de-smoothing, by assuming that funds in a currently held portfolio will perform like funds in the past.

Suppose an investor at time t_0 wants to determine the VaR of the portfolio of funds held for time t_1 in the future, typically the end of the year. To do this, the investor needs to determine the probability distribution for the valuation of a portfolio of funds at $t_1 > t_0$. A standard approach is a Monte Carlo simulation, randomly drawing returns for mature funds from a database that reflect the characteristics of the portfolio to be modelled.

- The higher the number of runs for the Monte Carlo simulation the more stable the results will be.
- For every fund in the limited partner's portfolio a specific cash flow scenario is generated (this will be discussed in detail in Chapter 11).
  - To project cash flows in every simulation run a new set of randomly chosen parameters is generated as input for a fund model.
  - Correlations are reflected by constraining the random draws to subsections of the database (e.g., specific vintage years or strategies).
- All individual fund scenarios are aggregated, resulting in a scenario for the entire portfolio of funds' cash flow.
- A suitable discount rate is applied to determine the PV for this portfolio scenario.
- All PVs of the simulated portfolio scenarios are compiled, which provides the distribution function.
- Based on this distribution function, the VaR for confidence level α is determined.

The annual standard deviation of returns can be derived from the terminal wealth dispersion by "annualizing backwards" (see Figure 9.5).

This analysis reflects the risks of an investor in a portfolio of limited partnership funds who has sufficient liquidity to respond to all capital calls and thus is under no pressure to sell his stake in the secondary market under potentially unfavourable market conditions during the portfolio's lifetime. This is a crucial assumption, which appears sensible for most large institutional investors who tend to have a relatively small allocation to private equity and similarly illiquid assets. However, as we have stressed before, there should be no room for complacency, given the experience of even some of the most sophisticated investors during the recent financial crisis. Instead, a funding test is required to confirm that the LP is in such a position.

How can we calculate a portfolio's cash flow-based VaR using the backward annualization technique? We propose two alternative approaches.

(i) **Time series calculation.** The first approach calculates the annual VaR based on the PV of one simulated cash flow series per fund over the entire lifetime (n periods) of this fund. The VaR for a given time period is calculated based on the differences between the PV of two periods.
(ii) **Fund growth calculation.** The second approach begins by calculating the fair value of a fund at time $t = 0$ based on m simulations of cash flow series over the entire lifetime

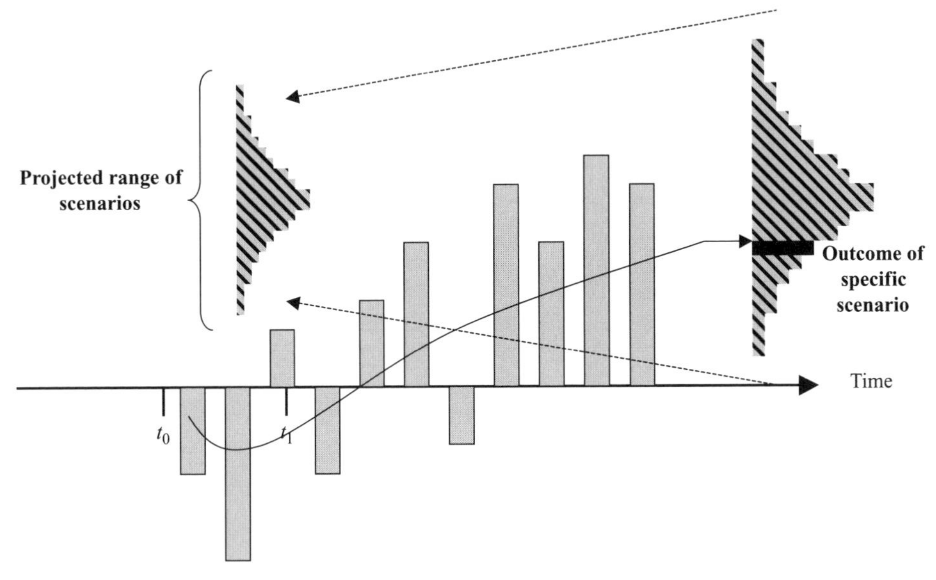

Figure 9.5 Annualizing final returns backwards.

(n periods) of this fund. For each scenario, the straight-line growth over its full lifetime and the resulting gain or loss per time period is calculated. The VaR for a given time period is derived from the projecting gains and losses under all scenarios starting from the fund's fair value at $t = 0$.

Generally, it is important that the risk manager understands the assumption as well as the implications and shortcomings of the various possible methodologies and then chooses the one most appropriate for his objectives.

9.3.1 Time series calculation

The starting point is a single fund with yearly cash flows in periods $n = 0$ to 10, i.e. the end of its lifetime (see Appendix Table 9.A.1). The fund receives contributions C_n from period $n = 0$ to 4, i.e. during its investment period, and generates distributions D_n thereafter. The fund returns a multiple of 1.55 times the invested capital with an IRR of 6.0%.

As a first step, we calculate the various PVs of the fund from each period until the end of its lifetime using a discount rate of $d = 5\%$ to reflect the opportunity cost for this asset.[7] For instance, at the beginning of period 3, we calculate the PV based on all cash flows from period 3 to 10:

$$\sum_{n=3}^{10} \frac{(D_n - C_n)}{(1+d)^n} = 94 \text{ EUR}$$

In a second step, we calculate the VaR for a portfolio of 10 funds over a period of 10 years with different investment and divestment periods and different returns (see Appendix

[7] With a discount rate of zero, the calculation would give the "default risk" of not returning the capital to the LP.

Table 9.A.2). In this example, we assume for simplicity that all funds start in one single year (this is not a requirement for the analysis, which can also be performed for a portfolio that contains funds with different degrees of maturity).

We adjust the PV with the cash flows between two observation periods. For instance, assuming a time interval of 1 year, the PV of the current period is the PV of the previous period adjusted by the cash flows. For longer time intervals, the cash flow adjustments themselves need to be compounded, too. For instance, for period 3, the cash flow of 50 EUR in the first period will be compounded over two periods, that in the second period (–20 EUR) over one period, etc. Hence, the cash flow adjustment (CFA) is the sum of the cash flows (80 EUR) plus the discount rate of 5% over the last periods:

$$\text{CFA}_{t=3} = \sum_{n=0}^{3} (D_n - C_n) * (1 + d)^n = -86.13 \text{ EUR}$$

The annual PV for period t, PV_t, is therefore the PV adjusted by the cash flows which took place in the previous periods. Hence, for this example, the annual $\text{PV}_{t=3}$ in period 3 is the PV of all cash flows from year 3 to 10 adjusted by all compounded cash flows from period 0, 1 and 2. These numbers build the basis for the VaR calculation of the underlying portfolio. Thus, for period 3 the annual PV is

$$\text{PV}_{t=3} = \sum_{n=3}^{10} \frac{(D_n - C_n)}{(1 + d)^n} + \text{CFA}_{t=3}$$

which results from the PV of 94 EUR adjusted by the negative cash flow of 86 EUR at a value of 7.55 EUR. For this, as well as for the other periods, the PV is positive as the fund is returning a higher return of 6% compared with the opportunity cost of 5%. If we assume

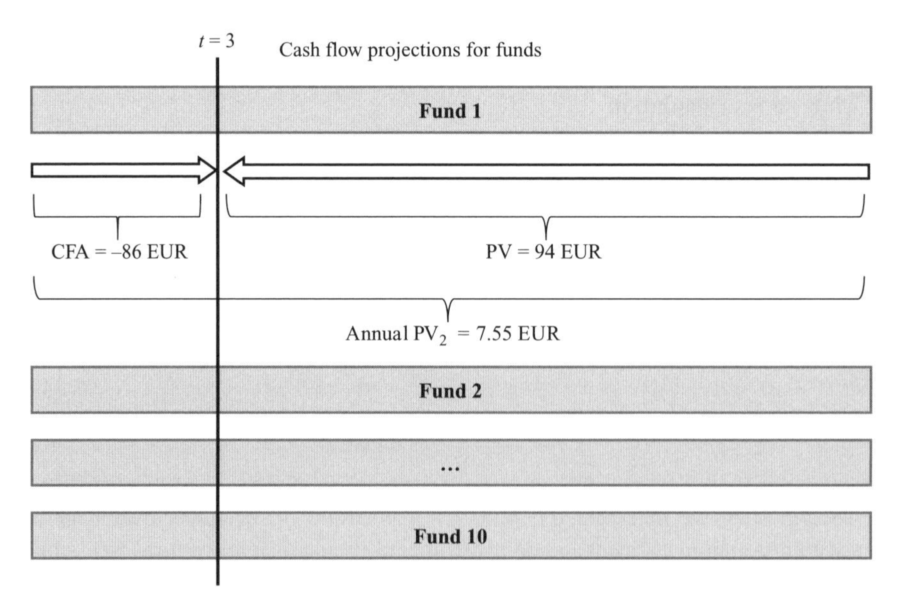

Figure 9.6 Time series calculation approach.

a higher opportunity cost of 8%, how would it affect the PV calculation? In this case, the annual PVs would be negative (such as funds 4, 9 and 10 in the example; see Appendix Table 9.A.2).

Appendix Table 9.A.3 shows the annual PV as well as the VaR for a 99% confidence level. The VaR is calculated over the cross-section of the various annual PVs of all funds of one period. In our example, the 99th percentile of the annual PV is negative for each of the periods. The relation between the net invested amount and the cumulative invested amount helps us to assess the VaR's relative magnitude. Note, however, that a portfolio with 10 funds is too small to be statistically significant and thus unlikely to reflect the characteristics of a large and well-diversified portfolio.

Figure 9.6 visualizes this approach. Based on the cash flow simulation of each fund, the PV is assessed by computing the future cash flows which will be adjusted by the compounded historical cash flows that have occurred. These annual PVs will be used to derive the annual VaR for the portfolio.

9.3.2 Fund growth calculation

In contrast to the time series approach, the fund growth approach is based on a number of simulation paths for each fund over its remaining lifetime. In addition, the VaR is calculated based on the difference between the PVs of each simulation run and its current value.

The higher uncertainty that results from the use of alternative scenarios should be expected to affect the distribution of the density function. Specifically, the VaR calculation follows five steps.

1. For each fund in the sample, m cash flow scenarios over the fund's full lifetime n are generated.
2. For each scenario i and a given discount rate, a PV_i is calculated.
3. The average present value of all scenarios of one fund is calculated in order to derive the fair value of the fund at time $t = 0$:

$$\text{Avg}\,(\text{PV}) = \frac{1}{m}\sum_{i=1}^{m} \text{PV}_i$$

4. The period gain or loss for a given scenario i is obtained by relating the difference between the fund's fair value and PV_i to the time period (depending on whether quarterly or annual VaRs are to be calculated). This linear approach eliminates the fund's J-curve or other fund lifecycle-induced distortions:

$$\text{gain/loss} = \frac{\text{Avg}\,(\text{PV}) - \text{PV}_i}{n}$$

5. Based on these results, the density function of the annual/quarterly gains and losses can be computed. This allows the portfolio's VaR to be calculated over the required period for a set confidence level.

A simple example may help illustrate this approach. Suppose we want to determine the VaR for 1 year for a single fund. For this fund we run three cash flow scenarios with a given discount rate, resulting in three PVs (Figure 9.7).

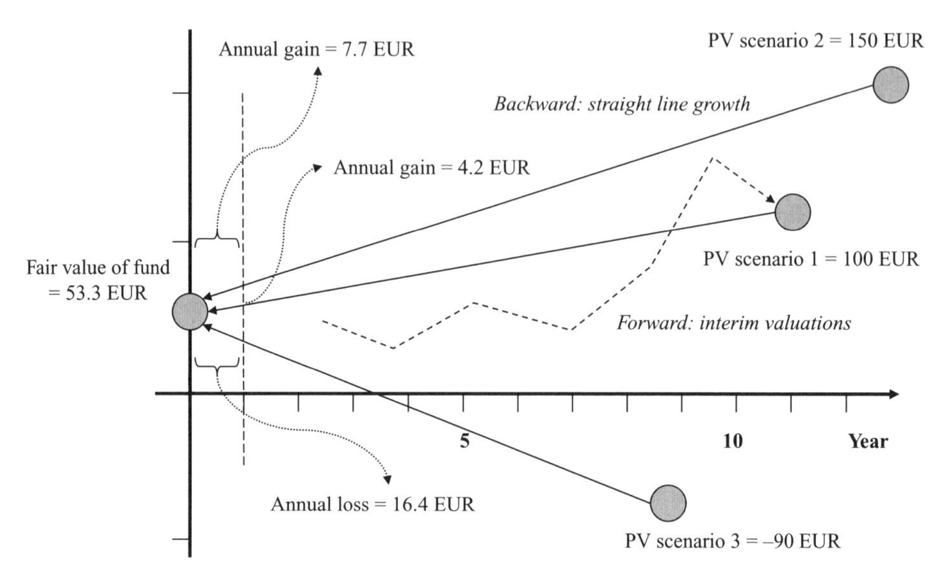

Figure 9.7 Fund growth calculation approach.

Scenario 1: fund's remaining expected lifetime 11 years, $PV_1 = 100$ EUR.
Scenario 2: fund's remaining expected lifetime 12.5 years, $PV_2 = 150$ EUR.
Scenario 3: fund's remaining expected lifetime 8.75 years, $PV_3 = -90$ EUR.

These three scenarios are based on different cash flow scenarios and, hence, reflect possible real outcomes of the fund. Assuming that they will materialize with equal probability, the fair value of the fund at time 0 is the average of these scenarios:

$$\frac{150\text{ EUR} + 100\text{ EUR} - 90\text{ EUR}}{3} = 53.3\text{ EUR}$$

We calculate the risk of this fund based on these scenarios and the gain/loss over a given time period. Under scenario 1 the fund would gain a value of 4.2 EUR p.a. over its projected lifetime:

$$\frac{100\text{ EUR} - 53.3\text{ EUR}}{11\text{ years}} = 4.2\text{ EUR p.a.}$$

Under scenario 2 the gain is 7.7 EUR p.a. while under scenario 3 the fund would lose 16.4 EUR p.a. Based on these results, the density function for the fund's valuation after 1 year can be determined as follows:

- Should scenario 1 materialize, after 1 year the fund would be worth 53.3 EUR + 4.2 EUR = 57.5 EUR.
- Should scenario 2 materialize, after 1 year the fund would be worth 53.3 EUR + 7.7 EUR = 61.0 EUR.
- Should scenario 3 materialize, after 1 year the fund would be worth 53.3 EUR − 16.4 EUR = 36.7 EUR.

These valuations allow us to determine the risk of losing capital on a 1-year horizon. Let us now discuss another example to compare the calculation method to the time series calculation approach described before.

We start by generating a set of scenarios. The first simulation path A results in the cash flow series that has already been shown in Appendix Table 9.A.1. In addition to this simulation, we run additional simulations (in reality, risk managers would typically run between 1,000 and 100,000 paths per fund). These results ("A" to "J") for fund 1 are shown in Appendix Table 9.A.4. After running the simulations for fund 1, we do the same for fund 2, 3, ..., 10. For simplicity, we only show the results of the cash flow scenarios for fund 1. However, they would look very similar for the other funds.

Having estimated all cash flow paths for each scenario m, we calculate the PVs for these scenarios. For scenario A, we obtain a PV = 6.85 EUR assuming a discount rate of 5%. Scenario B leads to a PV = –18.47 EUR. In order to determine the current fair value of the fund, we calculate the average of these numbers, which is 19.11 EUR. Now, we are ready to calculate the differences for each scenario. For example, for scenario A, we obtain 6.85 EUR − 19.11 EUR = −12.27 EUR, which represents the fund's total loss over its full life. To determine its annual loss, we need to divide this amount by the projected lifetime of 10 years, resulting in –1.23 EUR p.a.

Similarly, the annual loss under scenario B is estimated at 3.8 EUR, whereas the investor expects an annual gain of 0.12 EUR under scenario C.

Given these results, we can determine the histogram and density function for many scenarios of fund valuations at a future point in time. This forms the basis for determining the VaR over a required projection period (annually or quarterly). While the results become increasingly robust with a larger number of runs, the difference in the results is higher in our example for each new simulation. This also shows that in comparison to the time series-based approach, we have additional volatility through the simulations. This appears to be a better reflection of the true situation and the diversification of the portfolio. Therefore, this example might have a better coverage of the possible outcomes through higher variations but it is also more computation-intensive.

9.3.3 Underlying data

To be able to calculate a VaR we need to use representative market data (see also Box 9.2) or synthetic cash flows and be able to project the funds' future cash flows. In Chapter 11 we discuss in greater detail how such projections can be generated. In the preceding discussion, we have annualized the final returns "backwards" to calculate an annual VaR for a portfolio of limited partnership funds. Depending on an investor's objectives or specific financial regulations, there may be situations where quarterly, rather than annual, VaRs are required. In this case, PVs for each quarter would be calculated until each fund's end of lifetime, applying a quarterly interest rate. In addition, cash flows would need to be adjusted on a quarterly basis and compounded accordingly.

Large institutional investors with a long history of investing in private equity and real assets usually possess proprietary datasets which reflect their experience and investment strategies. By contrast, smaller LPs and those who have begun to invest in limited partnership funds only recently usually have to rely on publicly available data provided by data vendors (e.g., Preqin, Thomson VentureXpert) or specialized service providers (Burgiss, Cambridge Associates, State Street). Cornelius (2011) and Harris *et al.* (2012) provide a detailed analysis of these

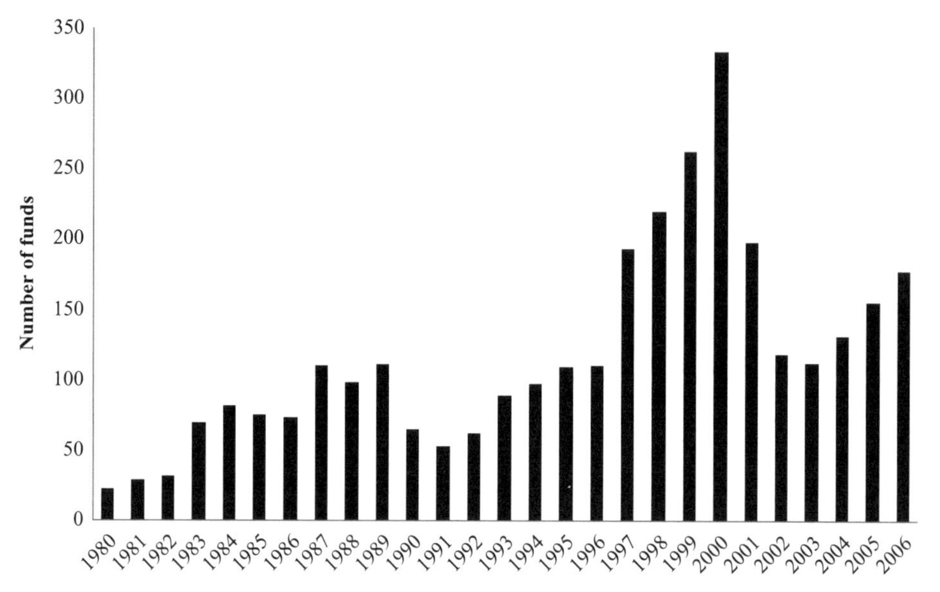

Figure 9.8 Distributions of vintage years in data sample.
Source: Thomson Reuters.

datasets and find significant differences in terms of sample periods, sample sizes, geographic coverage, mean returns and the dispersion of returns (see Chapter 5). No dataset is complete in the sense that it includes all funds that have ever been raised, which raises the issue of potential sample biases.

The choice of the dataset that is used to calculate the VaR already involves an important decision by the risk manager. For instance, the Thomson VentureXpert database has the longest sample period going back to the early 1980s, covering several market cycles, such as the first buyout wave in the second half of the 1980s, the tech bubble in the late 1990s and the second buyout wave in the mid-2000s (Figure 9.8). Thus, Thomson VentureXpert is widely used by practitioners as well as in academic research. However, Harris *et al.* (2012) and Stucke (2011) find evidence that the quality of the Thomson VentureXpert data might have been compromised by infrequent updates of NAVs. Against this background, risk managers are well advised to work with alternative datasets to examine the sensitivity of outcomes with respect to the underlying data.

Furthermore, since rarely will all relevant scenarios be covered by one or even several combined data providers, working with "synthetic" cash flows can be a – and in some situations the only – solution. This can mean adding stress factors, like lower distributions (affecting the performance) as well as faster contributions and slower distributions (affecting the holding period and, hence, having an impact on liquidity management). As we describe in Chapter 15, rating agencies use these kinds of approaches also for deriving the rating for bonds of securitized private equity portfolios.

9.4 DIVERSIFICATION

LPs typically hold portfolios of funds that are diversified across several dimensions, such as investment strategies, underlying assets, fund managers, vintage years, industries, geographies and currencies. Larger diversification over more funds has two important characteristics: first, there is more diversification across fund managers and their applied strategy, which usually has a positive effect. Second, and perhaps even more importantly, a greater degree of diversification at the fund level implies a greater degree of diversification in terms of portfolio companies. A portfolio of 10 private equity funds containing 80 to 150 underlying portfolio companies has different risk characteristics than a portfolio of, say, 150 funds with 1200 to 2250 companies, which have been acquired at different stages of the business cycle.

Let us consider just two dimensions of diversification, i.e. (1) the number of funds in a portfolio and (2) the vintage years during which the funds were raised. We employ data provided by Thomson VentureXpert for a sample of 3183 private equity partnerships. These partnerships include US and European buyout and venture capital funds raised between 1980 and 2006, with valuations as of end-September 2011. Choosing 2006 as a cut-off ensures that the sample includes only fully liquidated funds or those that are already relatively mature and in their divestment phase. For fully liquidated funds, we use their real cash flows (information on DPI); for the rest of the sample, we include the last NAV as a final cash flow similar to the TVPI calculation.

Suppose an investor picks randomly just one fund out of a randomly chosen vintage year in our sample between 1980 and 2006. As shown in Figure 9.9, the highest probability (i.e., the mode) for the distribution is located close to the multiple of 1. In other words, the most probable outcome of a random investment into a single private equity fund is that the investor will get his invested capital back. However, the distribution is clearly skewed to the right with some funds having generated TVPIs of 5 and more. The average TVPI is 1.62, which is higher than the median of 1.24. On the left-hand side of the distribution, losses are limited to a multiple of 0, with a very small number of funds having lost their entire capital (complete write-offs). The tenth percentile in the sample has achieved a multiple of 0.6, the fifth percentile a multiple of 0.43 and the first percentile a multiple of 0.14. This implies that the private equity investor has a confidence level of 99% to lose less than 86% of his investments at the end of the fund's

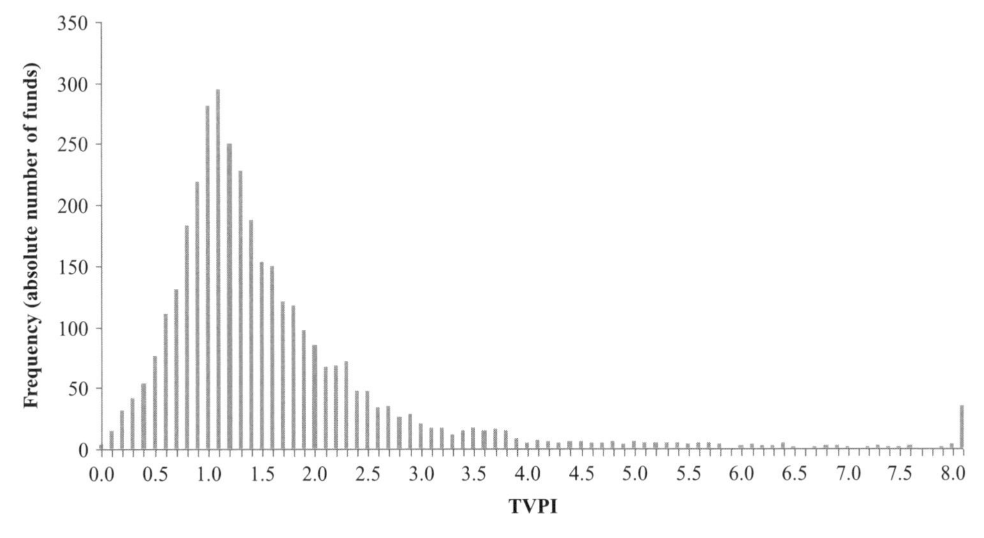

Figure 9.9 TVPI probability density function for randomly picked private equity fund (vintage years 1980 to 2006) – based on Thomson Reuters data.

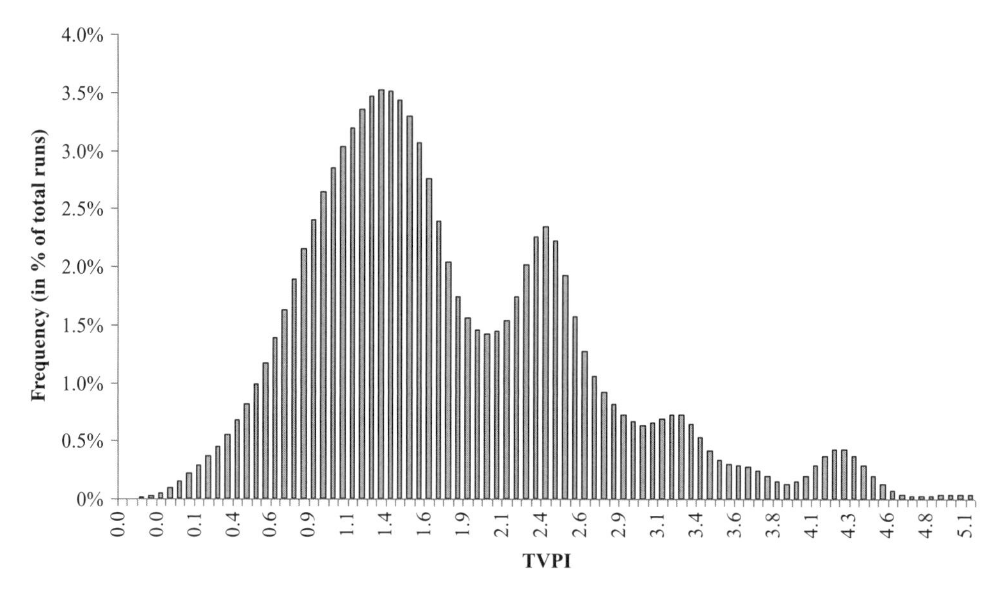

Figure 9.10 TVPI probability density function for randomly picked private equity fund (vintage years 1980 to 2006) – based on Preqin data.

lifetime. This corresponds to an invested capital-at-risk (iCaR) of 84%, a concept introduced by Diller and Herger (2008).

Let us repeat this analysis using a dataset provided by Preqin. The Preqin sample includes 1892 funds. While the sample is biased towards US funds, the results we obtain are broadly similar (Figure 9.10). Specifically, given a confidence level of 99% the investor is expected to lose less than 92% of his capital by choosing randomly a single fund in the sample.

As Weidig and Mathonet (2004) show, diversified portfolios are significantly less risky than an investment in any single fund, with well-performing funds compensating investors for the losses they may incur by committing capital to "defaulting" funds. While private equity is not unique in terms of diversification benefits, Weidig and Mathonet (2004) and Meyer and Mathonet (2005) find that significant gains can be reaped at relatively low levels of diversification. This is particularly true for investors diversifying across vintage years (Diller and Herger, 2008).

Consequently, the continuous monitoring and management of diversification is an integral component of a limited partner's risk management framework. Diversification reduces the long-term risk of a portfolio of funds. For large portfolios, diversification is found to increase the expected median returns – which, however, comes at the price of a reduced potential to harvest extraordinary returns (Mathonet and Meyer, 2007). Thus, investors who are confident of being able to select the best funds may decide to have a relatively less diversified portfolio. In this context, it is important to recognize that cash flows tend to become highly correlated during market downturns. Therefore, even funds following different strategies or targeting different geographies can become subject to similar degrees of liquidity risk in the short and medium term. The impact of diversification depends also on the interaction between the portfolio of funds and other assets held, for example, through the so-called denominator effect.

Using correlations as a measure of dependence between the funds within a portfolio has significant limitations as it builds on measuring the risks of funds and is thus faced with difficulties similar to those discussed before. Practitioners try to address this issue with different modelling approaches:

- Direct correlation modelling based on performance data observed for funds (or co-investments, as we discuss below) if available from either public or private sources.
- Implied correlation modelling based on systemic factors (i.e., value drivers) which are usually mapped to each fund and/or underlying portfolio company.

Alternatively, the relative dependence or independence of funds within a larger portfolio can be assessed through other tools such as cluster analysis. Cluster analysis is a technique to classify similar objects into relatively homogeneous groups and dissimilar objects into different groups (Lhabitant, 2004). It can be used to analyse the degree to which a portfolio of funds is "clogged", i.e. tends to form clusters of sub-portfolios of funds with a high degree of interdependence. Funds that belong to the same cluster should be modelled as moving in the same direction. In applying stress scenarios, it should be assumed that portfolios of funds tend to get increasingly clogged. Thus, in constructing portfolios of limited partnerships, investors should pursue highly heterogeneous strategies across a wide range of pre-identified dimensions, such as vintage years, stage focus, industry focus and geographical focus.

As already mentioned, vintage year diversification is generally found to be the most powerful dimension, at least in private equity. Vintage year diversification requires a high degree of discipline, however. Murphy (2007) shows that investors may reach their target allocation to private equity in a relatively short period of time. The downside, however, is that such a strategy inevitably results in highly concentrated portfolios, implying (other things being equal) higher risk. As funds are usually investing over a period of several years, the acquisition multiples, the debt environment and the price levels of these companies tend to vary significantly. While this can be observed at the fund level, it is even more pronounced at the portfolio company level. A larger degree of diversification over time also allows for a wider spread in terms of industry, geography, debt situation and stages in the lifecycle of underlying companies, which as a consequence are little correlated among each other.

In practice, of course, no investor invests in just one fund. Thus, let us come back to our previous example, but this time considering a strategy whereby the investor commits to several funds spread over several vintage years. In particular, we are interested in the relative importance of vintage year diversification as opposed to the benefits investors may obtain by investing in different funds in a single vintage year. Let us consider two investors with a portfolio of 36 randomly chosen funds. Investor A has built his portfolio over 4 years with 9 funds per year, whereas investor B has committed to only 4 funds per year but has allocated his capital over a period of 9 years.

The effects of the two strategies are depicted in Figures 9.11 and 9.12, respectively. Comparing the two strategies suggests that diversifying over time have a significantly larger risk-mitigating effect. In addition to the substantial reduction of risk on the left-hand side of the distribution, there is a significant shift of the entire distribution into the positive area as can be seen. Importantly, there is no risk for the investor to lose capital as the entire distribution lies in the positive multiple range. For investor A, the median of the distribution of multiples is 1.15, with the first percentile portfolio achieving a multiple of 1.06. As far as investor B is concerned, the median multiple is 1.35, with the first percentile portfolio generating a multiple of 1.20. At the same time, the tails of the distribution are flattened to a significant degree. Obviously, the price of pursuing a more diversified investment strategy is a more limited probability of achieving an extraordinarily large return.

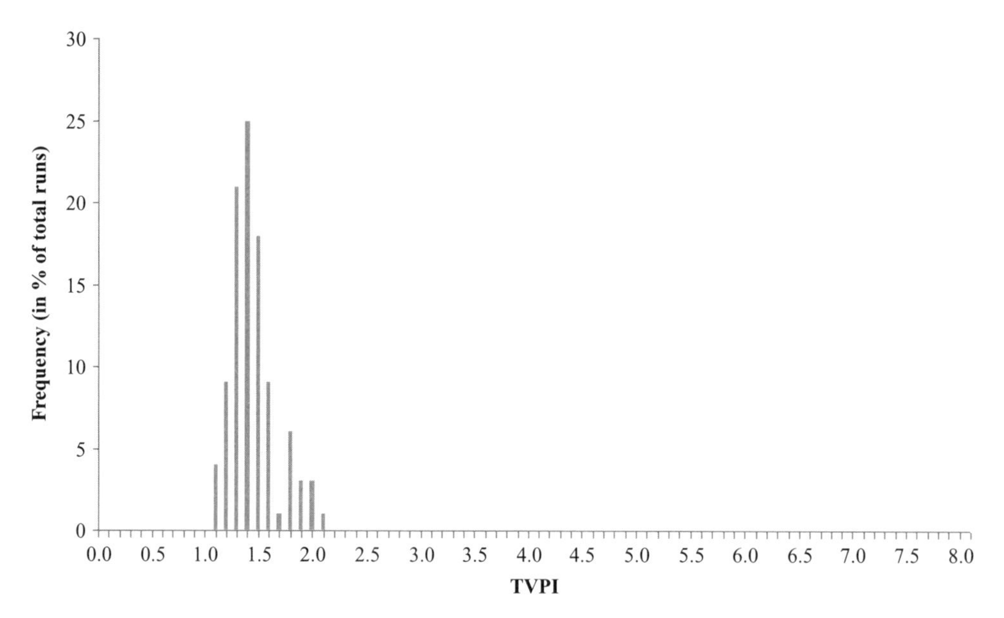

Figure 9.11 Investor A's portfolio built over 4 years with 9 funds per year – calculation based on Thomson Reuters data.

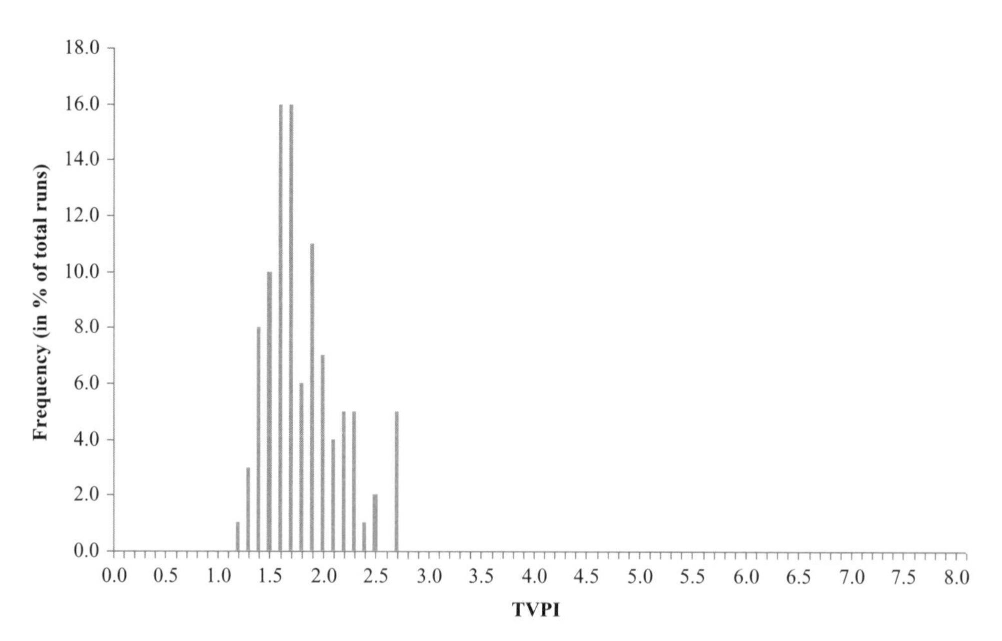

Figure 9.12 Investor B's portfolio built over 9 years with 4 funds per year – calculation based on Thomson Reuters data.

Thus far, we have focused exclusively on fund investments. Increasingly, however, investors also pursue co-investment strategies where an investor holds shares in portfolio companies alongside a fund where he is a limited partner. Generally, co-investments where exit decisions are solely taken by the GP can be covered within the model proposed above. For example, Smith *et al.* (2012) model co-investments in the form of artificial "co-investment funds" with the same structure as the primary private equity funds taken as reference, i.e. containing the same number of investments but with each co-investment from a different fund manager, from the same geography, roughly the same size and invested within 1 year of the reference investment in the primary fund. However, assumptions need to be made regarding the limited partner's selection skills and the resulting range for the multiples.

Generally, there is no contractual or legal obligation to fund additional financing rounds in the case of co-investments; consequently, funding risk is usually not an issue. Nevertheless, there is some funding risk in the case of expansion-related investments (e.g., buy-and-build strategies which might entail the acquisition of a competitor) or equity injections to comply with debt covenants and, in worst-case scenarios, to remain solvent.

Finally, some limited partners also pursue direct investment strategies. However, as in such cases investment and divestment decisions rest with the LP, they require specific risk management approaches that are beyond the scope of this book.[8]

9.5 FACTORING IN OPPORTUNITY COSTS

Given the time value of capital, investors need to factor in the opportunity costs of committing capital to limited partnerships. This issue is different from the risk that the fund manager might not be able to return the invested capital to the investor. Here, we are concerned with the issue of returns that fail to meet an investor's target return.

Opportunity costs can be viewed from different perspectives. To begin with, investors usually have the choice of investing in various asset classes. Therefore, the opportunity cost of investing in limited partnership funds is the expected return of other asset classes like bonds, stocks, real estate, hedge funds, etc. Benchmarking returns from private equity funds against, for instance, public equity indexes or high-yield bonds, the VaR can be calculated in such a way that it mirrors the risk of not achieving that benchmark. Alternatively, insurance companies and pension funds have guaranteed or fixed interest rates over the lifetime of the life insurance product in some countries.[9] In this case, the VaR could reflect the risk of not achieving this return with fund investments in private equity and real assets. Further, investors like insurance companies, banks or industrial enterprises also have a cost of capital for their enterprise.

In order to reflect such opportunity costs, it is necessary to project the cash flows over the portfolio of funds' entire lifetime. The reference base for the risk calculation is then the invested capital of the portfolio compounded by the annual yield of the opportunity cost over the average holding period.[10] Consider a randomly chosen portfolio of 50 funds an investor commits to over a period of 10 years (Figure 9.13). Incorporating opportunity costs in each of the Monte Carlo simulations has a non-trivial impact, as depicted in Figure 9.14, with

[8] For example, techniques such as the one proposed by Bongaerts and Charlier (2006) could be applied.

[9] In Germany, for example, there is a guaranteed but adjustable rate of interest on a life insurance policy. At the time of writing, this rate was 1.75%, down from 3.25% at the beginning of the century. In Japan, the high guaranteed return on life insurance policies in the 1990s caused several insurers to fail and be taken over.

[10] In conducting a Monte Carlo simulation, cash flows need to be simulated under the "risk-neutral" probability measure to take account of the risk properties of the cash flows. Simulating cash flows using historical means and variances and then still discounting such flows using a risk-free rate would overstate the value. We thank Per Stromberg for pointing this out.

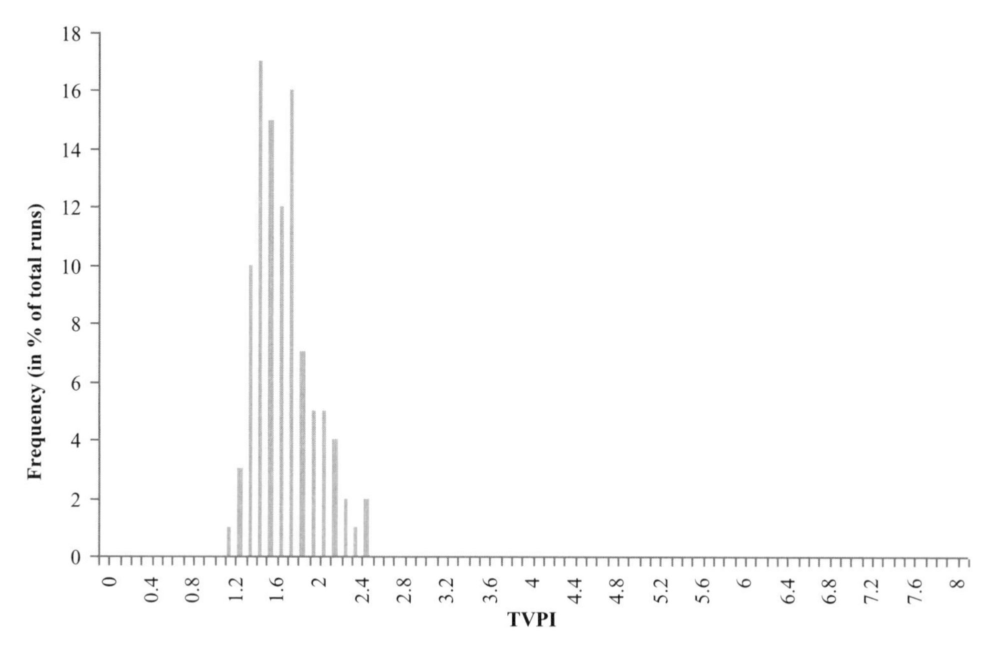

Figure 9.13 Distributions of TVPIs for 10-year investment period – calculation based on Thomson Reuters data.

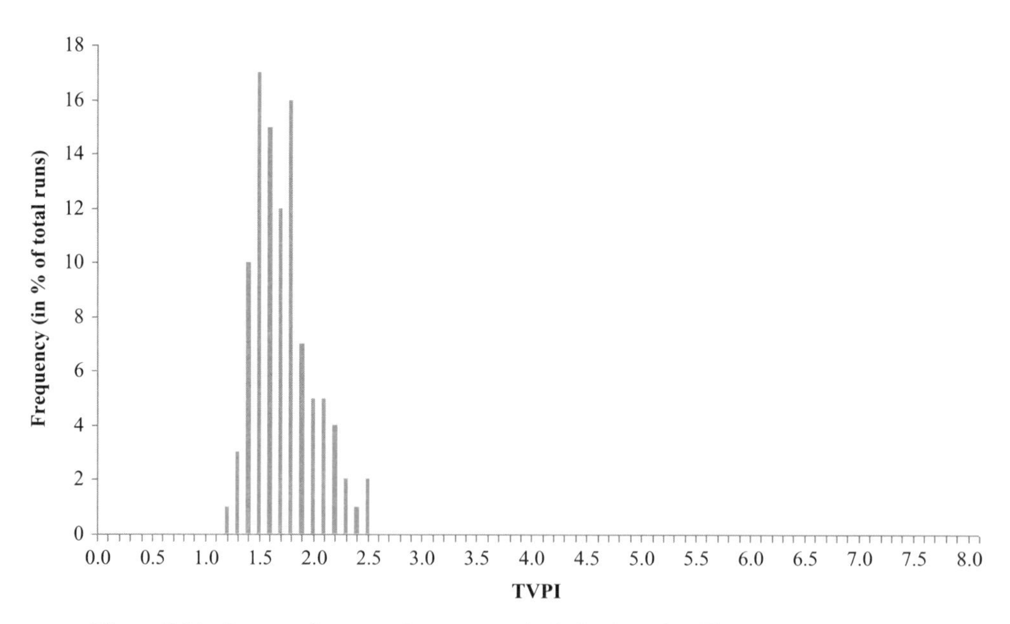

Figure 9.14 Impact of opportunity costs – calculation based on Thomson Reuters data.

opportunity costs assumed to be 4%: the distribution shifts to the left with an associated increase in VaR. Hence, a larger degree of diversification is necessary to reach the same risk exposure in percentage terms as without opportunity costs.

9.6 CASH-FLOW-AT-RISK

Investors use VaR as a basis for determining their capital adequacy and measuring traded risk. Non-financial firms, however, have found this concept difficult to apply in their risk management as value mainly takes the form of real investments in fixed assets that cannot be monetized easily. Industrial companies tend to look at the cash-flow-at-risk (CFaR) as a more relevant measure for their risk exposures. The CFaR is the maximum deviation between actual cash flows and a set level (e.g., a budget figure) due to changes in the underlying risk factors within a given time period for a given confidence level.

While in the case of tradable assets VaR is usually computed for very short time periods (days or weeks), CFaR relates to longer periods, typically quarters and sometimes even years (see Damodaran, undated). As far as financial firms are concerned, it has been argued that marked-to-market portfolios are convertible into cash at short notice and therefore their VaR is also their CFaR (see Damodaran, undated; Yan *et al.*, 2011). However, this argument does not apply to illiquid assets, which ties into our previous discussion of the cash flow volatility-based approach to calculating the VaR for portfolios of funds.

When looking at the CFaR for a portfolio of funds we focus on variations in cash flow within a given time interval $[t_1, t_2]$ (Figure 9.15). For a LP, both directions of cash flow are relevant as they play into the funding test: positive cash flows as they will be needed by the LP for new investments or to honour future capital calls, negative cash flows as they expose the LP to liquidity risks because available cash may not be sufficient to meet its financial obligations.

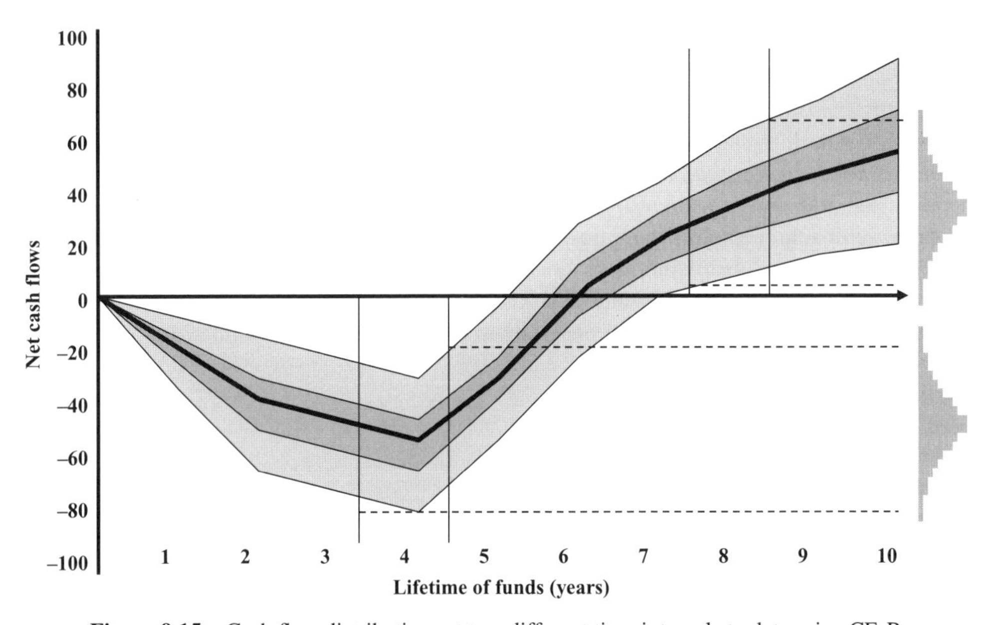

Figure 9.15 Cash flow distributions at two different time intervals to determine CFaR

9.7 CONCLUSIONS

In this chapter, we have presented a VaR approach for investments in limited partnership funds. Intuitively, the purpose of calculating a VaR for such funds is similar to the original idea behind the VaR concept, which has been designed for marketable assets – namely to estimate the maximum loss for a given portfolio, a given confidence level and a given time horizon. To be sure, the VaR concept has been criticized for a number of reasons, not least because it has not prevented a number of financial institutions from failing during periods of financial turmoil, notably the recent global financial crisis, the biggest casualty of which was Lehman Brothers. While investors need to be acutely aware of the shortcomings of VaR, its greatest benefit should be seen in the imposition of a structured methodology for critically thinking about risk (Jorion and Taleb, 1997).

Investors in illiquid funds face additional issues when they apply a VaR approach in order to determine the risk of their portfolios. Specifically, there are no observable market data that can be used as input. So what to do? We have proposed two alternatives: first, an approach based on NAV time series and second, one based on cash flows. While a NAV-based approach is relatively simple to implement, there are a number of important problems that limit its applicability, in particular with regard to relatively immature portfolios. As we have argued in this chapter, immature portfolios are characterized by a significant amount of unfunded commitments, thus favouring the use of cash flow-based VaR modelling.

We know from other asset classes that risk can be significantly reduced through diversification. Investments in private equity and real assets through limited partnerships are no different. However, there are many dimensions along which diversification can be achieved, including vintage years, investment strategies, stages and geographies. Among these, as we have shown, vintage year diversification provides the largest benefits.

While investment risk is generally seen as the probability of losing capital, this perspective ignores opportunity costs. Alternatively, the LP could have invested in a different asset class, such as a public equity index or high-yield bonds. This can be taken into account by a VaR that is adjusted for opportunity costs.

Finally, we have presented briefly a complementary approach, the CFaR. This approach is generally considered to be particularly relevant for non-financial firms, whose real assets cannot easily be liquidated. Although the VaR concept takes a prominent role in financial regulation, for illiquid assets, in fact, the CFaR may be of even higher relevance. Importantly, therefore, the cash flow-based VaR provides a tool to calculate the VaR and the CFaR following the same approach. Thus, the cash flow-based VaR approach ensures that the VaR and the CFaR concepts are reconcilable. This dovetails into our previous discussion in Chapter 8, highlighting the importance of a funding test to ensure that the investor is always in a position to respond to capital calls, which are uncertain in terms of their timing and size.

APPENDIX – EXAMPLES

Table 9.A.1 One-fund scenario, discount rate 5%

Year	0	1	2	3	4	5	6	7	8	9	10	TVPI	IRR
Cash flows	−50.00	−20.00	−10.00	−15.00	−5.00	5.00	10.00	20.00	30.00	40.00	50.00	1.55	6.0%
PV	6.85	57.19	80.05	94.05	113.75	124.44	125.66	121.95	108.04	83.45	47.62		
Cash flow adjusted/period	−50.00	−72.50	−86.13	−105.43	−115.70	−116.49	−112.31	−97.93	−72.82	−36.47	11.71		
Annual PV	6.85	7.19	7.55	7.93	8.32	8.74	9.18	9.63	10.12	10.62	11.15		

Table 9.A.2 Scenario for portfolio of 10 funds

Year	0	1	2	3	4	5	6	7	8	9	10	TVPI	IRR
Cash flow Fund 1	−50	−20	−10	−15	−5	5	10	20	30	40	50	1.55	6.0%
Cash flow Fund 2	−10	−30	−10	0	0	10	20	40	50	40	10	3.40	20.4%
Cash flow Fund 3	−30	−20	−10	0	10	20	40	20	10	0	0	1.80	10.1%
Cash flow Fund 4	−15	−15	−15	−15	15	15	15	10	5	5	5	1.22	3.4%
Cash flow Fund 5	−50	−20	−10	−15	20	10	20	20	50	40	50	2.53	12.3%
Cash flow Fund 6	−10	−30	−10	10	20	40	20	20	20	0	0	5.00	24.1%
Cash flow Fund 7	−5	−15	−20	−5	10	15	15	20	20	10	0	2.29	15.1%
Cash flow Fund 8	−5	−15	−20	−5	0	10	15	15	20	20	10	2.00	12.3%
Cash flow Fund 9	−50	−20	−10	−15	0	10	15	15	20	20	10	0.95	−0.8%
Cash flow Fund 10	−15	−15	−20	−5	0	10	15	5	5	2	0	0.67	−7.6%
Total	*−240*	*−200*	*−135*	*−65*	*70*	*145*	*185*	*185*	*230*	*177*	*135*		
Sum contr. cumulative	−240	−440	−575	−650	−655	−655	−655	−655	−655	−655	−655		
Sum distr. cumulative	0	0	0	10	85	230	415	600	830	1007	1142		
Sum net invested	−240	−440	−575	−640	−570	−425	−240	−55	0	0	0		

Table 9.A.3 Scenario portfolio of 10 funds – annual VaR calculation

Year	0	1	2	3	4	5	6	7	8	9	10	
Annual PV Fund 1	6.85	7.19	7.55	7.93	8.32	8.74	9.18	9.63	10.12	10.62	11.15	
Annual PV Fund 2	66.01	69.31	72.78	76.41	80.24	84.25	88.46	92.88	97.53	102.40	107.52	
Annual PV Fund 3	15.82	16.61	17.44	18.31	19.23	20.19	21.20	22.26	23.37	24.54	25.77	
Annual PV Fund 4	−3.60	−3.78	−3.97	−4.17	−4.37	−4.59	−4.82	−5.06	−5.32	−5.58	−5.86	
Annual PV Fund 5	50.17	52.67	55.31	58.07	60.98	64.03	67.23	70.59	74.12	77.82	81.71	
Annual PV Fund 6	49.02	51.47	54.04	56.74	59.58	62.56	65.69	68.97	72.42	76.04	79.84	
Annual PV Fund 7	22.50	23.62	24.81	26.05	27.35	28.72	30.15	31.66	33.24	34.90	36.65	
Annual PV Fund 8	19.53	20.51	21.54	22.61	23.74	24.93	26.18	27.49	28.86	30.30	31.82	
Annual PV Fund 9	−27.45	−28.82	−30.26	−31.77	−33.36	−35.03	−36.78	−38.62	−40.55	−42.58	−44.71	
Annual PV Fund 10	−23.32	−24.49	−25.71	−27.00	−28.35	−29.77	−31.26	−32.82	−34.46	−36.18	−37.99	
99th percentile annual VaR	*−27.08*	*−28.43*	*−29.85*	*−31.34*	*−32.91*	*−34.56*	*−36.28*	*−38.10*	*−40.00*	*−42.00*	*−44.10%*	***Average***
Net invested capital (%)	11.3%	6.5%	5.2%	4.9%	5.8%	8.1%	15.1%	69.3%	0.0%	0.0%	0.0%	*11.5%*
Cumulative invested capital (%)	11.3%	6.5%	5.2%	4.8%	5.0%	5.3%	5.5%	5.8%	6.1%	6.4%	6.7%	*6.2%*

Table 9.A.4 Ten different scenarios "A" to "J" for one fund – annual VaR calculation

Run	Year 0	1	2	3	4	5	6	7	8	9	10	$PV_m(t=0)$	$PV_m(t=0)$ – Avg(PV)	Lifetime (years)	Annual difference	TVPI
A	−50	−20	−10	−15	−5	5	10	20	30	40	50	6.85	−12.27	10	−1.23	1.55
B	0	−50	−20	−10	−15	0	5	10	20	30	40	−18.47	−37.58	10	−3.76	1.11
C	0	0	−50	−20	−20	0	10	20	30	40	50	20.35	1.23	10	0.12	1.67
D	−50	−20	−10	−15	25	55	65	65	30	10		89.56	70.44	9	7.83	2.63
E	0	−50	−20	−10	10	0	0	20	0	20		−39.07	−58.18	9	−6.46	0.63
F	−50	−20	−10	0	0	0	10	20	30	10	30	−10.74	−29.85	10	−2.99	1.25
G	−50	−20	−10	−15	−5	15	10	20	30	40	50	14.31	−4.80	10	−0.48	1.65
H	0	0	−50	−20	−20	0	10	70	80			33.89	14.78	8	1.85	1.78
I	−50	−20	−10	−15	25	55	65	65	30	10		89.56	70.44	9	7.83	2.63
J	0	−50	−20	−10	10	0	0	100				4.90	−14.22	7	−2.03	1.38
Average (PV(*t*))												**19.11**	**VaR (0.1)**		**−6.19**	

10
The Impact of Undrawn Commitments

As we have discussed in the preceding chapters, a number of LPs faced serious problems during the recent financial crisis because of the significant undrawn commitments they had made in their alternative investment portfolios. Their experience has caused increased interest from practitioners and academics alike in what has been coined "commitment risk" or "funding risk". However, academic research into this type of risk is still in its infancy. For instance, in reviewing the (risk-adjusted) performance of private equity, Harris *et al.* (2012) note that:

> "[...] investing in a portfolio of private equity funds across vintage years inevitably involves uncertainties and potential costs related to the timing of cash flows and the liquidity of holdings that differ from those in public markets. For instance, there is uncertainty regarding how much to commit to private equity funds to achieve a target portfolio allocation. This is due to the uncertain time profile of capital calls and realizations. Consequently, there exists 'commitment risk' when investing in private equity [...] Estimating plausible ranges for a commitment risk premium is a subject for future research [...]"

To the extent that academic research has begun to focus on commitment risk, it has typically approached it from the viewpoint of portfolio construction. For instance, Phalippou and Westerfield (2012) emphasize that

> "[b]ecause these capital calls and distributions are stochastic, investors may suddenly become significantly over-committed or under-committed. Such swings [...] may reduce diversification benefits and move investors away from their optimal portfolio."

In essence, this research aims to address the following issue. Suppose an investor wants to have $x\%$ of his assets in private equity. In order to hit this target the investor is bound to have to overcommit at $(x + y)\%$. Thus, the challenge he faces is to determine y, with higher or lower values causing deviations from the overall optimal portfolio.[1]

Thus defined, commitment risk exists whether or not the LP has sufficient liquidity at any given point in time – for instance, thanks to a contractual credit line – to honour the GP's capital calls. However, things get considerably more complex if the LP finds itself in a situation where he faces a sudden liquidity constraint. This was the situation for a number of LPs during the recent financial crisis, and as they were forced to sell their most liquid assets (such as public stocks) and/or to raise bonds to avoid defaulting on their commitments in private equity and other illiquid assets, their portfolios drifted even further away from their optimal position.

In this chapter, we do not attempt to quantify the commitment risk premium. Our objective is humbler. Instead, our focus is on managing commitment risk. In addressing this issue, our discussion is guided by the following questions. To what extent do overcommitments to funds represent leverage? Given that fund investments involve commitment risk, is there a limit beyond which overcommitments appear imprudent? From the viewpoint of individual

[1] We thank Tim Jenkinson for clarifying this point.

partnerships, do undrawn commitments matter for the valuation of a fund? And to the extent that they do matter, how should they be priced? These questions will help us clarify the key issues and identify possible avenues of future research in dealing with cash flow uncertainty.

10.1 DO OVERCOMMITMENTS REPRESENT LEVERAGE?

As we have explained in Chapter 8, overcommitments refer to a strategy whereby an investor commits more capital in aggregate than he actually has at his disposal, with the gap expected to be filled by future distributions from his existing portfolio.[2] Overcommitments are typically made by investors to ensure that their actual exposure to private equity and similar illiquid assets is aligned with the optimal portfolio weights of these assets. The portfolio weights are set with a view to maximizing the risk-adjusted returns of the portfolio, implying that deviations are costly. On the downside, an overcommitment ratio (OCR) of less than 100% suggests an inefficient use of resources, given the long lead times associated with the due diligence process and the negotiations of the limited partnership agreements.[3] On the upside, a ratio of greater than 100% signals increased commitment risk in the sense that the investors might not have the required cash to respond to unpredictable capital calls when they occur. Other things being equal, (commitment) risk-adjusted returns are lowered. As already mentioned, views differ as to the degree of overcommitment that would still be seen as prudent. Arguably, an investor only becomes "really" overcommitted at OCRs above 105% to 110%, with OCRs of 125% and even more found to be relatively common (Mathonet and Meyer, 2007).

There are similarly divergent views as to whether overcommitments represent leverage. Those who take the view that overcommitments should not be seen as leverage argue that such strategies do not involve debt. However, this view may be disputed. It would, for instance, seem to be at odds with the AIFMD, which defines "leverage" as "*any method* by which the AIFM increases the exposure of an AIF it manages whether through borrowing of cash or securities, or leverage embedded in derivative positions *or by any other means*" (authors' emphasis).

Fundamentally, leverage is used to magnify returns, which is exactly the motivation behind overcommitment strategies. What is more, overcommitments may result in the need to get external funding. LPs pursuing overcommitment strategies may therefore need to put in place some sort of contingency planning to mitigate commitment risk, for instance, in the form of credit lines. Thus, although *ex ante* overcommitments may not entail borrowing, *ex post* such a strategy may result in debt being used to make equity investments in limited partnership funds, thus leveraging an investor's alternative portfolio. An example we have referred to earlier is the Harvard Management Company, which, among other things, issued a bond to avoid a default on its commitments to limited partnership funds.

---

[2] Overcommitments by LPs need to be distinguished from what is sometimes also labelled overcommitments by individual funds. GPs usually draw down only between 80% and 95% of the capital they have raised, with proceeds from exited investments sometimes being reinvested (Conner, 2005). This recycling within a fund is different from a LP's overcommitment because the GP has no obligation to continue to finance a portfolio company or to reinvest the proceeds by acquiring new assets, whereas a LP is contractually obliged to honour the capital calls.

[3] Arguably, overcommitments are especially relevant for funds-of-funds. While the potential cash drag may result in lower returns, managers of funds-of-funds generally are subject to commitment risk only to the extent that their limited partners fail to honour their commitments. Thus, for the GP managing a fund-of-funds it is critical to work closely with his LPs regarding the modelling of cash flows.

Alternatively, an investor might rely on the secondary market in the belief that he can sell his stakes in case of a liquidity squeeze. As Harris *et al.* (2012) note, commitment risk "[...] could be mitigated, to some extent, by secondary transactions to sell commitments to private equity funds". However, as these authors hasten to add, "[...] the development of such trading is still in its infancy". In fact, during the Great Recession this route proved illusionary for many investors. As a large number of LPs found it increasingly difficult to honour their undrawn commitments, they were able to find buyers only at extreme discounts. CalPERS, another example we have referred to in our previous discussion, thus decided to liquidate what proved to be the most liquid assets under the circumstances – public equity. While CalPERS was thus able to avoid raising capital in the debt markets, this came at substantial costs in terms of foregone returns in the stock market rally that followed.

Against this background, we are leaning towards the view of treating overcommitments as leverage from the point of view of measuring and managing risk. Although overcommitments may not involve debt, they are motivated by similar considerations and entail similar risks that need to be monitored and managed carefully.

10.2 HOW SHOULD UNDRAWN COMMITMENTS BE VALUED?

If undrawn commitments matter from a risk standpoint, how should they be priced? Let us consider a simple example.[4] Suppose we want to value two different funds.

- Fund A has undrawn commitments of USD 100, which are expected to be invested in year 2, with a subsequent exit of USD 200 in year 5.
- Fund B has no undrawn commitments. There is one portfolio company that is expected to be exited in year 3 for USD 36.22.

Assuming a discount rate of 15%, the NPV of both funds is USD 23.82, as can easily be calculated. Thus, the funds have the same value according to standard finance theory.

For the standard finance model, undrawn commitments do not matter. Different investments and assets can be valued in isolation. Each project has its own NPV, which is calculated by discounting future cash flows using an appropriate discount rate. If the NPV exceeds zero, the investment is economically valuable, regardless of how the capital is raised and how interim cash flows are reinvested. According to the standard model, undrawn commitments can therefore be ignored because they do not represent actual cash flows. In other words, undrawn commitments have a NPV of zero.

This view is shared by many academics and the majority of investors. As far as large pension funds and insurance firms are concerned, many have viewed their undrawn commitments essentially as irrelevant from a liquidity standpoint, given their relatively small allocations to illiquid partnerships compared with their holdings of public equity and bonds. However, the recent financial crisis has raised serious doubts about this view, and although not all investors suffered losses as significant as those reported for CalPERS, allegedly many institutional investors actually asked their GPs to postpone investments and hence the capital calls for contributions during the crisis.

[4] Arguably, overcommitments are especially relevant for funds-of-funds. While the potential cash drag may result in lower returns, managers of funds-of-funds generally are subject to commitment risk only to the extent that their limited partners fail to honour their commitments. Thus, for the GP managing a fund-of-funds it is critical to work closely with his LPs regarding the modelling of cash flows.

To avoid commitment risk, investors may decide not to overcommit and to hold liquidity in risk-free extremely liquid instruments, such as treasury bills. According to the standard model, treasury bills are zero-NPV investments, with low returns reflecting the absence of risk. However, in pursuing this strategy, the risk-averse investor suffers opportunity costs in the sense of foregone returns stemming from private equity and real assets. For simplicity reasons, let us assume that a private equity investment returns 15% per year, while the risk-free rate is 5% per year. If the average investment rate in private equity is at 66%, while 33% of the capital is on average held at the risk-free rate, the average return of the investor is reduced to 11.6%.[5]

From the viewpoint of the standard model in finance, there is no particular issue with the lower overall returns, as the overall risk is lower accordingly. Each individual asset is priced correctly and hence the investment in private equity – including undrawn commitments – is priced correctly. Thus, there appears to be no need for investors to take unfunded commitments into account.

In practice, however, commitment risk is unknown and the academic literature has yet to produce even a broad range of estimates. While efforts to quantify commitment risk are still embryonic, Harris *et al.* (2012, p. 30) conjecture that:

> "(t)he size of the commitment risk premium is likely to depend upon the ability (or willingness) of the investor to diversify their holdings across vintage years and, within vintage years, between funds . . . furthermore, the cost of deviating from an 'optimal' portfolio allocation, and the impact of cash-flow uncertainty, will vary across investors. Hence it is likely that commitment risk will vary significantly across investors."

Commitment risk represents a special characteristic of the limited partnership model. However, since this risk is very difficult to quantify, it aggravates substantially the investor's task of achieving optimal portfolio allocation. To the extent that in our example the risk-averse investor overestimates commitment risk, he will end up with a sub-optimal exposure to private equity and similar illiquid assets. According to the standard CAPM model, asset allocators choose a particular point on the efficient frontier by specifying a utility function, with the optimal portfolio being represented by the tangency with the efficient frontier. By holding cash in highly liquid low-return, low-risk assets the investor mitigates or even eliminates his commitment risk. However, holding such assets may imply a lower utility than his utility function would suggest, given the efficient frontier (Figure 10.1).

This brings us back to the issue of overcommitment strategies where investors aim to reach higher returns by harvesting illiquidity risk premiums, given their risk appetite. Committing more capital than an investor actually has at his disposal entails risk, which he is compensated for by higher expected returns in line with his utility function. However, undrawn commitments play a critical role in achieving the investor's optimal allocation, and in this sense they should not be ignored as standard finance theory would suggest.

[5] Diller and Kaserer (2004) calculate the return difference between a pure private equity strategy and a mixed strategy consisting of private equity investments and bond investments or equity investments. Using a sample of European private equity funds, they calculate an average IRR of 12%. As far as the mixed strategy is concerned, it is assumed that the undrawn commitments are invested in the MSCI Europe and the JP Morgan Government Bond Index. Similarly, the distributions are held in the same assets until the end of the fund's lifetime. The returns of the liquid public equity and bond investments are estimated at 9.8% and 8.2%, respectively, shaving around 2–4% off a pure private equity investment in terms of expected returns.

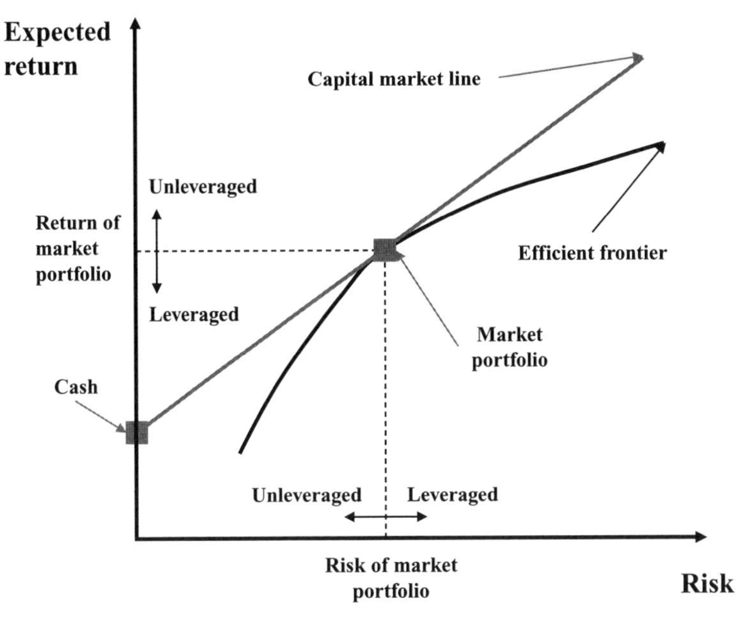

Figure 10.1 Capital market line, unleveraged and leveraged.

10.3 A POSSIBLE WAY FORWARD

In the standard model there is no straightforward way to deal with the particular characteristics of investments in limited partnership funds where investors have to hold enough cash to respond to capital calls at any given point in time. There are no liquidity constraints, and LPs are assumed to be able to finance negative cash flows in the market – an assumption that, we repeat, has proved to be misleading in the recent financial crisis. However, investors cannot simply toss out standard finance theory, unless the current model can be replaced by a superior coherent approach. Developing a model that deals explicitly with undrawn commitments is highly desirable, given the growing exposure of investors' portfolios to illiquid asset classes. While this sets an ambitious research agenda for years to come, the following discussion serves to clarify the issues that will need to be addressed in a revised framework.

10.3.1 Reconciling fund valuations with accounting view

In our preceding section we focused entirely on the real economic value of investments, ignoring entirely the accounting treatment of funds. However, accounting is important, as investors are required to report their allocations vis-à-vis internal agents as well as external parties, such as auditors and supervisors. Regulation requires reconciling risk measurement with the accounting view. In order to measure risk properly, valuations should mirror the true economic substance of an asset. Historically, limited partnership stakes have been valued and treated from an accounting standpoint in a relatively simple fashion. Specifically, investors have traditionally relied on the NAV reported by the GPs, a measure that is subject to considerable subjectivity, despite important regulatory reforms, such as the FAS 157. As we have argued above, the real value of a fund can only be realized over the long term, with NAVs reported on a quarterly basis providing at best a rough approximation.

Undrawn commitments are treated as off-balance-sheet items, and there is no link between the resources implicitly dedicated to the funds and the risk resulting from overcommitments. This can lead to a distorted picture and to investment decisions that fail to address risks and destroy value. If fund valuations based on cash flow projections do not reflect undrawn commitments, investors may find themselves in a situation where no resources are available for future capital calls – as they stem from future reflows from other funds.

How can we stay in the world of the standard finance model but make the impact of the undrawn commitments and the rewards and risks of overcommitting/overallocating to funds transparent? Traditionally, limited partnership funds have been modelled based on the funds' cash inflows and outflows. The commitment size (which determines the undrawn capital) as well as the change in the undrawn capital is usually not considered specifically. However, as argued above, liquidity risk is an essential part of risk management which needs to be reflected when modelling limited partnerships. This issue is important for two reasons: first, by modelling undrawn commitments as debt and overcommitments as leverage, it can be shown that a fund valuation model based on cash flow projections can be reconciled with an accounting view; second, even if investors are awash with liquidity, they want to optimize the use of undrawn commitments to ensure that their exposure is in line with their optimal portfolio.

10.3.2 Modelling undrawn commitments as debt

A possible solution may be sought in the modelling of a fund in its entirety as one financial instrument – the money managed by the GP – and the undrawn held by the LP essentially being a loan against this instrument. We have argued in the previous chapters that a LP stake in a fund has certain characteristics in common with a loan and that a limited partnership fund is somewhere between debt and equity. A standard valuation technique in finance is modelling one instrument as a combination of other instruments for which the values are known or easier to calculate.

Therefore, one way of approaching this issue is by viewing the LP as a bank which extends a credit line to the GP. The latter can draw it as he sees fit, like in any credit line with capital commitment being equal to the sum of capital calls and an interest-rate free loan that is being granted. Modelling undrawn commitments as a loan is not a new idea.[6] It is difficult (we are not saying it is impossible, but we have no proposal for it) when trying to model the limited partnership share as a loan given by the LP to the GP: the LP has no power to set the timing of the capital calls and the amount to be repaid by the GP is undefined (it can be less, but also much more) and cannot be enforced.

Instead of considering LPs as a lender, we suggest taking the opposite view. While this may seem counterintuitive, this approach is motivated by the observation that it is actually the GP who holds the power over the use of the undrawn commitments. From a modelling perspective, we thus assume that the GP calls the entire amount of commitments and then serves as a lender to his LPs. Seen from this perspective, the commitment size represents the principal, with the GP having a legal claim on the undrawn commitments. In parallel to a typical loan, the GP can restructure the relation with the LP if the latter defaults. In this situation the LP may lose the paid-in capital or suffer other penalties, with the GP holding the paid-in capital as collateral.

[6] We thank Ludovic Phalippou and Morten Sorensen for their detailed comments and suggestions on this section.

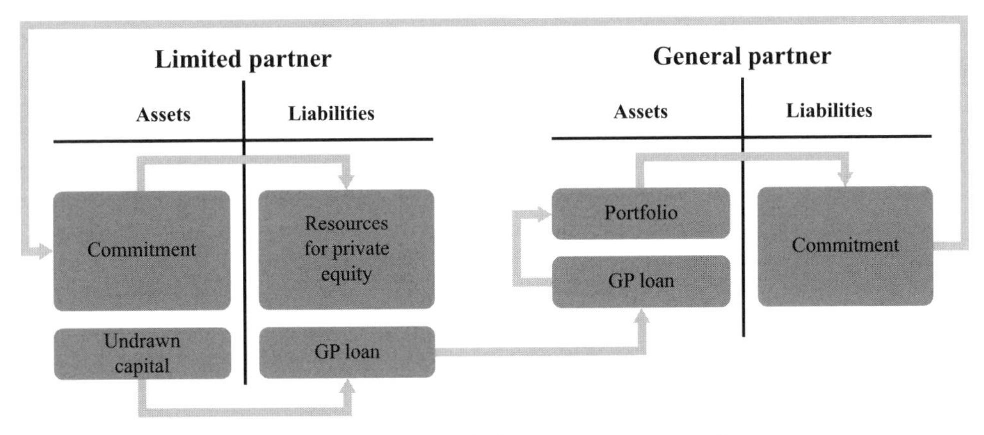

Figure 10.2 Flow of cash in first case: no overcommitment.

There is also a clearly specified time period during which the capital needs to be paid by the LP (i.e., the investment period[7]).

In essence, we consider two instruments: a commitment by the LP to the fund (reflecting a "virtual fund", i.e. commitment and distributions) and a loan by the GP to the LP (reflecting contributions). Cash flows from the LP to the GP and vice versa are not netted, as the required return for the loan provided by the GP is fixed at time of commitment and does not change afterwards (Figure 10.2).

From this perspective, many pieces of the puzzle start to fall into place. What we are interested in is the risk of default due to overcommitments. Considering the GP as a lender makes clear that a LP suffers a loss if he invests the loan in risk-free treasury assets. Measuring a fund's return exclusively on the basis of actual capital flows and ignoring the undrawn commitments thus provides the upper bound for the fund's performance. It is therefore necessary to optimize the resources dedicated to private equity and real assets even if sufficient liquidity is available, for example by following an overcommitment strategy (Figure 10.3)

The mental framework presented here is akin to a situation where a bank extends a loan to a GP, with the proceeds backed by the future capital calls from LPs. In our approach, the loan to the LP is modelled in a similar way as a loan from a bank. In fact, in recent years there have been cases where GPs have borrowed from banks to manage capital calls in challenging times. Importantly, banks have used the undrawn commitment of the LPs as security, analysing the creditworthiness of the LP. Since LPs pay interest to the bank, it is clear that unfunded commitments affect the returns of their investments in limited partnership funds.

10.3.3 The "virtual fund" as a basis for valuations

As our starting point, we treat a limited partnership fund as one entity, a "virtual fund" (VF), comprising the investment in the underlying alternative assets held by the fund as well as its undrawn capital. This treatment reflects the fact that commitments are contractually binding. In fact, until the mid-1980s it was common practice to call the entire capital at the time of the commitment or to draw down the commitment according to a predetermined schedule (Everts,

[7] In case there is a significant undrawn commitment left at the end of the investment period, this can be modelled by the LP paying back the remaining loan and the GP returning the same amount as capital instantaneously.

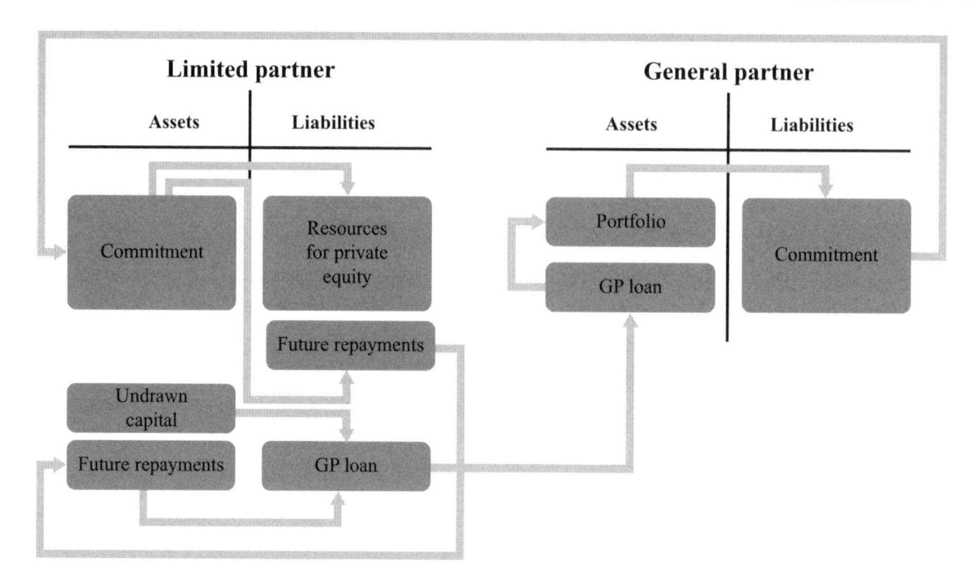

Figure 10.3 Flow of cash in second case: overcommitment.

2002). While the GP is assumed to manage the underlying assets, it is the LP's role to manage the undrawn capital. This arrangement is more efficient as LPs are typically institutional investors and thus are in a better position to pool and manage treasury assets. As we discussed in Chapter 4, however, timing and the use of undrawn commitments are under the GP's full discretion as if they were in "his hands" already.

Under such assumptions, the present value of the VF at the time of commitment is equal to the initial commitment size and thus the present value of future repayments from the fund:

$$\text{Commitment} = \sum_t \frac{D_t}{(1+d)^t}$$

with D_t denoting the distributions to VF in period t and d the discount rate, i.e. the rate of return that could be earned on an investment in the financial markets with similar risk. We model the fund's contributions C_t separately as a loan that the GP extends to the LP. Note that there are also returns resulting from the investment of the undrawn capital.

The discount rate d_{VF} for the VF can be determined by calculating the average IRR for one negative cash flow of the size of the commitment and the outflows from comparable funds taken from a historical cash flow library. Note that the discount rate for the VF's undrawn capital UC_{VF} will usually not be the LP's return d_{LP} on its undrawn capital: the discount rate for the VF's undrawn capital reflects the "market's" investment strategies, i.e. treasury assets and overcommitment level specific to all the other LPs.

How does the valuation of the VF change? For example, through "internal" changes such as the fund's PV or by accelerated drawdowns by the fund (reducing undrawn capital). When VF is returning capital, i.e. if there is an outflow of cash, its PV is reduced accordingly.

In order to assess the impact of overcommitments, we consider first the available resources for investing in funds. As explained before, the OCR is indicative of this risk:

$$\text{OCR} = \frac{\text{Signed commitments}}{\text{Resources available for commitments}}$$

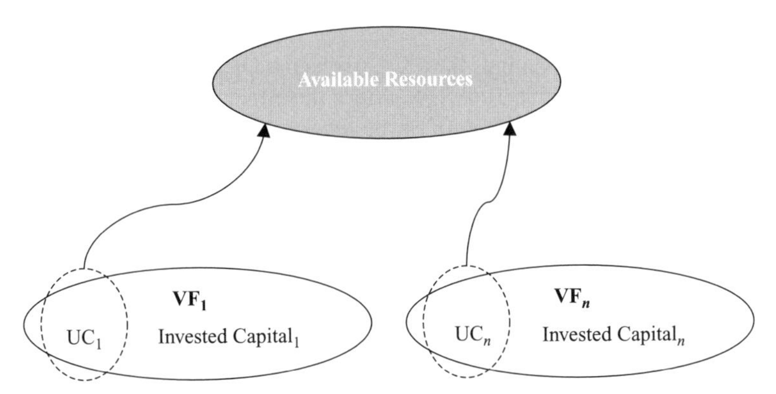

Figure 10.4 Modelling overcommitments.

If OCR > 100%, the difference between signed commitments and the resources available is the overcommitted capital (OCC):

$$\text{OCC} = \text{Signed commitments} - \text{Resources available for commitments}$$

What is the impact of overcommitments and how can we capture this in the LP's valuation of its portfolio of *n* funds? We model overcommitments as the *n* VFs "lending" their UC_{VF} to an account we call "available resources" (AR) (Figure 10.4).

The resources actually available are determined by

$$\text{AR} = \sum_{n} \text{UC}_n - \text{OCC}$$

For these resources, the LP has to pay opportunity costs of $d_{VF} - d_{LP}$. Why d_{VF} and not the average returns generated by investments in private equity and real assets? Within the framework of the standard finance model we can assume that the VF can borrow and lend at d_{VF}. These opportunity costs represent the so-called "cash drag" that can be reduced by the overcommitment. OCC can be reduced (and AR thus increased) by tapping into other sources of capital or by reinvesting returned capital from funds. However, for every capital call CC it has to be ensured that

$$\text{AR} \geq \text{CC}$$

Otherwise, the LP would become a defaulting investor. Because commitments are contractually binding, a LP who cannot meet his obligations is forced to default on payments and thus lose a substantial portion of his share in the partnership. Consequently, we need to factor in the expected losses potentially caused by becoming a defaulting investor. This overcommitment reserve (OR) increases proportionally with the OCR.

The size of the OR depends to a large degree on the other assets a LP has invested in. For an insurer, for example, with an immaterial allocation to alternative assets, treasury and cash stemming from the sell-off of liquid assets may be more than sufficient, so that the OR in fact would be negligible. EVCA's draft guidelines on private equity fund risk measurement suggest that liquidity shortfalls should be assessed conservatively, i.e. it should be assumed that existing individual fund positions will not provide any liquidity in the short term (EVCA,

2011). The valuation of the LP's portfolio is therefore the sum of the PVs of the VFs minus the opportunity costs for the AR minus the OCC minus the OR.

The example in Appendix Table 10.A.1 describes the effects of the value of the unfunded commitments and how it affects the return of the investor who has to reserve capital for the unfunded commitment. In this example, we consider the cash flows of a fund with a lifetime of 10 years. The commitment of 100 will be drawn down over 5 years in the investment period of the fund, whereas the first distributions start in year 4. Therefore, if the cash flows are netted, a capital amount of 80 is required to fund this commitment. Calculating the multiple of the fund shows that it returns twice the invested capital of 100. The IRR of this fund is 16%.

The virtual fund shows the cash flow stream given in Appendix Table 10.A.2. At the beginning, the investor lends capital from the virtual fund and pays back the "loan" through distributions resulting from the private equity investment. If the investor locks away available resources of 100, the virtual fund – that is, the investor – achieves an IRR of 11.7%, which implies a reduction of 4.3% compared to the pure private equity return of 16%. While in the standard model the lower return reflects comparatively less risk, this combination may be sub-optimal from the investor's standpoint given his utility function.

What can the investor do to achieve his optimal risk/return exposure? Let us consider in this framework an overcommitment strategy, whereby we assume that the investor holds reserves of less than 100 currency units. Figure 10.5 visualizes the impact of this strategy on returns. The return of the investor increases with the reduction of the available resources. When the available resources are equal to the maximum cash requirement – in our example 80 – the investor reaches the same return as in the pure private equity strategy. However, if the available resources of the investor fall to 70, the investor would default on his investment – unless of course he can borrow in the market at the given rate of interest. In the case of default, the investment return would be 0% – and most likely imply that the defaulting LP would no longer have access to investments in limited partnership funds.

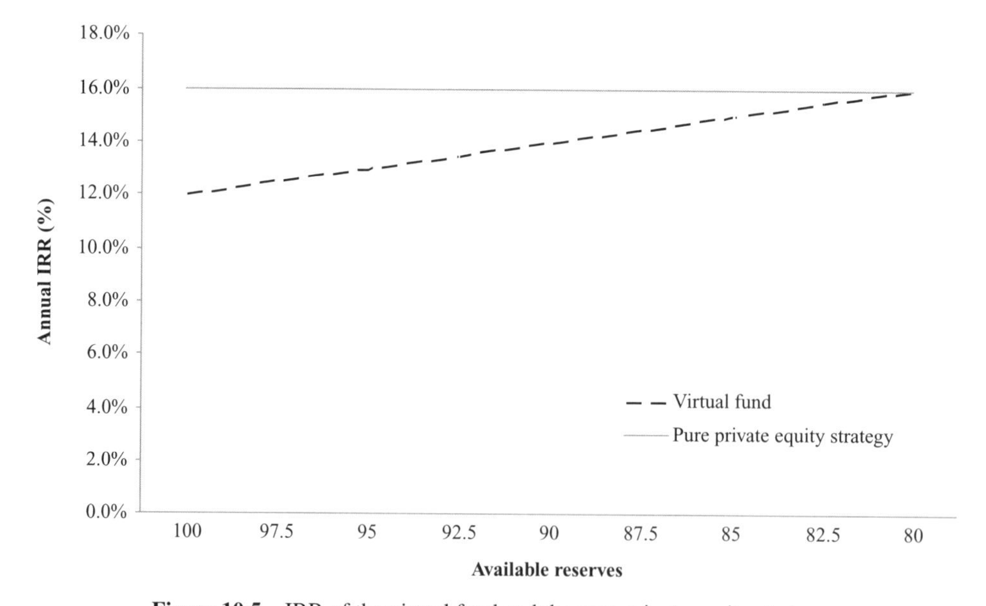

Figure 10.5 IRR of the virtual fund and the pure private equity strategy.

10.4 CONCLUSIONS

This chapter has focused on undrawn commitments, a critical characteristic of investments in illiquid limited partnership funds. Long ignored by investors and academics alike, there is growing interest in commitment risk thanks to the experience of several LPs during the recent financial crisis. Commonly, commitment risk is seen from the perspective of optimal portfolio allocation, with the risk premium being determined by the potential deviations from that allocation due to cash flow uncertainty.

Importantly, LPs are confronted with commitment risk, whether or not they are liquidity constrained. In reality, however, a non-trivial number of LPs found themselves in a situation where their overcommitment strategies led to sudden liquidity problems. In order to avoid defaulting on their commitments, several LPs were forced to sell their most liquid assets, such as public stocks, and/or to borrow in the debt capital markets at sharply higher rates, pushing their portfolios further away from the optimal diversification and raising the risk premium.

Although the quantification of commitment risk is subject to considerable challenges, and commitment risk is likely to vary across investors, the experience during the recent financial crisis suggests that the risk premium can be significant. If this is the case, unfunded commitments obviously matter. Against this background, this chapter has focused on three related issues. Do overcommitments represent leverage? Do undrawn commitments play a role in terms of fund valuations? And to the extent they do play a role, how should unfunded commitments be priced?

Although overcommitments do not involve debt *ex ante*, they share important commonalities with leveraged strategies, in our view. Importantly, overcommitments are made to magnify returns, just as leverage is used to amplify equity returns in buyouts. From the standpoint of standard finance models, this should not matter, however. To the extent that overcommitment strategies are used in order to achieve higher returns, they imply higher risk. Conversely, holding capital in low-yielding treasury bills to always be in a position to respond to capital calls reduces returns – but at the same time risk is reduced too.

Investors may therefore choose a commitment strategy that is consistent with a risk/return profile according to the investor's utility function – a conclusion that follows directly from standard finance theory. In practice, however, things are more complex. Given the tremendous difficulties in determining the (over-)commitment risk premium, the investor may end up in a sub-optimal portfolio position. Potentially, this position may turn out to be excessively risk-averse, implying opportunity costs in terms of foregone returns from illiquid investments. In the last section of this chapter, therefore, we have made an attempt to reconcile the accounting and economic perspectives on undrawn commitments. Clearly, this is a cutting-edge issue where views are still being developed and which undoubtedly will attract a huge amount of interest from both investors and academics alike in the years to come.

APPENDIX – EXAMPLES

Table 10.A.1 Cash flows for private equity fund example

Year	1	2	3	4	5	6	7	8	9	10
Contributions	25	25	20	20	10					
Distributions				10	20	30	40	45	30	25
Net cash flows	−25	−25	−20	−10	10	30	40	45	30	25
Cumulative net cash flows	−25	−50	−70	−80	−70	−40	0	45	75	100

Table 10.A.2 Cash flows and performance virtual fund compared with private equity fund for commitment size 100

Year	1	2	3	4	5	6	7	8	9	10	IRR	TVPI
Cash flow private equity fund	−25	−25	−20	−10	10	30	40	45	30	25	16.0%	2.25
Cash flow virtual fund	−100	0	0	10	20	30	40	45	30	25	11.7%	2.00

11 Cash Flow Modelling

"Any halfway decent portfolio manager can pick a few investments and beat the other institutional-grade asset classes on a return basis. Very real risks are hidden away from the naïve observer because they exist before the capital is drawn down, after the capital is distributed and, of course, with allocation shortfalls."

Kocis *et al.* (2009)

In this chapter we will discuss various techniques for generating cash flow samples for funds set up as illiquid limited partnerships. Such funds for assets like infrastructure, leveraged buyouts, VC, real estate and natural resources[1] share many characteristics and therefore can be modelled quite similarly, but between the various asset classes there are also statistically marked differences.[2] Rather than seeing limited partnership funds as an object that can be traded only with significant delays and at steep discounts, we see these vehicles as what could be called "cash flow assets": instead of trying to model prices they could fetch in a market, we see understanding their cash flows as critical to the successful construction of portfolios. Here modelling has a number of objectives, such as:

- Commitment pacing, i.e. the process by which the portfolio manager reaches the desired allocation to the asset class (Kocis *et al.*, 2009).
- Liquidity management, i.e. identifying excesses or shortfalls of capital, assessing the probability of becoming a defaulting investor and changing portfolios accordingly (Diller and Jäckel, 2010).
- Associated with this, risk management to achieve the targeted trade-off between risks and rewards. This can be achieved through, for example, determining the distribution of future cash flows per time period, the distribution of the final profit and loss, the distribution of the portfolio's final return or the probability of "defaulting" by not achieving a return target (Diller, 2007).
- Monitoring of projected against realized development to verify and if necessary correct the assumptions underlying the projections.

It would be dangerous to view the returns of such funds as the sole source of risk. There is significant risk pre- and post-investment and opportunity costs: pre-investment the funds' undrawn capital needs to be properly invested as well. The danger is that either insufficient cash is available to honour the funds' capital calls or that the undrawn capital is invested in securities and cannot be turned into cash without suffering a loss. How will capital returned by the funds be reinvested? Ideally, it should be recycled into other funds, but there is uncertainty regarding the timing of their capital calls. If too much of the capital is kept "in reserve", there is a shortfall risk related to the opportunity costs associated with not achieving the targeted allocation. This as well the discussion in the previous chapter illustrates that cash management

[1] Oil and gas, for example.

[2] Even within one asset class, such as private equity, this can be the case: Kocis *et al.* (2009) found differences between buyouts smaller than $1 billion, buyouts larger than $1 billion, early-stage VC, late-stage VC, mezzanine and distressed debt and base their modelling of future cash flows and valuations on this categorization.

is intertwined with portfolio and risk management. We intentionally use "management" for what is often referred to as "forecasting", but – in light of the long projection horizons and high uncertainty – this term may create inflated expectations.

11.1 PROJECTIONS AND FORECASTS

> "In public discussion about weather and climate, the words scenarios, projections, predictions, and forecasts are often used interchangeably, as if they are completely synonymous."
>
> MacCracken (2001)

Before the discussion of the various cash flow management techniques it is important to clarify what we are trying to achieve. For most investment managers the main justification and interest in modelling is related to decision making or problem solving. Here the general presumption is that a model's purpose is to predict with a reasonably high degree of precision,[3] which may work where stationary distributions are the regularities of interest. In the environment that characterizes alternative assets, however, distributions are not stationary and the ambition of modellers to be able to predict is questionable and unrealistic, almost naïve.

Indeed, as the quote above highlights, there is very little differentiation between scenarios, projections, predictions and forecasts. When talking about this subject there is clearly the expectation, or at least the hope, that a technique would be able to forecast with a meaningful degree of precision.[4] Or, to put it differently, what is the whole effort worth anyway if it cannot serve as a crystal ball to predict the future? One could suspect that there is ambiguity regarding these terms because expectations are often opposed: while the claim to be able to predict events over timeframes relevant for illiquid assets is questionable at best, many decision makers will reject results that do not fulfil this expectation. An example is the back-testing regulators require for internal models, which implicitly assumes a stable, predictable process where the past can be extended into the future – regulation remains silent on situations where this requirement cannot be met. The suggestion to look at ranges between best case and worst case is not addressing the issue. As van der Heijden (1996) points out, this does not add new concepts to the "forecasting" frame of mind.

If something is not a forecast and not reliable enough for the purpose intended, how can it be useful for decision making anyway? Most practitioners in this field would not feel comfortable with the claims of forecasting, and there is also the danger that such results will be accepted without question and thus lead to wrong decisions. Instead of believing in our ability to forecast, we rather rely on "projections" and for this purpose suggest the following distinctions.

- A projection is a conditional statement, i.e. something will happen provided that a condition is fulfilled. A model generating projections links future outcomes to conditions. Both conditions and outcomes can be probabilistic. Projections can be based on a relatively simple logic: we know that a fund's contributions in aggregate cannot exceed commitments and with a time lag such contributions are followed by distributions. While this does not allow for precise forecasts it nevertheless provides some useful information.

---

[3] See for example Palmer (2005), who put forward as features of good risk models that they have predictive qualities which can be used for decision-making purposes and that their predictions agree with known facts and can be validated.

[4] The distinction between the terms "prediction" and "forecast" is blurred. See for example Connolley (2007). For the purpose of this discussion we just use "forecast".

- For a forecast the condition is assumed to be fulfilled. In other words, a prediction is the maximum likelihood projection. Forecasts are a statistical summary of expert opinions (van der Heijden, 1996). As the "most likely" projection a forecast assumes a stable process that can be modelled and, as a consequence, that the model can be back-tested.
- Scenarios are a set of coherent, internally consistent, reasonably plausible, but structurally different futures (van der Heijden, 1996). Whereas projections and forecasts may be probabilistic, scenarios are alternative images without ascribed likelihoods of how the future might unfold.

Clearly, the objective of a forecast is to determine what will happen with a meaningful degree of precision but forecast accuracy will drop rapidly with lead time. The economy is a social and thus a complex system without a fixed cycle, where histories do not repeat themselves (Sherden, 1998). Projections, on the other hand, are based on the fact that even in a turbulent economy there is some degree of certainty about what will NOT happen. In such an environment we need to monitor the conditions underlying the projections with the aim of making them increasingly precise and reliable. We are more interested in "rolling forecasts" that may only be able to cover short time periods but mainly aim to ensure control of a portfolio. The techniques we are discussing are for projections to enable such rolling forecasts.

As opposed to forecasts, projections must go together with monitoring of assumptions and parameters. While projections are not a crystal ball and cannot predict the future, in regular intervals monitoring the assumptions and parameters and rerunning the projection model consistently allows changes in the environment to be picked up. The usefulness of projections stems from the disciplined and consistent execution of a control loop, where assumptions and data are monitored and adjusted over time.

11.2 WHAT IS A MODEL?

Before discussing the various possible modelling approaches we need to reflect on why we use models and what their limitations are. A model is a theoretical construct to describe and explain a real-life situation in a simplified way. In particular, a complex system needs to be modelled as one cannot comprehend it in its entirety. The model narrows the problem in question by focusing on only one aspect at a time. It has a set of variables and a set of logical relationships between them. These relationships are often – but not always – quantifiable by using mathematical techniques.

Because they are simplifications, models cannot be everything to everybody. To create value and despite many reservations, investment managers will at least try to forecast what will happen; whether they will succeed or not is a different matter. For risk management it is already valuable to know what will not happen. For this purpose, many models can be appropriate. Even if models cannot forecast, there are, according to Epstein (2008), other important reasons for modelling. To begin with, models are usually able to determine plausible ranges for outcomes. While within these ranges no real prediction with a reasonable degree of precision may be possible, this is often still of value from a risk management point of view. Models can illuminate core dynamics and uncertainties. In the alternative asset markets, where data is scarce and expensive, models can guide data collection and expose underlying market assumptions as incompatible with available data. Models can also point to inefficiencies and illustrate trade-offs. They help to structure the management dialogue around scenarios and to document decisions made to ensure the integrity of processes.

11.2.1 Model requirements

Often, practitioners debate whether one model is superior to another. As models are simplifications of reality and include only those elements that have broad effects or are judged as relevant to the given level of abstraction and the problem studied, there cannot be a definitive answer. In any case, models should never be treated as a "black box" and blindly followed. However, there are a number of criteria for cash flow models to be useful in practice:[5]

- The model must capture the essential features of limited partnership funds in a plausible manner. Therefore, it should be simple and sensible on a theoretical basis.
- The model should have the capability to treat a variety of fund types and their behaviour through setting of parameters.
- Since adequate data does not always exist for different fund types, there should be a continuous test of whether parameters are plausible and whether the behaviour of funds is different compared to the assumptions and to other illiquid fund types.
- Ideally, the model should not just generate a single value, but a range of potential outcomes.

Model outputs should be compared against actual outcomes and usually take the form of back-testing, which can be problematic as we discuss later in this chapter.

11.2.2 Model classification

When discussing approaches for generating projections we need to be clear that this cannot be the last word. To quote Kocis *et al.* (2009), even "with years of research and development on cash management, we continue to tinker with various approaches as our thinking evolves". Practitioners are faced with numerous trade-offs between conflicting requirements – like sophistication and simplicity, user-friendliness and frequency of running and checking models and their outcomes, flexibility and reliability, precision and robustness, etc. We are talking more about the "tricks of the trade" than about science. Projection approaches can be categorized in several ways, e.g. model-driven and data-driven, bottom-up and top-down, non-probabilistic and probabilistic.

Model-driven and data-driven

Weidig (2002a,b) differentiates between a model-driven and a data-driven approach. In the first case a phenomenon is described by a model with few input parameters. For such a model-driven projection approach the structure of a process and the factors influencing its behaviour need to be well understood. There is significant model risk because there is a high sensitivity to several input parameters that are difficult to observe and verify. Parameters can be based on judgment (i.e., they would be seen as "subjective") or on measurement (and thus seen as "objective"). However, subjectivity and objectivity are also not "black and white": to a large degree, even the selection of data to base the measurement on usually involves a high degree of subjectivity. The grading that we discuss in Chapter 13 tries to mitigate the subjectivity when selecting historical return figures as input to the projection model.

For a data-driven projection – also often referred to as bootstrapping – the structure and factors of a process do not need to be well understood and historical data sets the direction of

[5] See, for example, Takahashi and Alexander (2001) and Kocis *et al.* (2009).

future data. Weidig gives preference to a data-driven projection on a fund level as he sees model risk and sensitivity to be low: the description only reflects the past behaviour of comparable funds. In his view, a data-driven cash flow prediction at fund level is the conceptually most simple and efficient framework for a risk model. The problem we are faced with, however, is that for alternative assets too few historical data exist to allow this.

Bottom-up and top-down

A model can be constructed bottom-up or top-down. In a bottom-up approach, every portfolio company or project held by a fund is analysed in detail to determine the timing and size of its cash flows. A bottom-up analysis considers more factors that drive the overall risk but that individually also have a lower overall impact. Techniques for this purpose can be very simple – such as asking investment managers to give their estimates – or extremely complex, with all variations in between. What limits their usefulness for risk management is that the effort required is often too much for regular use, so a detailed discussion of such techniques is beyond the scope of this book.

Moreover, there are conceptual questions. In cases where the estimation of many of these factors requires judgment, biases can accumulate and the overall result will not necessarily be more precise than one generated by a top-down approach. With a top-down approach, many small factors can be encapsulated within a single one with significant impact, which also ensures that all material risks are identified. Here, funds are grouped according to their collectively coherent behaviour as reality can only be described at a reasonably high level of aggregation.

Very often decision makers express a preference for a bottom-up approach. They apparently expect this to give a better understanding of the underlying factors that drive risks and therefore ensure more reliable (i.e., more precise) results. Indeed, projections generated by bottom-up models often fall within narrower bands and thus appear to confirm this perception. What Tversky and Kahneman called "belief in the law of small numbers" may also play a role here. As few data are available in principle, decision makers could be subject to overconfidence in the stability of observed patterns (e.g., trust in the stability of early trends which are extrapolated from relatively little statistical information).

There are, however, conceptual as well as practical caveats. A bottom-up approach could be superior in situations where a fund's portfolio companies or projects develop independently. This assumption does not hold in all situations. The rule of thumb is that with approximately 20 reasonably independent positions the major amount of market risk is already diversified away. But LPs, through their diversified portfolios of funds, are often exposed to several hundred portfolio companies or projects. One answer to this puzzle is that we cannot assume a random process below the fund level, i.e. that portfolio companies or projects develop or fail independently from the rest of the portfolio held by a fund. For example, Inderst and Muennich (2003) looked at this question using a game-theoretical model. They found that funds having "shallow pockets" (i.e., commitments are unable to fully finance through all companies in a portfolio) is the optimum strategy in situations of high failure rates and high rewards, which characterizes VC financing. VC-funded companies require more than one injection of capital over time. Thus, shallow pockets give fund managers more bargaining power as entrepreneurs are forced to compete for scarce financing. This is a powerful incentive, since even small changes in performance may tip the balance in deciding whether new financing is provided to an entrepreneur or not. Without constraints, the fund managers cannot credibly threaten to withhold further financing. This implies that at least in the case of VC funds it does not make sense to follow a bottom-up approach. Additionally, changes in a fund's underlying portfolio do not translate directly into the cash flows to and from LPs.

It is understandable that one strives to incorporate specific terms, conditions and a range of variables and details into a model. However, caution is advisable: such bottom-up analyses are usually very cumbersome. Kocis *et al.* (2009) view this as a "leading cause of analysis paralysis in which no model is sufficient". Taking the high degree of uncertainty surrounding long-term illiquid asset classes into account, the returns to increasing modelling details are rapidly diminishing. Moreover, bottom-up analyses are often done for a specific purpose – i.e., the pricing of secondary fund positions, where there is a strong incentive for the buyer to have a systematic bias towards the pessimistic side. While a bottom-up approach clearly has its advantages in this context, biases in any form are detrimental for risk measurement, where a fair view of the economic substance is critical for the timely picking up of correct signals such as changes in trend.

Box 11.1 Look-through requirement

The bottom-up valuation approach should not be confused with the look-through required by auditors and regulators who need to know exactly how funds invest. For example, EC (2010) specifies that to properly assess the market risk inherent in collective investment funds their economic substance should be examined by applying a look-through approach in order to assess the risks applying to the assets underlying the investment vehicle *"[w]herever possible"*.

We need to differentiate between the look-through to ensure transparency and validate compliance with strategies and the bottom-up approach as a valuation technique that requires a comparable set of data. While the look-through treatment is designed to capture the risks of a fund's indirect holding of the underlying assets, in many cases the application of the look-through approach for funds can be impractical (Sourbes, 2012). The limited partnership fund's risk profile will not be appropriately captured by a look-through approach, which can only relate the existing assets that are reflected in the NAV but would not take the undrawn commitments into consideration. For their future use one could reference the fund's investment strategy and assume that this capital is invested in accordance and in line with past performance observed for this strategy – where a top-down approach is likely to produce more reliable results.

This does not mean, however, that the look-through principle is discarded. In order to decide which modelling approach should be applied, LPs still have to look through to the fund's portfolio companies in order to assess whether the approach is appropriate for the portfolio's composition and the underlying assumptions held.

Finally, what is "top-down" and what is "bottom-up" cannot be clearly defined and is largely a matter of perspective, depending on the object to be assessed: for example, a fund-of-funds could be modelled top-down, i.e. through looking at comparable funds-of-funds or bottom-up, by aggregating the individual funds in its portfolio. The individual funds again could be modelled top-down, i.e. by taking data from comparable funds as proxy or bottom-up, by analysing a fund's individual portfolio companies. A bottom-up perspective can calculate some measures, for example a return, which may be an input required for a top-down model.

Non-probabilistic and probabilistic

Related to the question of whether to go for a data-driven or a model-driven approach is the question of whether there is sufficient data to build a probabilistic model. Non-probabilistic models can be a solution in situations where too little data is available for a probabilistic approach. Instead, such models require a limited number of parameters which – due to the lack of data – will be highly subjective. As a consequence of these limitations, non-probabilistic models have to be robust and relatively simple. They can also only be applied in very specific situations. For example, the "Yale model" for limited partnership funds described below does not produce ranges for the outcomes and therefore does not capture volatility of cash flows and can only be used to manage liquidity risk for very large diversified portfolios of funds.[6]

Practitioners tend to prefer cash management models that are probabilistic because they show a range of potential outcomes (Kocis *et al.*, 2009). Probabilistic models base their forward-looking assumptions on historical data. In the end it comes down to whether data are available and what their quality is. For investors just starting to invest in an asset class and without access to large historical datasets, a non-probabilistic model may be the only feasible option. But also in situations where there are comprehensive datasets, there is a danger of being lost in a very sophisticated – but expensive to develop and maintain – model that, however, does not produce significantly better outputs. In reality the differentiation is less clear anyway, as many models are what could be described as "semi-probabilistic", i.e. not all but some of their input parameters are probabilistic.

11.3 NON-PROBABILISTIC MODELS

Takahashi and Alexander (2001) describe the "classic" non-probabilistic model for limited partnership funds[7] known simply as the "Yale model", which enables institutional investors to project future asset values and cash flows for funds in illiquid alternative asset classes.[8] Between 2001 and 2005 their paper "Illiquid Alternative Asset Fund Modelling" had been downloaded more than 10,000 times from the Yale School of Management International Center for Finance's website.[9] This demonstrates the wide acceptance of the Yale model and comparable techniques, which meanwhile has been followed up in a series of other papers, for example de Zwart *et al.* (2007), Hoek (2007) and Tolkamp (2007).

The Yale model mirrors the limited partnership's actual investment cycle, distinguishing contributions as cash inflows, distributions as cash outflows and the fund's underlying assets. The timing of all cash flows, as well as the return on the committed capital, is modelled as deterministic (i.e., for a given set of input parameters the model gives only one outcome). Nevertheless, according to the authors, the projections generated fit historical data surprisingly well. In fact, the model uses the best available information for each step (e.g., contributions are projected based on the undrawn commitment for the year and the remaining distributions are based on, among other factors, the current valuation).

---

[6] However, specific cases can be calculated by defining a worst, best and normal case with a defined set of input variables.

[7] Takahashi and Alexander (2001) use the term "illiquid funds".

[8] See, for example, Kocis *et al.* (2009). Note that several authors, for example Fraser-Sampson (2006), mean the multi-asset class investment strategy pioneered by the Yale endowment's David Swensen (see Swensen, 2009) when they confusingly also refer to the "Yale model".

[9] See http://icf.som.yale.edu/research/.

11.3.1 Characteristics of the Yale model

The purpose is to model the contributions and distributions for each time period of the fund's remaining life. Essentially, investment and divestment pace drive the contribution and distribution characteristics. Cash flows are modelled period-by-period and fund-by-fund and aggregated to the portfolio of funds level thereafter. The model proposed by Takahashi and Alexander (2001) works with yearly data. However, it can easily be expanded to incorporate the typical quarterly reporting intervals.

Investing in a fund starts with committing capital. The committed capital CC is not invested immediately and in full, but is called by the fund managers "just in time", i.e. whenever there is an investment opportunity. The paid-in capital in period t, PIC_t, consists of the total of capital contributions C_t in previous periods t:

$$\text{PIC}_t = \sum_{i=0}^{t-1} C_i$$

The remaining capital commitment, also often referred to as the "undrawn commitment", is CC minus the total of contributions in previous periods. The net contribution for the period is determined by the rate of contribution in period t, RC_t, which varies with the current age of the fund and defines what percentage of the remaining capital commitment is called. The contributions for period t depend on the initial amount of committed capital, the amount of capital already paid-in and RC_t:

$$C_t = \text{RC}_t{}^* \, (\text{CC} - \text{PIC}_t)$$

Theoretically, RC_t could be customized for each fund but in practice this is usually done per sub-asset class or vintage year. In situations where the undrawn commitment is zero there will obviously not be any contribution. A schedule based on contribution rates implies that the commitment will never be fully funded, but this is realistic as many funds underinvest and do not call all the capital pledged.[10]

In every period, a portion of the fund's NAV is distributed. The distributions D_t in period t depend on the rate of distribution RD, NAV_t as the valuation of the portfolio held by the fund and the fund's fixed growth rate G:

$$D_t = \text{RD}^* \text{NAV}_{t-1}{}^* \, (1 + G)$$

G combines realized and unrealized returns. The NAV increases with positive G and new contributions. It decreases with the distributions:

$$\text{NAV}_t = \text{NAV}_{t-1}{}^* \, (1 + G) + C_t - D_t$$

While the rate of contributions is set according to a schedule for each period, the Yale model assumes the rate of distribution to be dependent on the fund's lifetime L and the greater of the fixed yield Y and a rate proportional to the age of the fund, the so-called "bow factor" B:

$$\text{RD} = \text{Max}\left[Y, \left(\frac{t}{L}\right)^B\right]$$

[10] However, in reality funds also "overinvest" by reinvesting capital, a characteristic which is not captured directly by the model.

Essentially, this function describes whether the rate of distribution increases or decreases during the fund's life. The yield $Y \leq 1$ is introduced to make the Yale model useful for a variety of fund types. It sets a minimum distribution level and is used to model income-generating asset types such as real estate or infrastructure. Funds with assets like VC may not generate a periodic income. In such cases the yield is set to zero.

Depending on B, the rate of distribution is larger either at the beginning or end of the fund's lifetime. Plotting the relationship between a fund's age and its distribution rates for various values of B shows that for $B = 1$ it is a straight line whereas for $B \neq 1$ it follows a curve, hence the term "bow factor". For $B < 1$ the curve is concave, while $B = 0$ reflects the extreme case where the entire NAV_t for the year is always paid out immediately.[11] For $B > 1$ the curve is convex, with $B \to \infty$ we have the extreme where the entire NAV_t is paid out at the very end, i.e. when $t = L$ and

$$\text{RD} = \left(\frac{L}{L}\right)^B = 1$$

The rate of distribution can of course never be larger than 1, otherwise more than the NAV would be distributed:

$$\text{RD} = \text{Min}\left[1, \left(\frac{t}{L}\right)^B\right]$$

For $B = 1$ the rate of distribution does not change from time period to time period. For example, for a fund with lifetime $L = 10$ years each year 10% of the current NAV would be distributed. Note that while the rate remains constant here, the amount distributed every year is different. For $B > 1$ the rate of distribution increases with the age of the fund, while for $B < 1$ it is larger in the fund's early years. The higher the bow factor, the longer it takes for significant distributions to set in. So, for example, if $B = 2$ and the fund with an assumed lifetime of 10 years is in its eighth year, then the rate proportional to the age of the fund is

$$\left(\frac{8}{10}\right)^2 = 64\%$$

This rate appears to be quite large, but for this mature fund there are just 2 years to full liquidation. See Figure 11.1.

11.3.2 Extensions of the Yale model

Tolkamp (2007) proposes an extension of the Yale model where a performance index drives the returns of all individual vintage years of a portfolio of funds. This index can then be related to the macroeconomic environment which facilitates the funds' performance. It consists of growth rates G_t which the funds are able to generate in that specific year. Tolkamp's model does not assume fixed yearly NAV growth rates but a specific growth rate affects every vintage year. It is pooling cash flows and related performance numbers and models entire vintage years of funds. This modification of the Yale model is used to fit projected performance data to actual performance data for the purpose of deriving an index.

[11] As there can still be contributions for the fund it is possible that in the following periods there will again be a non-zero NAV.

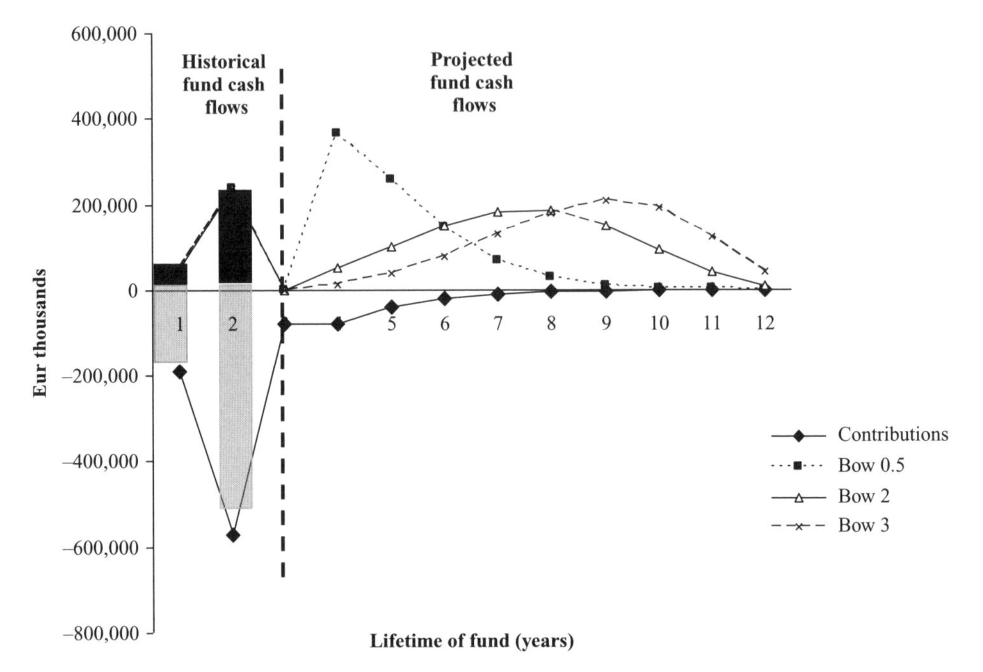

Figure 11.1 Yale model with different bow factors.

Hoek (2007) presented another version of the Yale model using aggregate data from Venture Economics for US buyouts and venture capital. A group of investment experts was consulted, in particular to critically evaluate whether the dynamics generated by the model are sufficiently in accordance with the behaviour of private equity in real life. Like Tolkamp (2007), Hoek (2007) also assumes that both the growth rate G_t and the distribution rate RD_t are stochastic, with G_t depending on the return of public equity but with "marking-to-market" valuations taking place with some delay. The author discusses further extensions of a stochastic model with regard to the contribution rate.

While Hoek describes his model as "stochastically extended", it nevertheless also creates just one result for one set of input parameters and not a range of outcomes. Clearly, and like with all other models, the longer the time horizon the less precise the Yale model's projections can be. While their mechanics are simple and allow for various scenarios by adjusting the input parameters, the relatively high number of parameters and the need to estimate them reduces the usefulness of non-probabilistic models. In particular, the inability to project widening ranges clearly restricts the usefulness of the Yale model and its extensions for risk management purposes.

The Yale model and its various extensions assume that the future cash flows can be generated from the reported NAV using a distribution scheme and require as input a growth rate and a distribution function. In the Yale model the growth rate equals the fund's IRR. As this is a non-linear measure the adjustment to new information – such as changes in a fund's expected lifetime – is not straightforward. Consistency requires that the modelled future cash flows discounted by the estimated IRR equals the value of the remaining portfolio, but Weidig (2002a) demonstrates that the generated cash flows plus the past cash flow do not always result in an IRR that equals the interim IRR.

11.3.3 Limitations of the Yale model

The Yale model is simple and easy to implement. There are relatively few input variables and it can be used even in situations where there are no or only insignificant historical data available. Clearly, this is also the Yale model's Achilles heel, as the output quality depends on how well the input parameters are chosen. This model is not intended to forecast in the sense that one can predict the fund's investment performance. The fund's expected final performance in the form of its growth rate G is an input parameter that drives the projections. In contrast to a probabilistic model, a single run of this model creates just one result for one set of input parameters and not a range of outcomes. Since the Yale model cannot reflect the volatility of annual cash flows it is of little use for managing liquidity risk and does not allow the calculation of a CFaR. It is difficult to track and compare the real development against the model and to capture stochastic processes and correlations between the different asset classes that are modelled.

The Yale model appears to explain the dynamics of limited partnership funds quite nicely, but caution is warranted with regard to the model's actual accuracy in concrete portfolios. The annual growth rate is assumed to be constant, i.e. identical to the final return realized by the fund, which is unobservable during its lifetime. The NAV figure is determined by the model's inner logic, which reconciles contribution and distribution schedules. It must not be confused with the real accounting figures for the NAV reported by the fund manager and will rarely be reconcilable with them.

In any case, it is unclear how to estimate the growth rate, i.e. the fund's final IRR, and the size of its random fluctuations. While it is standard practice to estimate the final IRR by the interim IRR (IIRR), the IIRR only becomes a reliable yardstick after the investment period has mostly been finished (Weidig, 2002a). We will return to this subject in more detail in the following chapters: during the investment period we essentially estimate the growth rates based on historically observed returns of comparable funds. As the IRR implicitly is a function of TVPI and lifetime, changing the lifetime of the fund and adjusting the various Yale model parameters so that the growth rate is equal to the IRR with the original lifetime is conceptually problematic. In the following we therefore do not consider the IRR but assume that lifetime and TVPI are two separate and independent inputs into a fund's model. The scaling of a fund's lifetime, with acceleration or deceleration of cash flows, allows a major component of its liquidity risk to be modelled. The scaling of its TVPI can help model a major driver of the fund's capital risk.

11.4 PROBABILISTIC MODELS

To be able to make investment decisions we need reliable averages or even better, ranges of possible outcomes. In most cases this will not be meaningful for individual funds but for portfolios of funds.[12] Kocis *et al.* (2009) built their model by summing contributions and

[12] One approach has been described by Buchner *et al.* (2010) as they develop a continuous-time model of the cash flow dynamics and equilibrium values of private equity funds, which implies the lifecycle of systematic fund risk and fund value. Based on their definition of the stochastic processes for contributions and distributions, the authors also derive equilibrium fund values based on Merton's intertemporal CAPM. Thereafter, the model is calibrated to a sample of 203 mature European private equity funds. Comparing the empirical results with the model shows a good fit of the stochastic approach. Bitsch *et al.* (2010) analyse the cash flow pattern of infrastructure funds. Another type of model that is based on Monte Carlo simulations is described in Diller and Herger (2009) and based on historical cash flow patterns of funds. In addition, a stochastic return for a public market is simulated. This PME-based approach allows the adjustment and stressing of fund returns.

distributions separately for each fund in a sample database for each year of its existence and recording the NAV at the end of the year for each fund. To allow comparisons to other funds, these amounts are then expressed as a percentage of the fund's size. Under the assumption that for each year in their life funds within each category behave differently, the statistics could help to answer questions like what percentage of a fund was drawn or what distributions can be expected for a given year. The main assumption of their model is that contributions, distributions and valuations are independent. This assumption could be challenged but as always when modelling, there are trade-offs between sophistication and robustness. Kocis *et al.* (2009) found that adding the additional layer of complexity involved in time-series analysis had mixed results and was not necessarily beneficial.

11.4.1 Cash flow libraries

We use historical data to model the behaviour of limited partnership funds. This approach is based on the major assumption that historical data are representative. The more data are available and the longer their history, the more likely it is that we fully capture the dynamics of the market. The main question is how to adjust the historical cash flows to fit the fund. Here, various approaches are possible. One method would be to compile the statistics of cash flows for each time period and draw from this independently for every cash flow. This assumes the absence of autocorrelation between consecutive cash flows, which might not always be justifiable (Weidig, 2002b). Taking account of autocorrelation would be more convincing but makes the model far more complicated and requires the introduction of other assumptions that will be difficult to justify as well.

Alternatively, we can base a model on libraries where for every fund the entire cash flow history is provided. We limit our discussion to this case. A historical library of comparable and liquidated funds with the same contractual structure H is defined as a set of library entries for the cash flows generated by m funds in the past:

$$H \equiv \{h_1, \ldots, h_m\}$$

Each library entry h_i for a fund with a lifetime of $L = n_i$ periods is defined as a set of its committed capital, contributions and distributions:

$$h_i \equiv \left\{\mathrm{CC}_i, C_1, \ldots, C_{n_i}, D_1, \ldots, D_{n_i}\right\}$$

To keep the discussion simple, we do not consider asymmetries between various investors in a fund.[13] The comparable funds are selected from H. The question is how to decide which historical funds can be seen as comparable. The greater the number of funds and the more diverse the vintage years, the more representative the sample becomes. The more restrictive the criteria, the fewer comparable funds are available. A few commercial data vendors provide cash flow data, while some investors may make use of their proprietary datasets (Figure 11.2).

In many situations, fund libraries are incomplete in the sense that individual cash flows are missing and the IRR and TVPI for each fund are given instead. These figures reflect the

[13] For example, we do not discuss the situation where the government is taking a subordinate stake in a VC fund.

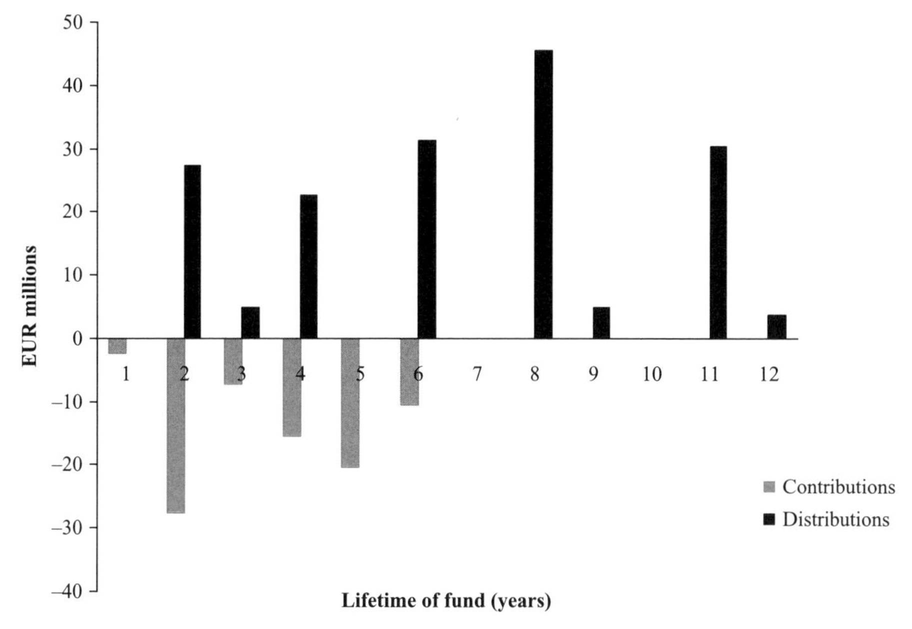

Figure 11.2 Probabilistic fund model.

aggregate of the cash flows but do not capture their full information. To generate consistent samples for cash flow projections requires several functions:

- Randomly select a cash flow series h_i from the library H.
- Randomly select a cash flow series h_i from the library H with constraints defined by parameters such as lifetime and TVPI.
- Build "synthetic" cash flows to fit the fund's actual age and the parameters of lifetime and TVPI.

To randomly select a cash flow series from H is consistent with the assumption that past behaviour characterizes future behaviour. Characteristics of future portfolios could then be derived by simulating combinations of such cash flow series. The problem is that generally too few historical observations are available to make this meaningful. How can we increase the sample size? We could take the cash flow series for one fund with a different lifetime and multiply and scale it accordingly to achieve a target lifetime and target multiple. This assumes that cash flow patterns of funds remain the same regardless of their performance and therefore cash flows of comparable funds can be adjusted to fit a fund and that adjusting is useful after all.

11.4.2 Projecting a fund's lifetime

For funds that have already achieved a certain maturity, we also need to predict their remaining cash flows. Again, we are faced with some challenges. For instance, what is the remaining lifetime to select for a fund? And how to ensure consistency between a fund's past and its future cash flows?

Internal age

The internal age is a measure of how far advanced the fund is at the time of the cash flows in the investment and divestment of its companies. The internal age at a given time is then half the sum of the investment and divestment ratio, giving a value between 0 and 1.

Modelling contributions is relatively simple, as they are normally clearly defined in the limited partnership agreement with a pre-agreed maximum and should thus evolve from 0 up to the fund size. However, to be accurate, it should be taken into account that the total fund size is not always fully drawn down and that some funds allow drawing down more than the fund size (e.g., reinvestment of management fees). Formally, using a scale of 0 to 1, the "contribution age"[14] can be written as

$$0 \leq \frac{\sum_{i=1}^{t} C_i}{\sum_{i=1}^{L} C_i} \leq 1$$

Distributions are more difficult to model, as their total will only be known at the end of the fund's life. One possible approach lies in estimating distributions based on general market statistics (average total repayments) or any other estimator of total repayment. For simplicity, the third component of the interim IRR, the NAV plus the undrawn, can be used as a proxy. Formally, using a scale of 0 to 1, the "distribution age"[15] can be written as

$$0 \leq \frac{\sum_{i=1}^{t} D_i}{\text{NAV}_t + \text{Undrawn}_t + \sum_{i=1}^{t} D_i} \leq 1$$

By combining the "contribution age" and the "distribution age", we get an estimator of the fund's internal age. Finally, for simplicity reasons, it is divided by 2 in order to have the internal age ranging from 0 to 1:

$$\text{IA} = {}^1\!/_2 * \left(\frac{\sum_{i=1}^{t} C_i}{\sum_{i=1}^{L} C_i} + \frac{\sum_{i=1}^{t} D_i}{\text{NAV}_t + \text{Undrawn}_t + \sum_{i=1}^{t} D_i} \right)$$

This internal age will allow us to align a fund's contractual lifetime and its current age to project its expected lifetime. See Figure 11.3.

Expected lifetime of a fund

To properly capture the increasing certainty in the projection over a fund's life, the range for projections of the lifetime volatility should be large for young funds, smaller for maturing funds and 0 for liquidated funds. Calculating the lifetime volatility needs to be dealt with in

[14] Called "drawdown age" by Weidig; see Meyer and Weidig (2003).
[15] Called "repayment age" by Weidig; see Meyer and Weidig (2003).

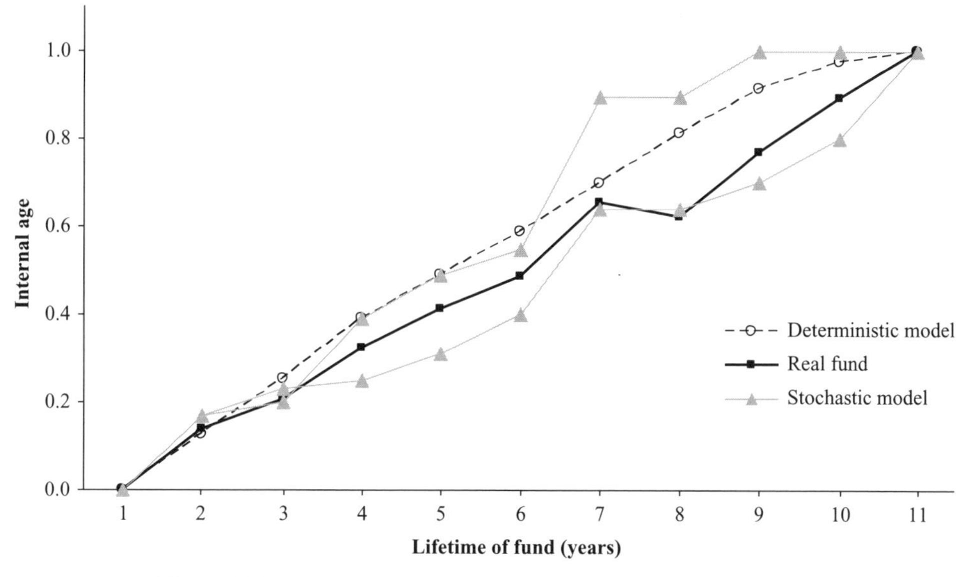

Figure 11.3 Internal age development of a limited partnership fund.

two steps: firstly, we have to determine the expected lifetime for a fund; secondly, we need to capture the minimum and maximum lifetime projected.

There are several reasonable approaches to estimating a fund's expected lifetime at time 0. For example, one could take a fund's contractual lifetime as first indicator for the expected lifetime. Another approach is to take the population of comparable funds (e.g., with the same contractual lifetime) and calculate the historical observed average lifetime for this population.

Regardless of which methodology is used for the estimate, the expected fund lifetime at time 0 is defined as $\bar{L}_0$. With the internal age we can project the expected lifetime at time $t+1$ based on the expected lifetime at time t as $\bar{L}_{t+1} = \bar{L}_t * (1 - \mathrm{IA}_{t+1}) + t + 1$. Note that $\bar{L}_t \geq t; \forall t \geq 0$.

The range for the lifetime poses another complication as we cannot assume it to be symmetrically distributed around $\bar{L}_0$. Experience suggests that the fund's lifetime can be significantly longer than the contractual lifetime, but that shorter lifetimes are rarely observed.

At the beginning of a fund's lifetime we assume a fund's maximum downward deviation as d time periods and set its maximum upward deviation as u time periods. We also need to cater for the situation where the current lifetime is already larger than the expected lifetime minus the downward deviation. One possibility is to run a Monte Carlo simulation of a fund at time t with expected lifetime $\bar{L}_t$, drawing one sample for the projected lifetime from the interval

$$\left[\max\left\{\bar{L}_t - (1 - \mathrm{IA}_t) * d\ ;\ t\right\}; \bar{L}_t + (1 - \mathrm{IA}_t) * u\right]$$

The parameters d and u can be determined based on historical experience, i.e. again taking the population of comparable funds (e.g., with the same contractual lifetime) and calculating the range between minimum and maximum lifetimes for this population. Often funds have a contractual lifetime of 10 years with a "1+1" extension. However, just 2 years as upward deviation appears too little for a fund at the time of commitment. In this case, for example, a reasonable estimate could be a 2-year downward and a 5-year upward deviation.

11.4.3 Scaling operations

Situations where a randomly selected cash flow series is scaled according to various parameters are consistent with the assumption that past cash flow patterns of funds are indicative of cash flow patterns of future funds. How can we scale a cash flow series h from the library H with a lifetime of $L^* = n$ and a multiple of TVPI* to a projected lifetime of $L = m$ or a projected multiple of TVPI, respectively?

Scaling of a fund's lifetime

We assume that the library entry gives us, for a fund, a lifetime of $L^* = n$ with contributions $\{C_1^*, \ldots, C_n^*\}$ and distributions $\{D_1^*, \ldots, D_n^*\}$. Adjusting to the projected lifetime while keeping the TVPI* unchanged requires spreading the cash flows over m instead of n quarters. As contributions tend to follow a more predictable and less volatile pattern – in the Yale model, a schedule is defined for this – they will typically not be affected by increases in a fund's lifetime. However, it is also possible to stretch the contributions proportionally with a different but lower factor: this may be necessary, for example, when $m < n$. For simplicity we just discuss the scaling of the lifetime for distributions.

Changing the fund's lifetime from L^* to $L = m$ requires spreading n distributions over m time periods. For this purpose we split D_i^* into m cash flows and define:

$$D_{i,j}^* = \frac{D_i^*}{m}; i = 1, \ldots, n; j = 1, \ldots, m$$

We re-label $D_{(i-1)*m+j}^+ = D_{i,j}^*$. Then for the fund with lifetime L the distribution for time period $j = 1, \ldots, m$ is:

$$D_j = \sum_{i=(j-1)*n+1}^{j*n} D_i^+$$

Note that this transformation does not change the fund's projected TVPI. See Figure 11.4.

Scaling of a fund's cash flows to a target TVPI

We assume that the library entry gives us, for a fund, contributions $\{C_1^*, \ldots, C_L^*\}$ and distributions $\{D_1^*, \ldots, D_L^*\}$, which results in a multiple

$$\text{TVPI}^* = \frac{\sum_{i=1}^{L} D_i^*}{\sum_{i=1}^{L} C_i^*}$$

Again, for simplicity, we assume that the rescaling just affects the distributions. We rescale the fund's distributions to a projected multiple of TVPI and keep its lifetime L^* unchanged. This gives, for the rescaled projection of contributions and distribution,

$$\left.\begin{aligned} C_i &= C_i^* \\ D_i &= \frac{\text{TVPI}}{\text{TVPI}^*} * D_i^* \end{aligned}\right\}; \quad i = 1, \ldots, n$$

See Figure 11.5.

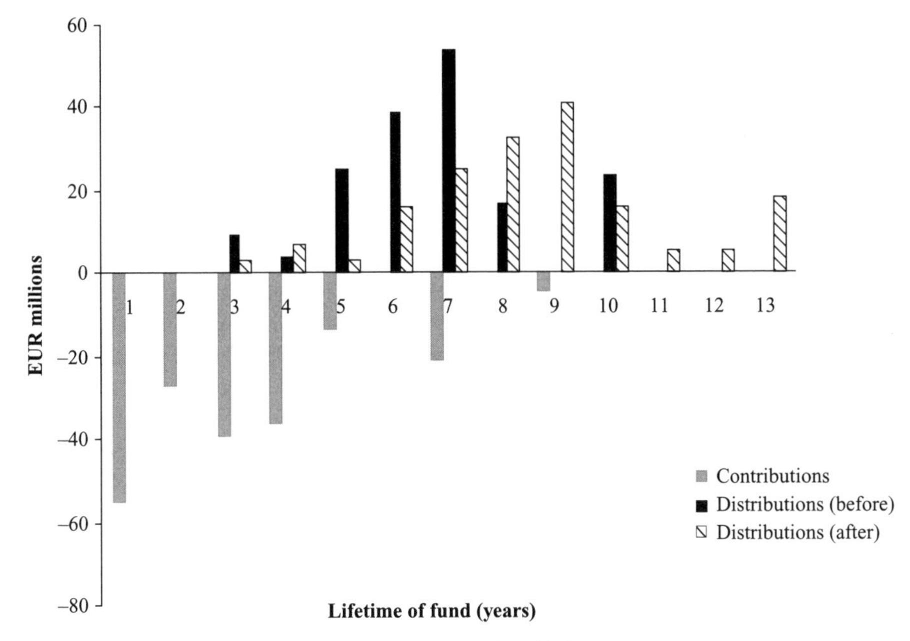

Figure 11.4 Scaling lifetime.

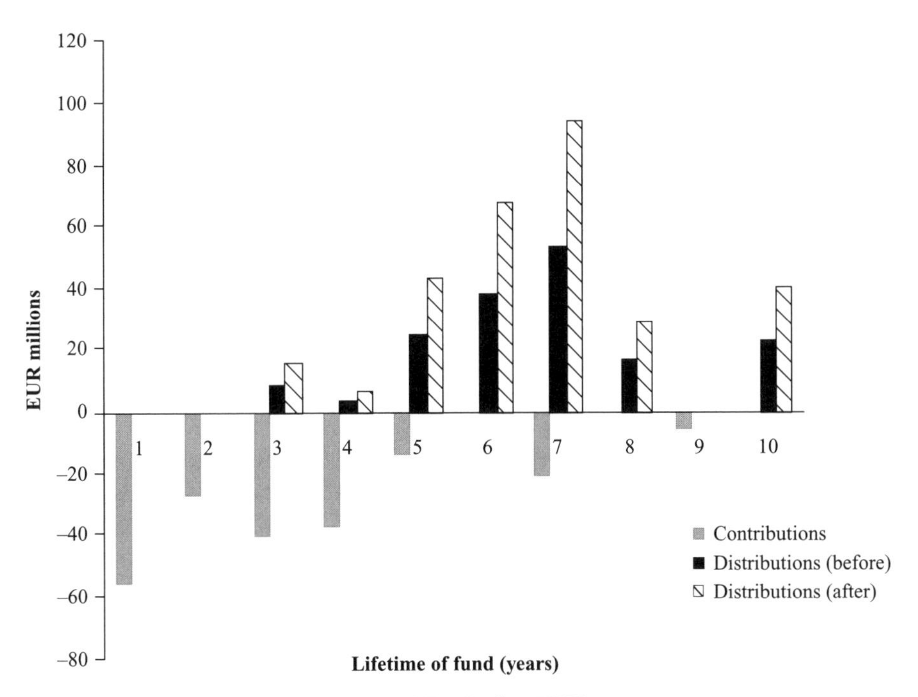

Figure 11.5 Scaling TVPI.

11.5 SCENARIOS

Any modelling approach has limitations, since it is so reliant on collecting actual internal and external data from cash flows that have occurred to determine frequency and severity distributions. It is dangerous to focus overly on historical data; instead, underlying latent conditions that arise from market shifts and where the impact spreads throughout the portfolio need to be addressed. Therefore, an important alternative approach is the use of scenarios, which for the purpose of this discussion are techniques that are heavily based on judgments and inputs by investment professionals rather than relying on a probabilistic or non-probabilistic model. What is relevant for projections is a matter of perspective and proportionality. One could argue that fund managers aim for and are thus exposed to rare events with high impact, such as IPOs. LPs, on the other hand, are mainly exposed to relatively frequent events with little to moderate individual impact.

Experience suggests that in alternative assets the major part of aggregate gains is driven by a small number of large events. The frequent minor events captured by statistics provide limited information and are almost irrelevant to the decision to invest in an asset class. One could argue that risk management for alternative assets cannot focus on eliminating smaller risks; it is rather about developing the right "drag net" for the high-impact events that are critical for success. As stakes in funds cannot be infinitely small, not all opportunities can be captured and not all markets can be covered. This also implies a much stronger integration of risk management in the overall investment process compared to more conventional asset classes.

There are also situations – VC is the "classical" one – where historical averages can only lead to the conclusion that the activity should not be pursued. In principle, there are two possible routes to overcome this in a meaningful way. The first route is to factor in selection skills (i.e., eliminate data from the statistics that is seen to give a too negative bias). How to improve investment strategy, etc. goes beyond the scope of this discussion, but how far can one realistically go in a competitive environment? The other route is to focus one's modelling attention on the outliers – large but infrequent and unpredictable payoffs – in the distribution.

High gains with high frequency would be the Holy Grail in alternative assets, but at least under usual circumstances (the dot-com bubble was one exception) this remains largely illusive. High gains are highly unlikely, as otherwise this would not be an alternative asset class in the first place (everybody would like to do it) and consequently there cannot be any reliable statistics, which restricts the use of probabilistic models.

This also has consequences regarding the back-testing requirement for a model: factors that are easy to quantify are not relevant, whereas for the factors that are most relevant for the asset class's raison d'être, little evidence beyond expert judgment can be provided. See Table 11.1.

In this situation the use of scenarios can be the most appropriate approach to determining figures for the high-impact, low-frequency events that drive the fund's cash flows. Utilizing relevant data and assessments of the business environment, scenarios rely heavily on expert judgment to determine relevance and fill in gaps in the data. High-level scenario analysis can ensure that all material factors are identified. In practice, this is a three-stage process where in the first step scenarios are identified and their parameters are determined. Then, the scenarios and parameters are reviewed by business experts. Finally, a senior management committee needs to review and approve this.

Scenarios not only apply to the rare high-impact events but also to projections over long timeframes with their potential fundamental shifts in overall conditions. Van der Heijden (1996) points out that scenarios cannot be proved or disproved, as there is no claim that

Table 11.1 Relationship gains and frequency of gains materializing

	Small gains	Large gains
Low frequency	Atypical, but can characterize long periods of drought in the market.	Typical "major" events that cause primary modelling challenge but constitute what alternative assets are about. Difficult to understand and anticipate, by definition.
High frequency	Usually "minor" events. Generally don't make the difference compared to conventional asset classes (or underperform by definition). Similarities make it difficult to differentiate between high and low performers among funds. Main basis for improving investment programme efficiencies. Main relevance for liquidity/cash flow management.	Atypical, only observed during bubble periods.

they will materialize as such in the first place, and they are not supposed to be used on that basis.

11.6 BLENDING OF PROJECTIONS GENERATED BY VARIOUS MODELS

Scenarios are a pragmatic approach that can give reasonable results and are cost-effective to implement. They are easy to adapt and adjust to changing circumstances. Generally, modellers should beware of the human desire for "the silver bullet" and avoid the simplistic preoccupation with a single technique. In practice, therefore, hybrids of scenarios and probabilistic models are recommended.

Stochastic approaches to cash flow projections can well capture small-impact, high-frequency events, whereas scenario techniques are better at dealing with large rare events. A "blending" of various approaches is often required, but this needs a rescaling of the fund's remaining cash flows to be consistent in the sense that its projected lifetime and projected TVPI do not change.

To be able to blend a projection derived from another model B for the time interval $[l_{\text{start}}; l_{\text{end}}]$ and $1 \leq l_{\text{start}} < l_{\text{end}} \leq L$ with that generated from a model A for the fund's entire lifetime L, the projection between $[l_{\text{start}}; l_{\text{end}}]$ has to have "full coverage" in the sense that during this interval model B has to cover cash flows for the entire fund. Before blending, model A has generated a projection for contributions C_i^* and distributions D_i^* for $i = 1, \ldots, L$ with

$$\text{TVPI}^* = \frac{\sum_{i=1}^{L} D_i^*}{\sum_{i=1}^{L} C_i^*}$$

Between $[l_{\text{start}}; l_{\text{end}}]$ cash flows D_i^* and C_i^* are replaced by those generated by model B, D_i^+ and C_i^+. To ensure consistency, the remaining cash flows generated by model A for the interval $[l_{\text{end}} + 1; L]$ need to be scaled by a factor s to ensure that

$$\frac{\sum_{i=1}^{l_{\text{start}}-1} D_i^*}{\sum_{i=1}^{l_{\text{start}}-1} C_i^*} + \frac{\sum_{i=l_{\text{start}}}^{l_{\text{end}}} D_i^+}{\sum_{i=l_{\text{start}}}^{l_{\text{end}}} C_i^+} + \frac{s * \sum_{i=l_{\text{end}}+1}^{L} D_i^*}{\sum_{i=l_{\text{end}}+1}^{L} C_i^*} = \text{TVPI}^*$$

This implies the scaling factor

$$s = \frac{\left(\text{TVPI}^* - \frac{\sum_{i=1}^{l_{\text{start}}-1} D_i^*}{\sum_{i=1}^{l_{\text{start}}-1} C_i^*} - \frac{\sum_{i=l_{\text{start}}}^{l_{\text{end}}} D_i^+}{\sum_{i=l_{\text{start}}}^{l_{\text{end}}} C_i^+}\right) * \sum_{i=l_{\text{end}}+1}^{L} C_i^*}{\sum_{i=l_{\text{end}}+1}^{L} D_i^*}$$

Note that it needs to be ensured that $\sum_{i=l_{\text{end}}+1}^{L} D_i^* > 0$ and

$$\text{TVPI}^* - \frac{\sum_{i=1}^{l_{\text{start}}-1} D_i^*}{\sum_{i=1}^{l_{\text{start}}-1} C_i^*} - \frac{\sum_{i=l_{\text{start}}}^{l_{\text{end}}} D_i^+}{\sum_{i=l_{\text{start}}}^{l_{\text{end}}} C_i^+} > 0$$

If these conditions are not met, the projections produced by model B do not allow a scaling of the remaining cash flows that would be consistent with multiple projections by model A for the fund's entire lifetime L. Also, model B may project $l_{\text{end}} > L$, i.e. a lifetime that stretches beyond the originally projected lifetime for the fund.

Such a result, however, will not necessarily be wrong: this can well happen in situations where there is better data for a fund available that "overwrites" the results for model A. This gives as new projection for the fund's contributions over its entire lifetime:

$$C_i = \begin{cases} C_i^*;\ i = 1, \ldots, l_{\text{start}} - 1 \\ C_i^+;\ i = l_{\text{start}}, \ldots, l_{\text{end}} \\ C_i^*;\ i = l_{\text{end}} + 1, \ldots, L \end{cases}$$

The distributions reflect the scaling factor

$$D_i = \begin{cases} D_i^*;\ i = 1, \ldots, l_{\text{start}} - 1 \\ D_i^+;\ i = l_{\text{start}}, \ldots, l_{\text{end}} \\ s * D_i^*;\ i = l_{\text{end}} + 1, \ldots, L \end{cases}$$

See Figure 11.6.

11.7 STRESS TESTING

Regularly innovative products such as alternative assets lack the data that could be used to feed models. In this environment of high uncertainty there are also limits to the predictive value of

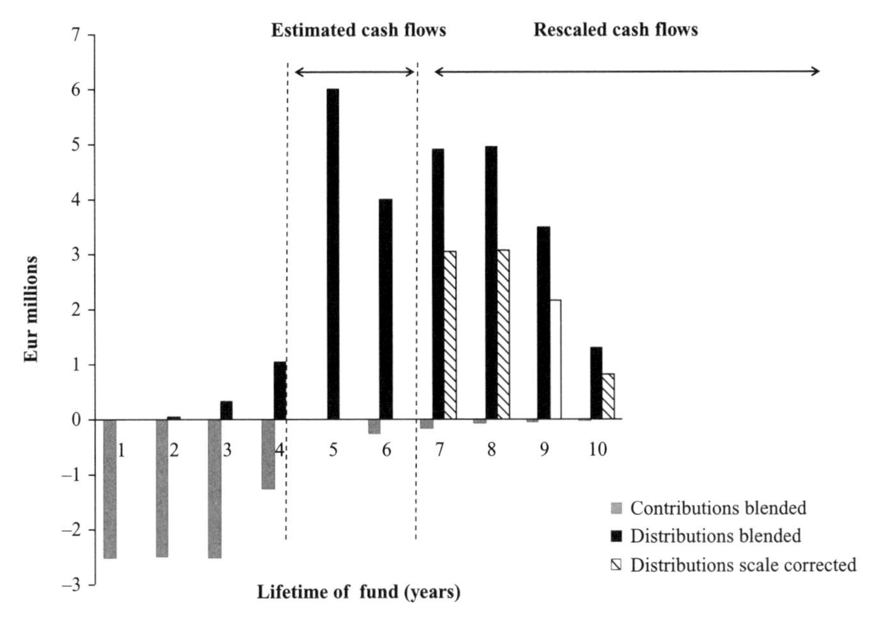

Figure 11.6 Blending deterministic model with estimates.

historic data, which causes concerns to decision makers and regulators alike. In fact, in the wake of the crisis starting in 2008 the Basel Committee on Banking Supervision has been considering abandoning VaR as the main measure on which market risk capital is calculated (Carver, 2012). Instead, many practitioners argue that VaR should be complemented by stress testing.

While it is not possible to anticipate outcomes, it is nevertheless possible and meaningful to evaluate and quantify the impact of shocks that would materially change projections and look at the effect of such extreme scenarios on the portfolio. For cash flow-based models of funds and the associated portfolio models a number of stresses should be applied in the simulation. Stress testing implies introducing more pessimistic assumptions, which makes it much more subjective than VaR because it accounts poorly for correlations and depends heavily on the choice of scenarios. Stress testing is primarily a tool for risk management where precision is less of an issue.

In addition to increasing a fund's projected lifetime and decreasing its projected TVPI, a number of other stresses should be applied in the simulation – e.g., assuming delayed distributions, accelerated contributions or increased volatility of a fund's cash flows.

11.7.1 Accelerated contributions

One way of accelerating contributions $\{C_1^*, \ldots, C_L^*\}$ over a fund's lifetime $L^* = n$ could be by "front loading", i.e. compressing the period for contributions to $m < n$:

$$C_{i,j}^* = \frac{C_i^*}{m}; i = 1, \ldots, n; j = 1, \ldots, m$$

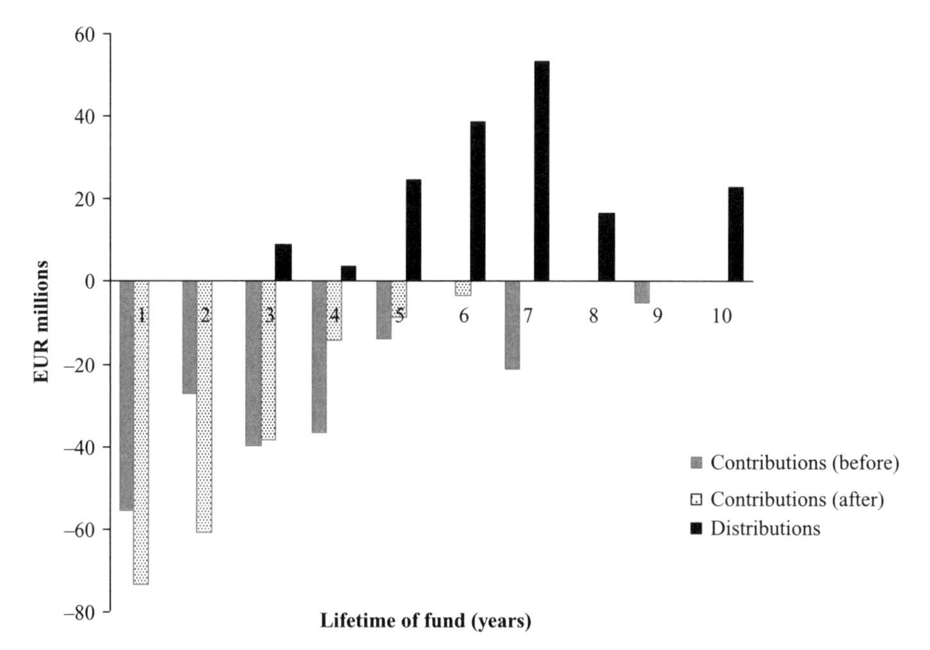

Figure 11.7 Accelerating contributions.

We re-label $C^{+}_{(i-1)*m+j} = C^{+}_{i,j}$.

$$C_j = \sum_{i=(j-1)*n+1}^{j*n} C^{+}_i;\ j = 1, \ldots, m \wedge C_j = 0;\ j = m+1, \ldots, n$$

This operation leaves the schedule for distributions unchanged, i.e.

$$D_i = D^{*}_i, \quad i = 1, \ldots, n$$

See Figure 11.7.

11.7.2 Decelerated distributions

In the same way distributions $\left\{D^{*}_1, \ldots, D^{*}_n\right\}$ can be decelerated during a fund's lifetime $L^{*} = n$ by "back loading", i.e. compressing the period for distributions to $m < n$:

$$D^{*}_{i,j} = \frac{D^{*}_j}{m};\ i = 1, \ldots, n;\ j = 1, \ldots, m$$

We re-label $D^{+}_{(i-1)*m+j} = D^{*}_{i,j}$ and set

$$D^{*}_j = 0;\ j = 1, \ldots, n-m \text{ and}$$

$$D_j = \sum_{i=(j-1)*n+1}^{j*n} D^{*}_i;\ j = n-m+1, \ldots, n$$

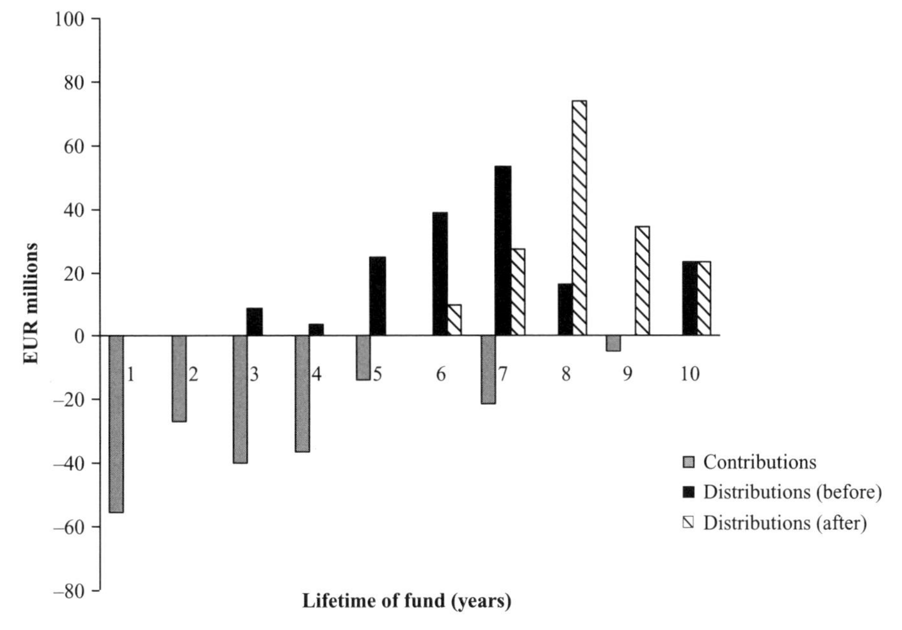

Figure 11.8 Decelerating distributions.

This operation leaves the schedule for distributions unchanged, i.e.

$$C_i = C_i^*, \quad i = 1, \ldots, n$$

See Figure 11.8.

Note that the fund's projected lifetime remains unchanged both for the acceleration of contributions as well as for the deceleration of distributions. In both cases cash flows are actually "squeezed" into shorter time intervals. In the case of decelerating distributions this could also be combined with further stretching the fund's projected lifetime.

11.7.3 Increasing volatility

Increasing a fund's projected lifetime (as discussed before) while maintaining its projected TVPI results in a lower IRR as distributions will be spread over longer time periods. Alternatively, the fund's lifetime could be kept but distributions scaled downwards, resulting in a lower multiple. Another way of introducing a stress could be by assuming that the distributions will set in later in the fund's life with its overall lifetime unchanged. To recall, in the Yale model this is controlled by the bow factor. Likewise, contributions could be accelerated by reducing the number of time periods during which they take place. In fact, various techniques are feasible and meaningful.

A simplistic way of increasing the volatility of cash flows of a fund would be by multiplying contributions C_i^* and distributions D_i^* by the same scaling factor $s > 1$ for $i = 1, \ldots, L$. The problem, however, is that contributions are typically less volatile. To increase the volatility of distributions while maintaining the fund's lifetime as well as its multiple requires more complex techniques under specific assumptions. An example for such a technique would be

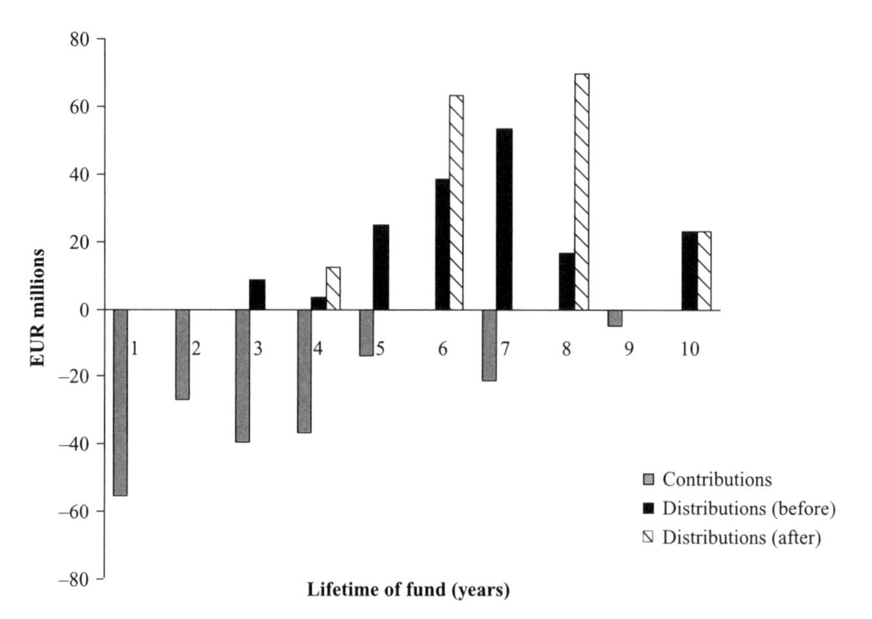

Figure 11.9 Increasing volatility of cash flows.

applying a scaling factor $0 \leq s \leq 1$ to the distributions and rearranging them:

$$\left.\begin{aligned} D_{L+2*(1-i)} &= D^*_{L+2*(1-i)} + s * D^*_{L+2*(1-i)-1} \\ D_{L+2*(1-i)-1} &= (1-s) * D^*_{L+2*(1-i)-1} \end{aligned}\right\} \quad i = 1, \ldots, \lfloor L/2 \rfloor$$

With $s = 1$ essentially the number of distributions is halved and every two distributions are aggregated. This scaling factor cannot be larger than 1 as otherwise the fund's multiple would increase. Likewise it cannot be negative as otherwise the distributions would change their sign. See Figure 11.9.

For individual stress scenarios, a higher degree of dependency between funds should also be assumed to capture the downturn scenario for the entire market. We outlined possible approaches for this in the discussion of correlations in the context of VaR in Chapter 9.

11.8 BACK-TESTING

"When regulators blithely ask us to calculate the once-in-a-thousand-years worst credit event, it is not just a matter of collecting more data. It is a matter of where to find the relevant data. There may well be a chapter 11 in Geoffrey Chaucer's books, but there was certainly no Chapter 11 in Geoffrey Chaucer's times."

Rebonato (2007)

Regulation requires that a financial institution's internal capital adequacy analysis is meaningfully tied to the identification, measurement, monitoring and evaluation of risk for its capital needs (Lopez and Saidenberg, 2001). Since models are a natural way to examine these issues, financial regulation has moved in this direction but their verification and validation is – as previously discussed – far from simple. The nature of the data poses a challenge for back-testing risk models for limited partnership funds.[16] For starters, it is difficult to detect deviations in quality (i.e., skills) between fund managers. Even for mutual funds, where there is much higher transparency regarding returns, the peer group composition is comparatively stable and valuations are far more frequent than in the case of limited partnership funds. Kothari and Warner (2001) found that it can take years of return observations to reliably identify skills.

The so-called "use test" requirement imposed by regulators could be interpreted as the way out. In essence, this requires that the model, its methodologies and results are fully embedded into the risk strategy and operational processes of regulated financial institutions. Regulators have to be convinced that senior management understand, trust and take appropriate account of model outputs within their key decisions. This is consistent with the observation that over time regulators have placed increasing emphasis on financial institutions' internal processes for measuring risks. Why should a regulator accept a model that the regulated institution's investment management does not buy into?

Only the real use of an internal model can be clear evidence that it is trusted, that it reflects all relevant information and that there is a best effort in keeping it up-to-date. In fact, Garnsworthy *et al.* (2010) observed that the use test is "one of the biggest headaches" to address and in many cases demands a "significant cultural shift" for regulated financial institutions. The discussion around the use test is relevant for the question of how often cash flow projections should be run to evaluate the exposure to limited partnership funds held by an institutional investor. Takahashi and Alexander (2001) and Hoek (2007) suggest that such an analysis be done yearly, a view shared by Kocis *et al.* (2009) who express concern that doing this too frequently creates a short-term focus. On the other hand, cash flow projections are the fundament of any risk model for funds. Since the use test requirement implies that risk management needs to be fully embedded in the investment decision-making process, the answer is, however, not clear and we do not want to give the impression that running the analysis, say, four times a year would be "enough".

Box 11.2 Validation and verification of financial models

Models incorporate relevant past data but, because of the long-term nature of asset classes, models of limited partnership funds cannot be static and need to evolve with new information, which suggests a Bayesian approach: while starting with an *ex-ante* "view of the world" the model adopts to a changing environment. Neither does the model discard new information entirely, nor does it accept them in full. Initial views are modified to a degree commensurate with the weight and reliability of both the evidence and of prior beliefs (Rebonato, 2007). Models are rarely completely wrong but rather, oversimplistic or less applicable in specific situations than alternative models. Therefore financial models, particularly when designed for risk management purposes, should be validated and verified.

Scope and process

Validation is the process of determining the degree to which a model is an accurate representation of the real world from the perspective of the intended uses of the model. It covers

[16] At the time of writing this book the Basel Committee had not given any recommendation on the choice of back-testing method. This is left to the financial organization, and how the back-testing was conducted must be disclosed to the local regulators. For an in-depth discussion of back-testing please refer, for example, to Lehikoinen (2007).

the entire model design and implementation process and begins during model development, and some validation activities should be performed before a model is ever used. A validation includes an evaluation of conceptual soundness and the ongoing monitoring and analysis of outcomes. Items to be validated are the model's theory and logic, and its assumptions and limitations, or its sensitivity to input data.

Verification refers to the process of determining that a model implementation accurately represents the developer's conceptual description of the model and the solution to the model. Through verification, management ensures that the process is consistent with policies and procedures. It relates to the accuracy and integrity of input data, the appropriate use of results and whether model validation procedures were properly followed.

To be objective and unbiased, the verification and validation processes should be conducted independently. This can be done by qualified internal staff or through an external independent review prior to actual reliance on a model, and periodically thereafter.

Internal and external consistency

A question in this context is whether models are internally and externally consistent. Internal consistency asks whether the logic followed by the model conforms to economic and mathematical principles and is covered within the validation process. External consistency is not about logic, but whether or not the output from the model conforms to experiences. This comparison of model output against actual outcomes is essentially tackling validation and verification at the same time and usually takes the form of back-testing.

Moreover, originally the back-testing required by regulators appeared to address mainly trading activities: The BIS (1996) specified that "the essence of all backtesting efforts is the comparison of actual trading results with model-generated risk measures" and described a back-testing framework involving the use of risk measures calibrated to a one-day holding period. Such a framework, however, is difficult to apply in the context of a long-term buy-and-hold asset like a portfolio of limited partnership funds. Essentially, back-testing assumes that the modelled environment is behaving in an orderly, predictable and rational manner. But this will not work for a Bayesian approach to probability, for large infrequent events that characterize situations that are chaotic, non-linear and subject to the force of personalities.[17]

---

[17] Notably in the context of investing in limited partnership funds:

- In any case all models' ability to forecast decreases with the length of the forecast horizon and considerably after a certain limit. Volatility as a measure for risk cannot be accurately forecasted beyond 10–15 trading days, whereas some long-term risk measures of up to a maximum of one year can be derived from short-term risk measures by scaling (see Lehikoinen, 2007). Funds can have lifetimes of beyond 10 years.
- Long historical observation periods provide the most accurate forecasts for models. Compared to conventional financial products, for alternative assets there are fewer data available and disclosure is incomplete. The small sample sizes in combination with the long-term nature of funds will render forecasts highly imprecise. Past performance of the funds may rather be a good measure for the overall "laws of gravity" in this industry.
- Back-testing a model assumes that what happens in the past will also happen in the future, taking market cycles into consideration this implies sampling over a time horizon which is far longer than the modern private equity industry has been in existence. Moreover, VC is dealing with innovation, where by definition historical data cannot be a reference.

The Basel Committee recognized in BIS (1996) that the back-tests in their framework have a limited power to even distinguish an accurate model from an inaccurate model. In the case of funds, the final return figures show wide variations and therefore it becomes even more problematic to compare between models.

Therefore, in practice back-testing takes place in the form of a qualitative evaluation of experiences with a model over a longer time period and whether the model is functioning as intended. In any case, back-testing will need to go beyond just looking at the model and also needs to cover aspects of model governance, such as setting of parameters and the collecting, cleaning and choosing of input data. To overcome the lack of historical data, Bongaerts and Charlier (2009) performed a sensitivity analysis to show that their results were still valid under more pessimistic conditions. These experiences are documented, and exceptions and limitations are described.

We have argued that in the highly uncertain and changing environment that characterizes alternative assets, forecasting will fail and therefore we need to rely on projections within the context of rolling forecasts – i.e., where assumptions of original projection are revisited, and a new projection, based on those new assumptions, is produced. Whether back-testing is of any meaning in this context is debatable. Nevertheless, regulators will insist that such tests are conducted, which poses a dilemma: as no forecasting model will work, institutions basically need to use the same models everybody else is using and feed them with the same data, which will necessarily be anchored in the past. Consequently, we see overly stringent back-testing standards as misguided and fundamentally at odds with the – far more relevant – use test requirement. Instead, we see the way out in the systematic review of the entire control process. Back-testing should take the form of a qualitative evaluation of experiences over a longer time period, helping identify limitations and areas for improvements. In essence, this boils down to the question of whether the control mechanism is functioning as intended. If not, appropriate remedies are to be put in place given the experience made with existing arrangements.

11.9 CONCLUSIONS

This chapter focussed on cash flow modelling concepts and how various models can be applied to estimate various risks. Given the high degree of liquidity risk associated with investments in private equity and real assets, cash flow modelling is a key challenge that needs to be addressed. Models can be generally built up from a top-down perspective and a bottom-up view. Top down models are mainly used in case of well-diversified portfolios.

In order to derive cash flows, two types of model approaches can be generally distinguished: Non-probabilistic and probabilistic models. Non-probabilistic models use a limited number of parameters and are very often applied in cases in which historical data is limited. A well-known model developed by Yale University derives the cash flows of private equity funds without historical data and through the use of various assumptions. While this model and its numerous variants that have been developed in recent years are relatively simple and easy to implement, they are subject to strict limitations. Importantly, non-probabilistic models do not provide for statistical outcome ranges. However, specific cases can be calculated by defining a worst, best and normal case with a defined set of input variables, which already provides many investors with valuable input.

By contrast, probabilistic models are typically more complex and pose important data challenges. Probabilistic models use either extensive cash flow libraries to project the cash flows of a given investment portfolio or use created synthetic cash flows. Scenarios are particularly useful to stress-test cash flow projections derived from probabilistic models in order to evaluate and quantify the impact of exogenous shocks.

Furthermore, we highlight the difficulties of back-testing in a highly uncertain environment and suggest to implement a systematic review of the entire risk process as described in more detail in Chapter 17.

12

Distribution Waterfall

Risk models for funds can be constructed bottom-up or top-down. In a bottom-up approach the limited partnership agreement's provisions related to the distribution waterfall are often the most complex part to model. The waterfall sets out how distributions from a fund will be split and in which priority and when they will be paid out, i.e. what amount must be distributed to the LPs before the fund managers can take a share from the fund's profits. One immediate reason to model the distribution waterfall is its relationship with the returns of the fund in question. A fund's economics has a significant impact on incentives and, as a consequence, on the behavioural drivers of the fund managers' performance (Mathonet and Meyer, 2007).

The design of the waterfall's terms and conditions is one of few opportunities where LPs can anticipate and manage risk: it will always have effects – sometimes even unintended ones – as it drives motivation and attitude, sense of responsibility, accountability and priorities of fund managers.

Box 12.1 Definitions for main waterfall components based on the EVCA glossary[1]

- Carried interest is "a share of the profit accruing to an investment fund management company or individual members of the fund management team, as a compensation for the own capital invested and their risk taken. Carried interest (typically up to 20% of the profits of the fund) becomes payable once the limited partners have achieved repayment of their original investment in the fund plus a defined hurdle rate."
- Hurdle rate is the "return ceiling that a private equity fund management company needs to return to the fund's investors in addition to the repayment of their initial commitment, before fund managers become entitled to carried interest payments from the fund". The term "preferred return" is often used as equivalent.
- A clawback clause or option "requires the general partners in an investment fund to return capital to the limited partners to the extent that the general partner has received more than its agreed profit split. A general partner clawback option ensures that, if an investment fund exits from strong performers early in its life and weaker performers are left at the end, the limited partners get back their capital contributions, expenses and any preferred return promised in the partnership agreement."

Waterfall structures influence incentives significantly and practices can differ significantly between geographies (USA, Europe and Asia) and types of fund (particularly in the case of VC). Notwithstanding these differences, however, this chapter is primarily the modelling of the waterfall in a bottom-up derived fund model. Another application of the principles presented in

[1] Available from http://www.evca.eu/toolbox/glossary.aspx?id=982 [accessed 24 July, 2009].

this chapter could be in the context of different classes of limited partners, such as government investors with subordinated stakes in the fund. This leads to additional refinements which also go beyond the scope of this book.

12.1 IMPORTANCE AS INCENTIVE

The main incentives that align interests between fund managers and their investors are based on management fees, GP investment in the fund, carried interest allocations and distribution provisions.

12.1.1 Waterfall components

These partnership agreement provisions, but also other terms and conditions such as investment limitations, vesting, transfers, withdrawals, indemnification or the handling of conflicts of interest tend to look quite similar between different fund agreements.

- **Management fees.** The purpose of management fees is to cover the basic costs of running and administering the fund. These costs comprise mainly salaries for investment managers and back-office personnel, expenses related to the development of investments, travel and even entertainment expenses, and office expenses such as rent, furnishings, utilities or supplies. Management fees are nearly always calculated as a percentage – in the case of private equity funds typically between 1% and 2.5% depending on the fund size – of the capital the LPs commit to the fund, but generally taper off after the investment period or when a successor fund is formed. While the management fee's calculation is relatively simple and fairly objective, there are controversies surrounding the finer details.
- **GP investment in fund.** GPs typically invest a significant amount of capital – typically about 1% – in their funds, which is treated in the same way as that contributed by the limited partners. There are a number of reasons for this, for example that GPs contribute a meaningful amount of capital to ensure their status as a partner of the fund for income tax reasons. More important, however, is putting "skin into the game" to help align the interests between fund managers and their investors.
- **Carried interest.** Management fees are paid regardless of the fund's performance and therefore fail to provide an incentive to work hard and generate superior returns. Excessive and quasi-guaranteed management fees stimulate tentative and risk-averse behaviour, such as following the herd. Consequently, the carried interest (i.e., the percentage of the profit that goes to the fund managers) is the most powerful incentive to create value. The typical carried interest split is 80/20 and gives the fund managers a share in the fund's net profits that is disproportional to their capital committed and is essential to attracting talented managers.

Somewhat surprisingly, fund terms have been relatively stable across market cycles. One explanation for this phenomenon might be sought in the fact that both fund managers and their investors have sufficient negotiation power to reject "off-market" terms sought by the other side, but not enough leverage to move the market in one direction or the other. In the case of private equity, to some degree the ILPA Private Equity Principles released in September 2009 may have initiated a shift in the power relationship between GPs and LPs but may also lead to further cementing of standardized terms.

12.1.2 Profit and loss

How is a fund's profit figure determined? For instance, the profit and loss can either be aggregated or the GP can be allowed to take a share of the profit on each individual investment. Depending on which approach is taken, it can lead to different amounts of carried interest being paid out to the fund managers.

Participating in every investment's profit can be problematic as the GP can make profits on successful investments but has little exposure to unsuccessful transactions. As the LPs thus cover the bulk of the capital risk, this approach significantly weakens the alignment of interests.

12.1.3 Distribution provisions

The distribution provisions govern the timing and content of payments in respect of the carried interest. While fund terms are by and large stable, the significant exception to this general rule appears to be the set of fund agreement provisions governing the timing and apportionment among the partners, and how to operate distributions.

This multiplicity of approaches arises because no single mechanism can satisfy all the economic goals of both the GP and LPs. Often one party's gain in the arrangement is the other party's loss. As a consequence, negotiations over such distribution provisions for capital and carried interest often are difficult and time-consuming.

12.1.4 Deal-by-deal vs. aggregated returns

Another important parameter is whether returns are aggregated or "deal-by-deal". The methods we describe in this chapter can be applied in both cases. When aggregating, no distributions are made to the GP until the LPs have received distributions equal to the amount of their overall capital contributions. Only thereafter are distributions made to the LPs and the GP according to the agreed carried interest split. This arrangement provides LPs with the greatest percentage of early distributions and minimizes the possibility that the GP will receive more than its agreed-upon percentage of the fund's cumulative net profits.

The other extreme is the "deal-by-deal" distribution approach where carried interest distributions are made following the return of capital contributions attributable to individual realized investments. From the viewpoint of the fund managers, "deal-by-deal" has a major advantage as it allows them to receive carried interest distributions sooner. It therefore creates perverse incentives for the fund manager to realize successful deals early and to delay the recognition of unsuccessful deals and write-downs of unprofitable investments. As a result, the "deal-by-deal" approach creates a clear possibility of overdistributions to the GP and thus requires a clawback provision.[2]

12.2 FUND HURDLES

Fund managers cannot take a share in the distributions until the LPs have received aggregate distributions equal to the sum of their capital contributions plus an additional amount determined by the set hurdle.[3] Without the hurdle, the GP would receive a "straight carry"

[2] The ILPA Private Equity Principles are commonly regarded as a response to the market excesses in the mid-2000s. Following these recommendations, "deal-by-deal" carried interest looks set to further lose in significance. However, it remains to be seen whether the current trend remains intact once a new investment cycle gains momentum.

[3] "Hurdle" is often used interchangeably with the term "preferred return", although CPEE (2004) interprets the preferred return as the limited partners' downside protection only, not as any sort of incentive for the fund managers.

and participate in any return of capital in excess of the original investment. The addition of the hurdle provision generally has the effect of further subordinating the GP's right to receive distributions, and is intended to align the interests of the GP and the LPs by giving the fund managers an additional incentive to outperform a traditional investment benchmark.

12.2.1 Hurdle definitions

For the hurdle, only the fund's ultimate performance matters. It does not offer the LPs the power to place the fund in default if it is not paid. From an investor perspective, it protects the return on investment in case of low return and gives the manager the incentive to achieve returns above this threshold. It is a standard term for illiquid funds worldwide, at it ensures that the LPs receive at least as much as they would have made on a safer investment.[4]

Most partnership agreements foresee that the hurdle rate – typically 8% – is defined on the basis of the compounded interest. In this case the GP has to first return an "amount as is equal to interest at an annual rate of 8% (compounded annually) on the daily amount of the partnership share" to the LPs before receiving carried interest.

A number of partnership agreements foresee that the hurdle rate and the catch-up should be applied just as a simple interest. Here, the preferred return calculation could be defined as a "return of 8% (simple rate) per annum with respect to all unreturned capital contributions made on the partnership shares in excess of the nominal value of such partnership shares". Compound interest is standard in finance and simple interest is used infrequently. For interest r on a principal P compounded over n periods, the final amount to be returned is $A = P * (1 + r)^n$. For simple interest, i.e. where the interest is not added to the principal, this amount is $A = P * r * n$. Another approach, which we will discuss later, is to define the hurdle rate not in terms of interest but on the TVPI to be achieved by the fund.

12.2.2 Option character and screening of fund managers

The hurdle gives the limited partnership fund an option-like character. The fund managers as holders of the carried interest, like the holder of a call option, enjoy the possibility of theoretically unlimited upside gain (Rouvinez, 2005). If the fund loses value, the fund managers – unless they invested a significant share of their personal wealth – have neither a gain nor a loss, just like when an option holder declines to exercise an option.

This option-like character is a main argument against hurdles in the case of VC funds. Venture capitalists have to be willing to take large but informed investment risks. Here, a hurdle can give sub-optimal incentives, e.g. large losses early on in a fund's life could put it so far under water that the fund managers are inclined to quit the game altogether or probably worse, fund managers might "swing for the fences" and become overly aggressive with subsequent investments to get back into the zone where they could receive carried interest.

[4] Hurdle rates typically range from 5% to 10% and are often tied to a spread over risk-free rates. Whether setting a hurdle makes sense or not ultimately depends on the importance of deal flow relative to deal harvesting. In cases where deal flow incentives are relevant, e.g. in the case of buyout or mezzanine funds, the fund managers should not be rewarded for investments that do not return at least the investor's cost of capital. Setting a hurdle achieves this objective, whereas a straight carried interest creates an incentive to go for low-risk, low-return investments. For VC funds, however, deal harvesting is clearly more relevant, and with the hurdle incentives they are even distorted when the option on the carried interest is "out-of-the-money". Here, a straight carried interest is more efficient than a hurdle in providing the proper incentives to the fund managers.

On the other hand, in the case of infrastructure or buyout funds where there is less volatility and the implied cost of capital is different from that of VC funds, setting a hurdle rate is argued for more fervently. Here, doing away with it entirely would create a moral hazard, as fund managers could then receive carried interest for pursuing a low-risk, low-return strategy (Fleischer, 2005).

12.3 BASIC WATERFALL STRUCTURE

It makes a huge difference whether the hurdle is defined as "soft" or "hard". The "soft" hurdle defines a sharing of all profits if a return of not lower than the hurdle rate is achieved. In this case, once a fund has returned the initial capital plus, say, 8% return, it has cleared the hurdle and thus becomes entitled to take the full carried interest. To achieve this objective, the agreement includes a so-called catch-up provision. Once the hurdle is cleared, profits are then allocated disproportionately to the GP until it catches up to the point where it would have been had it received its carried interest on the entire profit. See Figure 12.1.

The "hard" hurdle, on the other hand, defines a sharing of profits only that are above the hurdle rate. In contrast to the "soft" hurdle, which basically gets "extinguished" once passed, the "hard" hurdle is relevant for all scenarios where the fund's IRR is above the hurdle rate. This arrangement is also sometimes called a "floor" (Fleischer, 2005). In instances where there is a "floor" and therefore no catch-up has been agreed, the carried interest only applies to those net profits that exceed the hurdle.

12.3.1 Soft hurdle

We define a_x to be the amount required as the residual value of a fund's portfolio to give an IRR of $x\%$ or a multiple of x before splitting it up according to the waterfall. c is the carried

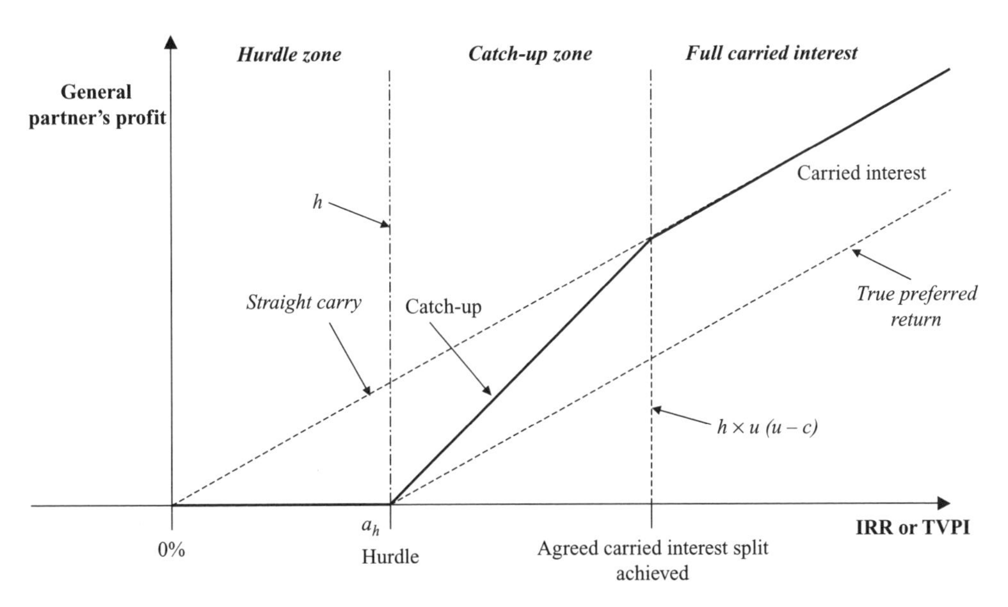

Figure 12.1 Basic waterfall structure.

Table 12.1 Payout split

	Return range (either IRR- or TVPI-based)	Distribution key for LPs	Distribution key for GP
Hurdle zone	return $\leq h$	a	0
Catch-up zone	$h \leq$ return $< \frac{h * u}{u - c}$	$a_h + (a - a_h) * (1 - u)$	$u * (a - a_h)$
Full carried interest	$\frac{h * u}{u - c} \leq$ return	$a * (1 - c)$	$a * c$

Table 12.2 Generalized waterfall

	LPs	GP	Total
Sale of investment for amount a			
Return of capital	d		d
Preferred return for LPs	$a_h - d$		$a_h - d$
Catch-up for GP	$(1 - u) * x$	$u * x$	x
Split of residual amount	$(1 - c) * y$	$c * y$	y
Closing balance	$(1 - c) * (a - d)$	$c * (a - d)$	$a - d$

interest due to the general partner, h the hurdle rate and u the catch-up (with $u > c$). The payout of the portfolio value a attributable to GP and LPs is shown in Table 12.1.

How can one determine the amount to be caught up and the residual amount to be split up as carried interest for $u < 100\%$? In the case of a soft hurdle, the waterfall can be generalized as in Table 12.2.

The "catch-up" provision allows the fund managers to participate faster in the gains, once the hurdle has been passed, whereas without catch-up they only participate in the proportion of its agreed carried interest. With a 100% catch-up (a "full catch-up") the hurdle will have no ultimate effect on the carried interest if the fund clearly exceeds its target IRR and does not terminate with returns still in the catch-up zone.

During a fund's life some investments may be exited earlier and distributions can already be made to the GP. However, this may be followed by years of losses, e.g. caused by failures of the underlying projects and portfolio companies or through lack of exit opportunities during prolonged economic downturns. This may mean that the GP receives more than the intended carried interest based on the overall performance of the fund. The GP should not receive profits in excess of the agreed carried interest percentage.[5] "Clawback" provisions aim to protect the economic split agreed between the GP and the LPs. The clawback provision is sometimes

[5] When talking about clawbacks, usually "GP clawbacks" are being referred to, i.e. corrective payments to prevent a windfall to the fund managers. Nevertheless, there can be, albeit rarely, situations where LPs have received more than their agreed percentage of carried interest (Mathonet and Meyer, 2007). Consequently, some partnership agreements address the question of the so-called "LP clawback" as well. LPs aim to minimize the risk that the GP lacks liquid assets and the clawback right would be unenforceable. The simplest and, from the viewpoint of the LPs, the most desirable solution is that the GP does not receive carried interest until all invested capital has been repaid to investors. But that can take several years before the fund's team sees any gains and it could demotivate the individuals. An accepted compromise for securing the clawback obligation is to put a fixed percentage, e.g. 25%, 30% or 50%, of their carried interest proceeds into an escrow account as a buffer against potential clawback liability.

Table 12.3 Example fund (all amounts in EUR)

	LPs		GP	
Year	Contributions	Distributions	Contributions	Distributions
1	−2,254,350	0	−118,650	0
2	−27,660,200	27,234,600	−1,455,800	1,433,400
3	−7,169,650	4,780,400	−377,350	251,600
4	−15,390,950	21,584,000	−810,050	1,136,000
5	−20,365,150	0	−1,071,850	0
6	−10,612,450	31,350,000	−558,550	1,650,000
7	0	0	0	0
8	0	45,600,000	0	2,400,000
9	0	0	0	0
10	0	34,200,000	0	1,800,000

called a "give-back" or a "look-back", because it requires a partnership to undergo a final accounting of all its capital and profit distributions at the end of a fund's lifetime.

12.4 EXAMPLES FOR CARRIED INTEREST CALCULATION

We discuss soft and hard hurdle rate-based carried interest calculations for compounded interest and multiples for the example in Table 12.3. In this example, it is assumed that the GP himself holds a 5% stake in the fund.

The fund's development over its lifetime is depicted in Figure 12.2.

For the purpose of this discussion and for simplicity, we just discuss yearly periods. The approach described bases the waterfall calculation on the previous period and the changes

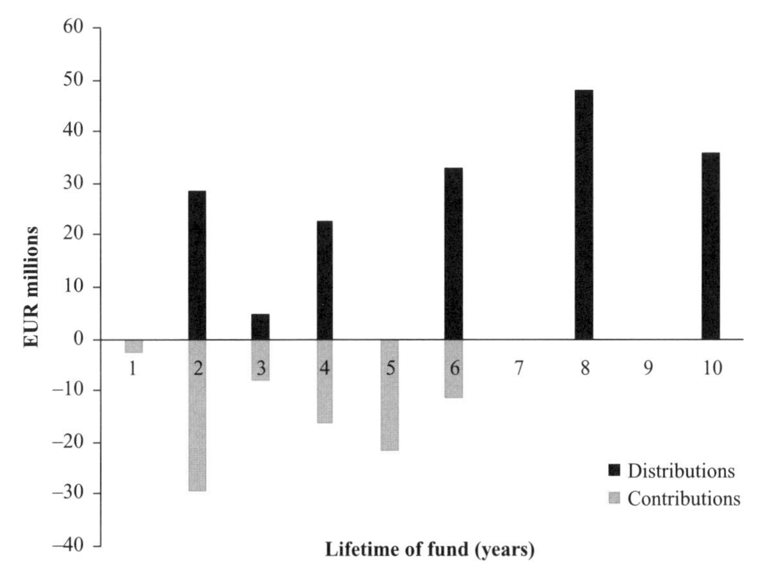

Figure 12.2 Development of example fund.

Table 12.4 Payout split for example fund (compound interest case)

	IRR range
Hurdle zone	IRR ≤ 8%
Catch-up zone	8% ≤ IRR < 12%
Full carried interest	12% ≤ IRR

during the year. It aims to determine the split of cash flows for the year and the amount of clawbacks that need to be returned to the LPs in case the fund terminates at year end. Only the shares held by the LPs are affected by the carried interest split and consequently we do not have to consider the GP's own stake in the fund.

12.4.1 Soft hurdle for compounded interest-based carried interest allocation

For this example (Table 12.4) we assume a hurdle rate of 8%, a catch-up of 60% and a carried interest of 20%. Appendix Table 12.A.1 shows the development over the fund's entire lifetime.

How do we determine the amount that the distributions need to exceed the threshold set by the hurdle? To calculate the amount to reach the hurdle at the end of the year we sum up the amount paid-in (i.e., the remaining aggregated contributions until then) in the beginning of the year, the interest payments on this amount and the changes within the year. See Table 12.5.

Table 12.5 warrants the following comments: (6) the interest is paid on the remaining amount paid-in (3)+(4)+(5). If this amount is positive a share of the distributions will be paid-out as carried interest. The paid-in (6) is brought forward to the next period (1). Until year 4 the fund is below its hurdle and the GP is not entitled to carried interest yet. In year 4 there is a significant distribution and the hurdle is exceeded by EUR 276,408.

In the case of compounded interest considered here there is an alternative way to calculate this amount based on the IRR and the resulting $a_{8\%}$ for the year. The IRR is the discount rate that gives a NPV equal to zero:

$$\sum_{n=1}^{n=L} \frac{(D_n - C_n)}{(1 + \text{IRR})^{t_n}} = 0$$

where C_n are the contributions and D_n the distributions in period t_n and L the lifetime. The interim IRR is a rough but widely used estimation of IRR performance and in the case of private

Table 12.5 Calculation of amount in excess of 8% hurdle (all amounts in EUR)

Year	1	2	3	4	5
(1) Beginning	0	−2,254,350	−2,860,298	−5,478,372	0
(2) Interest	0	−180,348	−228,824	−438,270	0
(3) Subtotal (1)+(3)	0	−2,434,698	−3,089,122	−5,916,642	0
(4) Paid-out before	0	0	0	0	276,408
(5) Change in year	−2,254,350	−425,600	−2,389,250	6,193,050	−20,365,150
(6) Paid-in	−2,254,350	−2,860,298	−5,478,372	0	−20,088,742
(7) Above hurdle	0	0	0	276,408	0

equity forms the basis of most published comparative performance statistics. For active funds, the IIRR is computed by taking the NAV as the last cash flow at time T:

$$\sum_{n=1}^{t_n<T} \frac{(D_n - C_n)}{(1+\text{IIRR})^{t_n}} + \frac{\text{NAV}}{(1+\text{IIRR})^T} = 0$$

a_x is the amount required as the residual value of a fund's portfolio to give an IRR of $x\%$ before splitting it up according to the waterfall:

$$\sum_{n=1}^{t_n<T} \frac{(D_n - C_n)}{(1+x)^{t_n}} + \frac{a_x}{(1+x)^T} = 0$$

This gives

$$a_x = -\sum_{n=1}^{t_n<T} (D_n - C_n) * (1+x)^{T-t_n}$$

Based on this formula we can calculate the amount to reach the hurdle of 8% as

$$\begin{aligned} a_{8\%} = &-(\text{EUR } 0 - \text{EUR } 2{,}254{,}350) * 1.08^3 \\ &-(\text{EUR } 27{,}234{,}600 - \text{EUR } 27{,}660{,}200) * 1.08^2 \\ &-(\text{EUR } 4{,}780{,}400 - \text{EUR } 7{,}169{,}650) * 1.08 = \text{EUR } 5{,}916{,}642 \end{aligned}$$

The net distribution in year 4 is EUR 21,584,000 – EUR 15,390,950 = EUR 6,193,050 exceeding this threshold by EUR 276,408. As the fund's IIRR in year 4 is 10.4% it is still within the catch-up zone. As a result, 60% of this amount, i.e. 165,845, is due to the GP. See Figure 12.3.

An alternative way of determining whether the fund is still in its catch-up zone is to determine the amount that exceeds the threshold of 12% in the same manner as for 8% (hurdle and start of catch-up zone). See Table 12.6.

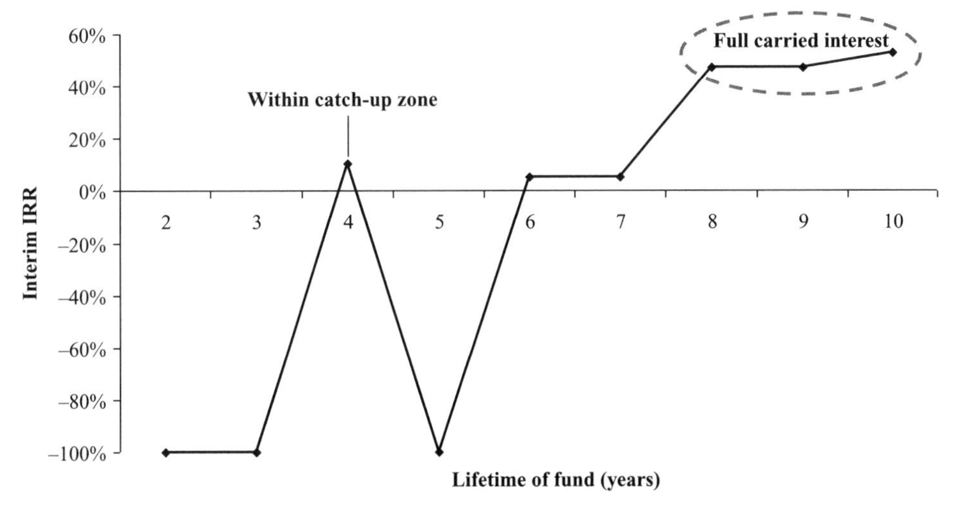

Figure 12.3 Development of interim IRR for example fund.

Table 12.6 Calculation of amount in excess of 12% (end of catch-up zone, in EUR)

Year	1	2	3	4	5
(1) Beginning	0	−2,254,350	−2,950,472	−5,693,779	−183,982
(2) Interest	0	−270,522	−354,057	−683,253	−22,078
(3) Sub-total (1)+(3)	0	−2,524,872	−3,304,529	−6,377,032	−206,060
(4) Paid-out before	0	0	0	0	0
(5) Change in year	−2,254,350	−425,600	−2,389,250	6,193,050	−20,365,150
(6) Paid-in	−2,254,350	−2,950,472	−5,693,779	−183,982	−20,571,210
(7) Above hurdle	0	0	0	0	0

A complication occurs in year 5, where we have just a contribution but no distribution and the IIRR drops below the hurdle rate (see Figure 12.3). Should the fund end in this year, the carried interest paid in the previous year would have to be clawed back from the fund managers. We assume that clawbacks will only be realized when the fund has come to the end of its lifetime and is wound up. As we see in the example, the fund recovers in later years and eventually no clawbacks are necessary.

In year 8 we have distributions that put the fund again in the carried interest area (see Appendix Table 12.A.1). Should the fund come to the end of its lifetime now, the carried interest of EUR 9,419,250 would need to be set off against the clawback of EUR 165,845 carried interest already paid out and would reduce it to EUR 9,253,405. In fact, the fund's repayments put it firmly above the threshold of 12% where the catch-up ends, essentially "extinguishing" the hurdle and giving the fund manager 20% of every repayment in excess of the capital called.

In this case, how do we split the LPs' shares' repayment of EUR 45,600,000 between the LPs and the GP? The LPs receive the difference between the LPs' shares' accumulated distributions until year 8 of EUR 121,129,750 and the accumulated distributions until year 7 of EUR 84,949,000 minus the reduction of clawback from year 7 to year 8 of EUR 165,845, giving a distribution of EUR 36,346,595 in year 8. See Figure 12.4.

Until year 8 the GP has to receive the distribution of its own 5% stake in the fund of EUR 6,871,000 plus the carried interest of EUR 9,419,250. For year 8 the GP receives the difference between his accumulated distribution until year 8 of EUR 16,290,250 and his accumulated distribution until year 7 of EUR 4,471,000 minus the change in clawback from year 7 to year 8 of EUR 165,845, giving a distribution of EUR 11,653,405 in year 8.

The fund's lifetime ends in year 10, where overall it has generated a return of 53%. The GP receives the full return of its own 5% stake in the fund of EUR 8,671,000 plus a carried interest of EUR 16,259,250, which is 20% of the difference between the LPs' shares' accumulated distributions of EUR 164,749,000 and the accumulated contributions of EUR 83,452,750 (see Table 12.3). The LPs receive EUR 83,452,750, i.e. the full amount of the distributions until the accumulated contributions are fully repaid plus 80% of the excess distributions, giving them a total of EUR 148,489,750.

12.4.2 Hard hurdle for compounded interest-based carried interest allocation

In the case of the hard hurdle we base the calculation of the carried interest again on the amount by which the accumulated distributions exceed the threshold set by the hurdle of 8%.

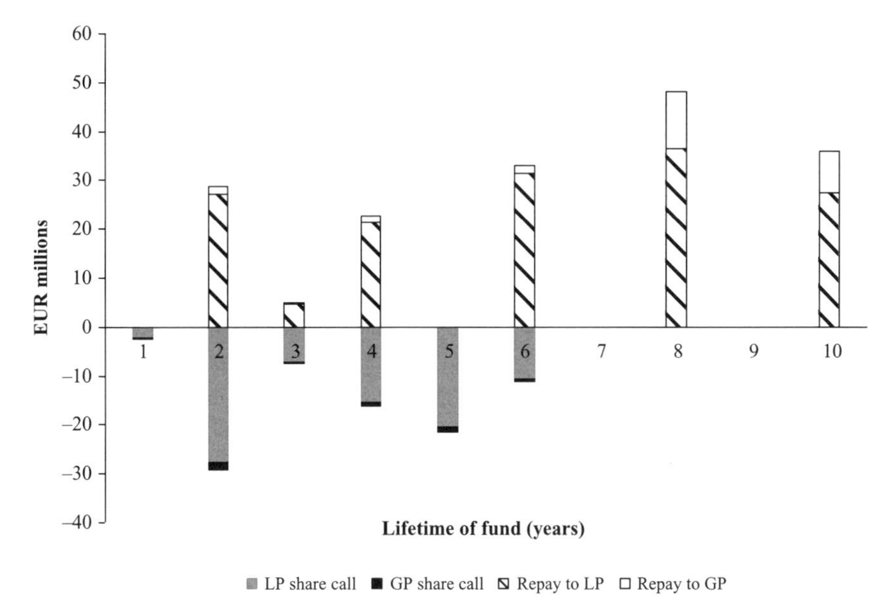

Figure 12.4 Split of cash flows between LPs and GP (soft hurdle, 8%).

As in the example before, for year 4 this amount is EUR 276,408. However, with a hard hurdle there is no catch-up and the GP only participates in distributions above 8%. In other words, the hurdle is never "extinguished", resulting in an overall lower aggregated carried interest for the GP. See Figure 12.5.

Compared to the aggregated carried interest of EUR 16,259,250 in the case of the soft hurdle, here the GP would just receive an aggregated amount of EUR 15,736,450. Note that

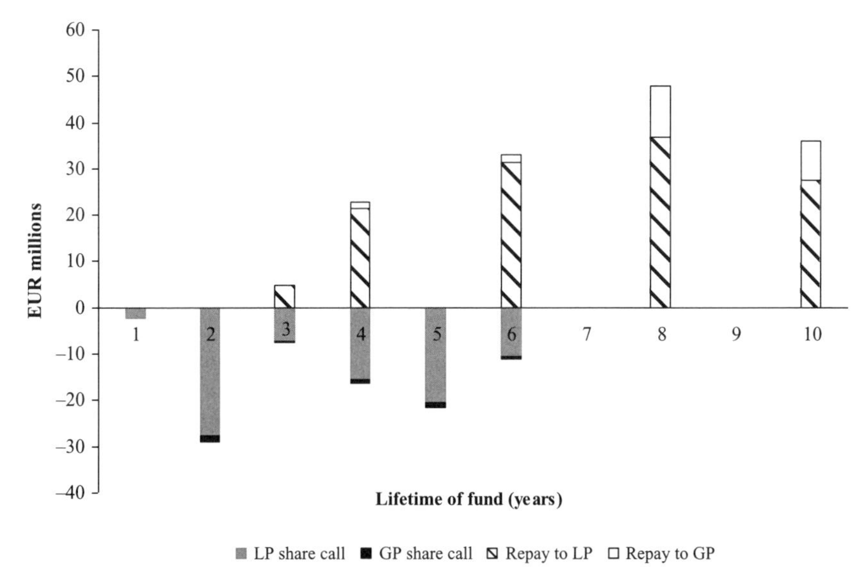

Figure 12.5 Split of cash flows between LPs and GP (hard hurdle, 8%).

Table 12.7 Payout split for example fund (multiple case)

	TVPI range
Hurdle zone	TVPI $\leq$ 1.5
Catch-up zone	1.5 $\leq$ TVPI < 1.75
Full carried interest	1.75 $\leq$ TVPI

just the amount is reduced compared to the soft hurdle case, but the timing when the GP receives carried interest (and also when it is clawed back) remains the same. Appendix Table 12.A.1 shows the development over the fund's entire lifetime.

12.4.3 Soft hurdle for multiple-based carried interest allocation

Another, albeit less often used, approach is a multiple-based hurdle rate. Here again, in principle, a soft and a hard hurdle are possible. For the example, we assume a hurdle multiple of 1.5× and again a catch-up of 60% and a carried interest of 20%. Note that it is not intended to draw a comparison between the payoffs of a compound interest and a multiple-based carried interest scheme. The purpose of this example is just to compare the calculation approaches.

How do we determine the end of the catch-up in this case? We follow the same approach as for the compounded interest in the soft hurdle case. For a hurdle multiple $m_h = 1.5\times$ the catch-up is between

$$1 + (1.5 - 0.5) \leq \text{TVPI} < 1 + \frac{(1.5 - 0.5) * 60\%}{60\% - 20\%}$$

See Table 12.7.

How do we determine for period t_n the threshold after which the GP receives carried interest? Accumulated distributions have to exceed

$$\sum_{n=1}^{t_n<T} D_n - m_h * \sum_{n=1}^{t_n} C_n{}^{n}$$

In the example, this does not happen before year 8 when finally the threshold set by m_h is exceeded by EUR 5,369,875. With an interim TVPI (ITVPI) of 1.56 this is still within the catch-up, which results in a carried interest payment of EUR 3,221,925.

As Figure 12.6 demonstrates, the ITVPIs develop more "steadily" and are less "volatile" than the IIRRs. Consequently, clawbacks are possible but less likely for a multiple-based carried interest.

When the end of the catch-up zone is reached in year 10, the hurdle is "extinguished" and the GP has received the same total amount of carried interest of EUR 16,259,250 as in the case of the soft hurdle for compounded interest-based carried interest allocation. See Figure 12.7.

For all figures over the fund's lifetime, please refer to Appendix Table 12.A.3.

12.4.4 Hard hurdle for multiple-based carried interest allocation

In the case of the hard hurdle we base the calculation of the carried interest again on the amount by which the accumulated distributions exceed the threshold set by the hurdle multiple

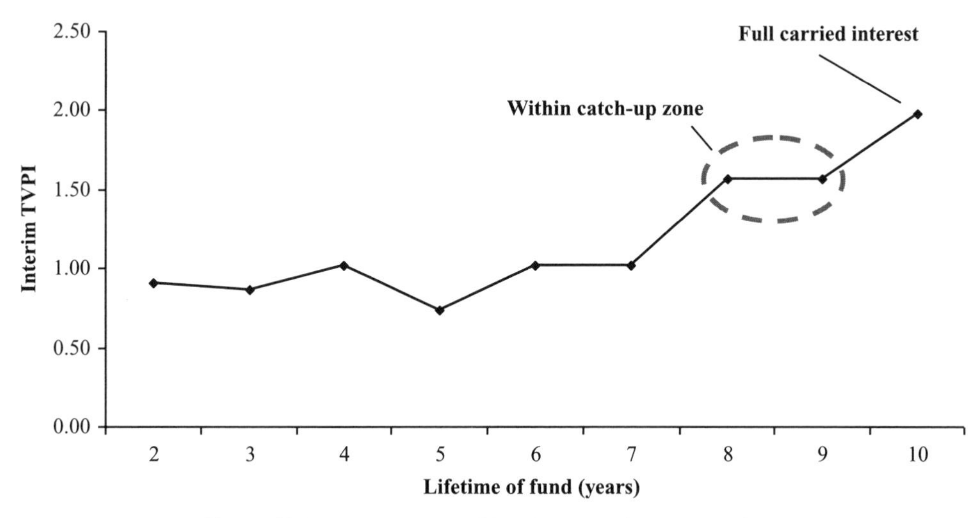

Figure 12.6 Development of interim TVPI for example fund.

$m_h = 1.5\times$. As in the example before, this does not happen before year 8 where the threshold set by m_h is exceeded by EUR 5,369,875.

With a hard hurdle there is no catch-up and the GP only participates in distributions above the target multiple and thus just receives EUR 1,073,975. See Figure 12.8.

Again in the hard hurdle case the aggregated carried interest of eventually EUR 7,913,975 is lower than that of EUR 16,259,250 in the soft hurdle case. The timing when the GP receives carried interest remains the same. For all figures over the fund's lifetime, please refer to Appendix Table 12.A.4.

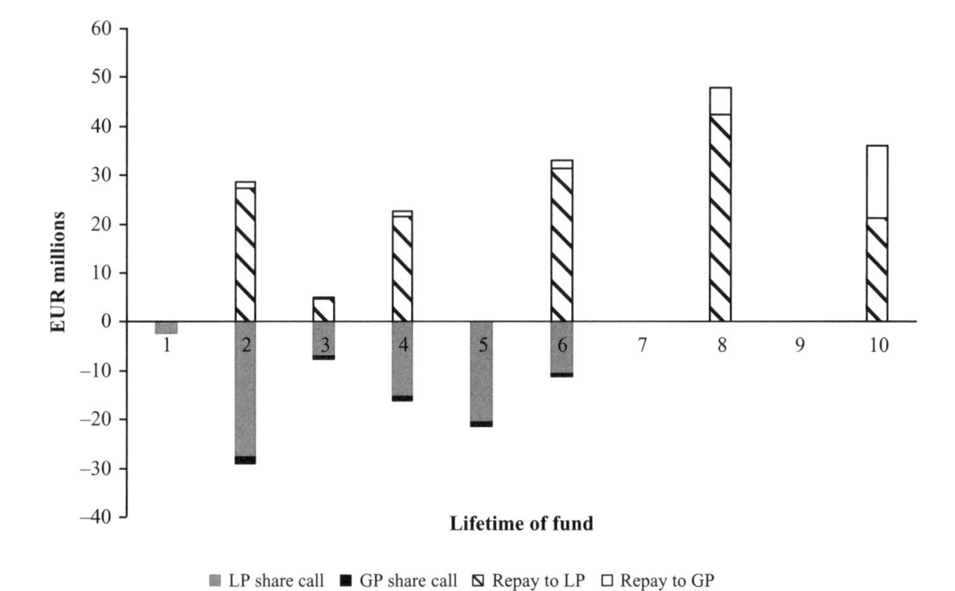

Figure 12.7 Split of cash flows between LPs and GP (soft hurdle, $1.5\times$).

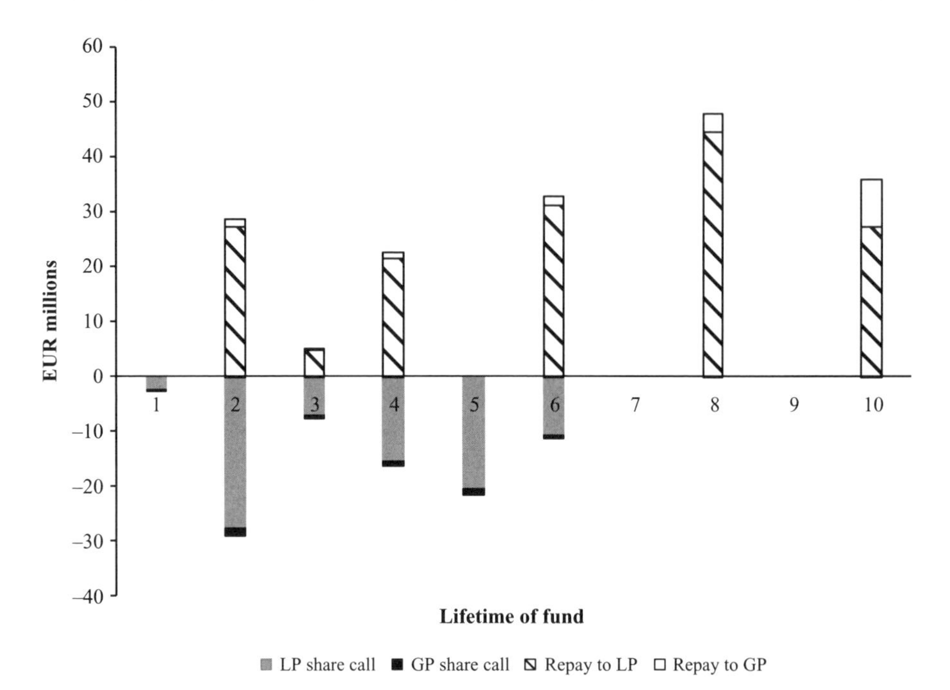

Figure 12.8 Split of cash flows between LPs and GP (hard hurdle, 1.5×).

12.5 CONCLUSIONS

In this chapter, we have presented the major principles of the waterfall determining the investment profits of the LPs and the GP. However, over the years, many new layers have been added to the basic approach making it increasingly complex and difficult to model the waterfall. CPEE (2004) found that some "newer GPs (who can tend to have fewer financial staff) might not even understand their own waterfall, let alone their LPs." Thus, the examples in this chapter can only be a broad description of the key fundamentals.

In determining the waterfall of the portfolio of illiquid fund investments, LPs can in principle follow either a bottom-up or top-down approach. A bottom-up approach requires tailor-made models for each fund to capture their specific terms, conditions and the range of possible variables. For risk management purposes, this may be too cumbersome, however, and in most situations a top-down modelling approach can be the preferred solution.

APPENDIX – EXAMPLES

Table 12.A.1 Example compounded interest-based carry calculation for soft hurdle 8% with 60% catch-up (all amounts in EUR)

Year	1	2	3	4	5	6	7	8	9	0
(1) LP share acc. distrib.	0	27,234,600	32,015,000	53,599,000	53,599,000	84,949,000	84,949,000	130,549,000	130,549,000	164,749,000
(2) GP share acc. distrib.	0	1,433,400	1,685,000	2,821,000	2,821,000	4,471,000	4,471,000	6,871,000	6,871,000	8,671,000
(3) Capital returned	0	0	0	1,123,850	0	1,496,250	1,496,250	47,096,250	47,096,250	81,296,250
(4) Above hurdle	0	0	0	276,408	0	0	0	44,482,249	44,482,249	78,682,249
(5) Distribution key	No carry	No carry	No carry	Catch-up	No carry	No carry	No carry	Full carry	Full carry	Full carry
(6) Carried interest due	0	0	0	165,845	0		0	9,419,250	9,419,250	16,259,250
(7) Payout to LP acc.	0	27,234,600	32,015,000	53,433,155	53,599,000	84,949,000	84,949,000	0	121,129,750	148,489,750
(8) Carry paid acc.	0	0	0	165,845	165,845	165,845	165,845	9,419,250	9,419,250	16,259,250
(9) Clawback	0	0	0	0	165,845	165,845	165,845	0	0	0
(10) Change in clawback	0	0	0	0	165,845	0	0	−165,845	0	0
(11) Payout to GP acc.	0	1,433,400	1,685,000	2,986,845	2,821,000	4,471,000	4,471,000	16,290,250	16,290,250	24,930,250
(12) LP payout year	0	27,234,600	4,780,400	21,418,155	0	31,350,000	0	36,346,595	0	27,360,000
(13) GP payout year	0	1,433,400	251,600	1,301,845	0	1,650,000	0	11,653,405	0	8,640,000

Table 12.A.2 Example compounded interest-based carry calculation for hard hurdle 8% (all amounts in EUR)

Year	1	2	3	4	5	6	7	8	9	0
(1) LP share acc. distrib.	0	27,234,600	32,015,000	53,599,000	53,599,000	84,949,000	84,949,000	130,549,000	130,549,000	164,749,000
(2) GP share acc. distrib.	0	1,433,400	1,685,000	2,821,000	2,821,000	4,471,000	4,471,000	6,871,000	6,871,000	8,671,000
(3) Capital returned	0	0	0	1,123,850	0	1,496,250	1,496,250	47,096,250	47,096,250	81,296,250
(4) Above hurdle	0	0	0	276,408	0	0	0	44,482,249	44,482,249	78,682,249
(5) Distribution key	No carry	No carry	No carry	Carry	No carry	No carry	No carry	Carry	Carry	Carry
(6) Carried interest due	0	0	0	55,282	0	0	0	8,896,450	8,896,450	15,736,450
(7) Payout to LP acc.	0	27,234,600	32,015,000	53,543,718	53,599,000	84,949,000	84,949,000	121,652,550	121,652,550	149,012,550
(8) Carry paid acc.	0	0	0	55,282	55,282	55,282	55,282	8,896,450	8,896,450	15,736,450
(9) Clawback	0	0	0	0	55,282	55,282	55,282	0	0	0
(10) Change in clawback	0	0	0	0	55,282	0	0	−55,282	0	0
(11) Payout to GP acc.	0	1,433,400	1,685,000	2,876,282	2,821,000	4,471,000	4,471,000	15,767,450	15,767,450	24,407,450
(12) LP payout year	0	27,234,600	4,780,400	21,528,718	0	31,350,000	0	36,758,832	0	27,360,000
(13) GP payout year	0	1,433,400	251,600	1,191,282	0	1,650,000	0	11,241,168	0	8,640,000

Table 12.A.3 Example multiple-based carried interest calculation for soft hurdle 1.5× with 60% catch-up (all amounts in EUR)

Year	1	2	3	4	5	6	7	8	9	0
(1) LP share acc. distrib.	0	27,234,600	32,015,000	53,599,000	53,599,000	84,949,000	84,949,000	130,549,000	130,549,000	164,749,000
(2) GP share acc. distrib.	0	1,433,400	1,685,000	2,821,000	2,821,000	4,471,000	4,471,000	6,871,000	6,871,000	8,671,000
(3) Capital returned	0	0	0	0	0	0	0	47,096,250	47,096,250	81,296,250
(4) Above hurdle	0	0	0	0	0	0	0	5,369,875	5,369,875	39,569,875
(5) Distribution key	No carry	No carry	No carry	No carry	No carry	No carry	No carry	Catch-up	Catch-up	Full carry
(6) Carried interest due	0	0	0	0	0	0	0	3,221,925	3,221,925	16,259,250
(7) Payout to LP acc.	0	27,234,600	32,015,000	53,599,000	53,599,000	84,949,000	84,949,000	127,327,075	127,327,075	148,489,750
(8) Carry paid acc.	0	0	0	0	0	0	0	3,221,925	3,221,925	16,259,250
(9) Clawback	0	0	0	0	0	0	0	0	0	0
(10) Change in clawback	0	0	0	0	0	0	0	0	0	0
(11) Payout to GP acc.	0	1,433,400	1,685,000	2,821,000	2,821,000	4,471,000	4,471,000	10,092,925	10,092,925	24,930,250
(12) LP payout year	0	27,234,600	4,780,400	21,584,000	0	31,350,000	0	42,378,075	0	21,162,675
(13) GP payout year		1,433,400	251,600	1,136,000	0	1,650,000	0	5,621,925	0	14,837,325

Table 12.A.4 Example multiple-based carried interest calculation for hard hurdle 1.5× (all amounts in EUR)

Year	1	2	3	4	5	6	7	8	9	0
(1) LP share acc. distrib.	0	27,234,600	32,015,000	53,599,000	53,599,000	84,949,000	84,949,000	130,549,000	130,549,000	164,749,000
(2) GP share acc. distrib.	0	1,433,400	1,685,000	2,821,000	2,821,000	4,471,000	4,471,000	6,871,000	6,871,000	8,671,000
(3) Capital returned	0	0	0	0	0	0	0	47,096,250	47,096,250	81,296,250
(4) Above hurdle	0	0	0	0	0	0	0	5,369,875	5,369,875	39,569,875
(5) Distribution key	No carry	No carry	No carry	No carry	No carry	No carry	No carry	Carry	Carry	Carry
(6) Carried interest due	0	0	0	0	0	0	0	1,073,975	1,073,975	7,913,975
(7) Payout to LP acc.	0	27,234,600	32,015,000	53,599,000	53,599,000	84,949,000	84,949,000	129,475,025	129,475,025	156,835,025
(8) Carry paid acc.	0	0	0	0	0	0	0	1,073,975	1,073,975	7,913,975
(9) Clawback	0	0	0	0	0	0	0	0	0	0
(10) Change in clawback	0	0	0	0	0	0	0	0	0	0
(11) Payout to GP acc.	0	1,433,400	1,685,000	2,821,000	2,821,000	4,471,000	4,471,000	7,944,975	7,944,975	16,584,975
(12) LP payout year	0	27,234,600	4,780,400	21,584,000	0	31,350,000	0	44,526,025	0	27,360,000
(13) GP payout year	0	1,433,400	251,600	1,136,000	0	1,650,000	0	3,473,975	0	8,640,000

13
Modelling Qualitative Data

In Chapter 11 we described how a fund's cash flows can be scaled to achieve a projected lifetime and a projected TVPI, but we have not discussed how projected TVPIs reflecting the fund's growth prospects could be determined. For investment in a new fund as a blind pool and in young funds with too little significant history, we need to use qualitative inputs to model such multiples. Therefore, we have to deal with the question of how we can use such data in a consistent manner to put funds into different classes according to their growth prospects.

Such classifications could, for example, take the form of what is commonly called a "fund rating". Another question relevant for this discussion – and to which we will turn in more detail later – is how to translate such a classification into quantification, again to determine ranges for growth rates as inputs for the cash flow models.

13.1 QUANTITATIVE VS. QUALITATIVE APPROACHES

Quantitative approaches are concerned with the statistical analysis of data that are collected from empirical observations. In order to derive meaningful conclusions from the statistical analysis, the data sample must be sufficiently large and representative (i.e., unbiased). Unfortunately, such samples often do not exist as far as alternative assets are concerned. As a result, risk managers face the challenge of working with imperfect data, strictly limiting the application of quantitative techniques regarding the *ex-ante* assessment of limited partnership funds. Instead, risk management in the area of illiquid assets has frequently to rely on the interpretation of sporadic, incomplete and often ambiguous information.

13.1.1 Relevance of qualitative approaches

In contrast to quantitative approaches, qualitative assessments focus on the classification of information, which is usually anecdotal and hence subject to interpretation as data samples are small and unrepresentative. Insights are sought from loosely structured qualitative information rather than quantitative data that allow the application of econometric techniques. However, working with small data samples and information that is difficult to measure – such as reputation, expertise or management style – inevitably introduces an element of subjectivity. Many risk management practitioners thus view qualitative analysis with suspicion: lack of repeatability and structure, inconsistencies in the analysis as well as problems in translating descriptive information into quantitative measures contribute to the perception that qualitative analysis is an inferior approach to be used only if data problems are insurmountable.

Another reason why many investment professionals feel uncomfortable with qualitative approaches is likely to be rooted in psychological factors: the principal weaknesses of such approaches may expose the decision maker to a higher degree of responsibility, whereas purely quantitative – and thus allegedly "objective" – models due to their "black box" nature are viewed as less subject to manipulation. Thus, their results tend to be more likely to be accepted by outside stakeholders, such as auditors and regulators. As Porter (1992) argues, "quantification appears as a strategy for overcoming distance and distrust [...] We need to understand quantification as a response to a set of political problems."

Nevertheless, regulators increasingly recognize that qualitative analysis can be of significant value as it may generate a more in-depth understanding about a particular issue (ESMA, 2011). Qualitative analysis can provide a competitive edge, as it is concerned with understanding the underlying dynamics. Arguably, therefore, it may be more forward looking than quantitative analysis, where information about key factors, such as management, may not be reflected in the data or may be available only with a substantial delay.

In order for qualitative analysis to provide meaningful input in the decision-making process, it has to be properly structured, for example, through a formalized scoring system. In this sense, qualitative analysis is principally no different from quantitative approaches, which are also subject to interpretation of the data and hence not entirely free from a potential decision bias. In this context, an important step in avoiding a decision bias in using qualitative analysis could lie in establishing an expert panel that is responsible for approving the evaluation and scoring of activities. Consistency and repeatability can be ensured through keeping matters as simple as possible, proper documentation of the methodologies used, training of analysts and through regular reviews.

13.1.2 Determining classifications

Classifications may take the form of ratings. To determine such ratings, two approaches are generally conceivable. First, the various classes and the delineation between them are clearly defined and described in as much detail as possible, but the methodology to arrive at the classification is left to analysts who are free to select the tools most appropriate for the purpose. Such an approach may be advantageous in situations where it is difficult to model how individual characteristics interact to produce outcomes and where combinations of factors determine the ultimate classification. There is certainly a high element of subjectivity and lack of transparency and consistency, but these problems could be mitigated, for example, through a structured review process.

Alternatively, the scoring methodology, and how the various rankings are to be aggregated to arrive at the classification, could be a formalized algorithm. The advantage of this approach is that the classification process is more transparent and repeatable. However, as mentioned above, aggregating various individual scores into one classification may be problematic in situations where combinations of factors determine the ultimate classification.

13.2 FUND RATING/GRADING

It has repeatedly been claimed that investing through limited partnership structures lends itself to techniques that are akin to assessing credit risk. For instance, the Basel Committee on Banking Supervision (BIS, 2001) has argued that it

> "is a sound practice to establish a system of internal risk ratings for equity investments [...]. For example, rating factors for investments in private equity funds could include an assessment of the fund's diversification, management experience, liquidity, and actual and expected performance. Rating systems should be used for assessments of both new investment opportunities and existing

portfolio investments. The quantification of such risk ratings will vary based on the institution's needs [...]. The policies, procedures and results of such quantitative efforts should be fully documented and periodically validated."

Similarly, the International Swaps and Derivatives Association (ISDA, 2001) has taken the view that

"... some traded assets with little or low liquidity (e.g. private equity) may require risk rather [sic] analysis closer to that which accompanies assessment of bankruptcy or default risk rather than a market risk paradigm."

Importantly, the traditional approach to assess credit risk is a rating system. The rating of borrowers is a widespread practice in capital markets. It is meant to summarize the quality of a debtor and, in particular, to inform the market about repayment prospects. All credit rating approaches are based on a combination of quantitative and qualitative components.[1] The more limited the quantitative data, the more the rating will have to depend on the qualitative assessments.

13.2.1 Academic work on fund rating

Unfortunately, the views expressed by institutions like the Basel Committee and the ISDA have failed to encourage academic research in this field. To the extent that work on rating systems in private equity and similar asset classes has been done, it has been led by practitioners and commercial entities. Examples include Troche (2003) on private equity, Giannotti and Mattarocci (2009) on real estate and Ruso (2008), who discusses a rating system comprising a governance and risk rating for closed-end real estate, ship and private equity funds. In many ways, the proposed techniques are similar in the sense that the risk rating consists of several criteria for which either negative or positive points are awarded, depending on whether they increase or decrease the risk level. However, none of these studies link rating classes to quantitative measures.

13.2.2 Techniques

Studies on investment management and qualitative methods often use the terms "scoring", "ranking" and "rating" interchangeably, which can lead to confusion. For our purpose, we differentiate between qualitative and quantitative methods to determine a ranking, the scores derived from a ranking and the various rankings or scores which are aggregated to come to a classification, such as a rating or grading (Meyer and Mathonet, 2005).

Ranking

Rankings from "best" to "worst" are usually designed to help users make decisions. Rankings, sometimes called "league tables", are based on various measures (Bromley, 2002). Typically, several relevant dimensions are ranked independently: for example, in university league tables "research assessment", "teaching assessment", "staff/student ratio" are often ranked separately,

[1] For example, in the case of credit ratings, qualitative factors can have a weight of more than 50% of the total rating analysis. See O'Sullivan, B. and Weston, I. (2006) *Challenges in Validating Rating Systems for IRB under Basel II.* Standard & Poor's, October. Quoted in Rebonato (2007).

as users may be interested in the individual factors that drive the overall rankings or have a particular interest in a single dimension. While rankings are generally quite straightforward as long as they entail only one dimension, it is far more challenging to aggregate rankings of different dimensions as a basis for making a decision about two or several alternative investments. This requires translating rankings of a set of items or attributes translated into numerical scores.

Scoring

A scoring aims to assign a set of criteria that are relevant for the measurement within a meaningful categorization in predefined classes. When designing a scoring template, important questions relate to the number of dimensions that should be reflected in the evaluation and the weighting of these dimensions. For example, for an infrastructure fund it might be assumed that the ability to take advantage of cheap debt financing is more important than being able to provide operational support to the portfolio company. By contrast, while venture capital investments typically involve very little, if any, debt, operational factors are critical. Given the relative importance of various dimensions, the question arises as to how one may assign specific weights.

13.2.3 Practical considerations

There are a number of limitations and trade-offs that need to be taken into consideration. First, while practitioners generally try to develop a single collective ranking from a set of rankings of different criteria, the aim of coming up with a "perfect ranking" is illusive. In fact, such a ranking cannot exist, a classical paradox in social choice theory as shown by Condorcet and Arrow.[2]

A good scoring method will result in classes where the intra-class similarity is high while the inter-class similarity is low. These classes should be somehow "similar" to one another, so that the population of funds within the class can be treated collectively as one group. But the more classes we look at, the higher the probability that the proposal is assigned to the "wrong" class, i.e. that there is another class that fits its characteristics better. Consequently, the lower the number of classes, the more robust the scoring method will be. Weighting the various dimensions will often be difficult and ambiguous. In such situations, a pragmatic and robust approach may lie in assigning equal weights to each dimension.

A simple approach to guide decisions is "tallying". In this approach, analysts look for cues that might help to make a choice between two or several options, with the preferred option being determined by the greatest excess of positive over negative cues without bothering to try to rate them in order of importance (Fisher, 2009). Tallying looks oversimplistic as it takes no account of the relative importance of different factors, but this simple method was found to do consistently better in predicting outcomes than experts' intuition (Dawes, 1979). Statistical weighting of the different factors is a better fit for known data. However, risk managers are dealing with situations of high uncertainty where it is not known which weights to give to these factors. For extrapolating data into the future – what risk managers should primarily be

[2] According to Nobel laureate Kenneth Arrow, the impossibility theorem states that no voting system based on the ranking of candidates can be converted into a community-wide ranking while also satisfying a particular set of four criteria – unrestricted domain, non-dictatorship, Pareto efficiency and independence of irrelevant alternatives.

concerned with – simple tallying works just as well and sometimes even better. Rather than operating with "absolute truths", in essence a risk manager – like a judge in a legal case – can only weight evidence pro and con. Terry Smith followed a comparable approach in his 1992 analysis of accounting techniques (Smith, 1996). He introduced "blob" scores for companies (with a "blob" representing the use of creative accounting techniques). For the companies he analysed, this "blob" scoring has proved to be a remarkably robust methodology for predicting financial distress.

It also does not make sense to look at too many dimensions and be overly sophisticated with the scoring. The more dimensions that have to be taken into account for the scoring, the more pronounced the reversion to the mean will be: statistically speaking, an extreme event is likely to be followed by a less extreme event. The more dimensions are taken into consideration, the closer the aggregations are to the average.

13.3 APPROACHES TO FUND RATINGS

To review the different approaches to fund ratings that are currently in use, we differentiate between (i) assessments that are conducted by independent external parties and (ii) techniques for fund evaluation that are employed internally by investors. The term "rating" is typically used in the context of credit risk models and is associated with default probabilities of loans or bonds. While ratings are sometimes mentioned in the context of limited partnership funds, funds – as we argued in Chapter 8 – do not "default" in the sense of a credit default, which is generally defined as an event where the debtor misses a regular contractually agreed repayment of interest or principal. Later in this chapter, we shall discuss a classification of limited partnership funds that we call a "grading", i.e. an assessment based on comparisons against a peer group population.

13.3.1 Rating by external agencies

As far as mutual funds are concerned, the term "rating" is the norm, although such ratings are fundamentally different from credit ratings in terms of their objectives and underlying methodologies. Ratings of mutual funds are conducted by independent agencies like Feri (Financial and Economic Research International), Lipper, Morningstar or S&P. According to the Feri Trust Funds Guide 2002, "fund 'rating' is a standardised valuation with a forward-looking prognosis". For a fund to be rated by Morningstar, for example, it needs to have a minimum history of 5 years and at least 20 comparable funds. S&P, by contrast, requires a fund history of at least 3 years and a sufficient number of comparable funds. In contrast to mutual funds, however, limited partnership funds are typically not covered by external rating agencies. The concept of a rating assigned by an independent agency is difficult to apply to private equity and real assets.

Fiduciary rating of firms

Fiduciary rating measures the risk of investors who entrust their money to third-party organizations. Fiduciary risk is the risk of breaching the investor's trust by failing to perform their contractual obligations. It reflects weaknesses, deficiencies and failure of systems, processes and organization of an investment firm. According to RCP & Partners, a fiduciary rating is "a methodology for assessing, rating and monitoring asset management organisations through application of standardised process".

The rating evaluates the stability of a firm and its ability to sustain relative performance over time and takes criteria such as the quality of the investment process, the financial strength, the quality of risk management, the avoidance or mitigation of conflicts of interest, the quality of controlling, customer service or management strategy into consideration. RCP & Partners assesses management companies by reviewing two families of risk:[3]

- *Structural risk*, which relates to the "hardware" of a firm, covering overall resource allocation, risk control, compliance, administration and back-office, middle office, sales and marketing.
- *Performance risk*, which relates to the firm's "software" and depends on the whole investment management process, from research to trade execution, including the firm's own investment track record.

A fiduciary rating is based on the assumption that a necessary condition for good investment performance lies in the appropriate organization of the investment process. The advantage of this approach is that it does not require a long investment history and therefore might help overcome a main obstacle to investing in private equity and real assets. However, there is no direct link between fiduciary rating and future performance, and a good fiduciary rating is not a sufficient condition for good investment returns. RCP & Partners use the same scale as Standard & Poor's, which could cause confusion, as the RCP & Partners' scale is not based on the same investment risk model.

There is an additional challenge. Fiduciary rating relies on voluntary participation, a precondition that might be difficult to meet in the alternative investing industry. Ruso (2008), for example, bases his governance rating on information disclosed in the issuance prospects: 12 main criteria are used to evaluate different fund features that determine the quality of a fund's governance structure. However, high-quality firms may not even be interested in providing more granulated information, as they have an established investor base for the funds they raise.

Importantly, a fiduciary rating should not be confused with due diligence. Instead, it should be regarded as a complement, possibly suited for the monitoring phase and as a standard input for a fund's qualitative assessment. Such "ratings" signal the quality of a fund (typically focusing on the quality of the investment team or organization) but are not designed to predict performance.

Rating of firms

Instead of rating individual funds, Gottschalg focuses on what he labels the fitness of private equity firms.[4] These fitness rankings have been published since 2009 as a joint product by HEC (the French business school) and Dow Jones. The HEC-Dow Jones Private Equity Fitness Ranking™ aims to list the best private equity firms "... in terms of their competitive fitness, specifically, their expected ability to yield a superior performance over the next 5–10 years".[5] More specifically, the rankings are designed to evaluate each firm's competitive positioning

[3] See http://www.globalcustody.net/rcp-and-partners/?149 [accessed 10 February 2012].

[4] This work should not be confused with his proposed approach of selecting funds, which is described in Gottschalg (2010).

[5] See press release of 19 May 2011 (Professor Oliver Gottschalg publishes the Spring 2011 HEC-Dow Jones Private Equity Fitness Ranking™. http://www.hec.edu/var/fre/storage/original/application/b3034f561b8dc60a51887e9d6d7d849e.pdf, accessed 5 November 2012). See also Primack (2011).

based on 10 different criteria, deriving an overall future competitiveness score based on the historic link between firm performance and each of the criteria. The criteria are chosen out of more than 30 criteria because collectively they are found to capture some of the most important value drivers. The calibration of the model is based on the proprietary HEC buyout database, which contains information on the investment characteristics and performance of a large sample of private equity transactions over the past 30 years.

The criteria thus selected include the scale of current activities, the ability to take advantage of cheap debt financing, the ability to time the stock market to benefit from market trends over the holding period, the ability to time the stock market to exit at high exit valuations, the level of industry focus, the change in the level of industry focus, the quality of deal flow (defined as the ability to continue to invest during periods when all other private equity firms are decreasing their investment pace), the flexibility to take advantage of investment opportunities of different sizes, the level of strategic uniqueness and differentiation and recent changes in the scale of activity.

While the fitness rankings are supposed to be forward-looking, they are thought to complement the HEC-Dow Jones Private Equity Performance Ranking™, which aims to rank the top GPs in terms of their past performance.

The actual rankings are based on data provided by Thomson Reuters VentureXpert, a large private equity database. For the 2012 rankings, this dataset includes a total of 33,025 investments of USD 631 billion by 2,544 funds and 1,295 firms into 15,690 distinct portfolio companies. From this large universe, private equity firms are selected which had (i) completed at least 50 transactions, (ii) raised at least 4 funds, (iii) invested at least USD 1 billion and (iv) been active for at least 10 years. These filters reduced the sample to 238 firms with over 1,000 funds that had raised almost USD 1 trillion and made investments in over 20,000 portfolio companies. Missing variables reduced the sample further to 217 private equity firms.

While the statistical tests suggest a high explanatory power of the model, the methodology is inevitably subject to two important limitations. As Gottschalg himself points out, the ranking of competitive fitness is based on the historic relationship between the criteria and subsequent performance. In situations where these criteria or their relationships change, the model's accuracy decreases. Furthermore, the analysis is based on data that are observable but do not reflect factors like the departure of key personnel or future changes in strategy that are not yet reflected in recent investment decisions but may influence the future performance of the firm. The ranking's value as a decision support tool thus rests heavily on the assumption of performance persistence, an assumption that is far from perfect despite its wide acceptance among practitioners.

Investment rating of funds

Introduced in 2000, Feri's investment rating of closed-end funds differentiates between the following asset classes: real estate, ships, aircraft, new energy, private equity, infrastructure, multi-assets.[6] The objective of the rating is similar to traditional ratings of mutual funds, i.e. to help users select individual funds following a transparent, standardized and effective evaluation method, based on a defined list of criteria which include qualitative and quantitative factors: "The outcomes of fund managers' due diligence are benchmarked. The quantitative

[6] See http://frr.feri.de/en/products-services/funds/closed-end-funds/ and http://ft.feri.de/en/investment-segments/private-equity/ [accessed 8 February 2012].

aspects of a fund are then compensated by qualitative aspects and both result in a fund rating from A to E, where A is the best rating." Feri uses a scoring model to combine the various criteria into a single rating. The rating of funds is conducted at the request of Feri's clients, who require a systematic and independent analysis to ensure that their investment decisions are sound. The ratings are not made available to the general public. As far as real estate funds are concerned, a fund's rating is based on the evaluation of its structure (e.g., contract analyses, guarantees, financing and earnings, exit options), the quality of management and the property or properties under management. By contrast, Feri's private equity fund selection criteria are management[7] (60%), economics[8] (32.5%) and customer service[9] (7.5%) (Söhnholz, 2002).

There are other advisers who have developed a rating process for limited partnership funds. One example is Mackewicz & Partner and its successor firm Fleischhauer, Hoyer & Partner (FHP), who regard the rating of private equity and VC funds as broadly comparable to traditional funds rating.[10] The objective of their approach is to provide reliable decision-making support for potential investors in funds and in funds-of-funds. Its focus is on evaluating the probability of losses and gains for the capital invested. FHP uses a scoring model which is based heavily on qualitative criteria for five main assessment dimensions.[11] This results in an "FHP-Rating" for the fund of either "very bad" (weighted aggregate score 0–39), "bad" (weighted aggregate score 40–59), "good" (weighted aggregate score 60–79), "very good" (weighted aggregate score 80–89) or "outstanding" (weighted aggregate score 90–100).

Limitations of fund assessments by external agencies

The following issues may render the rating of limited partnership funds by external agencies problematic.

- If an external agency cannot base its opinion on a sufficient number of objective criteria, it will be difficult to defend an assigned "rating". Alternative investments are an appraised and speculative asset class. Therefore, the assessment of a fund will predominantly be based on qualitative factors which could make the rating highly subjective.
- A rating usually does not imply any recommendation by an agency. As an external rating for a limited partnership fund would only be relevant pre-investment and there is no efficient risk-adjusted pricing, it implicitly forms an investment recommendation. Post-investment, the investor has access to far better in-depth information on the fund than any rating agency.
- There are too few potential investors as customers to make an external rating service viable.[12] As this is an unregulated industry, only qualified and experienced investors can become LPs, and they cannot invest without proper due diligence.

---

[7] Business concept, management experience, management resources, past performance, deal and exit generation, manager risk, management participation.

[8] Management fee, incentive fee, other costs, cash flow, fund risk.

[9] Tax and legal structure, customer relationship management.

[10] See http://www.fhpe.de/investors/vc-pe.htm [accessed 8 February 2012].

[11] The dimensions of management team and experience (30%), track record (30%), structure and terms of fund (20%), investment strategy (10%) and investment process (10%) are assigned scores from 1 (very poor) to 5 (very good). See http://www.fhpe.de/investoren/FHP_Flyer_Rating%20internet.pdf [accessed 8 February 2012].

[12] Mutual funds are more scalable in terms of number of investors (mainly retail investors) and investment volume: interest for rating services like Morningstar and the mutual fund managers is higher and no due diligence is necessary, as it is a regulated industry. The rating for alternatives assigned by Feri should rather be seen as a standardized due diligence; its results are, to our knowledge, only made available to Feri customers.

Table 13.1 CalPERS fund performance assessment

Exceeds expectations
As expected
Below expectations
Below expectations/with concern
Too early to tell

Source: CalPERS.

Table 13.2 Internal fund performance assessment

Assessment scale	Description
A	Clear evidence of $X\%+$ rate of return over the life of the fund.
B	An immature fund managed by a strong VC team or a fund set to generate a return in the low to high teens range.
C	An underlying portfolio which may generate a return in the high single figure to low teen range, or an unproven or less talented management team.
D	A fund set to produce a single figure return or major concerns about the management team.
E	A fund expected to produce a negative return or minimal positive return.

- Committing capital to a fund is possible only during the fundraising period or through a secondary transaction. This is fundamentally different from mutual funds, where investors can continuously adjust their portfolios in response to an external rating.

13.3.2 Internal fund assessment approaches

Some private equity investment programmes use grading-like assessments to manage their portfolios. CalPERS, for instance, uses the categories listed in Table 13.1.

"Too early to tell" does not mean that CalPERS has no opinion on a fund before they invest. The underlying assumption is that the investment is done in a fund that meets the declared return expectations. Return expectations carry over the cycle and across asset classes. According to Braunschweig (2001), CalPERS based their commitment decisions for seed capital investments on an expected return of at least 30% at the beginning of the century. While the target return for early and late-stage VC was set at 25% at that time, buyout and mezzanine investments were subject to an expected return of 20% and 15%, respectively.

Table 13.2 provides an alternative example for an assessment framework developed for VC funds.

Both examples in Tables 13.1 and 13.2 define static benchmarks for grades that, to some degree, take a specific market environment into consideration.[13] Raschle and Jaeggi (2004) refer to another approach based on probabilities and quartiling; see Table 13.3.

[13] See Healy (2001): "Calpers [sic] may have gotten greedy after that ITV fund. The Silicon Valley fund's 1998 portfolio was up 69.9% through the end of last year – yet was ranked 'below expectations.' A Thomas H. Lee fund of the same year (a buyout fund, vs. a start-up tech fund) had gained 19.2% by year-end and was seen to be performing 'as expected' . . . Still, over the long term, Calpers [sic] has been doing something right. As of March 31, its average annual return for 10 years of private equity investing was 17.5%. The Wilshire 2500 Index, a broad stock market benchmark, was up 13.9% in that period."

Table 13.3 Adveq fund performance assessment

Manager quality	Quality definition
Outstanding	50% probability of reaching top quartile
Solid	35% probability of reaching top quartile
Average	25% probability of reaching top quartile
Poor	Less than 20% probability of reaching top quartile
Unproven	Too young

Source: Adveq analysis 2002.

Such fund assessments are mainly used for internal purposes and are rarely published. Based on discussions with industry practitioners, it appears that fund "grading" approaches – whether published or internal – are often "unpopular".[14] One reason might be that a low grade would typically be interpreted as a failure of the initial investment selection method. The probability of making it into the first quartile is also time-dependent. A mature top-performing fund will most likely make it to the first quartile, while in its early years the same fund's probability of reaching this objective will certainly be lower. Consequently, in the Adveq scale a fund would go through different stages, although the fund's quality is essentially unchanged. That could make comparisons over several vintage years difficult.

13.4 USE OF RATING/GRADING AS INPUT FOR MODELS

The choice of a rating/grading system and the techniques to be applied depends critically on the decision maker's main objective. Is the rating/grading system supposed to support investment decisions as part of the due diligence process? Alternatively, is its main purpose seen in the area of portfolio management and risk budgeting? Or is such a system expected to support the monitoring of investment decisions? For example, to the extent that ratings/grades are primarily employed as a tool in investment decision making, the main interest is in picking superior investment proposals. Therefore, the ratings described before could be interpreted mainly as indicators for success.

It is well understood that there can be no excess return without incurring risks. In fact, often there is the expectation that this works in reverse, too, and in return for taking the risk an investor would automatically get rewarded. This, however, requires a risk-adjusted pricing mechanism that establishes a link between the risk taken and the premium sought by the investor. Alternatively, as we will discuss below, investors can seek risk by exploring for opportunities thus undetected and unexploited by other market participants.

13.4.1 Assessing downside risk

The typical limited partnership structure does not allow for risk-adjusted pricing. All primary positions are bought at par (i.e., without premium or discount) and there is no predefined coupon payment but only an uncertain performance and a predefined cost structure. Only in the case of secondary transactions is it possible to translate a fund's underperformance

[14] See Healy (2001): "Even now, managers of venture funds and other private portfolios are talking about the posting, aghast that the numbers – good, bad, and ugly – are there for all to see. Said one private equity executive, 'If you show up in the "below expectations" column, you're done'."

into respective discounts (Mathonet and Meyer, 2007). As a consequence, the elimination of critical issues is usually tackled during the due diligence pre-investment phase. If critical issues remain (often called "deal-breakers"), an investment proposal is typically rejected. However, during the lifetime of a fund things can change, and a fund that was given a high rating may encounter unexpected problems. While ideally the rating should anticipate possible issues that may arise over the life of the fund, it is important to recall (Chapter 8) that default models for limited partnership funds are problematic as they ignore the upside potential compensating investors for the downside risk they accept.

13.4.2 Assessing upside potential

While a structured approach should result in a higher degree of consistency, there remain doubts as to whether rating techniques per se can actually lead to additional insights that allow superior investment decisions. A single rating or grading can be derived from a profile of different scores, but not vice versa. For investment decisions a profile offers more insights than an assignment to a single class. In any case, the value of any methodology for investment decision making rests on its ability to predict future outcomes compared to peers – a proposition that has yet to be proved by robust empirical evidence.

13.4.3 Is success repeatable?

Rating systems are explicitly or implicitly predicated on the assumption that returns are persistent. In fact, many practitioners subscribe to this view, which takes into account that success in private equity requires a special skill set, with fund managers typically going through a learning process. Kaplan and Schoar (2005) find support for the persistence hypothesis in private equity and Hendershott (2007) argues that there is at least an 80% probability of a fund being top-quartile, if its three predecessors were top-quartile as well. However, given the substantial data issues researchers are confronted with, more research is required to draw meaningful conclusions from the point of view of making investment decisions. Specifically, the following points should be taken into account.

- Rouvinez (2006) points to the fact that more than a quarter of the funds in the market are being labelled "top quartile" and that there is about a 40% probability that managers with lower quartile funds do not come back to the market.[15] As a consequence, investors tend to only meet top-quartile managers. The high attrition rate with a combined repetition of upper performance seems to be the signature characteristic of the private equity asset class. This makes it difficult for investors to use top-quartile performance as an effective screening criterion.
- Peer groups cannot be compared over different vintage years. Private equity firms raise funds at irregular intervals, and therefore the firms that raised the funds comprising the

[15] See Rouvinez (2006): "One reason is that except for the 25 percent ratio itself, nothing in the definition is cast in stone. Whether 'best performance' refers to total value or internal rate of return, net or gross, realised or not, is open to interpretation, as is the question of who are the 'peers'." Good fund managers can also be unlucky, e.g. backing a good company where an exceptional CEO suddenly died or where the entire sector then goes into a protracted downturn. Long-term exposure to market extremes can disproportionately favour one strategy over another even if fund managers are equally competent. Likewise, Hendershott (2007) calculated that for the best 250 of 1,000 private equity funds one would expect to find that 146 of them or 58.4% were managed by top-quartile managers. That still leaves 41.6% of the good funds managed by the 13.9% of ordinary managers who happened to be lucky.

previous vintage year peer group may not be in the market looking for investors the same time again. With peer group compositions continuously changing, the persistence claim is difficult to verify.

- Studies on return persistence are typically based on data for mature funds. At a minimum, funds are at least 6 years old to be included in a sample as the performance of younger funds is still subject to considerable variation.[16] However, a typical fundraising cycle is 4 years and at the peak of the last private equity boom it was not uncommon for funds to return to market after less than 3 years. In fact, in the dataset for venture capital funds used by Conner (2005), firms raised a successor fund on average after just 2.9 years. Nearly half of these firms in his sample raised a successor fund in years 2 or 3. This implies that the performance of a fund is not reliably visible at the time when investors have to take their re-up decision. In fact, at that time a non-trivial part of the fund's committed capital is still to be called, and the investments that have already been made are often too recent to draw conclusions with a sufficiently high degree of confidence.
- To the extent that persistence exists, the question arises as to whether this is due to superior skills or other factors. Recent research by Chung (2010), for example, finds that market conditions are likely to play an important role, with outperforming funds operating in markets that have enjoyed particularly strong growth. However, this makes success less predictable as market conditions can change and new competitors may enter the market, affecting the incumbents' potential for achieving excess returns.
- Finally, the performance of a fund manager may be undermined by his own success. As a fund outperforms its peers, its successor fund will find it easier to attract more capital. However, as the size of the fund (and its successor fund) grows, its performance might suffer. In fact, Kaplan and Schoar (2005) find a concave relationship between fund size and performance for VC funds, although not for buyout funds. Robinson and Sensoy (2011) find that PMEs for both buyout and VC funds are modestly concave in the log of fund size. Harris *et al.* (2012), finally, report a concave relation between PME and the log of fund size for both buyout and VC funds controlling for vintage year. However, the regression coefficients are significant only at the 12% level for buyouts and are not at all significant for VC funds.

13.5 ASSESSING THE DEGREE OF SIMILARITY WITH COMPARABLE FUNDS

Against this background, we suggest focusing on the degree of similarity of a fund with respect to its peer group as a reference point for quantification. The scoring aims to measure the deviation in relevant dimensions from this peer group. Using such a comparison for *ex-ante* assessment is based on the assumption that membership in a group of funds has significant performance implications (Porter, 1979). Our concept of a qualitative risk assessment is based on how closely a fund is aligned with best practices in a given market environment at the time when it is launched. A fund that is well adjusted today is assumed to perform in line with earlier funds that were well adjusted at the time when they were raised, even if the criteria of what constitutes best practice have changed since.

[16] See Burgel (2000) and Conner (2005).

13.5.1 The AMH framework

The adaptive market hypothesis (AMH) reflects an evolutionary model of the alternative asset industry: market participants often make mistakes but they also learn. Competition drives adaptation and innovation, natural selection shapes market ecology and evolution determines market dynamics. Speculative opportunities do exist in the market, but appear and disappear over time, so innovation in the form of continuous search for new opportunities is critical for survival and growth. The AMH originated in the hedge fund world, where a significant number of funds focus on generating returns from arbitrage strategies, which should not be possible if the efficient market hypothesis (EMH) holds. The AMH is a relatively new framework developed by Lo, although the application of evolutionary ideas to economic behaviour is not new.[17]

The grading technique based on the idea of "similarity" is questionable in the context of the EMH: without a risk-adjusted pricing mechanism it would not seem to make sense to invest in a fund that has any apparent weaknesses or structural deviations from industry standards. However, as a tool the fund grading is consistent with the AMH: it is measuring the deviation of a fund structure from market best practices representing the "average" population. Kukla (2011) finds that several successful strategies exist in the private equity sector. Strategic groups evolve, with successful firms monitoring other firms in their strategic group as reference points and converging to each other over time.

13.5.2 Strategic groups in alternative assets

Kukla (2011) identifies strategic centre points, i.e. "centroids", such as "sector specialist", "product specialist", "sector-focused investment firm", "multi-business investment firm" and "small cap generalist". He interprets centroids as the mathematical equivalent of a strategic pattern of a group of firms and finds significant inter-group differences. He reports evidence which suggests that private equity firms affiliated with a more successful strategic group gravitate towards their centroids over time.

The LPA ratings tool developed by ILPA could be interpreted as falling into this category.[18] Its purpose is to rate the degree to which a particular partnership agreement adheres to the ILPA's best practice approach, PE Principles V 2.0. These principles are meant to serve as a tool in connection with due diligence and to monitor and evaluate investments in private equity. While the rating tool is based on a ranking and weighting process that mirrors the more measurable aspects of a fund's governance, it is stressed that qualitative analysis is equally important – sometimes necessitating judgment calls by the LP. As every partnership agreement is different, it can also be subject to varying interpretations. Thus, the LPA ratings tool mainly forms a basis for comparing funds against peers, helping identify relative strengths and weaknesses. Although adherence to the ILPA principles plays an increasingly important role for LPs in the fund selection process,[19] it is important for investors to recognize their limitations, given their qualitative nature.

[17] See Lo (2005) or Lo and Mueller (2010). In fact, Thomas Malthus already used biological arguments to predict rather dire economic consequences. Vice versa, the evolutionary biologists Charles Darwin and Alfred Russel Wallace were strongly influenced by Malthus. His arguments became an intellectual stepping-stone to the idea of natural selection. Also, Schumpeter's notions of "creative destruction" and "burst of entrepreneurial activity" are consistent with the concept of evolution.

[18] See http://ilpa.org/lpa-ratings-tool/ [accessed 7 February 2012].

[19] According to a recent survey by Preqin, a data vendor, the majority of surveyed investors see non-adherence to the ILPA principles as a reason not to invest in a fund. To the extent that deviations exist, only those funds for which a case can be made – e.g., where there are strengths or differentiation compared to competing proposals – are likely to attract investors described as "increasingly terms and conditions-sensitive". See http://www.cpifinancial.net [accessed 23 June 2011].

13.5.3 Linking grading to quantification

Measuring deviations from the strategic group "centroids" could result in a grading as "standard", "mainstream", "niche" or "experiment", depending on how strong the deviations are. Quotes from industry practitioners like "[w]e categorise managers from A to D, with A being the managers in our portfolio and D being managers that we regard as non-institutional quality. We target our resources towards the A's and B's, essentially, but we would also be meeting the C's on a regular basis"[20] suggest that comparable methodologies for evaluating limited partnership funds are finding increasing acceptance.

13.6 CONCLUSIONS

The line between the "classical" approach to due diligence and the various fund ratings discussed in this chapter is blurred. Generally, such ratings aim to predict investment success for individual funds, but there remains considerable scepticism and investment managers often feel that such an "algorithmic" approach is unlikely to work. At the same time, many investment managers view due diligence as a major – or even the only – risk management tool in alternative assets. However, Kahneman (2011) finds that in situations of high uncertainty and unpredictability, expert views are often inferior to relatively simple formula. He concedes that intuition can lead to better results if the environment is sufficiently regular and the expert had a chance to learn its regularities. This, however, is typically not the case for investments in limited partnership funds as the investment environment is continuously changing and the long life of a fund makes observations too infrequent for investment managers to identify performance-relevant patterns and learn from their experience. This debate goes beyond the scope of this book, but we conclude that "best practices" and "lessons learned" can usefully be formalized in an algorithm that produces grades for limited partnership funds as input risk measurement purposes.

Consistent with the AMH, we therefore advocate an approach that aims to identify the closest similar benchmark population for the purpose of translating expected performance grades into quantifications. In Chapter 14 we discuss how, with this qualitative input, the index of comparable funds can be translated into a range of multiples.

[20] See Institutional Investor Profile, Colin Wimsett, Managing Partner, Pantheon Ventures at http://www.altassets.com/features/arc/2008/nz13106.php [accessed 3 July 2008].

14 Translating Fund Grades into Quantification

To value and measure risks for limited partnership funds, we have to overcome a series of problems. The quantitative analysis focuses on the financial strength and on the portfolio. But the relevance of the portfolio analysis follows the fund's lifecycle, with its importance increasing over time. As the investment is usually in a blind pool, any assessment has to rely – at least during the early years of the fund's life – to a high degree on qualitative criteria.

We follow on from the previous chapter and discuss a so-called fund grading system that draws upon analogies from established rating techniques for credit risk. The purpose of this discussion is not an exhaustive description of possible scoring techniques, which can be found in Crouhy *et al.* (2001) and Meyer and Mathonet (2005); instead, we focus on the question of how fund grades can be translated into a consistent quantification to determine ranges for growth rates as inputs for the cash flow projection models. This grading system comprises two components; that is (i) "expected performance" (P-A, P-B, P-C, P-D) and (ii) "operational status" (O-A, O-B, O-C, O-D) grades. The expected performance is assessed through benchmarking comparable funds with similar characteristics, and by identifying possible weaknesses in the fund's structure. This approach aims to provide a consistent framework for the *ex-ante* assessment, monitoring and *ex-post* performance measurement of partnerships. During the monitoring phase, the operational status grades aim to capture the risk that an unforeseen event (e.g., loss of a key person of the GP's investment team) can have a negative impact on the expected performance grades.

14.1 EXPECTED PERFORMANCE GRADES

The expected performance grades are assigned on the basis of both quantitative and qualitative criteria, the internal age to combine the two evaluations, a review and, if necessary, an adjustment of the grade. The grade reflects many attributes that are weighted depending on the specific stage within a fund's life. The quantitative score is derived through benchmarking against the fund's vintage-year peer group. The fund's internal age drives the model's sensitivity to qualitative inputs. Following this approach, the grading approach uses Bayesian inference in which evidence or observations are used to update the projections. Whereas projections for a young fund depend mainly on the subset of historical data as determined by the qualitative score, for funds with an internal age approaching 100% the model does not react to qualitative scores at all. See Figure 14.1.

The model is essentially designed top-down, i.e. it is marked to comparable funds. As the fund progresses through its lifecycle and undrawn commitments decline, the quantitative score becomes increasingly important relative to qualitative factors. At the same time, increasing weight is attached to individual portfolio companies, resulting in a growing role for bottom-up analysis.

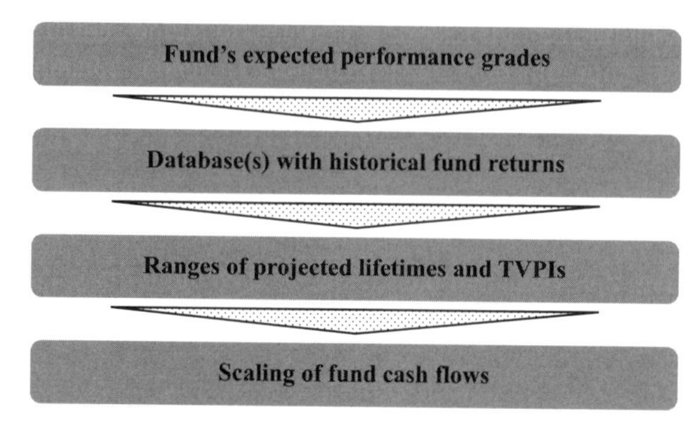

Figure 14.1 Basic approach.

14.1.1 Determine quantitative score

While the IRR is used universally as a key measure in the evaluation of fund performance, it is highly dependent on both the NAV calculation and cash flow timing. Therefore, we treat a fund's lifetime as well as its TVPI at the end of its lifetime as dimensions that are assessed separately. The quantitative score is calculated by benchmarking a fund's ITVPI against the interim multiples of its peer-group population.

The peer group for a fund allows a LP to see how a particular fund is performing relative to other funds at a given point in time. To determine this peer group various data vendors, such as Preqin or Thomson VentureXpert, are used to define the sample of funds raised in the same vintage year, controlling for the stage and geographical focus of the partnerships in the sample. The comparison against the benchmark is translated into a quantitative score: consistent with the objective of determining a fund's quartile rank within the peer group, the fund's relative position within its benchmark is converted as a linear combination between the quartile limits, with the maximum being equal to 1, the minimum to 4, the median to 2.5, the top quartile minimum to 1.75 and, finally, the lower quartile maximum to 3.25.[1]

As far as smaller and less developed market segments are concerned, such as partnerships targeting distressed assets or growth capital deals in emerging markets, it may be challenging to identify a sample of benchmark funds with similar characteristics. While available databases vary in terms of their market coverage, in practice some markets are just too thin and in their infancy so it will be difficult to grade a fund against comparator funds. In such cases, an alternative solution might be sought in comparing a fund with similar funds in different markets, as long as their fundamental characteristics are sufficiently comparable. For instance, in grading a growth capital fund in emerging markets, a LP may decide to use comparable growth capital funds in other geographies as a benchmark sample.

Importantly, the relative performance of funds is found to vary substantially over their life. As far as venture capital is concerned, Schäli *et al.* (2002) report that only 14% of partnerships with an interim IRR in the first quartile after year 1 end in the first quartile upon maturity. After year 4, however, 50% of top-quartile funds based on interim IRRs actually end up in the first quartile upon maturity. This suggests that the best performers can be identified relatively late

[1] In cases where the fund's ITPVI is higher than the maximum ITVPI of the benchmark, the quantitative score remains at 1; likewise, in cases where the fund's ITPVI is lower than the minimum ITVPI of the benchmark, the quantitative score remains at 4.

in the lifecycle of partnerships. Therefore, the interim top-quartile composition will change continuously – which underlines the importance of qualitative scoring.

14.1.2 Determine qualitative score

The objective of qualitative scoring is to determine a limited partnership fund's degree of compliance with industry standards applying to its closest peer group. It may be seen as a measure of how well adapted a fund is to the alternative asset market environment at a given point in time. Based on this, funds can be ranked according to their deviation from standard characteristics.

The qualitative scoring is used to evaluate several criteria related to the fund characteristics. There are multiple performance-relevant dimensions which the qualitative scoring aims to capture. The purpose of the qualitative scoring is to benchmark the fund against standard market practices. In assessing private equity funds, a scoring of the following dimensions (with several sub-dimensions) has proved to be useful (Meyer and Mathonet, 2005).

- Management team skills: private equity experience, operational experience, industry sector experience, country/regional experience, team size, team dynamics and key man, balance and coverage.
- Management team stability: cohesion of the management team, historical stability, sharing within the team, succession planning, financial stability.
- Management team motivation: incentive structure, reputation, team independence, outside activities, conflicts of interest, managers' investment into the fund.
- Fund strategy: deal flow strategy and sourcing, hands-on approach, investment focus and "sweet spot", fund size, exit strategy, overall strategy fit.
- Fund structure: compliance with standards, cost of the structure, corporate governance.
- External validation: previous funds' track record analysis, performance of comparable funds, quality of co-investors, recurrent investors.

Points are awarded for the various criteria, depending on whether or not the fund is in compliance with standard industry practices and structures. To determine the scores, it is important to evaluate whether sufficient information is available and whether it is relevant for forming an opinion. Moreover, criteria such as the robustness of evidence (i.e., can it be observed over longer time periods and under alternative conditions?) or persistence (i.e., is this expected to continue?) need to be taken into account. As a matter of course, scores are not strictly additive, but within the "continuum" of operating funds that have attracted sufficient institutional investments, it appears to be a reasonable heuristics.

In parallel with the quantitative scoring, and assuming that n criteria are assessed, the following applies: if all n criteria are found to be in line with standards, the highest score of 1 is awarded; conversely, if none of the n criteria is fulfilled, the lowest score of 4 is given. The qualitative scoring is based on the assessment of an investment proposal's key dimensions and uses a peer-group population as a yardstick. Therefore, the first step is to identify the "peer-group" universe, which will be used as a reference.

Prior to the investment, the benchmarking peer group of the same vintage year is usually unknown. Its composition needs to be "estimated", based on the current conditions and the prevailing standards in the fundraising market. The scoring is based on the assumption that the unknown future peer group will be comparable to the population of recent vintages. Even if the composition of the peer group is not known, to a high degree the investment decision

Table 14.1 Linking scores to expected performance grades

1 ≤ Aggregate weighted score < 1.75	P-A
1.75 ≤ Aggregate weighted score < 2.5	P-B
2.5 ≤ Aggregate weighted score < 3.25	P-C
3.25 ≤ Aggregate weighted score ≤ 4	P-D

is based on a list of criteria that is generally seen as consistent with the best-performing funds.[2] In this context, we suggest differentiating between two peer groups. Because of the long investment cycles, statistics on the historical peer group for fully realized vintage years will be "stale". Reliable quantitative information will relate to vintage-year cohorts that, in the extreme, date back more than 10 years. Therefore, qualitative scores are mainly based on interim data, anecdotal evidence and lessons learned from relatively young funds. The qualitative scoring cannot be seen as "static". The scoring methodology needs to be continuously updated and calibrated as new mainstream characteristics emerge and industry players do not further apply certain established practices.

14.1.3 Combine the two scores, review and adjust

As the fund in question continues to mature, quantitative information becomes increasingly available. In the early years of the fund, quantitative information complements qualitative factors, but as the fund approaches the final phase of its life quantitative information eventually fully replaces the qualitative judgment. The method used to combine the qualitative and quantitative scores is based on a parameter that summarizes the predictive power of each. There are two endpoints, the start and the end of a fund's life. While at the beginning only the qualitative score is relevant, at the end of the fund's life the opposite is true. At this stage, the TVPI is known, making a qualitative assessment obsolete. Therefore, once the quantitative and qualitative scores have been calculated, they are aggregated weighted by the fund's internal age (IA):

$$\text{Aggregate weighted score} = (1 - \text{IA})^{*}\ \text{qualitative score} + \text{IA}^{*}\text{quantitative score}$$

As long as the fund is young, the performance grade is fully weighted towards the qualitative score. As the internal age approaches 1, which is equivalent to the fund having distributed the majority of its value, the performance grade becomes more heavily weighted towards the quantitative score. The expected performance grades are then determined as in Table 14.1.

The last step for determining a fund's expected performance grade is the review and adjustment of the grade. The grade can be adjusted based on such qualitative factors as diversification of a fund's portfolio or its operational status grade (O-grade). While these are all valid reasons, there is room for bias and, to some degree, abuse, since this adjustment can significantly change the projected performance of a fund. Introducing quality controls into this process would allow it to become less subjective and more consistent. Such quality controls could take a number of "red-flag" criteria into consideration. For example, is the fund's portfolio

[2] Admittedly, it is difficult to perform consistent benchmarking focusing on particular industries and/or regions. In some market segments, relatively few funds are raised, and the sample in publicly available databases is likely to be even smaller as typically not all funds raised are actually captured. Thus, LPs may be confronted with a trade-off between using a larger sample with fewer similarities and employing a sample that shows a high degree of similar characteristics, which, however, includes only few funds.

overdiversified or is too much exposure taken. Is the fund's remaining liquidity insufficient to support its investment strategy? And to what extent are there questions about the quality of portfolio companies?

If the sum of these "red flags" reaches a predefined threshold, the fund should be downgraded. For this purpose, a grading review policy should be put in place. It should, for example, incorporate the operational status grades or insights gained from the cross-checking of portfolio company valuations between various funds. Such a system of checks, not dissimilar to the qualitative scoring method, would remove some of the potential bias and ensure the integrity of the grading system.

Generally, it is important to note that the scoring should not be considered as an assessment of the various pieces of a puzzle. More often than not, the assessment of the various dimensions will not be clear-cut and therefore requires taking a look at the investment proposal's "big picture". The overall fit of all these components is essential, notably the fit between the team and the fund strategy, but also the relation between the fund structure and the fund strategy. Finally, if too many dimensions cannot be assessed or too little evidence is found in the course of due diligence, this lack of completeness can set limits on the overall qualitative score assigned.

14.2 LINKING GRADES WITH QUANTIFICATIONS

After the fund's grade is determined, we would like to know the range of its projected TVPI. One approach lies in the collection of historical statistical data for funds according to their grades. This approach makes sense in situations where there is a sufficient amount of historical data, the environment is relatively stable and where categories do not change significantly. It is, however, problematic for alternative investments where historical data are rare and the investment environment is subject to material changes. Alternatively, classifications can be used to look for comparables with similar characteristics – either from the not too distant past or from the actual peer group – and take their observable quantitative characteristics as a reference.

14.2.1 Estimate likely TVPIs

We estimate a fund's likely TVPI by taking into account the fund's current grade and its internal age, and use a Monte Carlo simulation to select a scenario from historical TVPIs. For the simulation, historical TVPI figures are drawn out of the basket according to a schedule that reflects the grade of the fund and its internal age.[3]

Existing public databases on fund returns do not allow *ex-ante* conditions to be linked to outcomes. Additional risks, such as leverage or foreign exchange exposure, do not necessarily require specific modelling as the historical return statistics relate to funds that were leveraged and/or had foreign exchange exposure within the fund. However, details about the intended future strategy are generally not captured at inception, and there may be style drifts as a fund needs to adapt to a changing environment. Therefore, assumptions must be made regarding the relationship between the risks and rewards *ex ante*. Such assumptions should be sufficiently conservative in the sense that investors should be assumed not to be able to consistently

[3] Alternative schedules may be considered. However, in simulations we have found that the results are fairly insensitive to the schedule chosen.

Table 14.2 Weight of quartile basket for risk budgeting

$M_{i;j}$ (0)	Standard (P-A)	Mainstream (P-B)	Niche (P-C)	Experiment (P-D)
Weight of first-quartile basket	1/4	1/6	1/12	0
Weight of second-quartile basket	1/4	1/6	1/12	0
Weight of third-quartile basket	1/4	1/6	1/12	0
Weight of fourth-quartile basket	1/4	1/2	3/4	1

pick above-average funds or avoid underperforming partnerships. In fact, it is important to be cautious about what is described as a "random pick" when selecting the portfolio of funds. The samples are drawn out of *ex-post* statistics for funds, i.e. funds that LPs invested in because they believed they would get "outperforming returns" thanks to rigorous due diligence.

Box 14.1 Potential inconsistency between interim and final TVPI

There can be situations where a fund has already realized a higher interim TVPI than the projected multiple drawn from the statistics. In fact, the following relationship has to hold:

$$\frac{\text{Distributed capital}}{\text{Total amount committed}} \leq \text{Final multiple}$$

If this condition does not hold in the top-down model, the NAV would need to be negative, which obviously cannot be the case.[4] In fact, what we would need to know is the conditional projected multiple. Given a realized interim multiple, what would be the multiple at the end of the fund's lifetime? As such statistics are not available, two strategies are possible.

One is to draw another sample from the statistics in cases where the projected TVPI is smaller than the already realized multiple. This strategy leads to an overoptimistic bias towards higher projected multiples, particularly where larger multiples were realized early in the portfolio of funds' lifetime. Alternatively, one may discard the sample without replacing it if the projected multiple is smaller than the already realized multiple. This strategy leads to a pessimistic bias in case the portfolio is doing better than the market and is the recommended approach.

Table 14.2 shows the weights of the baskets at a fund's internal age of 0 for all grades.[5]

Essentially, it is assumed that without superior selection skills, selecting a "standard" fund will result in average returns. "Experiment" funds, i.e. partnerships managed by emerging managers in new markets, should not be invested in unless financial resources are sufficient to absorb the poor returns or losses associated with a fourth-quartile performance.

[4] The same problem can apply to bottom-up models. Also, here it can happen that one "case" has already been realized and it is no longer possible to employ the model with a scenario parameter for a different case.

[5] For the rationale underlying these weights, see Meyer and Mathonet (2005).

Table 14.3 Weight of quartile basket for risk/reward relationship

$M_{i;j}$ (0)	Standard (P-A)	Mainstream (P-B)	Niche (P-C)	Experiment (P-D)
Weight of first-quartile basket	0.2	0.25	0.3	0.5
Weight of second-quartile basket	0.3	0.25	0.2	0
Weight of third-quartile basket	0.3	0.25	0.2	0
Weight of fourth-quartile basket	0.2	0.25	0.3	0.5

However, this quantification is not taking the potential upside into consideration: conceptually, this is in line with a risk-budgeting approach. Alternatively, we could be neutral and assume that there are rewards commensurate with the amount of risk that is being taken. This could, for instance, be modelled with a matrix as shown in Table 14.3.

Calibrating the matrix as depicted in Table 14.3 assumes that for a commitment in a "standard fund" one could expect returns close to the average with a lower probability of extreme performance than a "mainstream" fund. For an "experiment" fund the expected outcome would be either extremely good or poor. Rather than predicting the portfolio's performance, such a calibration would be in line with an investment strategy that aims to give more weight to contrarian investing and searching for unexplored areas of the alternative asset market. In fact, it might be argued that portfolio management in the alternative investment arena should aim at maximizing the allocation to "experiments" and "niches" within the set limits that are based on this risk budget. In this sense, the assumed risk-taking behaviour is consistent with exploring new areas in the alternative asset space.

For any internal age $0 < t < 1$, the weights given to the baskets are determined by the following matrix:

$$M_{i;j}(t) = (1-t)^* M_{i;j}(0) + t^* M_{i;j}(1)$$

At the end of a fund's lifetime (with an internal age of 1), its grade is equivalent to its performance quartile within the benchmark (Table 14.4). Let $s_{i;j}(t)$ be the fund's final TVPI (i.e., the multiple achieved at the end of the fund's lifetime) under a scenario i for a fund graded j at internal age t.

To deal with the issue of the J-curve, we base our projections during the initial years of a fund on the TVPI statistics for realized historical funds only, rather than on the fund's interim multiples. Burgel (2000) reports that after 7 to 8 years, large changes in performance become unlikely and interim IRRs and final IRRs converge. After a few years, IIRRs can already provide a good approximation to the fund's overall return. To capture this behaviour, we foresee a trigger point, T, from which time onwards the interim multiple receives an

Table 14.4 Weight of quartile basket at end of fund's lifetime

$M_{i;j}$ (1)	P-A	P-B	P-C	P-D
Weight of first-quartile basket	1	0	0	0
Weight of second-quartile basket	0	1	0	0
Weight of third-quartile basket	0	0	1	0
Weight of fourth-quartile basket	0	0	0	1

increasing weight in the projections. As long as the fund's internal age is lower than a given T, the interim multiple is ignored entirely. If the internal age $t \leq T$, the projected final TVPI for this scenario is

$$\overline{\text{TVPI}}_{i;j} = s_{i;j}(t)$$

Only after the fund has reached an internal age higher than a set trigger do we start to take the interim TVPI into consideration. If $t > T$:

$$\overline{\text{TVPI}}_{i;j} = s_{i;j}(t)^{*}(1-t) + \text{ITVPI}_{i}(t)$$

Thus, we now have a method that helps us determine the range of the final TVPIs and the range of the final life (discussed previously), which converge towards a fund's true final TVPI and its true lifetime.

14.2.2 Practical considerations

Qualitative scoring is not a substitute for due diligence, but instead is based on its results. The aim is to categorize and compare investment proposals. While there is a sort of "market view" of what represents an "ideal fund" in terms of structure, industry and geographical focus, team, etc., in this unregulated and opaque asset class there is ongoing innovation. Therefore, the definition of what constitutes "standard" is continuously evolving.

It is important to avoid a conservative bias in assigning grades. While such a bias would be an understandable reaction in an environment of high uncertainty, to be able to identify risks at the portfolio level, assessments need to be as unbiased as possible. It is certainly good investment management to be conservative in decision-making, but assessments have to be as free from biases as possible to allow the decision-maker to form an opinion.

Finally, the grade should not be confused with pricing. Even if a fund has a low grade, the price on the secondary market can be highly attractive. This is comparable to a bond rating, where the premium required by investors is not reflected in the rating. The two questions "what is the quality?" and "how much should we pay for?" are conceptually different.

14.3 OPERATIONAL STATUS GRADES

The expected performance grades are complemented by the operational status grades gained during the course of monitoring (Figure 14.2). The operational status grades capture information that is conceptually close to event risk. These events – unless a mitigating action follows within the short to medium timeframe – are expected to have a negative impact on a fund's performance.

We also suggest four grading classes for the operational status grade depending on the severity of the operational issue (Table 14.5).

The operational status grade aims to identify these events and to form a judgment on its severity. In essence, the grades have two functions. One function is to alert the investor in cases where "red-flag" events could have such an adverse impact that they need to be addressed without delay. The second function concerns diagnosis, i.e. forming a judgment on the degree of potential impact resulting in a priority setting for monitoring corrective actions.

Assessing the severity of the event's impact is typically highly subjective. As there are all kinds of events possible depending on the investment area, no exhaustive list can be given.

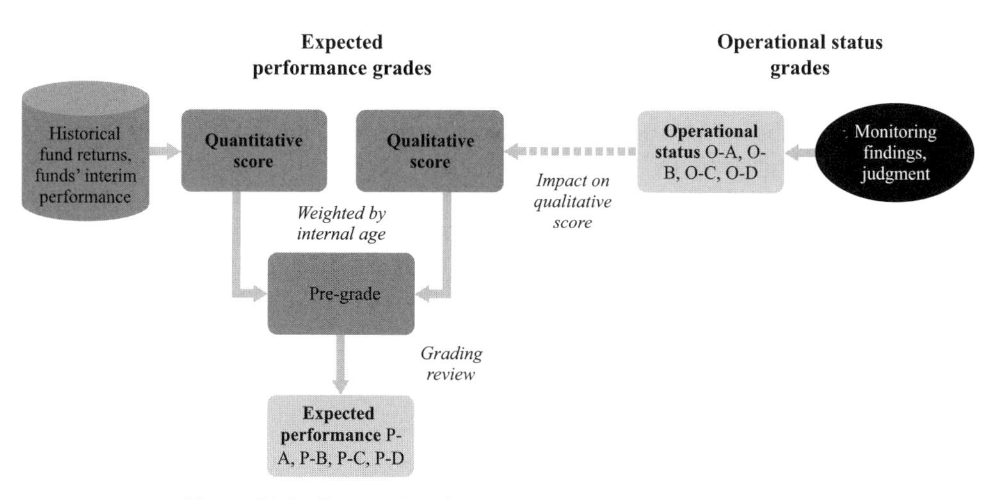

Figure 14.2 Expected performance and operational status grades.

Accumulation of such events may be taken as a sign that a fund is veering off track and may show substandard performance. As these operational status grades can be indicative of a possible impairment, they should always be reflected in an updated expected performance grade and, therefore, tied into the fund's valuation.

14.4 CONCLUSIONS

As we discussed in Chapter 7, "objective" risk in illiquid asset classes is extremely difficult, if not impossible, to determine in the absence of observable market prices. Investment professionals therefore need to use subjective probabilities to operationally define perceived uncertainty. Under these circumstances, a more practical question is whether a risk metric is "useful", in the sense that it promotes behaviour that is desirable in a given application. The

Table 14.5 Operational status grades

Grade	Description
Neutral	No adverse signals or information so far.
Problems	Presence of signals or information that – if no appropriate measures are quickly put in place – would be atypical for a first-quartile fund. Absence of signals or information that would be inconsistent with an expected second-quartile performance.
Failure likely	Presence of signals or information that – if no appropriate measures are quickly put in place – would be atypical for an above-average fund. Absence of signals or information that would be inconsistent with an expected third-quartile performance.
Failure happened	Events that – if no appropriate measures are quickly put in place – will result in a substandard performance or even a failure or collapse of the fund.

purpose of the techniques presented in this chapter is mainly to encourage disciplined, meaningful investment behaviour and the efficient incorporation of relevant up-to-date information in the investment process.

The definition of the expected performance grades ensures that projections converge towards the fund's final lifetime and TVPI, and that the grades converge to the fund's final quartile within its benchmark population. The degree of the projections' precision depends on how far a fund is advanced in its lifecycle.

Part III

Risk Management and Its Governance

15
Securitization

Securitizations of portfolios of illiquid assets make use of the general techniques widely known in the context of collateralized debt obligations (CDOs) or collateralized fund obligations (CFOs) (Fabozzi and Kothari, 2008). As discussed in previous chapters of this book, risk management for illiquid asset classes has to address the non-tradability and lack of a continuous price discovery. One of the main ideas of securitization is the transformation of a pool of illiquid assets into various tranches for tradable notes with different risk and return characteristics. These notes can be quoted on exchanges and, hence, traded. Through "layering" the pool of assets into tranches, the risk is also transferred into different notes. Each different note has more standardized risk characteristics, thus investors feel more comfortable valuing it and trading such notes.

Securitizations of portfolios of limited partnership funds establish a link between the default risk element (similar to a bond) and market risk (similar to equity). In this chapter, we demonstrate how, even for such illiquid assets, one risk dimension can be transformed into another and trade-offs between risk dimensions can be managed: e.g., equity into debt, market into credit risk, illiquidity into liquidity, liquidity risk into capital risk. While the structural elements of the transactions are very similar, the modelling and understanding of the different illiquid asset classes are different, creating specific challenges. Therefore, it is very important to understand cash flow projections in general as described in Chapter 11 to be able to model CFOs.

15.1 DEFINITION OF SECURITIZATION

In general, securitization is a financial technology where assets are pooled and sold to a special purpose vehicle (SPV). The SPV refinances itself by issuing debt instruments and equity tranches. Therefore, transactions backed by illiquid asset classes represent only an adaption of traditional methodologies (used, for instance, to securitize mortgages) to portfolios of illiquid funds.

Figure 15.1 shows an outline of a securitization in which a portfolio of private equity funds is moved to a SPV and refinanced through the issuance of various classes of notes. The underlying portfolio usually consists of limited partnership funds that contain investments in companies (i.e., private equity), projects (like infrastructure or real estate) or financial instruments (like hedge funds). On the other hand, the financial structure typically consists of an equity tranche, a mezzanine tranche and one or more debt tranches, which can be rated by the rating agencies (Henzler, 2008).

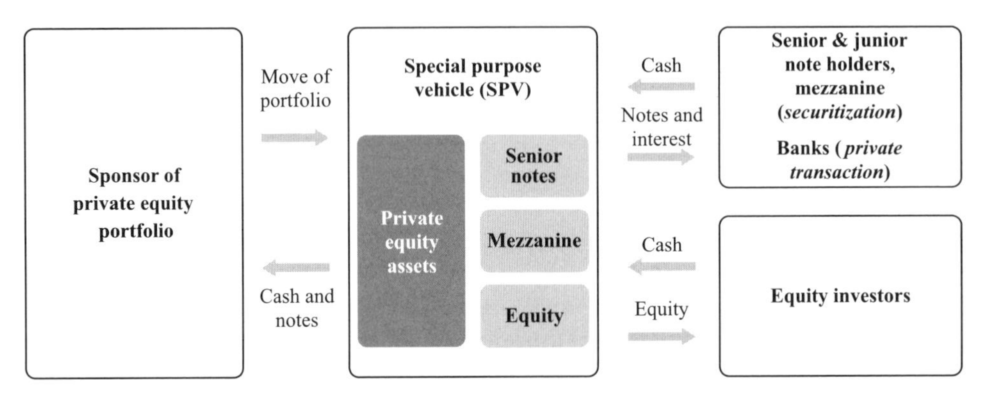

Figure 15.1 Overview of main players and key characteristics of securitization.

Box 15.1 The history and state of the securitization market for illiquid assets

Princess was one of the first transactions using structural elements of securitizations. However, it cannot be considered a "true" securitization but rather a publicly listed vehicle with a convertible note. Princess had private equity funds as assets which were financed with a listed convertible bond that paid interest. Although if it was not a pure securitization, it already displayed some of a CFO's characteristics. A vehicle called Pearl had a similar structure and a size of EUR 550 million, a volume that is EUR 150 million higher compared with the volume at the closing of the transaction.[1]

One of the first CFOs that can actually be considered a true securitization, comprising different senior notes and ratings on the notes, was Prime Edge in 2001 (*The Economist*, 2001). This product was a leveraged fund-of-funds which was financed with two senior notes with AA ratings. In addition to the normal coverage of the risk of these notes, an insurance company insured the payback of the senior notes at maturity.

This transaction was followed by Pine Street, which is a structure in which AIG sold parts of their portfolio with the objective of seeking regulatory capital relief, to free up cash for new investment opportunities and to reduce the cost of financing.[2] Pine Street was closed in 2002 with a diversified portfolio of interests in 64 different private equity funds with a total exposure of USD 1 billion. This portfolio was backed by six classes of notes, with various levels of seniority issued. The most senior class A notes had a principal amount of USD 250 million and received an AAA rating from rating agencies (Standard & Poor's, 2010).

These early structures were put together by large asset managers and small specialist investment boutiques. Given the success of such transactions, investment banks subsequently tried to enter the market: Deutsche Bank with Silver Leaf in 2003 and BNP with Tenzing in 2004. Silver Leaf was a USD 480 million structure with dual currency notes in EUR and USD matching roughly the structure of the underlying assets. Around 25% of the assets were covered by senior notes rated AAA with a maturity in 2013 and another 17%

[1] See published annual reports of Princess and Pearl on their respective webpages and in *The Economist* (2001).
[2] For information regarding Pine Street, see Henzler (2004).

by class-B notes. The single A-rated class-C notes accounted for another 9%, while mezzanine and equity holders held around 49% of the structure.[3]

At the same time, a programme to kick off the Greek VC market, called Taneo (the New Economy Development Fund), was arranged by Deutsche Bank, EFG Telesis Finance and NBG International in 2003.[4] Taneo securitized a fund-of-funds with senior notes of EUR 105 million raised from third-party investors and a EUR 45 million equity tranche that was fully held by the Greek government. The debt notes are listed on the Irish stock exchange and mature in 2013. Standard & Poor's and Fitch at that time rated these notes A, as they were also guaranteed by the Greek Treasury. The objective was to invest the capital in 10 to 12 VC funds focusing on Greece. However, this target allocation was not reached by the end of 2005 and thus the investment period was extended to 2008.

In addition, between 2004 and 2007 SVG created structures like Diamond I, II and III with sizes between EUR 400 million and 600 million NAV. While Diamond I and II were public transactions with listed senior notes and equity tranches, the debt tranches of Diamond III were financed through a private placement. All Diamond transactions have been based on the concept of a leveraged fund-of-funds.

Diamond I's senior notes were issued partially in EUR and USD according to the expected split of the underlying assets. This approach achieves a natural hedge between the asset and liability side. SVG issued AAA-rated bonds of EUR 40 million and USD 55 million at closing. Diamond II had a total amount of EUR 500 million with senior A notes (AAA-rated at closing; downgraded in the financial crisis to AA) of EUR 55 million and USD 72 million. The EUR tranche of class-B notes accounted for EUR 76 million and the USD part for USD 40 million; both with an AA rating at closing. In Diamond III, the debt was provided by a bank and hence no public information is available.

One of the last transactions closed before the financial crisis was Astrea, a structure backed by a large portfolio of private equity funds from Temasek Holding in Singapore (Henzler and Etter, 2008). Astrea is a securitization of a diversified portfolio of limited partnership interests in 46 different private equity funds with a total exposure of USD 810 million. The owner of the portfolio received cash on a non-recourse basis equalling approximately the portfolio's reported value and parts of the junior securities issued. The senior debt was structured into two classes of notes that were rated AAA and AA, respectively and sold to capital market investors. In the meantime, all debt has been paid back (see Standard & Poor's Rating Reports 2012).

All these structures weathered the turmoil of the Great Recession and none of them faltered. Like all CFOs, these private equity structures also appeared on the watch list of rating agencies in 2009. Some structures were downgraded from AAA to AA, while other structures were able to retain the highest rating. Some of them have already successfully paid down their debt tranches without defaulting on interest rate payments or amortization, as indicated by rating agency reports of the years 2010 to 2012. Figure 15.2 summarizes the evolution of securitization of illiquid assets.

[3] See Amblard (2007) and Standard & Poor's different announcements on ratings of private equity CFOs; published on their webpage at www.sandp.com.

[4] For more information and a detailed description, see Amblard in Mathonet and Meyer (2007).

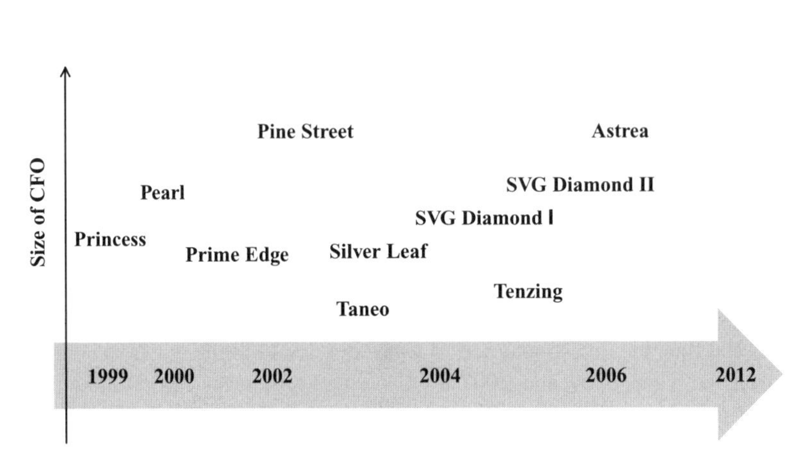

Figure 15.2 Overview of different CFOs.

During the Great Recession no new CFO was issued as these structures came under public scrutiny and debt markets dried up. Nevertheless, since 2010 there have been some green shoots and together with the recovery of the debt markets and the significantly increased secondary market, securitizations might experience a revival.

Typically, the senior notes and equity tranches of securitizations have been listed on stock exchanges in Luxemburg, Ireland or other market places. Therefore, investors are able to sell their bonds, mezzanine and equity participation in public markets. Even if the trading volume of these notes has been rather small, for investors there is the possibility of trading the bonds and other notes in a transparent and standardized way, offering a method to assess the risk of the different financial instruments employed.

15.1.1 Size, quality and maturity

The size of the portfolio is critical for rated transactions. To achieve a sufficient degree of diversification, typically more than 25 funds with hundreds of portfolio companies are required. Not only the diversification is an issue, but also the costs for placing the senior and junior notes and for the rating requires a minimum portfolio size. For a securitization of private equity funds and the listing of its notes to be economically viable, the minimum portfolio size would be above a NAV of EUR 300 million. With such a portfolio size, the costs as well as the diversification parameters start to become acceptable.

Furthermore, the quality of the assets that are to be securitized is key. In such a process, common criteria for fund manager quality will also be assessed. The historical track record of the fund manager, team stability and the behaviour of the manager with investment in the crisis play important roles. In today's market, a key issue is also the probability of the manager successfully raising a follow-on fund, as this might have an important influence on the exit behaviour.

If the transaction is to be built on an existing portfolio – similar to a secondary transaction – then an analysis of the underlying companies will be performed as well. The techniques used for a typical bottom-up analysis come into play, and the underlying investments will be valued and their return drivers and possible exit timing assessed. Companies with stable financials are preferred as well as funds with long-standing experience and where recession-proven strategies can provide some degree of downside protection.

Furthermore, the maturity of the assets also affects the characteristics of senior and junior notes. The ratio between open commitments and existing assets plays a role as it determines the net cash requirement for the future portfolio. The more mature the portfolio is, the shorter the expected remaining lifetime of the senior notes. If the average age of the portfolio is already advanced, the net funding requirement of the portfolio is lower and exits can be expected relatively earlier. Earlier exits and cash flows also mean earlier repayment of the notes and hence the maturity of the assets also influences total interest rate costs.

15.1.2 Treatment of other types of assets

Another question that arises in this context is whether adding co-investments has a positive influence on the structure. The short answer is: it depends. To begin with, co-investments as well as minority investments in other companies generally increase the diversification of the underlying asset pool, which is a plus. However, if co-investments result in a more concentrated portfolio, this would have a negative effect as it increases the probability that notes default. At the same time, however, co-investments influence the ratio between funded and unfunded commitments positively, as co-investments usually have no or less open commitments (at least not as a contractual obligation) and thus mitigate risks associated with leverage – i.e., that the structure becomes a defaulting LP. Therefore, the maturity of the portfolio as well as its asset coverage can be improved through co-investments.

To sum up, the degree of diversification combined with the size of the portfolio has the same degree of importance as the quality of the assets and its maturity. Also, adding other types of assets and strategies for diversification purposes can have a positive effect.

15.2 FINANCIAL STRUCTURE

The financial structure of the portfolio is typically very simple with four different tranches: two senior notes, a mezzanine tranche and equity.

15.2.1 Senior notes of a securitization

The senior notes in a securitization backed by illiquid assets are usually structured as a typical coupon-based bond with quarterly interest rate payments. Although the underlying assets are illiquid, there is some degree of liquidity generated by the assets that supports the regular interest rate payment. As this liquidity is subject to random swings, an additional safety mechanism is usually put in place. Other characteristics of the senior notes are as follows.

- **Interest rate type.** Senior notes are either structured as a floating rate note (FRN) or as a fixed interest rate (FRI). The majority of transactions in the past in private equity have been structured as FRNs. The FRNs are based on a reference interest rate, like LIBOR or EURIBOR, depending on the currency plus a spread for the additional risk of the illiquid asset class.
- **Repayment schedule.** The repayment of the notes is typically structured in a flexible way, i.e. whenever the portfolio produces excess cash flows, the most senior notes can be paid down according to a "payment waterfall" that determines the priority of payments and is at the heart of a securitization.

- **Security.** Bonds or senior notes of such a transaction have the highest priority in the payment waterfall. These bonds typically have the first right on all cash flows out of the asset portfolio. In case of default, the holders of these notes also have the first right on the remaining value.
- **Rating.** Since the loan-to-value ratio of the senior notes is usually moderate, the probability of loss is relatively low, which is also reflected in the rating by the rating agencies. Hence, it is possible to receive ratings in the AAA/AA area on the most senior tranches and investment grade ratings on most of the senior notes. Given the diversification of the portfolio, the risk profile of the senior notes is accordingly low.

For further calculations, let us define the interest rate of class-A notes (most senior tranche) as r_A and the outstanding amount A of these notes. At the close of the transaction, the notional amount of the notes equals the outstanding amount. This amount will be paid down over time through distributions. The second highest tranche (class-B notes) shall have an interest rate of r_B and an outstanding amount B.

Assuming that the senior notes are issued as FRNs, the interest rates r_A and r_B depend on the development of LIBOR plus a spread which reflects the risk of the underlying asset class as well as the market conditions at the close of the transaction:

$$r_A = \text{LIBOR} + s_A$$

$$r_B = \text{LIBOR} + s_B$$

The additional spreads s_A on the class-A notes have ranged from 40 bps in the case of the Astrea transaction to around 125 bps in the case of Silver Leaf, but certainly depend on the actual level of the credit markets. The spread s_B of class-B notes ranges in the area of 55 bps to 200 bps and can be even higher depending on the loan-to-value ratio.[5]

15.2.2 Junior notes/mezzanine tranche of a securitization

Investors in junior notes can expect a higher interest rate than for senior notes. The notes can have a regular interest rate payment which can be deferred if necessary or is already paid in kind up-front. The interest rate might also be fixed and structured as a FRN. However, in most historical transactions, the interest rate has been fixed without any floating element. As the cumulative loan-to-value ratio is higher, investors in these notes face higher risk for which they want to be compensated. Therefore, there are also warrants attached to some senior notes which can be converted into equity. We define the return for junior notes as the interest rate r_C and the outstanding amount as C.

15.2.3 Equity of a securitization

Investors in the equity tranche of such a product look for enhanced returns r_D as they invest in a levered pool of limited partnership interests. The experience and results of simulations show that equity investors have the potential to receive extraordinary returns when the portfolio returns are good, but also hold the first-loss stake if the portfolio loses value. Later in this chapter we discuss the leverage effect and how it influences the risk in more detail.

[5] See Standard & Poor's different announcements on ratings of private equity CFOs, published on their webpage at www.sandp.com and Henzler and Etter (2008) on the Astrea transaction.

15.3 RISK MODELLING AND RATING OF SENIOR NOTES

As described, one driving factor of a securitization is the diversification and quality of the portfolio, which results in the risk and, connected with it, the rating of the senior notes. Typically, capital market securitizations received a rating from leading rating agencies at the close of the transaction and most of them went through a re-rating process in the wake of the financial crisis in 2009. The models applied by the rating agencies to derive the ratings are published in various articles.[6] The methodology of these approaches is based on cash flow simulations as described in Chapter 11. In order to access the risk of such transactions, two main questions arise for the note holders and rating agencies:

1. Is the underlying asset of the SPV able to pay the regular interest rate payments?
2. What is the probability of default on the principal of the notes?

In many default situations it is still possible to "cure" these events over a relatively short time period. However, as fallback it is always better to have standby financing in place before such an event happens.

15.3.1 Payment waterfall

The risk/return characteristics of the notes help structure the priority of payments (i.e., the payment waterfall) and, vice versa, the priority of payments determines the risk-return profile of the different tranches. Depending on each individual structure, the market environment for debt and equity and the negotiations between the various parties involved in structuring the transaction and placing the notes, the payment waterfall of each transaction is different. Sometimes exceptions are possible for a defined time period or until different milestones are reached. It is difficult to generalize a payment waterfall and we can give here only a broad sketch of possible arrangements. Typically, payment days are defined in a regular time period, for example quarters. On each payment day, distributions generated by the portfolio are split according to the payment waterfall.

Box 15.2 Overview of a general payment waterfall – priorities of payment

(0) Funding source: Distributions of underlying assets DI_t
(1) Capital calls of underlying assets C_t
(2) Interest rate payment of class-A notes (based on outstanding amount): $r_A^* A_{t-1}$
(3) Interest rate payment of class-B notes (based on outstanding amount): $r_B^* B_{t-1}$
(4) Interest rate payment of class-C notes if not deferred (based on outstanding amount): $r_C^* C_{t-1}$
(5) If remaining excess cash flow available, repayment and amortization of class-A notes:

$$\text{IF } \mathrm{DI}_t - C_t - r_A^* A_{t-1} - r_B^* B_{t-1} > 0$$

$$\text{THEN } A_t = A_{t-1} - \mathrm{DI}_t - C_t - r_A^* A_{t-1} - r_B^* B_{t-1}$$

[6] See Standard & Poor's (2006, 2008) as well as Diller and Kaserer (2009), Diller and Herger (2008), Meyer and Mathonet (2005) and de Malherbe (2003).

(6) If remaining excess cash flow is available, the repayment and amortization of class B notes are determined as follows:

$$\text{IF DI}_t - C_t - r_A^* A_{t-1} - r_B^* B_{t-1} > 0 \text{ AND } A_t = 0$$

$$\text{THEN } B_t = B_{t-1} - \text{DI}_t - C_t - r_A^* A_{t-1} - r_B^* B_{t-1}$$

(7) If interest payments of class-C notes have been deferred, then the payment of class-C note interest, including all compounded interest rate payments, is determined as follows:

$$\text{IF } A_t = 0 \text{ AND } B_t = 0$$

$$\text{THEN } C_t = \sum_{i=1}^{t} r_C^* C_{t-1}^* (1 + r_C)$$

(8) If remaining excess cash flow is available, repayment and amortization of class-C notes is determined as follows:

$$\text{IF DI}_t - C_t - r_A^* A_{t-1} - r_B^* B_{t-1} - r_C^* C_{t-1} > 0 \text{ AND } A_t = 0 \text{ AND } B_t = 0$$

$$\text{THEN } C_t = C_{t-1} - \text{DI}_t - C_t - r_A^* A_{t-1} - r_B^* B_{t-1} - r_C^* C_{t-1}$$

(9) All remaining cash flows go to equity (class D notes):

$$\text{IF } A_t = 0 \text{ AND } B_t = 0 \text{ AND } C_t = 0$$

$$\text{THEN } D_t = \text{DI}_t - C_t$$

In general, the first priority is the payment of the interest rates of the senior notes, the fees and the junior notes' interest rates, which are in most cases also deferrable. After paying off all these quarterly expenses, any additional excess net cash flow will be used to pay down the principal of the notes. The repayment starts with the most senior class-A notes. After all these notes are paid back, the holders of the class-B notes start receiving their capital and so on. At the end – after paying down all other notes – equity investors will typically receive the remaining cash flows.

In addition to the cash flows for the note holders, fees for third-party service providers have to be paid on a regular basis (i.e., administrator, legal advisor, rating agencies, etc.). These payments will be put into the payment waterfall typically after position (3) as they have to be paid on a regular basis. Figure 15.3 shows a possible structure and repayment of the notes. After repaying the class-A, class-B and class-C notes will be paid back.

15.3.2 Modelling of default risk and rating on notes

In order to receive a rating for the senior notes, it is necessary to model the characteristics of the underlying limited partnership funds and the proposed structure.

- The main model is the one that reflects the priority of payment schedule for the newly created structure – see below.
- A quantitative model projects the various cash flow scenarios of the underlying assets (see Chapter 11).
- In addition, a sub-model derives the different risk ratings of the fund and transforms the qualitative input into a quantitative model (see Chapter 14).

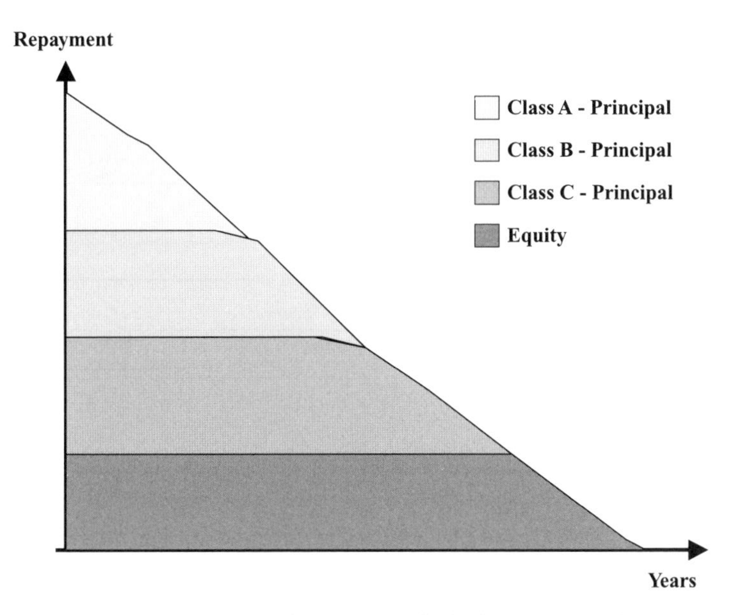

Figure 15.3 Payment schedule of repayment of principal amounts of various notes.

- Another sub-model reflects the foreign exchange rate movements.
- A sub-model for the waterfall simulation reflects the changes in the LIBOR rates in case the senior notes are FRNs.

Figure 15.4 gives an overview of the various models and an outline for the rating process.

Historical cash flows can be used to assess the risk under normal market conditions. Standard & Poor's (2006) explain how they analyze historical cash flow patterns to assess the J-curve's impact. Here, they focus on four main criteria: money multiple, IRR, speed of drawdowns and depth of curve. In their standard case the J-curve reaches its deepest point after 4 years at 60%

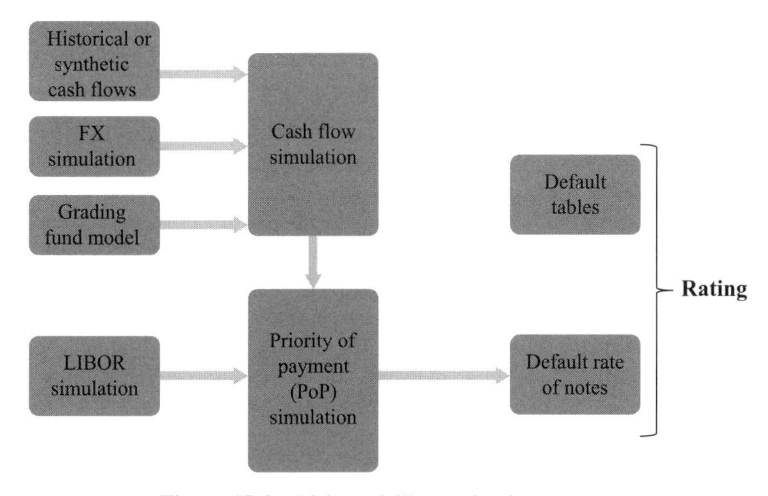

Figure 15.4 Risk modelling and rating process.

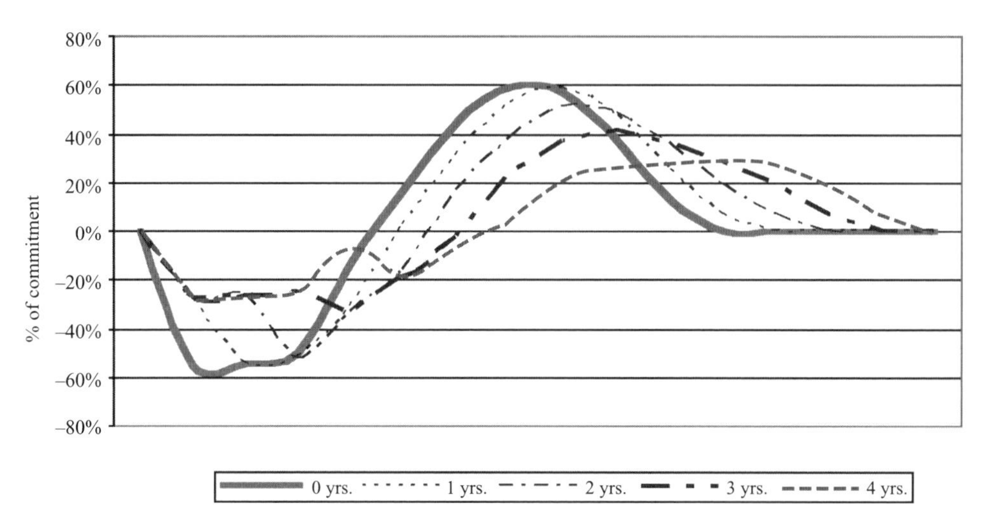

Figure 15.5 Impact of vintage year diversification on J-curve (two-fund example) See also Standard & Poor's (2006).

of the committed capital. In addition, Standard & Poor's highlights the fact that vintage year diversification mitigates the J-curve, as illustrated in Figure 15.5.

In addition, analyses of more extreme cases (stress scenarios) have to be performed to examine how the structure would behave in situations with very limited net distributions or even contributions. These stress scenarios can either be derived by focusing on extreme cases in the past like the 5th or 1st percentile of dispersions of cash flows within a CFaR framework, or looking at more hypothetical situations which can be also derived from simple models assuming some obvious stress scenarios.

Standard & Poor's (2006) points out that considering stress scenarios for cash flows is extremely important. Therefore, they propose to create synthetic cash flows through linking the funds' cash flows to a simulated stochastic path of a public market index. Standard & Poor's also describes the principles of such a simulation algorithm.[7]

An important lesson of the Great Recession was that the exit markets were closed in 2008 and 2009, which resulted in longer holding periods, delayed distributions or no distributions at all. Standard & Poor's models always incorporated such stress factors, but they now receive an even higher recognition and relevance. Therefore, new approaches combine historical behaviour with a range of different stress scenarios. Based on the experience gained during the financial crisis in 2009, stress tests of rating agencies include situations in which exit markets are closed and, hence, holding periods of companies are prolonged and default rates are higher. Therefore, new stress scenarios include a combination of a stressed dispersion of returns with a stressed dispersion of holding periods – i.e., accelerated drawdowns and prolonged distributions – techniques we discussed in Chapter 11. Scenarios are modelled totally independently from the development of the public market component, which is one of the main differences from the models that have been used before. In addition, the weight of the bottom-up analyses in the top-down cash flow simulation increases. This methodology represents the current state-of-the-art and is essentially a two-step approach.

[7] See Standard & Poor's (2006, 2008) as well as Diller and Kaserer (2009), Diller and Herger (2008), Meyer and Mathonet (2005) and de Malherbe (2003).

As described in Chapter 11, the idea is to use a historical cash flow library H of m liquidated funds. For each fund, the commitment CC, capital calls $C_1, \ldots, C_n$ and distributions $D_1, \ldots, D_n$ are saved as well as fund characteristics like geography G, currency FX, vintage year VY, fund type FT and fund grading RA. Hence, each fund h_i is characterized through the following vector:

$$h_i = \{\text{G}, \text{FX}, \text{FT}, \text{VY}, \text{RA}, \text{CC}, C_1, \ldots, C_n, D_1, \ldots, D_n\}$$

In order to create a cash flow projection, the following steps are performed.

- Randomly select a cash flow series h_i from the library H matching fund characteristics G, FX and FT.
- Randomly pick from the return distribution for TVPIs (or IRRs) for limited partnership funds using dispersions of returns and introduce a stress factor. In addition, the return of a fund h_i can be adjusted to the fund grading RA of the fund.
- Randomly pick from the distribution for the lifetime of funds and add additional stress to these periods and change the time period for distributions accordingly.
- Build synthetic cash flows based on the new stress scenarios.

The advantage of these scenarios is that no information from other asset classes like public markets is needed to derive cash flow information, and stress scenarios reflect extreme cases and can as far as possible reflect a financial crisis.

Another element that should be highlighted is the fact that most of the securitizations are based on mature portfolios acquired on the secondary market. This has an additional implication on the degree of risk of a portfolio, which is lower than the risk of a primary portfolio. As secondary transactions are performed during the lifetime of a fund, the investor has already more information about the underlying investments. Take the example of a single fund interest: while the primary investor commits to a strategy and team without assets, i.e. a "blind pool", the secondary investor who would like to acquire the portfolio after 4 years can already analyse the portfolio companies acquired by that time. The advantage is that the secondary investor has already seen the first write-offs, first exits and changes or adjustments in valuation. For the remaining companies, the acquirer can already get a good picture of whether the underlying investments are in line with their business plans, above or below. Moreover, a portfolio of secondary positions is more advanced in its lifecycle and the outcome volatility of the investment is lower compared with a portfolio of primary fund positions.

Hence, the difference between a primary and a secondary transaction is that the investor acquires a future cash flow stream (i.e., dividends and exits of the underlying investments) at a later stage and at a different price than the primary investor. While the price for the primary investor is the commitment which results in capital being called by the fund managers, the secondary buyer usually acquires (more or less) tangible assets at a discount (or premium) relative to the last valuation (see discussion on pricing secondary transactions in Chapter 6). Note that in both cases the simulation methodology is the same cash flow simulation. Figure 15.6 illustrates this in more detail.

After deriving many – stressed and normal – cases for the development of the underlying assets, the proposed CFO's "payment waterfall" and its priorities are modelled. In such a model the objective is to reflect the structure of the CFO as realistically as possible.

Based on the results of the cash flow simulation and the payment waterfall, the default rate for the different notes can be assessed. This default rate can be compared with tables of rating agencies, which derives the rating of a note from its expected default rate and expected

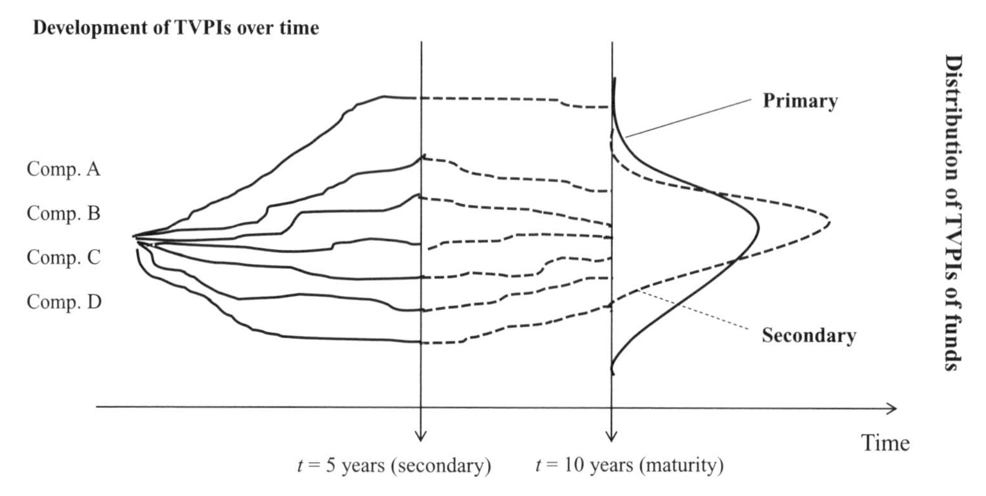

Figure 15.6 Outcome volatility of primary and secondary transactions.

lifetime. Depending on the results of the simulations for the CFO, the rating for the different tranches can be determined.

15.4 TRANSFORMATION OF NON-TRADABLE RISK FACTORS INTO TRADABLE FINANCIAL SECURITIES

Securitizations are good examples of how financial engineering techniques can be used in order to help evaluate various risks and influence their characteristics. CFOs allow four main transformations, as shown in Figure 15.7.

The first – and one of the main – advantages of securitizations is that they transform the illiquid limited partnership interest of private equity, infrastructure or real-estate funds into various groups of securities – notably bonds, mezzanine and equity – that are listed on an exchange.

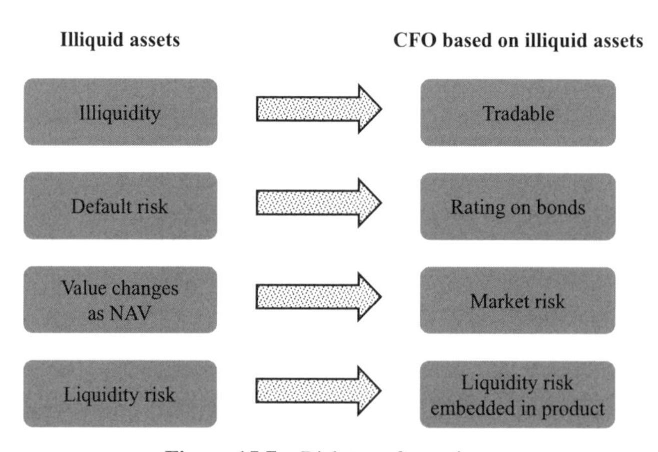

Figure 15.7 Risk transformations.

While CFOs have proved to be an efficient portfolio management tool, they have also opened the illiquid asset classes to a broader investor base as the portfolio is split into fixed-income products and levered-equity portions. This new investor group has access to a new underlying asset type offering low correlation to the other, more traditional asset-backed securities (ABSs), which are typically backed by loans, bonds, credit cards, other receivables, etc. Although in particular subprime-backed loan products ran into trouble and were confronted with negative publicity during the financial crisis, the private equity-backed CFOs managed to weather the storm and therefore provide evidence that these structures are a proven concept for efficient risk management of portfolios of limited partnership funds.

15.4.1 CFOs as good example for risk and liquidity management practices

Why do we see CFOs as a good example for sophisticated risk and liquidity management practices? The answer is simple: because CFOs operate under the strictest rules, constraints and guidelines and they have a clearly identifiable asset and liability side. Senior notes of rated structures are not only monitored by rating agencies but also by market participants. Moreover, they can be seen as an (albeit simple) case of an asset liability management. Therefore, such securitizations are highly instructive for LPs facing comparable issues, e.g. pension plans and insurance companies.

The interest and the notes to be amortized need to be paid by the proceeds of the portfolio of funds. Hence, the objective is that none of the notes run into a default situation when reflows from the funds slow down or temporarily dry up and that there is no breach of the value coverage, usually expressed by the loan-to-value ratio. CFOs prove that risk management systems for LPs most of all have to focus on liquidity management. Looking at rating criteria from rating agencies and drawing upon practical experiences and publications on the rating of such transactions[8] as well as on the experience of managing these structures, it is evident that cash flows and liquidity risk play the most prominent role. Even if the investor does not face liquidity risk or funding risk directly through its own investment, the liquidity management in the structure is the basis for properly controlling a portfolio of private equity funds.

The liquidity requirements of a CFO come from two directions: their assets, mainly comprising the portfolio of funds and the associated undrawn commitments on one side, and their schedule of liabilities on the other.

- The first dimension refers to the funding test in the context of liquidity risk (see Chapter 8). As discussed, it is necessary to monitor the liquidity of the portfolio of funds and that the capital calls of the portfolio can always be funded by any source of capital. The special situation for a CFO is that there is no other source of capital available and no other continuous cash inflow from regular business activities like in insurance companies or pension funds. Therefore, the overcommitment ratios of CFOs tend to be very low.
- The second dimension is that the liability side of the structure needs additional funding for the payment of the interest rates of the senior notes. This additional cash requirement lowers the availability for the payment of capital calls.

Therefore, OCRs for the CFO need to be adjusted in such a way that they also reflect the liability side. In Chapter 8 we defined the OCR as the ratio of "undrawn commitments" to

[8] See Standard & Poor's (2006, 2008).

"resources available for commitments". Resources available in this case is not the cash balance only (in case of OCR 1), but the cash balance at the current time reduced by the interest rate payments of the senior notes for the next payment days. Depending on the security mechanism, this ratio can be applied for various time periods:

$$\text{OCR (CFO)} = \frac{\text{Undrawn commitments}}{\text{Resources available} - \sum_{i=1}^{4} \left(r_A^* A - r_B^* B - r_C^* C \right)}$$

A more sophisticated approach is the use of models for projecting cash flows. Based on the experience and our knowledge gained through the management of these products, we see that these rules and methods are also applicable for typical LPs even if there are no such strict constraints on the liability side.

15.4.2 Risk of coupon bonds as one part of the risk of illiquid asset classes

The rating for the various classes of notes transforms the long-term default risk of interests in limited partnership funds in bonds with a fixed maturity and a default rate that can be assessed and rated like other ABS transactions. The market value of bonds is based mainly on the general interest rate development and the probability of default of the notes as well as the rating. From the perspective of most LPs it is arguably the long-term default risk of investments in private equity and real assets which is of most relevance. While this risk measure is purely focused on cash flows – contributions and distributions – it represents the true risk of the investor of losing capital or not achieving the target return. The CFO creates new tranches which are affected by the long-term default rate over a fixed lifetime. While it is difficult to measure the risk based on a credit risk rating approach only, using the default probability of a bond not achieving its interest rate and amortization is one way of quantifying the actual risk of a portfolio of funds.[9]

Regulation forces investors to look at the long-term as well as the short-term perspective. New regulations like Solvency II and Basel II/III base the risk management approaches on a 1-year time horizon. Even investors with long-term investment duration, like life insurance companies and pension funds, will or might be regulated in such a way. Methodologies along the lines we discuss here exist to bring these two perspectives together.

In order to assess the risk of these bonds, cash flow simulations have to be performed to calculate the probability of default. The tranching of a portfolio of funds into bonds and equity allows the quantification of the senior notes through typical risk models. These models for bonds are usually driven by two main factors: duration and convexity. As a coupon bond makes a series of payments over its life, fixed-income investors need a measure of the average maturity of the bond's promised cash flow to serve as a summary statistic of the effective maturity of the bond. Also needed is a measure that could be used as a guide to the sensitivity of a bond to interest rate changes, since price sensitivity tends to increase with time to maturity. Duration as a measure aids investors in both cases.

[9] An additional risk is the risk of the equity tranche.

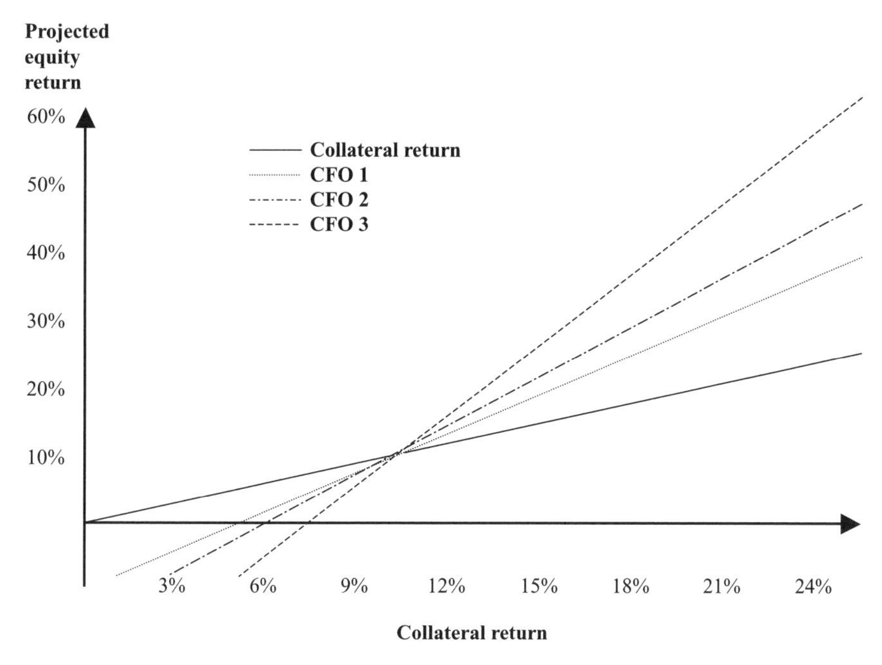

Figure 15.8 Collateral return vs. projected equity return.

15.4.3 Market risk as second part of the risk of illiquid asset classes

While the risk of the bonds can be derived based on the default risk, the bonds do not reflect directly the market risk of the illiquid asset class; i.e., the change in valuation of the underlying illiquid assets. The market risk of private equity and real assets and their valuation changes will be reflected in the CFO's equity portion in the short term. However, in the long term the equity risk will be driven by the long-term characteristics of the underlying illiquid asset class. Depending on the realizations of these investments, equity investors will receive excess returns.

The short-term changes in illiquid asset classes will be reflected fully in the movement of the equity portion of such a securitization. It is important that the absolute change in the underlying assets is reflected fully in the absolute value of the equity. As the amount of equity is lower than the total amount of assets, the relative change in the equity tranche is much higher than the change in value of the underlying portfolio. The leverage effect can result in relatively higher changes, typically in the range of 2x, 3x or even higher depending on the leverage and performance of the underlying portfolio.

Figure 15.8 gives an overview of the leverage effect of a CFO structure and shows three examples of structures with different degrees of leverage. The axes represent the return of the collateral relative to the equity return of the investor. In this case the equity investors would be indifferent to investing in a structure or the collateral if it generates a return of 10%, but would certainly prefer a structure if the expected return was higher.[10]

[10] See also Mahadevan and Schwartz (2002) and Stone and Zissu (2004) for a more detailed description of hedge fund CFOs.

The total return of a securitization needs to equal the return of the underlying illiquid asset class r_{IA}. Formally:

$$r_{\mathrm{IA}} = r_A^* A + r_B^* B + r_c^* C + r_D^* D$$

The return for equity investors r_D increases with an increased debt-to-equity ratio $\frac{A+B+C}{D}$ if the return of the underlying asset r_{IA} is higher than the weighted average cost of debt:

$$r_{\mathrm{WDebt}} = \frac{A}{T} * r_A + \frac{B}{T} * r_B + \frac{C}{T} * r_C$$

with T = A + B + C + D. Hence,

$$r_D = r_{\mathrm{IA}} + \frac{A+B+C}{D} * (r_{\mathrm{IA}} - r_{\mathrm{WDebt}})$$

The equity tranche's risk and accordingly also the risk weighting in regulatory frameworks is high. However, Shady *et al.* (2011) show in an analysis that the leveraged exposure of the equity investors in hedge fund portfolios created value for their portfolio, even during the financial crisis. Missinhoun and Chacowry (2005) observed this in 80% of their sample. This is also the case for private equity CFOs, as most of the equity investors created value from their portfolios.

15.5 CONCLUSIONS

To summarize, a CFO transforms the risk of an investment in illiquid limited partnership funds into two different sub-categories: default risk of a bond and levered long-term risk of equity. This is a very important finding for our discussion on risk management in illiquid asset classes, as it shows that the long-term risk is a combination of credit risk and equity risk. As we discussed in Chapter 8, credit risk models are not suitable as models for portfolios of limited partnership funds since they fail to capture the significant upside potential. The risk of the equity tranche of the structure is comparable to the risk of a leveraged position.

16 Role of the Risk Manager

"Fearing failure, he did not try to win."
John Keegan about General McClellan (Commander of the Union Armies, 1861–62)[1]

In this chapter, we discuss the role of the risk manager overseeing portfolios of illiquid assets. While the recent financial crisis and the subsequent regulatory changes have caused a shift in investors' attitude towards risk management for illiquid assets, the adoption of new risk management standards has often been relatively slow. This inertia may be attributed to a combination of factors. A key reason may be sought in the fact that while the value of risk management for minimizing downside risk is largely uncontroversial, the boundaries with compliance have sometimes remained vague. However, as we have emphasized throughout this book, risk management is not just about protection against downside risks. Instead, risk management deals with the question of whether portfolio risk is adequate, which includes upside risk as well. Risk managers in the investment industry, and especially in alternative assets, cannot just focus on risk avoidance; instead, their chief responsibility is to ensure an adequate degree of risk taking, which is consistent with the institution's risk appetite and expected returns.

16.1 SETTING THE RISK MANAGEMENT AGENDA

Risk managers are tasked to develop specific policies, including quantifying the appetite for risk and setting risk limits accordingly. To monitor and report key risk exposures and to develop early warning indicators, appropriate risk metrics need to be defined. The risk manager intervenes in the investment process by allocating economic capital to investment activities based on risk and by setting incentives through risk-based performance measurement. To support this process, the appropriate methods and data management and analytical systems need to be put in place.

The management of risks in illiquid asset classes has frequently been perceived as falling into the remit of the compliance officer. This type of "risk management" is based on the argument that the inability to deal with operational risk[2] and/or the failure to comply with legal and regulatory requirements poses the main risks to the organization. As a consequence, the risk manager's role is widely perceived to be centred on these areas. In this book, however, we focus on financial risks and largely ignore functions related to compliance and operational risk, which we consider as separate tasks.

[1] Keegan, J. (2009) *The American Civil War*. Vintage.

[2] The Basel Committee defines operational risk as "the risk of loss resulting from inadequate or failed internal processes, people and systems or from external events". This definition includes legal risk, but excludes strategic and reputational risk.

16.1.1 What risk taking is rewarded?

Among academics and practitioners, it is widely accepted that risk taking is rewarded. What is less clear, however, are the mechanisms through which risk taking can be translated into higher returns for illiquid assets. In principle, two channels are relevant for this discussion. One channel involves the risk-adjusted pricing mechanism, where the downside risk is quantified and the investor requires a premium for taking the risk when purchasing the asset. This implies a major role for risk management to quantify the risk, which should be reflected in the price of the asset.[3] A second channel, and one that plays a particularly important role in the context of alternative investing, refers to risk taking by searching for overlooked niches and opportunities in the market. Generally, failure rates are high and only sustainable if balanced by more predictable sources for financial gains or by a sufficient number of wins. Risk management can do little to mitigate risks for individual transactions, but its main value is in keeping the portfolio of funds in balance.

16.1.2 Risk management: financial risk, operational risk or compliance?

The risk management agenda is generally set by institutional investors, who allocate the major part of their portfolio to traditional assets where risk-adjusted pricing is the main mechanism to balance risk and rewards. However, for primary investments in limited partnership funds, a risk-adjusted pricing mechanism does not exist (Mathonet and Meyer, 2007), arguably contributing to the widespread confusion about the role of the compliance function versus the role of the risk management function. Sharon (undated) argues that merging the risk management and compliance functions would create a vacuum in the sense that there would be no oversight of risk management whereas compliance would need to deal with a complex task it is conceptually not made for. Managing risks is not just about assessing and quantifying all that could go wrong, but, perhaps more importantly, understanding all the things that need to go right for the investment strategy to be successful. Clouding the boundaries between risk management and the compliance function reduces their value and is ultimately dangerous. Clearly, compliance is an extremely important function in a modern regulatory environment. Ensuring conformity with regulatory requirements and dealing with operational risk is fundamental to good business practice, but it is not the management of financial risks in the sense of seeking a trade-off of risks versus rewards in a market.

That risk management is often reduced to focusing on issues which could contribute to failure has often led to the marginalization of this function as an overhead to the business process, not a contributor to its success. It is, however, rather the taking of calculated risks at a portfolio level that is the driving force behind successful investing and cannot just be a box-ticking exercise of all the things that have and might go wrong in individual transactions.

When searching for overlooked niches and opportunities in the market, risk management has to provide decision-makers with an assessment of the potential for success, both quantitatively and qualitatively, and of the overall ability to cope with possible failure. Compliance has to ensure that those methodologies and processes are being followed in the manner intended, but risk management has to provide methodologies and processes in the first place to support decision-making for achieving the strategic objectives. In this respect, risk management plays a potentially far more important role than widely perceived and hence should be an integral

[3] See, for example, FSA (2010) where the remuneration principle "stresses the importance of risk adjustment in measuring performance, and the importance within that process of applying judgment and common sense. A firm should ask the risk management function to validate and assess risk-adjustment techniques, and to attend a meeting of the governing body or remuneration committee for this purpose."

part of the organization. For portfolios of limited partnership funds, the risk manager needs to help shape the investment strategy.

16.1.3 A gap of perceptions?

In the context of hedge funds, Lo (2001) finds that there is a gap between how institutional investors and alternative asset managers perceive the risk management agenda. Specifically, in explaining this gap, he emphasizes the very different perspectives that these two groups have on the investment process. Importantly, however, this is by no means just a phenomenon of the hedge fund industry, but characterizes alternative assets in general. Frequently, investment managers in alternative asset classes do not view risk management as central to the success but often see risk management as something that is imposed by regulation without adding any value. With the focus being on individual transactions, risk management – and the numerous compliance issues associated with it – is seen by many investment managers as costly and a potential drag on performance.

The perspective of the typical institutional investor is markedly different. Such institutions operate in a highly regulated environment and as fiduciaries need to understand a fund's investment process before committing capital to it. This investment process has to be institutionalized and should not be dependent on any single individual; risk management and risk transparency are essential for this purpose. The investment return of a specific transaction is not the overriding priority. What matters also is the fit within the overall portfolio, the consistency of the investment with the institution's objectives and notably liquidity constraints, and the degree of correlation with overall assets and liabilities.

16.2 RISK MANAGEMENT AS PART OF A FIRM'S CORPORATE GOVERNANCE

Regulation in relation to corporate governance as set out under Europe's Alternative Investment Fund Manager Directive (AIFMD) is instructive. Under this regulation, AIFMs are required to put in place appropriate conflict and liquidity management policies as well as a risk management function that is separate from the portfolio management function. Independence is viewed as necessary, as risk managers are hoped to be less "deal-driven", more objective and detached from personal relationships, and more consistent, process-oriented and systematic. The philosophy behind this is that risk managers cannot provide effective checks and balances unless they are truly independent from the risk takers.

How can it be ensured that risk management is fulfilling its role in corporate governance? Basically, two approaches are conceivable. While the "democratic" approach favours investment decisions by a group of partners whose interests are aligned, including with outside stakeholders, the "hierarchical" approach foresees a risk management function with a clearly defined line of reporting.

16.2.1 "Democratic" approach

In a partnership – the typical vehicle for alternative assets[4] – essentially all the partners have similar exposure to risks and rewards, are sharing risk aversion and risk appetite, and are

[4] The Free Dictionary gives several definitions for partnership, e.g. "contractual relationship between two or more persons carrying on a joint business venture with a view to profit, each incurring liability for losses and the right to share in the profits" and a "relationship between individuals or groups that is characterized by mutual cooperation and responsibility, as for the achievement of a specified goal". *Source:* http://www.thefreedictionary.com/partnership [accessed 7 June 2011].

managing risks and the trade-offs against competing long- and short-term objectives, discrepant priorities, conflicting interests and expectations of various stakeholders like investors, finance professionals and regulators. Arguably, the partnership itself is a response to the challenge posed by risks associated with highly uncertain outcomes that require experience and judgment and where the common direction of individual investment professionals needs to be rationally aligned with the firm's long-term interest.

But in such a setup, what is the role of an independent risk manager who either has no equity, and thus no say, or whose interests are fully aligned with those of the other partners? In this setting, there is a high probability that the risk manager will be focused on the downside: Ellis (2008), in his study on Goldman Sachs, a private partnership until 1999, quotes Bob Rubin who explained, "I can see for myself what could go right. Concentrate your analysis on what can go wrong. That's where you can really be most helpful."[5] Most investment managers would subscribe to this view and see risk management (read: analysis) as something done solely as an early-warning system for senior executives. The danger is that such a system is usually designed to give too many rather than too few signals. False alarms, however, may eventually lead the investment managers to decide to ignore the risk manager.

16.2.2 "Hierarchic" approach

In the hierarchical setup, which is typical for financial institutions like banks, insurers and pension funds, the primary responsibility for risk management is vested in the chief executive and overseen by the board of directors that has overall responsibility for ensuring risks are managed and there is an adequate risk management system in place. In many instances, risk managers report to the chief executive or to the CFO, and some have a direct reporting line to the board of directors.[6]

The risk manager cannot be subordinated to the investment functions, but it is not straightforward to draw a clear line: for example, is monitoring related to the investment function or to risk management and/or compliance? A factor that supports the first interpretation is that in the case of alternative assets, insights gained through monitoring are valuable inputs for due diligence related to the reinvestment decision. By contrast, the second interpretation could be justified by the fact that monitoring is also, and in fact to a large degree, concerned with the financial impact of changes in the fund's development, operational risk and ESG-related matters. What makes risk management for limited partnership funds particularly challenging as far as "balance sheet investors" are concerned is that the major part of their portfolios consist of traditional asset classes. As a result, there is limited interest in developing specific approaches for immaterial allocations to alternatives.

[5] According to the author, one of the most important units at Goldman Sachs is the commitment committee which focuses on making certain that the firm never makes a life-threatening bet, i.e. all the risks in every capital commitment decision should be fully identified, discussed and understood before any significant commitment of the firm's capital.

[6] The OECD sees risk management in a corporate-wide perspective where the risk management system is adjusted continuously to corporate strategy and risk appetite and recommends that the risk manager report directly to the board of directors and not via the CEO. See http://www.oecd.org/document/49/0,3746,en_2649_34813_43063537_1_1_1_1,00.html [accessed 21 February 2012].

16.3 BUILT-IN TENSIONS

A narrow interpretation would see risk management merely as an addition to the toolbox of financial instruments with a focus on analysing and modelling risks. Thus interpreted, risk management helps price individual transactions, transforming risks into quantifiable return premia.

16.3.1 Risk managers as "goal keepers"

Risk managers are often seen as "goal keepers", confronted with investment managers who seek approval for deals. There is no reason, however, to assume that the risk manager can make "better" investment decisions. If things go wrong, there will be immediate allegations that the risk manager should have been better prepared. Avoiding mistakes at the deal level is fundamentally a front-office job that needs to be fulfilled by the investment manager. This is particularly true for alternative investments, where there is generally no independent data source for verification. In fact, the full universe of investment opportunities is unknown: the risk manager only knows about the deals that are put forward, but does not know about the ones that were rejected. Consequently, the risk manager has a more conservative bias almost by definition and has limited scope for managing risk on the portfolio level.

16.3.2 Different perspectives – internal vs. external

For alternative assets, we can differentiate between an internal and an external point of view. Sometimes, risk managers are seen as presenting the "fair" view of outside stakeholders[7] whereas it is the investment managers whose responsibility it is to identify potentially attractive deals, requiring them to take views that may be contrary to those held by external observers. In line with the idea that risk taking for alternative assets means doing different things or things differently, the firm's internal views on deals often does – and actually should – deviate significantly from the external standard assessment. This will, by definition, create tensions between outside stakeholders represented by the risk manager on the one hand and the investment manager and decision-makers on the other.

Clearly, the investment industry recognizes the need for risk management, and its corporate governance bodies support this function. "But when it comes to the crunch, resources are diverted to activities which have a direct and immediate impact on the bottom line" (NSM, 2008). This diversion of resources is usually due to deliberate decisions by the firm's CEO and board, highlighting that investment management and risk management are often seen as playing two different roles, which may collide in the short term. This is particularly true for illiquid assets where, as we discussed in Chapter 10, accounting presentation might deviate significantly from economic substance, which risk management should focus on.

16.3.3 Analysing and modelling risks

While risk modelling plays an important role in the investment process, it is important to recognize the limitations of models. Models, no matter how complex they are, can only

[7] This is particularly true for asset managers having a client risk manager who acts as an interface between the investment team and the mandators.

be an approximation of the numerous interdependencies in the real world. In mapping the potential financial outcomes with a reasonable degree of plausibility, modelling illiquid assets requires both quantitative information and judgment. As an integrated framework, risk management has to look at the overall portfolio and therefore needs to model all the firm's assets and liabilities.

Risk measurement and the associated metrics should be used widely in the investment process. However, tensions are almost pre-programmed if risk metrics result in constraining investment activities (Holton, 2004). Golub and Crum (2010) refer to such cases: "For instance, if a risk manager finds himself or herself in conflict with a large revenue producer, the actions taken by senior management in resolving the conflict will speak a hundred times louder than simply mouthing slogans but not backing them with action." A key challenge for the risk manager, however, is that he is expected to present an "irresistible, quantifiable" (Sher, 2010) business case that runs the risk of ignoring non-quantifiable, but potentially highly relevant, risk factors.

16.3.4 Remuneration

While the organizational setting of risk management plays a key role for the efficacy of this function, which is well recognized by regulators, in some jurisdictions compensation structures have become subject to regulatory interest. Potentially, this may have important implications for the "functional and hierarchical" independence of risk management and compliance. If the remuneration policy is not fully aligned with effective risk management, it is likely that employees will have incentives to act in ways that are detrimental to the organization's objectives. Consequently, regulators like the UK's Financial Services Authority (FSA) require that remuneration policies must promote effective risk management and do not create excessive risk exposure (FSA, 2010). Specifically, the FSA stipulates that a "firm's risk management and compliance functions [. . .] have appropriate input into setting remuneration for other business areas. The procedures for setting remuneration should allow risk and compliance functions to have significant input into the setting of individual remuneration awards where those functions have concerns about the behaviour of the individuals concerned or the riskiness of the business undertaken."[8]

Some regulators have also provided guidance in terms of the remuneration of risk managers themselves. The European Securities and Markets Authority (ESMA), for example, has declared that "those engaged in the performance of the risk management function are compensated in accordance with the achievement of the objectives linked to that function, independent of the performance of the other conflicting business area."[9] This suggests that the regulatory authorities put considerable emphasis on managing the conflicts of interest that might arise if other business areas have undue influence over the remuneration of employees within the control functions in general and to prevent situations by which the remuneration's structure of these same employees would blur their objectives (FSA, 2010). However, despite the importance of this dimension, incentives and compensation for risk managers still remains an under-researched area.

[8] See FSA (2010). Apparently, the FSA stepped backwards slightly from its original position where it required "significant input" (see FSA, 2009).

[9] See ESMA (2011, p. 70) and also FSA (2009).

16.4 CONCLUSIONS

Despite disastrous financial losses, risk management still does not always play the key role it should. Indeed some, like Sher (2010), have claimed that there is "a huge 'placebo effect' in so much of what passes for risk management nowadays". While risk management is generally regarded as an instrument that focuses exclusively on avoiding losses, few actually see risk management in a more symmetric way that can help maximize risk-adjusted returns, taking into account the risk appetite of the organization. As this chapter has argued, the risk manager can and should play a key role in shaping investment strategies, requiring that his functions are deeply embedded in the decision-making process.[10]

Unfortunately, financial risk management in the area of illiquid investments is still under-developed, and there remains considerable confusion as to how the precise role of the risk manager should be defined. In our view, risk management should focus on financial risks and minimize overlaps with compliance and operational risk management, which should be dealt with by separate business functions. In focusing on financial risks, the risk manager should take a portfolio view that considers both downside and upside risks – instead of concentrating exclusively on the potential losses of individual funds. To fulfil his role in helping build a robust portfolio, the risk manager has to be involved in the early stages of developing an investment strategy. This aspect of the function should be performed by a dedicated manager within the firm even when the risk management function is outsourced to a third party.

In assessing financial risks in illiquid investments, the risk manager will often have to blend quantitative data with qualitative information. In fact, at the beginning of an investment in a long-term partnership fund, risk management will need to rely primarily on risk parameters that are usually not quantifiable. Gradually, this will change as the investment matures and more hard data become available that allows a more quantitative approach. Importantly, as we have stressed in this chapter, the management of financial risk is an ongoing process that aims to ensure strategy adjustments can be made if unexpected events cause deviations from the planned risk profile of the portfolio. This process requires a clearly defined risk management policy aimed at ensuring the portfolio's risk exposure is consistent with the institution's expected returns and risk appetite. This leads us to the final chapter of this book, where we discuss best practices for setting a policy framework for risk management.

[10] In fact, this is what regulators want to achieve when they put the "use test" requirement for risk models in place.

17

Risk Management Policy

The final chapter of this book is concerned with risk management policy, which links a firm's investment strategy with its organizational setup and its systems and procedures. Essentially, risk management policy sets the framework for a financial institution to coordinate and execute its activities and hence plays a key role in the decision-making process. There is a growing awareness that failures and near-misses within financial institutions have been caused, or at least perpetuated, by deficiencies in risk management systems and policies. Against this background, the European Securities and Markets Authority (ESMA, 2011) has recently identified three areas of particular importance for the management of financial risks:

(i) the establishment, organization, role and responsibilities of a permanent risk management function, including requirements in respect of its reporting to senior management and its functional and hierarchical separation from other operating units including portfolio management;
(ii) the establishment of a risk management policy and the process and frequency for the assessment, monitoring and review of this policy; and
(iii) the processes and techniques for the measurement and management of risk including the use of qualitative and quantitative risk limits for certain types of risk.

In many financial organizations, the development and implementation of an effective risk management policy has therefore been given high priority. Although regulatory initiatives have often been an important driver for financial services firms to upgrade their risk management tools, regulations usually set only a broader framework within which individual organizations design their specific policies. This approach recognizes that investors may differ substantially, for example, in terms of their asset and liabilities profile, their internal governance structures, their size and their asset portfolios, including their exposure to alternatives.

Within the broader context of regulations, this chapter aims to help investors design a risk management policy that takes into account the specific characteristics of investments in illiquid limited partnership funds. In pursuing this objective, we address the following issues. To what extent should a risk management policy be based on concrete rules as opposed to broader principles? What is the exact scope of an effective risk management policy? And how does a risk management policy fit into the organizational structure of the firm?

In addressing these issues, our discussion focuses primarily on the management of financial risks through appropriate policies. However, we do recognize the importance of operational risk for an effective risk management policy. As we emphasize in this chapter, for the management of financial risk to achieve its objectives, it is critical that it be supported by adequate reporting systems and a robust IT infrastructure. In fact, this discussion is consistent with recent financial regulations which consider operational risk explicitly.[1]

[1] As far as Basel III is concerned, for example, regulatory capital is calculated for three major components of risk: credit risk, operational risk and market risk. Solvency II considers market risk, credit risk, liquidity risk, insurance risk and operational risk.

17.1 RULES OR PRINCIPLES?

17.1.1 "Trust me – I know what I'm doing"

In alternative investing, concrete rules generally do not exist, which explains why historically there has been substantial reliance on principles. Principles-based approaches specify desired outcomes and allow the charting of an organization-specific path to those results, usually based on self-regulation and confidence in the skills and experience of the investment managers. Principles are general almost by definition; they set normative goals with respect to, for instance, integrity and proper standards of market conduct. As Quintyn (undated) argues, principles-based approaches to corporate governance and regulation were historically the preferred *modus operandi* of the British banking system, which was managed as a "small gentlemen's club" through self-regulation, i.e. the use of "moral suasion". Moral suasion was widely seen as "best practice" for guiding and supervising this system. In a number of ways, the alternative asset industry appears to have preserved this culture – at least until recently. While a principles-based approach is generally preferable in situations where it is difficult to set clear rules, the recent financial crisis has undermined the confidence in the former and resulted in tighter regulation in the European Union as well as in the USA.

17.1.2 "Trust but verify"

To be sure, a principles-based approach in and of itself does not necessarily result in excessive risk taking. In fact, it is conceivable that investment managers operating under such a system are too risk-averse, given the substantial amount of uncertainty in long-term investing. While rules are meant to provide clarity and certainty for a financial institution's management, their disadvantage lies in their rigidity. Importantly, regulation recognizes that risk management methodologies are generally proprietary and contribute significantly to the investment performance. For instance, ESMA did not consider it appropriate to provide advice on the types of risk management methodology to be employed. Given the governance structure, there is a broad range of systems that can be employed to facilitate the risk management process, with different methodologies potentially being applied in different situations.

If principles-based approaches are seen as too weak or ambiguous and rules-based approaches are too rigid and unable to keep up with the pace of change in the investment environment, what is the way out? New regulatory initiatives, such as Europe's AIFM Directive, appear to favour an approach that Quintyn has called a "principles-cum-rules system" for a governance-driven financial industry. Under this system, rules are used in support of the broad principles, to explain them or direct their implementation. Put differently, the regulatory principle is that every institution investing in alternative assets needs to develop and regularly update its own system of specific rules. This set of rules can then be assessed by external stakeholders, who "trust but verify".

17.2 RISK MANAGEMENT POLICY CONTEXT

While regulatory initiatives such as the AIFM Directive, the Dodd–Frank Act, Basel III or Solvency II target different classes of investors in the financial industry, there is clear convergence between these regimes in terms of their general thrust. As long as investors' exposure to alternative asset classes was small, private equity and similar investments remained below the radar screen of the regulatory bodies. However, this has changed significantly in recent years. Perhaps not surprisingly, the new regulatory interest in alternative investing has prompted a considerable pushback by the industry (Acharya *et al.*, 2011), albeit with limited success. Thus, LPs and GPs alike have begun to upgrade their risk management policies in compliance with new regulatory requirements.

Importantly, risk management policy has to follow a dynamic approach that reflects best practices, requiring a periodic review of the specific arrangements, processes and techniques. Many LPs have adopted internal models, which have to pass a so-called "use test": this requires that the model is embedded within the system of governance, is a key tool in decision-making processes and is updated regularly to reflect the risk profile. Investors using internal models need to monitor their investment programme's compliance with the risk management policy and to act in case of deviations.

An effective risk management policy represents a holistic approach that links investment strategies, the firm's business plan, the organizational setting and the IT systems environment to ensure consistency of the overall process. For each of these areas, a separate document should be prepared that is consistent with the firm's overall risk management policy.

17.2.1 Investment strategy

Haight *et al.* (2007) define investment strategy as "the plan(s) and methods that will be employed to realize the investment return goals". This, of course, requires setting clearly defined objectives that are to be pursued (Fraser-Sampson, 2006). A critical ingredient in this process is the explicit determination of the investor's risk tolerance, according to which certain return goals may simply not be attainable. Objectives should be consistent, realistic and clearly stated, using measurable criteria on the basis of which deviations can be determined.

Investment strategies are formulated under uncertainty – especially in illiquid asset classes where the investment horizon is 10 years or even longer. This does not mean that strategies are obsolete, however. In fact, strategy is about choice between different outcomes in the future, and while the range of outcomes tends to widen as the horizon increases in length, strategic thinking arguably gains in importance as a competitive differentiator. In this context, it should be made clear why a particular strategy is pursued and how this strategy may deviate from expected market developments to achieve excess returns, given the investor's risk appetite. Furthermore, a good strategy needs to spell out specific rules about strategic adjustments to market changes. Importantly, strategic planning is a dynamic process rather than a static set of instructions.

A useful framework for strategic thinking about investing and portfolio construction has been developed by Black and Litterman (1992). Although their model was designed originally for diversified portfolios of marketable instruments, its fundamental ideas are applicable to the context of alternative investing as well. The point of departure of the Black–Litterman model, which is based on a Bayesian approach, is the observation that investment managers tend to think in terms of weights in portfolios rather than balancing expected returns against the contribution to portfolio risk as assumed in the traditional CAPM (Cornelius, 2011).

The reference point in the Black–Litterman model is a market-neutral allocation to different asset classes and market segments (e.g., US venture capital funds, European middle-market buyout funds, growth capital funds targeting Asia). The expected returns from holding the market portfolio represent the market equilibrium. To deviate from market neutrality, investors must formulate explicitly their own return expectations and specify the degree of confidence they have in their stated views. This is precisely where risk management comes in: the optimal portfolio is simply a set of deviations from neutral market capitalization weights in the directions about which views are expressed (Cornelius, 2011).

17.2.2 Business plan

In its technical advice to the European Commission on possible measures of the AIFM Directive, the ESMA defines as an additional due diligence requirement for investing in a partnership interest the specification of a "business plan".[2] In the consultation process, the majority of respondents did not agree with the use of this term and proposed several alternatives. In the end, however, the ESMA decided to continue to refer to the "business plan" as no clearly superior and more appropriate term emerged from the consultation process. Despite this, the process helped clarify what a business plan is actually meant to be in the context of investing and portfolio construction. For example, an alternative term suggested by one respondent was "risk appetite statement". Although perhaps not the most elegant term, it underlines the importance of the business plan as a tool that is closely related to the risk management policy of the firm. The business plan explains how the firm's investment strategy is applied in the market place to achieve the desired objectives. Given that investment decisions are made under uncertainty, the business plan has to specify the assumptions under which a particular strategy is developed.

- In order to allow a judgment about the risk/return profile of the portfolio, the business plan has to describe the broad investment universe and reflect on the investment manager's skills regarding selection and access to opportunities.[3]
- Given the high degree of uncertainty in investment decisions, the business plan needs to give ranges of possible outcomes and simulate various scenarios.
- Market developments need to be monitored continuously against the business plan in order to design adjustments as conditions change and new opportunities and/or threats emerge.[4] If the original strategy in due course is found to be impossible to implement, changes need to be reported to the institution's senior governance and its investors.
- The business plan helps investors monitor progress, but should also give indications as to the possible need for tactical changes in the broader strategy; in the extreme case, this monitoring process may suggest abandoning the original strategy altogether.

Whereas policies and strategies are designed for the longer term and are therefore typically revisited relatively infrequently (usually only every 3 years, sometimes after even longer intervals), business plans need to be updated regularly and whenever material changes in the investment environment occur. To regularly revise business plans based on rolling forecasts ensures responsiveness in the volatile market environment, and forces a forward-looking management.

[2] According to Wikipedia, the online dictionary, a business plan is a "formal statement of a set of business goals, the reasons why they are believed attainable, and the plan for reaching those goals. It may also contain background information about the organization or team attempting to reach those goals." See http://en.wikipedia.org/wiki/Business_plan [accessed 23 January 2012].

[3] The AIFM Directive's requirements regarding documentation of deal flow pipeline could be interpreted as such (see ESMA, 2011).

[4] See http://www.businessdictionary.com/definition/business-plan.html [accessed 23 January 2012].

17.2.3 Organizational setting

Investment firms have to establish, implement and maintain an organizational structure that allocates specific investment functions, responsibilities and duties as well as reporting lines within the organization. This organization needs to be documented clearly in order to ensure accountability in the investment process. In this context, best practices include:

- The risk management and compliance functions should be independent from other operating units, including portfolio management. To be effective, they must have the necessary authority, resources, expertise and access to all information.
- In cases where the risk management function is not functionally or hierarchically separate, the safeguards that allow for its independence need to be described. This has to cover the nature of the potential conflicts of interest as well as the remedial measures to deal with such conflicts if they arise. Importantly, from the document it should be clear why the measures can reasonably be expected to result in the risk management function's independent performance.
- The organizational setting should ensure an adequate structure of supervision and remuneration with regard to different responsibilities. Furthermore, effective processes and procedures are required in terms of the exchange of information.
- The risk management function is a permanent instrument that is charged on an ongoing basis with identifying, measuring, managing and monitoring all relevant risks the investment strategy is exposed to.

A conflicts-of-interest policy needs to include procedures to be followed and measures to be adopted in order to manage such conflicts. It has to describe how it is ensured that the safeguards are consistently effective.

17.2.4 System environment

A well-designed risk management policy also specifies the reporting vis-à-vis the firm's governance bodies and senior management and, where appropriate, supervisory institutions. Terms, contents and frequency of reporting depend on the nature, scale and complexity of the specific investment activity; there is no formulaic answer.

In order for the risk management function to be effective, it is important that all relevant investment activities are well documented. Only then will it be possible to demonstrate consistency with the business plan and identify any deviations from it. Specifically, the documentation of the investment process should include the minutes of the relevant meetings and any supporting evidence, such as economic and financial analyses that are undertaken in the context of the due diligence work. Importantly, this includes documents that are provided by the fundraising partnership (such as private placement memoranda) as well as internal research on a particular opportunity. These documentation requirements apply regardless of whether an investment opportunity actually leads to a capital commitment. Records must be kept in order to allow risk managers to identify any potential source – including potential conflicts of interest – that could lead to an unintended deviation of the portfolio exposure from the institution's defined risk appetite.

To a large extent, record-keeping will take the form of electronic records, which poses considerable challenges in terms of IT systems. Furthermore, risk managers have to carry out documented stress tests and scenario analyses at regular intervals to identify potential changes in market conditions and examine their potential impact on the portfolio. In addition, periodic back-testing is required to review the validity of risk measurement arrangements that include model-based forecasts and estimates. All this is necessary to ensure that the risks of positions taken and their contribution to the overall risk profile are measured accurately on the basis of sound and reliable data and that the risk measurement arrangements, processes and techniques are documented adequately.

Given the high dependence on financial models in institutional investing, operational risk has become an increasingly important concern, not least from a regulatory perspective. The ESMA (2011) stipulates, for instance, that IT systems and tools used for the computation of investments be integrated with one another and/or with the front office and accounting applications. Moreover, arrangements need to be put in place to secure essential data in the case of an unexpected interruption of the IT system. At the same time, a high degree of confidentiality must be guaranteed. It should be obvious that these IT requirements by far exceed the possibilities offered by simple spreadsheets.

17.3 DEVELOPING A RISK MANAGEMENT POLICY

A policy can be interpreted as a "statement of intent" for which governance bodies can be held accountable.[5] It needs to be sufficiently forward-looking and stable for a period that is in line with the long-term orientation of an institution's activities in alternative assets. A policy needs to express the expectations of the various stakeholders in a language that accurately reflects their thinking. Procedures deal with the operational processes required to implement a policy. Depending upon the level of operational processes being described in the statements, the line between policy and procedures is difficult to draw.

17.3.1 Design considerations

A potential dilemma in designing a well-functioning risk management policy is to set restrictions that limit portfolio risk in a way that is consistent with the firm's risk appetite without imposing excessive constraints that result in an under-exposure to risk – with potentially significant effects on portfolio returns. Even apparently small restrictions can hamper severely the investment manager's ability to meet his defined objectives and lead to unintended consequences. However, to the extent that these restrictions are ignored, the lack of investment discipline may create significant and unforeseen risks. Thus, compliance with the risk management policy and specifically with its arrangements, processes and techniques should be subjected to permanent monitoring.

The broad principles of designing an effective risk management policy are already codified in the prudent investor rule (see Chapter 3). To repeat, these principles require that investments are made with judgment and care, taking into account the circumstances that prevail at the time of the investment decision. According to these principles, investment managers should act as persons of prudence – not speculators – as if they were managing their own affairs, considering the protection of their capital as well as the probable income to be derived from the investment.

[5] See http://en.wikipedia.org/wiki/Policy [accessed 23 January 2012].

In developing more specific policies, guidance may be sought in the "investment policy statements" developed by several US university endowments and public pension schemes, which have been long-term investors in alternative asset classes. Notwithstanding significant differences between the policy statements of individual institutions, there are a number of important commonalities with respect to governance issues (Mathonet and Meyer, 2007):

- A risk management policy should contain details about the effective procedures and appropriate systems that are put in place to ensure that the actual risk profile of the portfolio is consistent with the risk targets.
- The risk management policy should be laid out in a separate document that provides details as to how responsibilities relating to risk management are allocated within the organization. Furthermore, safeguards should be specified to ensure the independence of the risk management function.
- The frequency of reporting should be determined in the policy document. It should be clear who the addressees are – the governance bodies of the institution and those charged with setting the risk limits. Furthermore, details should be given regarding the techniques and models used to monitor and manage different types of risk.
- Roles and responsibilities are to be described in a transparent way. Any limitations concerning discretionary decisions by the institution's investment managers are to be stated clearly.

Furthermore, the risk management policy should address key issues in terms of the investment strategy and focus. This includes, but is not limited to, the following issues:

- The risk management policy should specify the universe of permissible investments in terms of strategies as well as market segments. At the broadest level, it will need to be determined, for example, whether the permissible universe includes secondary funds and co-investments and perhaps even direct investments, in addition to primary fund investments.
- Within the primary funds mandate, the risk management policy may introduce additional restrictions. For example, some investors may decide not to commit capital to funds investing in frontier markets. Investments that fall into the permissible universe should be guided by clear eligibility criteria. For example, are investments in first-time funds allowed? The definition of the permissible market universe and the eligibility criteria should be reviewed periodically.
- To the extent that the definition of the permissible market universe and possible eligibility criteria are adjusted, the risk management policy should specify whether existing investments in the portfolio that are no longer consistent with the new policy should be subject to grandfathering or would need to be divested.
- The risk management policy should clarify whether, and to what extent, overcommitment strategies are allowed. Similarly, it should be clear whether and to what degree illiquid portfolios may be leveraged.
- As far as distributions "in kind" (i.e., shares in listed portfolio companies) are concerned, the risk management policy should provide guidance as to the liquidation of such holdings.
- There should be clarity as to how performance is measured and which benchmarks are to be used.
- To the extent that regulated investors use an internal model, as opposed to the standard model (e.g., under Basel III and Solvency II), its main features need to be explained in the risk management policy document, with a view to its underlying rationale, the assumptions

made and the data used. The model needs to be validated by an external expert, with the validation process being documented appropriately.
- Finally, the risk management policy should also address the issue of monitoring the compliance of funds where investments have been made with the terms specified in the limited partnership agreement.

In sum, the risk management policy serves to outline internal controls, determining the remit of the investment managers and the criteria that are used to monitor the implementation of the investment strategy with regard to portfolio risk. Moreover, the risk management policy should provide specific guidance as to the communication of risk monitoring vis-à-vis senior management, the board and outside addressees, such as auditors and regulators.

17.3.2 Risk limits

Setting specific risk limits is a central responsibility of a well-defined risk management policy, with the risk manager tasked to monitor closely the compliance with such limits. Consistent with existing regulation, limits typically cover market risks, credit risks, counterparty risks, operational risks and liquidity risks. For illiquid assets, it is important to note that the enforcement of limits may be challenging as portfolios cannot easily be rebalanced, as we have already noted in Chapter 6. This is also recognized by the ESMA (2011), which clarifies that the breaching of a risk limit may not necessarily require immediate action by the investment manager.

Nevertheless, a system of risk limits requires procedures that, in the event of actual or anticipated breaches, trigger remedial actions in a timely fashion. Thus, risk managers need to monitor compliance with the risk limits on a forward-looking basis and alert senior management accordingly, taking into account that adjustments in illiquid asset classes will take a considerable amount of time.

More specifically, as far as liquidity risk is concerned, the risk management policy should address anticipated or actual liquidity shortages. In this context, it is particularly important to factor in the risk of market turbulences as a result of which liquidity may dry up literally overnight. This leads us back to our introductory discussion at the beginning of this book. In fact, as we emphasized in Part I, the Great Recession provides numerous examples where investors were essentially unable to liquidate their holdings in the secondary market (or only at extremely steep discounts) and could borrow only at exceedingly high interest rates. Putting in place a risk management policy that focuses on possible liquidity constraints will be essential for avoiding similar mistakes in the future.

17.4 CONCLUSIONS

In the final chapter of this book, we have presented the contours of a comprehensive risk management policy for investors in illiquid assets. To be effective, a risk management policy should be viewed as a holistic approach that links the firm's investment strategy, its organizational setting and its systems and procedures. This is one of the key lessons learned from the recent financial crisis, where risk management often had an isolated function, or worse, was embryonic or plainly non-existent.

In describing best practices in terms of risk management policies, this chapter started with a fundamental question about the pros and cons of a rules-based versus a principles-based approach. Advocating a hybrid model, we have then turned to the broader context of a well-functioning risk management policy, which is set by the strategic objectives of the firm, its business plan and organization. Finally, our discussion has focused on the design of a risk management policy itself, identifying some key pillars in terms of governance and investment strategy issues.

Importantly, the risk management policies we have outlined in this chapter should be understood as a generic framework. Within this framework, investors will need to develop their own policies and procedures in accordance with their specific regulatory environment, history and experience, their existing portfolio, ownership structures and resources. Putting in place a risk management policy that aims to help avoid the mistakes made in previous episodes is an evolutionary process, and as we continue to learn about the specific risks in alternative investing, risk management policies will need to be adjusted accordingly.

References

Acharya, V.V. and Pedersen, L.H. (2005) Asset pricing with liquidity risk. *Journal of Financial Economics*, 77, 375–410.

Acharya, V.V., Hamrick, L.W. and Bellini, C.J. (2011) The regulatory tangle. *Private Equity Findings*, 5. London Business School, Coller Institute of Private Equity.

Acharya, V.V., Gottschalg, O.F., Hahn, M. and Kehoe, C. (2013) Corporate governance and value creation: Evidence from private equity. *Review of Financial Studies*, 26(2), 368–402.

Achleitner, P. and Albrecht, S. (2011) Private equity in an insurance company's strategic asset allocation. In *Inside the Limited Partner – A compendium of investor attitudes to private equity*. PEI Media Ltd.

Achleitner, A.-K., Braun, R. and Engel, N. (2011) Value creation and pricing in buyouts: Empirical evidence from Europe and North America. *Review of Financial Economics*, 20(4), 146–161.

Akerlof, G. (1970) The market for 'lemons': Quality uncertainty and the market mechanism. *Quarterly Journal of Economics*, 84, 488–500.

Almeida Capital (2002) The advent of liquidity. Private Equity Secondaries. www.Almeidacapital.com.

Amblard, O. (2007) Securitization. In Mathonet, P.-Y. and Meyer, T. (eds), *J-Curve Exposure*. John Wiley & Sons, Chichester.

Amihud, Y. and Mendelson, H. (2006) Stock and bond liquidity and its effect on prices and financial policies. *Financial Markets and Portfolio Management*, 20(1), 19–32.

Ang, A. and Kjaer, K. (2011) Investing for the long run. Available at http://papers.ssrn.com/sol3/papers.cfm?abstract_id=1958258 [accessed 14 June 2012].

Ang, A. and Sorensen, M. (2011) Risk, returns, and optimal holdings of private equity. http://www.columbia.edu/~aa610/ [accessed 30 May 2012].

Ang, A., Papanikolaou, D. and Westerfield, M.M. (2011) Portfolio choice with illiquid assets. Available at http://www.kellogg.northwestern.edu/faculty/papanikolaou/htm/APW-101024.pdf [accessed 17 August 2011].

Arlen, J., Spitzer, M.L. and Talley, E. (2002) Endowment effects within corporate agency relationships. New York University Law and Economics Working Papers, No. 139. Available at http://lsr.nellco.org/nyu_lewp/139 [accessed 8 May 2012].

Axelson, U., Jenkinson, T., Strömberg, P. and Weisbach, M.S. (2009) Why are buyouts levered? The financial structure of private equity funds. *Journal of Finance*, 64, 1549–1582.

Bénéplanc, G. and Rochet, J.C. (2011) *Risk Management in Turbulent Times*. Oxford University Press, Oxford.

Bernstein, S., Lerner, J. and Schoar, A. (2009) The investment strategies of sovereign wealth funds. National Bureau of Economic Research, Working Paper No. 14861.

BIS (1996) Supervisory Framework for the Use of "Backtesting" in Conjunction with the Internal Models Approach to Market Risk Capital Requirements. Basel Committee on Banking Supervision, January. Available at http://www.bis.org/publ/bcbsc223.pdf [accessed 1 July 2008].

BIS (2001) Working Paper on Risk Sensitive Approaches for Equity Exposures in the Banking Book for IRB Banks. Basel Committee on Banking Supervision, August. Available at http://www.bis.org/publ/bcbs_wp6.pdf?noframes=1 [accessed 1 July 2008].

BIS (2008) Principles for sound liquidity risk management and supervision. Basel Committee on Banking Supervision, September.

Bitsch, F., Buchner, A. and Kaserer, C. (2010) Risk, return and cash flow characteristics of infrastructure fund investments. EIB Papers, Vol. 15, No. 1, pp. 106–136. Available at http://ssrn.com/abstract=1992961 [accessed 21 August 2012].

Black, F. and Litterman, R. (1992) Global portfolio optimization. *Financial Analysts Journal*, 48(5), 28–43.

Blackburn, R. (2002) *Banking on Death: Or, Investing in Life: The History and Future of Pensions*. Verso, London.

Blake, C. (2008) *The Art of Decisions. How to manage in an uncertain world*. Pearson Education Limited, Oxford.

Bongaerts, D. and Charlier, E. (2006) Risk management for LBOs in buy-and-hold portfolios, 27 August. Available at http://www.greta.it/credit/credit2006/poster/2_Bongaersts_Charlier.pdf [accessed 30 June 2008].

Bongaerts, D. and Charlier, E. (2009) Private equity and regulatory capital. *Journal of Banking and Finance*, 33(7), 1211–1220.

Borden, B.T. (2009) The aggregate-plus theory of partnership taxation. *Georgia Law Review*, 43. Available at http://ssrn.com/abstract=1121351 [accessed 18 July 2008].

Borensztein, E., Levy Yeyati, E. and Panizza, U. (eds) (2006) Living with Debt. How to Limit the Risks of Sovereign Finance. Economic and Social Progress in Latin America. Inter-American Development Bank, Washington, DC.

Braunschweig, C. (2001) Beset by falling IRRs, CalPERS plays defence. *Venture Capital Journal*, October.

Bromley, D. (2002) Comparing corporate reputations: League tables, quotients, benchmarks, or case studies? *Corporate Reputation Review*, 5(1), 35–50.

Brunnhuber, U. (2007) (Pre-) Islamic finance and venture capital. In Mathonet, P.-Y. and Meyer, T. (eds), *J-Curve Exposure*. John Wiley & Sons, Chichester.

Buchner, A., Kaserer, C. and Wagner, N.F. (2010). Private equity funds: Valuation, systematic risk and illiquidity. Available at http://dx.doi.org/10.2139/ssrn.1102471 [accessed 21 August 2012].

Buhl, C. (2004) Liquidität im Risikomanagement. PhD thesis, University of St. Gallen.

Burgel, O. (2000) *UK Venture Capital and Venture Capital as an Asset Class for Institutional Investors*. BVCA, London.

Buttonwood (2008) Requiem for a prudent man – A fund manager's career has lessons for today's investors. *The Economist*, 27 March.

CalPERS (2010) California Public Employees' Retirement System – Statement of Investment Strategy for Alternative Investment Management (AIM) Program, February 16. Available at http://www.calpers.ca.gov/eip-docs/investments/policies/inv-asset-classes/aim/altern-invest-man-prog.pdf [accessed 29 June 2011].

Cambridge Associates (2011) Pension Risk Management. https://www.cambridgeassociates.com/research_center/research_reports.html [accessed 23 March 2012].

Cao, J. and Lerner, J. (2009) The performance of reverse leveraged buyouts. *Journal of Financial Economics*, 91(2), 139–157.

Carver, L. (2012) Goodbye VAR? Basel to consider other risk metrics. *Risk Magazine*, February. Available at http://www.risk.net/risk-magazine/news/2154611/goodbye-var-basel-consider-risk-metrics [accessed 7 June 2012].

Chacko, G. (2005) Liquidity risk in corporate bond markets, http://papers.ssrn.com/sol3/papers.cfm?abstract_id=687619 [accessed 10 January 2012].

Chan-Lau, J.A. (2004) Pension funds and emerging markets. IMF Working Paper WP/04/181. http://www.imf.org/external/pubs/cat/longres.cfm?sk=17504.0 [accessed 2 February 2012].

Chung, J.-W. (2010) Performance persistence in private equity funds. Available at http://ssrn.com/abstract=1686112 [accessed 10 February 2011].

Cochrane, J. (2005) The risk and return of venture capital. *Journal of Financial Economics*, 75, 3–52.

Cogent Partners (2012) Secondary pricing trends and analysis, January. Cogent Papers, 27.

Conner, A. (2005) Persistence in venture capital returns. *Private Equity International*, March.

Connolley, W.M. (2007) Projection/prediction. Available at http://scienceblogs.com/stoat/2007/08/projection_prediction.php [accessed 15 November 2011].

Conroy, R.M. and Harris, R.S. (2007) How good are private equity returns? *Journal of Applied Corporate Finance*, 19, 96–108.
Cornelius, P. (2011) *International Investments in Private Equity*. Academic Press, Burlington, MA.
CPEE (2004) Limited Partnership Agreement Conference. Tuck School of Business at Dartmouth, Center for Private Equity and Entrepreneurship, 20–21 July. Available at http://mba.tuck.dartmouth.edu/pecenter/research/pdfs/LPA_conference.pdf [accessed 13 September 2006].
Crouhy, M., Galai, D. and Mark, R. (2001) Prototype risk rating system. *Journal of Banking and Finance*, No. 25.
Damodaran, A. (2007) *Strategic Risk Taking*. Pearson Prentice Hall, New York.
Damodaran, A. (undated) Value at Risk (VaR). Available at http://people.stern.nyu.edu/adamodar/pdfiles/papers/VAR.pdf [accessed 9 October 2012].
Danielsson, J. (2008) The paradox of models. Conference Paper, London School of Economics. Available at http://fmg.lse.ac.uk/upload_file/1027_J_Danielsson.pdf [accessed 13 October 2008].
Dawes, R. (1979) The robust beauty of improper linear models in decision making. *American Psychologist*, 34(7), 571–582.
Day, S. and Diller, C. (2010) Benchmarking private equity investments. In *Risk Management Handbook*. Private Equity International.
de Malherbe, E. (2003) Modeling private equity funds and private equity collateralized fund obligations. *International Journal of Theoretical and Applied Finance*, 7(3), 193–230.
de Zwart, G., Frieser, B. and van Dijk, D. (2007) *A Recommitment Strategy for Long Term Private Equity Fund Investors*. ERIM Report Series, Research in Management, December. Available at http://publishing.eur.nl/ir/repub/asset/10892/ERS-2007-097-F&A.pdf [accessed 2 July 2008].
Diller, C. (2007) *Private Equity: Rendite, Risiko und Markteinflussfaktoren – Eine empirische Analyse europäischer Private-Equity-Fonds*. Uhlenbruch Verlag, Bad Soden.
Diller, C. and Herger, I. (2008) Private equity – will you take the risk? *Private Equity International*, May, pp. 106–109.
Diller, C. and Herger, I. (2009) Assessing the risk of private equity fund investments. In *Private Equity Mathematics*. Private Equity International.
Diller, C. and Jäckel, C. (2010) Asset allocation and exposure management in private equity. In *Risk Management Handbook*. Private Equity International.
Diller, C. and Kaserer, C. (2004) European private equity funds – a cash flow based performance analysis. In *Performance Measurement and Asset Allocation of European Private Equity Funds*, EVCA Research Paper, Brussels.
Diller, C. and Kaserer, C. (2009) What drives private equity returns – fund inflows, skilled GPs, and/or risk? *European Financial Management*, 15(3), 643–675.
Diller, C. and Wulff, M. (2011) The private equity performance puzzle – let there be light! In Montana Capital Partners (ed.), *Performance Measurement and Benchmarking in Private Equity*. Private Equity International.
Dimson, E. (1979) Risk measurement when securities are subject to infrequent trading. *Journal of Financial Economics*, 7(2), 197–226.
Dowd, K. (2001) *Beyond Value at Risk – The New Science of Risk Management*. John Wiley & Sons, Chichester.
Dowd, K., Blake, D. and Cairns, A. (2004) Long-term value at risk. *Journal of Risk Finance*, 5, 52–57.
Drehmann, M. and Nikolaou, K. (2008) Funding liquidity risk: Definition and measurement. ECB Working Paper.
Driessen, J., Lin, T.C. and Phalippou, P. (2011) A new method to estimate risk and return of non-traded assets from cash flows: The case of private equity funds. *Journal of Financial and Quantitative Analysis*, forthcoming.
Duffie, D. and Pan, J. (1997) An overview of value at risk. *Journal of Derivatives*, 7, 7–49.
Dunbar, N. (2001) *Inventing Money*. John Wiley & Sons, Chichester.
EC (2010) QIS5 Technical Specifications – Annex to Call for Advice from CEIOPS on QIS5. European Commission, DG Internal Market and Services, Financial Institutions, Insurance and Pensions, 5 July. Available at http://ec.europa.eu/internal_market/insurance/docs/solvency/qis5/201007/technical_specifications_en.pdf [accessed 5 June 2012].
The Economist (2001) Private equity in Europe: The princess and the pearl. *The Economist*, 6 December.

EIOPA (2012) Technical Specifications for the Solvency II Valuation and Solvency Capital Requirements Calculations. Part I. Available at https://eiopa.europa.eu/fileadmin/tx_dam/files/consultations/QIS/Preparatory_forthcoming_assessments/EIOPA_12-362__A_-Tech_Spec_for_the_SII_valuation_and_SCR_calc__Part_I_.pdf [accessed 26 October 2012].

Ellis, C.D. (2008) *The Partnership – A History of Goldman Sachs*. Allen Lane, London.

Emery, K. (2003) Private equity risk and reward: Assessing the stale pricing problem. *Journal of Private Equity*, 6, 43–50.

EMPEA (2011) *Local Pension Capital in Latin America*. EMPEA, Washington, DC.

Epstein, J.M. (2008) Why model? Speaker notes. Available at http://www.mit.edu/~scienceprogram/Materials/Monday%20Materials/WhyModel.pdf [accessed 19 September 2011].

ESMA (2011) Final Report – ESMA's Technical Advice to the European Commission on Possible Measures of the Alternative Investment Fund Managers Directive. ESMA/2011/379.

EVCA (2005) International Private Equity and Venture Capital Valuation Guidelines.

EVCA (2011) Private Equity Fund Risk Measurement Guidelines. Exposure Draft for Consultation. Available at http://www.evca.eu/uploadedFiles/Home/Public_And_Regulatory_Affairs/Consultations/Consultation_Paper_EVCA_Risk_Measurement_Guidelines.pdf [accessed 8 June 2011].

EVCA (2012) Research paper: "Calibration of Risk and Correlation in Private Equity" – A proposal for a new approach for the development of a private equity index; authored by Neil Chakravarty and Christian Diller; published by European Venture Capital and Private Equity Association, May 2012.

Everts, M. (2002) Cash dilution in illiquid funds. MPRA Paper No. 4655. Available at http://mpra.ub.uni-muenchen.de/4655/ [accessed 30 September 2011].

Fabozzi, F.J. and Kothari, V. (2008) Introduction to collateralized debt obligations. In *Introduction to Securitization*. John Wiley & Sons, Hoboken, NJ.

Fama, E.F. and French, K.R. (1993) Common factors in the returns on stocks and bonds. *Journal of Financial Economics*, 33(1), 3–56.

Fang, L., Ivashina, V. and Lerner, J. (2012) The disintermediation of financial markets: Direct investing in private equity. Available at http://www.stern.nyu.edu/cons/groups/content/documents/webasset/con_037960.pdf [accessed 17 October 2012].

FDIC (2005) Trust Examination Manual. Section 3 – Asset Management – Part I. Investment Principles, Policies and Products. Federal Deposit Insurance Company. Last updated 5 October 2005. Available at http://www.fdic.gov/regulations/examinations/trustmanual/section_3/fdic_section_3-asset_management.html#c [accessed 29 June 2011].

Fisher, L. (2009) *The Perfect Swarm – The Science of Complexity in Everyday Life*. Basic Books, New York.

Fleischer, V. (2004) Fickle investors, reputation, and the clientele effect in venture capital funds. UCLA School of Law, Law-Econ Research Paper No. 04-14, 2 October. Available at SSRN: http://ssrn.com/abstract=600044 [accessed 5 May 2006].

Fleischer, V. (2005) The missing preferred return. UCLA School of Law. Law and Economics Working Paper Series, No. 465, 22 February.

Frankel, J.A. and Rose, A.K. (1996) Currency crashes in emerging markets: An empirical treatment. *Journal of International Economics*, 41, 351–368.

Franzen, D. (2010) Managing investment risk in defined benefit pension funds. OECD Working Papers on Insurance and Private Pensions, No. 38.

Franzoni, F., Novak, E. and Phalippou, L. (2012) Private equity performance and liquidity risk. *Journal of Finance*, 67(6), 2341–2373.

Fraser-Sampson, G. (2006) *Multi-Asset Class Investment Strategy: A Multi-Asset Class Approach to Investment Strategy*. John Wiley & Sons, Chichester.

Fraser-Sampson, G. (2011) *Alternative Assets – Investments for a Post-Crisis World*. John Wiley & Sons, Chichester.

Froot, K.A. (1993) Currency hedging over long horizons. NBER Working Paper 4355. National Bureau of Economic Research, Cambridge, MA.

FSA (2009) FSA draft code on remuneration practices. Financial Services Authority, 18 March. Available at http://www.fsa.gov.uk/pubs/other/remuneration.pdf [accessed 21 March 2012].

FSA (2010) Revising the remuneration code – feedback on CP10/19 and final rules. Financial Services Authority, December. Available at http://www.fsa.gov.uk/pubs/policy/ps10_20.pdf [accessed 21 February 2012].

Garnsworthy, C., Tuley, J. and Moore, A. (2010) Worth using: Meeting the use test for model approval. Available at http://www.pwc.com/gx/en/insurance/solvency-ii/countdown/0510-worth-using.html [accessed 12 October 2011].

Geltner, D., MacGregor, B.D. and Schwann, M.G. (2003) Appraisal smoothing and price discovery in real estate markets. *Urban Studies*, 40(5&6), 1047–1064. Available at http://usj.sagepub.com/content/40/5-6/1047.abstract.

Getmansky, M., Lo, A. and Makarov, I. (2004) An econometric model of serial correlation and illiquidity in hedge fund returns. *Journal of Financial Economics*, 74(3), 529–609.

Giannotti, C. and Mattarocci, G. (2009) How to evaluate risk for Italian real estate funds. *Journal of European Real Estate Research*, 2(2), 132–150.

Golub, B.W. and Crum, C.C. (2010) Risk management lessons worth remembering. BlackRock Report. Available at https://www2.blackrock.com/webcore/litService/search/getDocument.seam?contentId=1111106147&Source=SEARCH&Venue=PUB_INS [accessed 6 June 2011].

Gompers, P.A. and Lerner, J. (1997) Risk and reward in private equity investments: The challenge of performance assessment. *Journal of Private Equity*, 1, 5–12.

Gompers, P.A. and Lerner, J. (2000) Money chasing deals? The impact of fund inflows on private equity valuations. *Journal of Financial Economics*, 55, 281–325.

Gompers, P.A. and Lerner, J. (2001) The venture capital revolution. *Journal of Economic Perspectives*, 15(2), 145–168.

Gottschalg, O.F. (2010) Private equity fund selection. How to find true top-quartile performers. In Cumming, D. (ed.), *Private Equity. Fund Types, Risk and Returns, and Regulation*. John Wiley & Sons, Hoboken, NJ.

Guo, S., Hotchkiss, E.S. and Song, W. (2011) Do buyouts (still) create value? *Journal of Finance*, 66(2), 479–515.

Haight, G.T., Morrell, S.O. and Ross, G.E. (2007) *How to Select Investment Managers & Evaluate Performance*. John Wiley & Sons, Hoboken, NJ.

Hansmann, H., Kraakman, R. and Squire, R. (2005) Law and the rise of the firm. Available at http://law.usc.edu/academics/centers/cleo/workshops/05-06/documents/Kraakman.pdf [accessed 4 August 2008].

Hardymon, F., Lerner, J. and Leamon, A. (2009) The Canadian Pension Plan Investment Board. Harvard Business School, N9-809-073.

Harris, R., Jenkinson, T. and Stucke, R. (2010) A White Paper on Private Equity and Research. UAI Foundation Working Paper, University of Virginia.

Harris, R., Jenkinson, T. and Kaplan, S.N. (2012) Private equity performance: What do we know? NBER Working Paper No. 17874.

Hayden, R.M. (2008) Trustee delegations and the prudent investor act: Filling the gaps. *Rutgers Law Record*, 32(64). Available at http://lawrecord.com/files/32_Rutgers_L_Rec_64.pdf [accessed 30 June 2011].

Healy, B. (2001) Calpers posts fund's record on website – money managers aghast that pension investor shows returns, rankings. *Boston Globe*, August.

Heikkilä, T. (2004) European single market and the globalisation of private equity fundraising: Barriers and determinants of foreign commitments in private equity funds. MSc Eng. thesis, Helsinki University of Technology.

Hendershott, R. (2007) Using past performance to infer investment manager ability. Preliminary paper. Available at http://www.scu.edu/business/mindwork/winter08/upload/hendershott-past_performance_nov07.pdf [accessed 12 May 2008].

Hendricks, D. (1996) Evaluation of value at risk models: Using historical data. *Federal Reserve Bank of New York Economic Policy Review*, April, pp. 39–69.

Henzler, F. (2004) Pine Street I LLC: A case study in securitisation. In *Routes to Liquidity*. Private Equity International.

Henzler, F. (2008) Alternative routes to liquidity: Securitising private equity. In *The Private Equity Secondaries Market*. Private Equity International.

Henzler, F. and Etter, M. (2008) Astrea – securitisation as a path to secondary liquidity. In *The Private Equity Secondaries Market*. Private Equity International.
Higson, C. and Stucke, R. (2012) The performance of private equity, 2 March. Available at http://dx.doi.org/10.2139/ssrn.2009067 [accessed 21 August 2012].
Hoek, H. (2007) An ALM analysis of private equity. ORTEC Centre for Financial Research, January. Available at http://files.ortec-finance.com/Publications/research/OCFR_App_WP_2007_01.pdf [accessed 2 July 2008].
Hoevenaars, R. (2008) Strategic asset allocation. Asset liability management. Dissertation, University of Maastricht.
Holton, G.A. (2004) Defining risk. *Financial Analysts Journal*, 60(6), 19–25.
Hsu, D.H. and Kenney, M. (2004) Organising venture capital: The rise and demise of American Research & Development Corporation. Available at http://ssrn.com/abstract=628661.
Hubbard, D.W. (2009) *The Failure of Risk Management: Why It's Broken and How to Fix It*. John Wiley & Sons, Hoboken, NJ.
IMF (2011) Global Financial Stability Report. International Monetary Fund, Washington, DC.
IMF (2012) Global Financial Stability Report. The Quest for Lasting Stability. International Monetary Fund, Washington, DC.
Inderst, R. and Muennich, F. (2003) The benefits of shallow pockets. London School of Economics.
ISDA (2001) Modelling equity risk exposure – response to the Models Task Force. International Swaps and Derivatives Association's letter to Models Task Force of FSA.
Jorion, P. (2006) *Value at Risk: The New Benchmark for Managing Financial Risk*, 3rd edn. McGraw-Hill, New York.
Jorion, P. and Taleb, N. (1997) The Jorion–Taleb debate. *Derivatives Strategy*, April. Available at http://www.derivativesstrategy.com/magazine/archive/1997/0497fea2.asp [accessed 7 June 2012].
Kahneman, D. (2011) *Thinking Fast and Slow*. Allen Lane, London.
Kaplan, S. and Schoar, A. (2005) Private equity performance: Returns, persistence, and capital flows. *Journal of Finance*, 60, 1791–1823.
Kaplan, S.N. and Strömberg, P. (2009) Leveraged buyouts and private equity. *Journal of Economic Perspectives*, 23, 121–146.
Kaplan, S.N., Sensoy, B.A. and Strömberg, P. (2009) Should investors bet on the jockey or the horse? Evidence from the evolution of firms from early business plans to public companies. *Journal of Finance*, 64, 75–115.
Karmin, C. and Lublin, J.S. (2008) Calpers Sells Stock Amid Rout to Raise Cash for Obligations, *Wall Street Journal*, October 25.
Kaserer, C. (2011) Return attribution in mid-market buy-out transactions – new evidence from Europe, 19 October. Available at http://dx.doi.org/10.2139/ssrn.1946110 [accessed 21 August 2012].
Kaserer, C. and Diller, C. (2004a) Beyond IRR once more. *Private Equity International*, August.
Kaserer, C. and Diller, C. (2004b) European private equity funds – a cash flow based performance analysis. *EVCA Research Paper*.
Kaserer, C., Wagner, N. and Achleitner, A.-K. (2003) Managing investment risks of institutional private equity investors – the challenge of illiquidity. Center for Entrepreneurial and Financial Studies, Working Paper No. 2003-01. Available at http://www.cefs.de/files/200301-cefs-wp.pdf [accessed 1 July 2008].
Knight, F.H. (1921) *Risk, Uncertainty, and Profit*. Houghton Mifflin, Boston, MA.
Kocis, J.M., Bachman, J.C., Long, A.M. and Nickels, C.G. (2009) *Inside Private Equity – The Professional Investor's Handbook*. John Wiley & Sons, Hoboken, NJ.
Korteweg, M. and Sorensen, M. (2011) Risk and return characteristics of venture-capital backed entrepreneurial companies. *Review of Financial Studies*, forthcoming.
Kothari, P. and Warner, J. (2001) Evaluating mutual fund performance. *The Journal of Finance*, 56, 1985–2010.
Kreutzer, L. (2008) Managing risk takes center stage as GPs put out fires and LPs watch cash. *Dow Jones Private Equity Analyst*, November.
Krohmer, P. and Man, K.-S. (2007) Modeling default risk of private equity funds – a market-based framework. In Krohmer, P. (ed.), *Essays in Financial Economics: Risk and Return of Private Equity*.

Inaugural-Dissertation, Matrikelnummer 2473635, Fachbereich Wirtschaftswissenschaften, Johann Wolfgang Goethe Universität, Frankfurt am Main, April.
Kukla, D. (2011) Competitive strategy of private equity: Boundary of the investment firm. Doctoral thesis, Technische Universität Berlin.
Langbein, J.H. and Posner, R.A. (1976) Market funds and trust-investment law. Yale Law School, Faculty Scholarship Series, Paper 498. Available at http://digitalcommons.law.yale.edu/fss_papers/498 [accessed 26 July 2011].
Lehikoinen, K. (2007) Development of systematic backtesting processes of value-at-risk. Master's thesis, Helsinki University of Technology, Department of Engineering Physics and Mathematics, 21 May.
Lerner, J. and Leamon, A. (2011) Yale University Investments Office. Harvard Business School, Case Study N9-812-062.
Lerner, J. and Schoar, A. (2002) The illiquidity puzzle: Theory and evidence from private equity. *Journal of Financial Economics*, 72, 3–40.
Lerner, J., Schoar, A. and Wong, W. (2007) Smart institutions, foolish choices?: The limited partner performance puzzle. *Journal of Finance*, 62, 731–764.
Lhabitant, F.-S. (2004) *Hedge Funds – Quantitative Insights*. John Wiley & Sons, Chichester.
Lintner, J. (1965) The valuation of risk assets and the selection of risky investments in stock portfolios and capital budgets. *Review of Economics and Statistics*, 47, 13–37.
Litvak, K. (2004) Governance through exit: Default penalties and walkaway options in venture capital partnership agreements. University of Texas, Law and Economics Research Paper No. 34, October. Available at http://ssrn.com/abstract=613142 [accessed 5 May 2006].
Ljungqvist, A. and Richardson, M.P. (2003) The cash flow, return and risk characteristics of private equity. NBER Working Paper, No. 9454.
Lo, A.W. (2001) Risk management for hedge funds: Introduction and overview. *Financial Analysts Journal*, Nov/Dec.
Lo, A.W. (2005) The Adaptive Market Hypothesis. *Journal of Investment Consulting*, 7(2), 21–44.
Lo, A.W. and Mueller, M.T. (2010) WARNING: Physics envy may be hazardous to your wealth. Available at http://papers.ssrn.com/sol3/papers.cfm?abstract_id=1563882 [accessed 21 June 2010].
Lopez, J.A. and Saidenberg, M.R. (2001) The development of internal models approaches to bank regulation and supervision: Lessons from the market risk amendment. Available at http://www.frbsf.org [accessed 12 October 2011].
Lorenz, D., Trück, S. and Lützkendorf, T. (2006) Addressing risk and uncertainty in property valuations: a viewpoint from Germany. *Journal of Property Investment & Finance*, 24(5), 400–433.
Love, G. (2009) Praise for evergreen funds. *Venture Capital Journal*, 1 December.
MacCracken, M. (2001) Prediction versus projection – forecast versus possibility. *WeatherZine*, No. 26, February. Available at http://sciencepolicy.colorado.edu/zine/archives/1-29/26/guest.html [accessed 17 November 2011].
Mahadevan, S. and Schwartz, D. (2002) Hedge fund collateralized fund obligations. *Journal of Alternative Investments*, 5, 45–62.
Maloney, E.F. (1999) The investment process required by the uniform Prudent Investor Act. *FPA Journal*, November.
Markowitz, H. (1952) Portfolio selection. *Journal of Finance*, 7, 77–91.
Mathonet, P.-Y. and Meyer, T. (2007) *J-Curve Exposure*. John Wiley & Sons, Chichester.
McCrystal, A. and Chakravarty, N. (2011) Solvency II: Private equity, the LPX50 and risk calibration. Pantheon Ventures paper, November.
McKinsey Global Institute (2011) Farewell to cheap capital? The implications of long-term shifts in global investment and saving. http://www.mckinsey.com/Insights/MGI/Research/Financial_Markets/Farewell_cheap_capital [accessed 15 January 2012].
Metrick, A. (2007) *Venture Capital and the Finance of Innovation*. John Wiley & Sons, Hoboken, NJ.
Metrick, A. and Yasuda, A. (2009) The economics of private equity funds. *Review of Financial Studies*, 23, 2303–2341.
Meyer, T. and Mathonet, P.-Y. (2005) *Beyond the J Curve*. John Wiley & Sons, Chichester.
Meyer, T. and Weidig, T. (2003) Modelling venture capital funds. *Risk Magazine*, October.
Missinhoun, J. and Chacowry, L. (2005) Collateralized fund obligations: The value of investing in the equity tranche. *Journal of Structured Finance*, 10(4), 32–37.

Mittnik, S. (2011) Solvency II calibrations: Where curiosity meets spuriosity. Center for Quantitative Risk Analysis, Department of Statistics, University of Munich, Working Paper No. 4.

Möllmann, C. (2007) How to govern pension provision? The struggle over the "prudent person standard" in EU pension fund regulation. Paper presented at the 6th Pan-European Conference on International Relations ECPR Standing Group on International Relations, Turin, September, pp. 12–15. Available at http://turin.sgir.eu/uploads/Moellmann-Moellmann-Turin.pdf [accessed 29 June 2011].

Mossin, J. (1966) Equilibrium in a capital asset market. *Econometrica*, 34, 768–783.

Mulcahy, D., Weeks, B. and Bradley, H.S. (2012) We have met the enemy . . . and he is us. Ewing Marion Kauffman Foundation, May.

Murphy, D.J. (2007) *A Practical Guide to Managing Private Equity Commitments*. Goldman Sachs Asset Management, Strategic Research, June.

Myners, P. (2001) Institutional Investment in the United Kingdom: A Review. http://archive.treasury.gov.uk/docs/2001/myners_report0602.html.

NSM (2008) Today's risk manager – a strategic risk report. Newsquest Specialist Media Business Intelligence. Available at http://www.qbeeurope.com/documents/comms/TodaysRiskManagerReport.pdf [accessed 26 May 2011].

OECD (2006) OECD Guidelines on Pension Fund Asset Management. Recommendations of the Council. Available at www.oecd.org/dataoecd/59/53/36316399.pdf [accessed 26 March 2012].

OECD (2011) Pensions at a Glance Asia/Pacific 2011. OECD Publishing. Available at http://www.oecd.org/document/27/0,3746,en_2649_37419_49427099_1_1_1_37419,00.html#Download [accessed 27 March 2012].

Palmer, D. (2005) Using scenario analysis to estimate operational risk capital. Credit Suisse First Boston, presentation, OpRisk Europe, 17 March.

Partners Group (2011) Value-based secondary investing across market cycles. http://www.partnersgroup.com/g3.cms/s_page/80480/s_name/researchflashes [accessed 12 April 2012].

Pastor, L. and Stambaugh, R.F. (2003) Liquidity risk and expected stock returns. *Journal of Political Economy*, 111, 642–685.

Phalippou, L. (2009) Beware of venturing into private equity. *Journal of Economic Perspectives*, 23, 147–148.

Phalippou, L. (2011) An evaluation of the potential for GPFG to achieve above average returns from investments in private equity and recommendations regarding benchmarking. Available at www.regjeringen.no/Upload/FIN/.../Phalippo [accessed 24 August 2012].

Phalippou, L. (2012) Performance of buyout funds revisited? Available at http://papers.ssrn.com/sol3/papers.cfm?abstract_id=1969101 [accessed 17 October 2012].

Phalippou, L. and Gottschalg, O. (2009) The performance of private equity funds. *Review of Financial Studies*, 22, 1747–1776.

Phalippou, L. and Westerfield, M.M. (2012) Commitment risk in private partnerships. Preliminary and incomplete manuscript.

Porter, M. (1979) The structure within industries and companies performance. *Review of Economics and Statistics*, 61, 214–227.

Porter, T.M. (1992) Quantification and the accounting ideal in science. *Social Studies of Science*, 22, 633–651.

Primack, D. (2011) The best private equity firm is . . . *Fortune*. Available at http://finance.fortune.cnn.com/2011/11/14/best-private-equity-firm/ [accessed 8 February 2012].

Quintyn, M. (undated) *Principles versus Rules in Financial Supervision – Is there One Superior Approach?* Available at http://www.qfinance.com/regulation-best-practice/principles-versus-rules-in-financial-supervisionis-there-one-superior-approach?page=3, [accessed 10 January 2012].

Raschle, B.E. and Jaeggi, A. (2004) The quality of the fund manager is crucial in private equity investments. Adveq Management.

Rebonato, R. (2007) *Plight of the Fortune Tellers*. Princeton University Press, Princeton, NJ.

Reinhardt, C.M. and Rogoff, K.S. (2009) *This Time is Different. Eight centuries of financial folly*. Princeton University Press, Princeton, NJ.

Robinson, D.T. and Sensoy, B.A. (2011) Cyclicality, performance measurement, and cash flow liquidity in private equity. Charles A. Dice Center for Research in Financial Economics, Fisher College of Business, Ohio State University, WP 2010-021.

Romaine, K. (2012) Rethinking LP funds. *Unquote*, March.

Rouvinez, C. (2005) The value of the carry. *Private Equity International*, July/August.
Rouvinez, C. (2006) Top quartile persistence in private equity. *Private Equity International*, June.
Rouvinez, C. (2007) Looking for the premium. *Private Equity International*, June.
Ruso, S. (2008) A governance-focused rating system for closed-end funds in Germany. Diplomarbeit, Swiss Banking Institute.
Sanyal, D. (2009) Bank participation in private equity funds: Risk implication and capital adequacy, 23 August. Available at http://papers.ssrn.com/sol3/papers.cfm?abstract_id=1460577 [accessed 1 September 2008].
Schäli, S., Frei, A. and Studer, M. (2002) Top Quartile als umstrittener Benchmark. *Neue Züricher Zeitung*.
Scott, B. (2012) LP model in the dock. *Real Deals*, 8 March.
Shady, A.-E., Dionne, G. and Papageorgiou, N. (2011) Performance analysis of a collateralized fund obligation (CFO) equity tranche. *The European Journal of Finance*, August.
Sharon, B. (undated) Operational risk management: The difference between risk management and compliance. Available at http://www.continuitycentral.com/feature0243.htm [accessed 21 February 2012].
Sharpe, W.F. (1964) Capital asset prices – a theory of market equilibrium under conditions of risk. *Journal of Finance*, 19, 425–442.
Sharpe, W.F. (1966) Mutual fund performance. *Journal of Business*, 39, 119–138.
Sharpe, W.F. (2007) *Investors and Markets*. Princeton University Press, Princeton, NJ.
Sher, M. (2010) *Understanding the Psychology of Regulation*. Centre for Parliamentary Studies. International Symposium 2010 – Remapping the Regulatory Landscape. Available at http://www.regulation.org.uk/psychologyofregulation.pdf, [accessed 24 May 2011].
Sherden, W.A. (1998) *The Fortune Sellers*. John Wiley & Sons, New York.
Shin, H.S. (2010) *Risk and Liquidity*. Oxford University Press, Oxford.
Smith, D., Beaton, A., Herger, I. and Prieto, M. (2012) Why it pays to be diversified. *Private Equity International*, March.
Smith, T. (1996) *Accounting for Growth – Stripping the Camouflage from Company Accounts*, 2nd edn. Arrow, London.
Söhnholz, D. (2002) Private equity fund rating: Increasing the transparency of fund selection by using an 'objective' approach. Super Investor Conference, Paris.
Solnik, B. and McLeavey, D. (2009) *Global Investments*, 6th edn. Pearson Prentice Hall, Boston, MA.
Sorensen, M., Wang, N. and Yang, J. (2012) Valuing private equity. Columbia University working paper. Available at http://papers.ssrn.com/sol3/papers.cfm?abstract_id=2041715&download=yes [accessed 2 November 2012].
Sourbes, C. (2012) Solvency II 'look through' approach a threat to fund managers. *Investments & Pensions Europe*, 10 May. Available at http://www.ipe.com/news/solvency-ii-look-through-approach-a-threat-to-fund-managers-state-street_45434.php [accessed 5 June 2012].
Spence, M.A. (2009) Periodic systemic risk and investment strategy. PIMCO. http://www.pimco.com/EN/Insights/Pages/Periodic%20Systemic%20Risk%20Spence%20October.aspx [accessed 10 June 2012].
Spiteri, A. (2011) Running to stand still. Nordics Report 2011. *funds europe*.
Standard & Poor's (2006) Ratings Definitions Global Criteria for Private Equity Securitization. Standard & Poor's, New York, 18 January.
Standard & Poor's (2008) Rating Private Equity Companies' Debt and Counterparty Obligations. Standard & Poor's, New York, 11 March.
Standard & Poor's (2010) Rating Report on Pine Street. Pine Street I LLC Ratings Affirmed on Three Classes. Standard & Poor's, New York.
Stange, S. and Kaserer, C. (2009) Market liquidity risk – an overview, March 18. CEFS Working Paper Series 2009, No. 4. Available at SSRN: http://ssrn.com/abstract=1362537.
Stone, C.A. and Zissu, A. (2004) Fund of fund securitizations. *Journal of Derivatives*, 11(4), 62–68.
Stucke, R. (2011) Updating history. http://papers.ssrn.com/sol3/papers.cfm?abstract_id=1967636 [accessed 14 April 2012].
Studer, M. and Wicki, M. (2010) Private equity allocations under Solvency II. Partners Group Research Flash, July.

Swensen, D. (2009) *Pioneering Portfolio Management. An Unconventional Approach to Institutional Investment*, 2nd edn. Free Press, New York.
Takahashi, D. and Alexander, S. (2001) Illiquid alternative asset fund modelling. Yale University Investment Office.
Talmor, E. and Vasvari, F. (2011) *International Private Equity*. John Wiley & Sons, Chichester.
Thaler, R. (1980) Toward a positive theory of consumer choice. *Journal of Economic Behavior and Organization*, Issue 1.
Tirole, J. (2011) Illiquidity and all its friends. *Journal of Economic Literature*, 49, 287–325.
Tolkamp, C. (2007) Predicting private equity performance – the development of a private equity performance-forecasting model for AEGON asset management. Master's thesis, University of Twente, The Netherlands.
Treynor, J.L. (1962) Toward a theory of market value of risky assets. Unpublished manuscript. Finally published in 1999 in Korajczyk, R.A. (ed.), *Asset Pricing and Portfolio Performance: Models, Strategy and Performance Metrics*. Risk Books, London, pp. 15–22.
Troche, C.J. (2003) Development of a rating instrument for private equity funds. MBA Management Project Report, NIMBAS Graduate School of Management.
van der Heijden, K. (1996) *Scenarios – The Art of Strategic Conversation*. John Wiley & Sons, Chichester.
WEF (2011) The Future of Long-Term Investing. World Economic Forum, Geneva.
Weidig, T. (2002a) Towards a risk model for venture capital funds: Liquidity and performance forecasting. Available at http://ssrn.com/abstract=353562 [accessed 30 April 2009].
Weidig, T. (2002b) A risk model for venture capital funds. Available at http://papers.ssrn.com/sol3/papers.cfm?abstract_id=365881 [accessed 21 September 2011].
Weidig, T. and Mathonet, P.-Y. (2004) The risk profile of private equity, January. Available at http://ssrn.com/abstract=495482 [accessed 16 June 2008].
Witkowsky, C. (2012) OMERS PE loses fund investments expert, 12 March. Available at http://www.privateequityinternational.com/article.aspx?article=66254 [accessed 25 May 2012].
Woodward, S.E. and Hall, R.E. (2003) Benchmarking the returns to venture. NBER Working Paper, No. 10202.
Yan, M., Hall, M.J.B. and Turner, P. (2011) Estimating liquidity risk using the exposure-based cash-flow-at-risk approach: An application to the UK banking sector. Loughborough University, School of Business and Economics, Working Paper 2011-06.

Abbreviations

ABS	asset-backed security
ACR	adjusted current ratio
ADIA	Abu Dhabi Investment Authority
AIF	alternative investment fund
AIFM	alternative investment fund manager
ALM	asset liability management
AMH	adaptive market hypothesis
AuM	assets under management
AVM	asset value model
B	bow factor
bps	basis points
C	contributions, drawdowns, capital calls of funds
CalPERS	California Public Employees' Retirement System
CalSTRS	California State Teachers' Retirement System
CAPM	capital asset pricing model
CC	committed capital
CDO	collateralized debt obligation
CFA	cash flow adjustment
CFaR	cash-flow-at-risk
CFO	collateralized fund obligation
CIC	China Investment Corporation
CR	current ratio
D	distributions, capital repayments of funds
DB	defined benefit plan
DC	defined contribution plan
DCF	discounted cash flows
DMM	default mode model
EIOPA	European Insurance and Occupational Pensions Authority
ESG	environmental, social and corporate governance
ESMA	European Securities and Markets Authority
EUR	euro
EVCA	European Venture Capital and Private Equity Association
FoF	fund-of-funds
FOIA	Freedom of Information Act

FRI	fixed interest rate
FRN	floating-rate note
G	growth rate
GIC	Government of Singapore Investment Corporation
GP	general partner
HMC	Harvard Management Corporation
HNW	high net worth
iCaR	invested-capital-at-risk
IFRS	International Financial Reporting Standard
IIRR	interim IRR
IMF	International Monetary Fund
IORP Directive	Directive on the activities and supervision of institutions for occupational retirement provisions
IPEV	International private equity and venture capital valuation guidelines
IRR	internal rate of return
ITVPI	interim TVPI
KIA	Kuwait Investment Authority
L	lifetime of fund
LBO	leveraged buyout
LDI	liability-driven investing
LP	limited partner
M&A	mergers and acquisitions
MPT	modern portfolio theory
NAV	net asset value
NPI	net paid-in
NPV	net present value
OCL	outstanding commitment level
OCR	overcommitment ratio
OMERS	Ontario Municipal Employees Retirement System
p.a.	per annum
PD/LGD	probability of default/loss given default
PIC	paid-in capital
PME	public market equivalent
PPM	private placement memorandum
RC	rate of contribution
S&P	Standard & Poor's
SPV	special purpose vehicle
SWF	sovereign wealth fund
T	trigger point
TVPI	total value to paid-in
UBS	Union Bank of Switzerland
UCGL	unrealized capital gains and losses
USD	US dollar
VaR	value-at-risk
VC	venture capital
WEF	World Economic Forum
Y	yield

Index

Index compiled by Terry Halliday